February 7th, 2006

To the KING family,

— With Very Best Wishes
from the Author, &
Enjoy All your Hikes
& Climbs and Summits
together!

Sincerely,
Ed Webster...

SNOW
IN THE

KINGDOM

MY STORM·YEARS
ON EVEREST

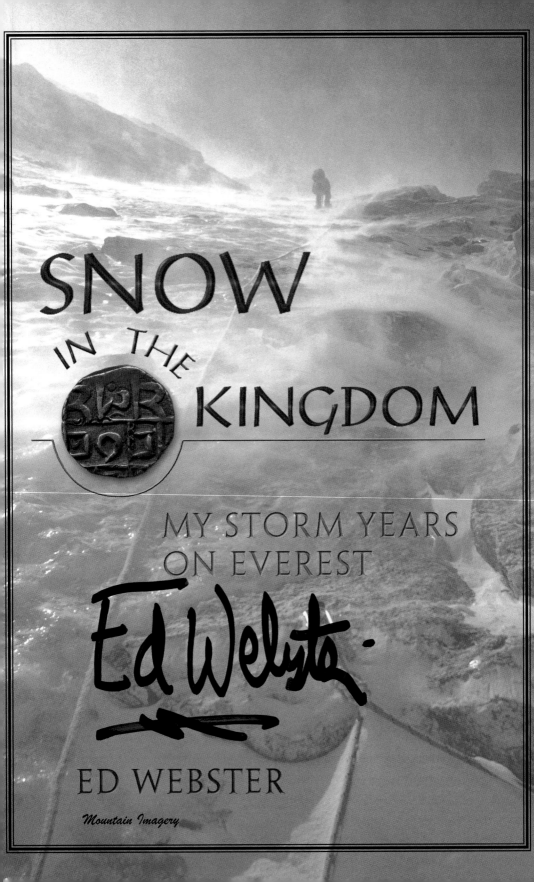

SNOW
IN THE
KINGDOM

MY STORM YEARS
ON EVEREST

Ed Webster

ED WEBSTER

Mountain Imagery

Published by *Mountain Imagery* PO Box 210, Eldorado Springs, Colorado 80025 USA

To order autographed copies of this book, or the Team signed edition, or the Deluxe signed edition, see our website at www.mtnimagery.com
Also available: the 1924 Mallory & Irvine British Everest Expedition photographs of Noel Odell.

Library of Congress Card Number: 00-192041
ISBN: 0-9653199-1-1

1 2 3 4 5 6 7 8 9 10

First Edition

To the mountaineers who first inspired me:

Edmund Hillary

Tenzing Norgay

Lute Jerstad

Barry Bishop

Tom Hornbein

Willi Unsoeld

and to

Fritz Wiessner

who encouraged me to climb at high altitude without bottled oxygen,
and whose strong spirit guided us during our descent.

And affectionately to Lisa, with all my love

We had already ... taken time to observe the great Eastern face of Mount Everest, and more particularly the lower edge of the hanging glacier; it required but little further gazing to be convinced—to know that almost everywhere the rocks below must be exposed to ice falling from this glacier; that if, elsewhere, it might be possible to climb up, the performance would be too arduous, would take too much time and would lead to no convenient platform; that, in short, other men, less wise, would attempt this way if they would, but, emphatically, it was not for us.

—George Mallory
Mount Everest, The Reconnaissance, 1921

The passions of the long trail bring out the best in men and the worst, and all in scarlet; and while the law of compensation, which keeps life livable, provides that in the after-memories which form existence, only what is pleasant survives, I hold that it is unfair to nature and the blessed weaknesses which make us human to divert by one hair's breadth in any record of the trail from facts as you saw them, emotions as you felt them at the time. To distort or hide, in deference to any custom, or so-called sense of pride or honor, simply is to lie. The tragic moments in the heat of the trail's struggle, *the event as it affected you as you then were*—to note that with all the passions or heroism, the beastliness or triumph, of the moment—must not such a record in the end turn out fair? And true as can be?

—Robert Dunn
The Shameless Diary of an Explorer

A mountaineer may be satisfied to nurse his athletic infancy upon home rocks, and he may be happy to pass the later years of his experience among the more elusive impressions and more subtle romance of our old and quiet hills. But in the storm years of his strength he should test his powers, learn his craft and earn his triumphs in conflict with the abrupt youth and warlike habit of great glacial ranges.

—Geoffrey Winthrop Young
Mountain Craft

Photograph by George Mallory, courtesy of the Royal Geographical Society

*E*verest's most daunting aspect is its East or Kangshung Face in Tibet. This stunning sunrise view of the mountain was taken by George Mallory during the very first Mount Everest expedition, the 1921 British reconnaissance. Lhotse—the world's fourth-tallest peak—is on the left, the South Col dips in the center, and Mount Everest rises on the right. Also visible are two prominent buttresses situated below the South Col; these challenging ramparts form the only existing routes up this "forgotten face" of Earth's tallest peak. The *Neverest Buttress*—first climbed in 1988, and the subject of this book—is just left of center. The large, central *American Buttress* was successfully ascended in 1983, after a prior attempt in 1981. (For more information, see route photo-diagram on page 462.)

John Hunt
Leader, 1953 British Mount Everest Expedition
Patron, 1988 International Everest Expedition

Foreword

Lord Hunt of Llanfairwaterdine

*F*or a mountaineer whose active life is long since over, one of my delights is to be kept in touch with the aspirations and achievements of younger generations of climbers who continue to reach for the limits of skill and daring on mountains. For myself, I have long discovered, as I hope they will, that there is a great deal more to be enjoyed in the mountain environment than climbing them by the hard ways.

Of the many expeditions whose members have paid me the compliment of making me their Patron, the 1988 International Everest Expedition is one of the most remarkable. As was the case with the Matterhorn in 1865, the sensation created by the first ascent of Mount Everest in 1953 has been followed by numerous climbs on that mountain which have not been deemed worthy of a mention by the news media. But there have been a few exceptions; one of these was the epic achievement in 1988 on Everest's East (or Kangshung) Face by Ed Webster with his three companions. They attempted a route of unknown difficulty, which they had viewed in a photograph taken from some distance. They were a team of four men with no reserves; they used no oxygen; they did not have the support of Sherpas; they employed a bare minimum of technical equipment; they were exposed to the dangers of bad weather and variable snow conditions. This band of heroes went to the very limits of human endeavour.

The question remains: was it worthwhile? Only they themselves can answer this at the personal level. More generally, I believe that it was. I am full of admiration for the outstanding achievement of their team in pushing through a new route of exceptional difficulty on this much-climbed mountain. In the future, Everest may become as commonplace a climb as the ascent of the Matterhorn by its Hörnli Ridge. But these men have shown the world the high value of courage, determination and comradeship in adversity—of challenging the near-impossible. The world stands in need of such examples.

I am honoured to have known them.

Aston, Henley-On-Thames
England   April 2, 1998

Tom Hornbein on Zummie's Thumb, Longs Peak, Colorado. Jim Detterline

Introduction

Great things are done when men and mountains meet.
This is not done by jostling in the street.

—*William Blake*

Thomas F. Hornbein

As this 20th century closes, more than a thousand pairs of feet will have trod upon Earth's highest point. Although for each of the many who now aspire to summit Everest, the effort is a serious and challenging undertaking, in the overall history of man's courtship with this mountain only a handful of moments of special creativity—those meetings when "great things are done"—shine forth as precious gems in the total matrix of human striving at the top of our planet. The tale told here by Ed Webster about what he, Robert Anderson, Paul Teare and Stephen Venables accomplished on the Kangshung (East) Face in 1988 describes an endeavor that is among those special moments on my personal list of landmark Everest events.

Among these events are Edmund Hillary and Tenzing Norgay's first ascent on May 29, 1953. Yet summiting is not an essential criterion. I would cite, for example, Edward F. Norton's remarkable climb above twenty-eight thousand feet without the use of supplemental bottled oxygen in 1924, an altitude not to be exceeded for nearly three decades. And from that same expedition we are left with the mystery of whether George Mallory and Andrew Irvine might have actually reached the summit before they disappeared.

For those at the cutting edge of mountaineering or indeed any act of creativity, uncertainty regarding outcome is an essential ingredient to the undertaking. Thus once Everest was climbed, the next stage in the game was the search for new, more challenging ways to its summit. Among subsequent climbs that raised the bar were those of the Southwest Face by Doug Scott and Dougal Haston in 1975, the Kangshung Face by a large American team in 1983, and the tenacious efforts to find a way through the forbidding gauntlet of obstacles on the Northeast Ridge.

And then, in 1980, Reinhold Messner's solo ascent over four days from the base of the North Col without supplemental oxygen augured a revolutionary change in style for climbing Everest. Now there was an alternative to the ponderous siege tactics that characterized earlier efforts. In 1986 Erhard Loretan and Jean Troillet in a forty-five hour round-trip journey up the *Super Couloir* on the North Face, further exploited that capacity for skilled, acclimatized mountaineers to move quickly over difficult terrain in the rarefied atmosphere at the top of the world.

In 1963 Willi Unsoeld and I made the first ascent of Everest's West Ridge and the first traverse of a major Himalayan peak. I would like to believe that our adventure helped set the stage for the climb which is the culmination of this book. Though our effort perhaps anticipated what was to come, mainly in the small size of our team and the extent of commitment on our summit push, there are important differences. We West Ridgers were part of a classical expedition, each successive camp being placed and stocked with the help of Sherpas. And we used supplemental oxygen; the first ascent without bottled oxygen would come fifteen years later, by Messner and Peter Habeler.

Each of these climbs is a piece of the creative history that underpins why I look upon what Ed Webster and his companions accomplished on this new route on Everest's Kangshung Face as a beautiful example of what David Brower, marveling at the magic of the human soul, described as "this inclination to inquire, this drive to go higher than need be, this innate ability to carry it off, this radiance in the heart when it happens.... " It's not just the boldness of a new route, one where the mix of difficulty and danger would give pause to most of the world's best climbers. But along with the boldness (some would say foolhardiness, and not without justification) was style: four savvy mountaineers, no Sherpas, no radios, no supplemental oxygen. Then, after days of punishing effort getting to the South Col, the final determined push for the summit stretched the metaphorical cord connecting Webster, Venables and Anderson to the world below—almost to the breaking point.

Getting up, remarkable though it was, seems but preamble to the ultimate challenge: getting down. Here, exhausted bodies and poorly functioning brains summoned that inner will to survive, combining with it an inexplicable luck ("Luck is what you make it," a Nepali told me in 1963). In a small way, this final, climactic struggle of these three (compelled predominantly by Ed) brings back memories of Shackleton's incredible Antarctic epic in 1914-15. All these elements combine to give us one of the more precious moments in our history with Mount Everest, transforming Ed Webster's account into a story that elicits admiration and adds meaning to our lives.

Yet Ed's story is more than Everest. Although we share common roots (and routes) on crags above Boulder, Colorado, and on the granite verticality of Longs Peak's East Face, Ed is someone I have come to know other than by reputation only in the last decade. This book is primarily about his captivation with Everest, covering three separate attempts upon its summit, but it evolved from the death in his arms of the young woman he loved, Lauren Husted, following a fall in the Black Canyon of the Gunnison. His memorial to her, perhaps in part an almost suicidal search for his own salvation from grief, was to climb alone a new route up the Diamond, the vertical upper wall on the East Face of Longs Peak. This climb, *Bright Star,* was both Ed's tribute to Lauren and the beginning of a search for salvation as his dreams carried him on to Everest.

One more comment would I make before you embark upon Ed's journey. This book is about one man's venture through a phase of life that is intense in its searching outward for something lurking inside. Ed Webster is a consummate photographer; in a certain sense he also writes pictures, seeing both vast panoramas but also their tiny, lovely parts: the flowers, the smells, the people. His perspective complements Stephen Venables' fine chronicle of their Everest ascent, *Everest Kangshung Face,* and we experience the same events through another set of eyes and emotions. For me this journey with Ed has been more than climbing yet another mountain. I have been privileged to journey with one who sees the world in ways different from my own, a person who takes me to places and into spaces I would otherwise not have known.

Seattle, Washington
July 1, 1998

Maps

Climbing Route Photo-diagrams

*Note: The book's Maps and Photo-diagrams utilize Mount Everest's
Year 2000 survey height of 29,035 feet / 8850 meters. The text uses
the prior accepted height of 29,028 feet / 8848 meters.*

CONTENTS

An End
and
a Beginning

Security is mostly a superstition. It does not exist in nature,
nor do the children of men as a whole experience it.
Avoiding danger is no safer in the long run than outright exposure.
Life is either a daring adventure, or nothing.

—Helen Keller

Twelve years ago, I determinedly began to write this book, typing out the words in agonizing taps with my black, mummified, frostbitten fingertips—and with thankfulness and disbelief that I'd survived my ordeal on Mount Everest's Kangshung Face. I was still alive. And although some of my life's ambitions had been realized, many others were now destroyed.

Several years earlier, I was convinced that I might never have the chance to climb in the Himalaya, let alone on Everest, the mountain of my dreams. Even though I'd rock climbed avidly since age eleven and by my midtwenties had accomplished many of my youthful goals—like scaling El Capitan's three-thousand-foot granite walls in Yosemite Valley—my greatest desire, to join a Himalayan expedition, lay unfulfilled. After graduating from Colorado College in 1978, I spent several happy wandering years rock climbing in many parts of

Left: *The summit of Mount Everest from Kala Pattar, Nepal.*

America, Great Britain, and France. My life's inspiration was my climbing, but earning a living as a climber was virtually impossible. My fledgling career as an adventure journalist earned only rejection slips. Then, in 1983, at age twenty-eight, I landed a job running a climbing school back in Colorado.

Overjoyed to return to the West from the deep woods of Maine where I had been living, I reveled once again under the sunny skies of the Rocky Mountains with their panoramic vistas. Below the Flatirons, in the university town of Boulder, I also met a beautiful young woman. Lauren Husted and I dated that summer, hiking and rock climbing locally before Lauren returned to college in Vermont. By June the next spring, Lauren had graduated, and we were living together in Boulder. My life was changing. Slowly, inexorably, even somewhat painfully, I could feel myself drifting farther away from full-time climbing.

I had to grow up sometime, didn't I? True, I had never achieved my dream of climbing in the Himalaya—and maybe now that Lauren and I were involved in a serious relationship I never would. How much longer could I delay life's expected rites of passage: getting married, settling down, working a nine-to-five job, maybe even having children? When would I come to my senses?

At twenty-two, Lauren was energetic and talented, brown-haired and blue-eyed. Born and raised in Boulder, she lived for the unbridled joy of being outdoors. But Lauren was no cardboard cutout. Bright and articulate—she'd graduated with honors—literature and writing were her motivating passions. Her career, too, was well begun; she'd just landed a job as a paid intern for *Denver Magazine*. Yet Lauren was also often uncomfortable in social settings, intensely jealous of her privacy, and she frequently needed time to be alone.

As our relationship blossomed and we overcame our inevitable ups and downs, Lauren could still surprise me, as she did one evening when I told her of the recent exploits of a climbing partner of mine. Bryan Becker and I had climbed together for years, and just two years earlier we'd successfully climbed the five-thousand-foot North Face of Mount Robson, an avalanche-raked precipice on British Columbia's highest peak. Now Bryan had taken this high-stakes alpine game a notch higher, forging a grueling new route, the *Denali Diamond,* up Mount McKinley in Alaska. I felt jealous of Bryan's pioneering climb, and my thoughts had become increasingly preoccupied with dreams of challenging a big mountain—a peak exceeding twenty thousand feet in elevation. Although the rigors and risks of climbing at high altitude felt daunting, going on a long expedition, hopefully overseas, and testing myself at altitude was the one type of mountaineering I hadn't experienced.

But one evening as we sat in our living room and I confided to Lauren that I'd give anything to go on a Himalayan expedition, her response couldn't have been more the reverse of what I'd expected. Instead of showing her usual vigorous enthusiasm for the outdoors, she suddenly and inexplicably broke down and began to sob as if seized by an unseen force. "No!" she burst out, startling me, her voice anguished and vehement, her fists clenched.

"No—I don't want you to go!" Then her body started to tremble.

"I'll die before you go to the Himalaya!" she exclaimed.

Of course I did not take her words literally—yet what she had said shocked me. Why had she spoken these disturbing words, and what did she mean by them? I hadn't meant to upset her, but I did feel strongly that one day I wanted to go on a Himalayan mountaineering expedition. As a climber herself, Lauren was well aware of the beauty and the danger of climbing, but a high-altitude ascent, we both knew, represented a greatly elevated level of seriousness above mere weekend rock climbing. However, although I'd lost several close friends in climbing accidents, my own twenty-year climbing record was injury free.

I was utterly stunned at the depth of Lauren's anguish and emotion. After immediately reassuring her that I'd be careful if I did go on an expedition, I hugged her as she wiped the tears from her eyes. I didn't know what more I could say to calm her fears. I only knew that testing myself on a big expedition and at high altitude were important goals to me. I hoped Lauren would eventually understand my need to fulfill these dreams, and as we hugged, I tried to put aside her initial, adamantly negative reaction to what I'd said.

*   *   *   *   *   *   *   *   *   *   *   *   *

A week later, Lauren and I spent Saturday and Sunday rock climbing in the Black Canyon of the Gunnison River, a twenty-five-hundred-foot chasm carved into the bedrock of Colorado's Western Slope. On Sunday, the sun was merciless. It was stiflingly hot, and we hadn't carried enough water. Dehydrated and worn out after ten rope lengths of climbing, we sat resting on a narrow ledge two hundred feet below the juniper-forested canyon rim—and safety.

"Next time we go away, let's try to relax a bit more," Lauren said. "Maybe we shouldn't do so much climbing."

"Maybe we shouldn't climb at all," I replied, somewhat out of character. "We'll have plenty of time to hike up in the mountains this summer."

Lauren nodded in quick approval; she loved the Rockies' wealth of alpine

The Black Canyon of the Gunnison River, Colorado.

flowers. After sharing some final sips of water from our water bottle, we caught our breath for several minutes, then I slapped my hands on my knees.

"Shall we?" I asked, rising.

"Let's go," Lauren replied.

Twenty minutes earlier, we'd decided to untie from our climbing rope in order to finish our ascent more quickly. The terrain had become easy—just scrambling along twenty-foot-wide ledges—and to stop and belay and safeguard each other with the rope, while obviously safer than climbing unroped, was also considerably more complicated and time consuming. To complete the climb, we now decided to traverse right across a narrower horizontal ledge system into a rocky, bush-filled gully that led to the canyon rim. The traverse was about three hundred feet long. And while the ledges looked relatively straightforward, in places they narrowed to only a foot or two wide, there was some loose rock, too—and below loomed a two-hundred-foot drop.

For the past month, Lauren had been leading her own rock climbs, going first on the rope and scouting out the route. Like a bird preparing to fly from the nest, she obviously enjoyed testing her strength and stamina, and increasingly she wanted to make her own decisions when we climbed together.

Yesterday, we'd done another route in the Black Canyon. Just below the top, Lauren had insisted that we climb solo—without the security of the climbing rope—up an eighty-foot-high crack. "No," I spoke firmly to her: "It's harder than it looks." When she refused my advice, I insisted we rope together and take the time to belay each other safely up the crack. And when she declined to tie into our climbing rope a second time, I took one end of it and, somewhat angrily, tied it into her harness. At the top, Lauren laughed. She was glad we'd roped up.

Today the situation was similar. Although the difficulty of the climbing was considerably easier, it was not without danger. The traverse ledges appeared to provide a natural and obvious line of escape. Once more Lauren assured me that she'd be okay climbing without the rope. And letting down my guard for the first time since we'd begun climbing together, I didn't question or analyze her judgment. We were both tired. I didn't want to argue. If she doesn't want to use the rope, fine, I thought. She seemed completely self-confident.

I went first; Lauren followed just behind me. She wore the coiled rope tied around her back; I carried the rest of our equipment. I threw most of the loose rock off, cleaning the handholds as I went. Ahead, I could see that the difficulties appeared to be ending. The climb would be over in a minute or two. A wide and spacious ledge was twenty-five feet away from me, but below our feet, the cliff still dropped precipitously for about one hundred feet. The potential for disaster never registered in my thoughts.

"Almost there!" I yelled, and then, as I turned around to watch her progress, I asked, "Are you okay?" Lauren stood twenty feet to my left.

"I'm coming!" she replied.

Then I witnessed the unthinkable. I saw her right hand reach for the next handhold. But she did not test it with a gentle tap to see if it was reliable. Instead, she pulled on the rock a little too hard—and it broke. Then I thought I saw her right foot slip, and Lauren lost her balance. She inhaled a breath in surprise. The look on her face was startled, but unafraid . . . then she cried out, helplessly—and fell, disappearing from view.

Horrified, I screamed her name repeatedly, but I heard only silence. Trembling with shock and disbelief, I ran over to the main gully, then angled back down it a short ways until I found Lauren lying on her side near the trail, bloodied and broken limbed, alive, yes, but breathing with great difficulty. It was the most horrible moment. Gently, ever so gently, careful of her head and neck, I rolled her over so she lay on her back. I cradled her head in my lap, trying to ease her pain and to stop the bleeding, but Lauren was very badly injured. Fortunately, some nearby hikers answered my shouts for help, then they ran to call for a rescue.

Twenty minutes later several people arrived, including Chester Dreiman, my best friend and a frequent climbing partner. Luckily, Chester had failed on his climb and was in the campground when the call came; he was also a skilled emergency medical technician. A woman hiker who was a registered nurse also rushed to the scene. They tended to Lauren's injuries for several minutes, then the nurse looked up. Staring directly at me, she spoke with a shocking calm.

"You know, she might not make it. Maybe you'd better prepare yourself."

Might not make it? Until that moment, I had never considered the possibility that Lauren could die. Now, on hearing the nurse's words, I contemplated anew the severity of Lauren's wounds. Yet as I lovingly cradled her head in my lap, I simply could not accept the possibility that Lauren would die. Was God so uncaring as to let such a young and vibrant woman die? Could fate be this unspeakably cruel? Lauren could not die.

But as the sun sank toward the canyon's western rim, Lauren did die. Her head rested upon my lap. In the passing of those eternally long and yet forever lost seconds, Lauren's face became serenely peaceful as her struggle for life ended. Her blue eyes, gazing upward, were both tranquil and open. Gradually her gentle breathing slowed, became imperceptible, and her heart quieted. Then Lauren became perfectly still. With tear-filled eyes and trembling limbs I held her close, and tried to understand why, why she had died.

My grief over her death and my sense of guilt for letting her die in a rock climbing accident—one so preventable in hindsight—were overwhelming. Lauren died in my arms that afternoon on the date of our one-year anniversary. She also died, much more tragically, on Father's Day. The date was June 17, 1984. That evening, as I struggled to control my shock and grief, a police officer drove me to a pay phone where I called her beloved father to tell him that his eldest daughter had died. Several days later, I joined her family and friends at an outdoor memorial service in the mountains above Boulder, and Lauren Ann Husted was buried in her hometown, within sight of the Flatirons and the snow-capped Rocky Mountains she had loved.

* * * * * * * * * * * * *

I lived alone that summer in the basement apartment Lauren and I had shared on Pine Street in Boulder. A month after her death, while visiting friends in Aspen, I forced myself to go rock climbing again. I sobbed uncontrollably. Climbing had always been so life affirming, my greatest source of joy and self-expression, and a constant stabilizing force for me. In my pursuit of climbing, I had seen incredible natural beauty and made many lasting friends—but how could I have let Lauren die? Why hadn't I foreseen the danger and insisted that we remain roped together for safety? Could I continue to climb? I wondered—and doubted—that climbing would ever give me the same joy that it once had.

Wanting to know Lauren better, I read several short stories that she had written, her recent diaries, and two of her college textbooks about the English poet John Keats. I knew she'd experienced a profound—and at the time, an inexplicable—kinship with Keats, who also died young, at the age of twenty-six. Lauren was twenty-two when she died. She had greatly enjoyed reading Keats's poetry aloud. Her favorite was the sonnet "Bright Star":

> Bright star, would I were steadfast as thou art—
>   Not in lone splendour hung aloft the night
> And watching, with eternal lids apart,
>   Like nature's patient, sleepless Eremite,
> The moving waters at their priestlike task
>   Of pure ablution round earth's human shores,
> Or gazing on the new soft fallen mask
>   Of snow upon the mountains and the moors—
> No—yet still steadfast, still unchangeable,
>   Pillow'd upon my fair love's ripening breast,
> To feel for ever its soft fall and swell,
>   Awake for ever in a sweet unrest,
> Still, still to hear her tender-taken breath,
> And so live ever—or else swoon to death.

In retrospect, I believe Lauren left me her writing and Keats's poetry to guide me through my anguish. The months following her death brought about a difficult and yet deeply spiritual awakening in me. As I read her diaries, I also learned Lauren had experienced premonitions of her own death, although she never mentioned them to me. I sensed Lauren's spirit had returned home to Boulder, and I often palpably felt her soft gaze consoling me over one shoulder.

Lauren and I were climbers because of our mutual delight in living life to its absolute fullest. She had filled her all-too-short number of years with such

The East Face of Longs Peak in Rocky Mountain National Park, Colorado.
The Diamond is the vertical granite precipice beneath the summit.

vitality that I decided I had to do something to equal her passion for living. The young woman who had bicycled alone through Scotland, biked down the California and Oregon coast, sailed along the Turkish coastline, hiked Colorado's high country, and climbed so elegantly, deserved a fitting memorial.

* * * * * * * * * * * * * *

The preceding spring, Lauren and I had discussed hiking up Longs Peak, which at 14,256 feet is the tallest mountain in northern Colorado. Longs was my favorite local summit; I'd already hiked and climbed it a half dozen times. Longs also boasts Colorado's most difficult alpine rock wall, the thousand-foot vertical granite face called the Diamond.

I first climbed the Diamond at age twenty-one in 1977, completing a four-day rope-solo ascent of the *D1 Route*. Getting caught in a violent hailstorm just below the peak's weather-blasted summit, I had been forced to make an emergency bivouac. Would I be able to find my way down the next morning? I had no map, and just a rough idea of where the descent route was located. Snow fell thick around me that night, and tossing and turning through the long dark hours, wet, shivering, and cold, I began to wonder if I'd survive.

Then, not knowing if I was awake or asleep, I floated upwards. Separating from my physical body, I rose into a warm and comforting sky. From this vantage point, I looked down at my suffering, bent body clinging to life amongst the iron-cold boulders and swirling snowflakes. A moment later, a female figure hovered beside me. We drifted together; I knew her identity immediately. She was my mother, Irene, who had died from a heart attack brought on by diabetes when I was a baby. The sensation of being surrounded by her caring love intensified. Irene was watching out for me, as she always had. She would protect me. I would survive the storm, and she was my guardian. Without a single word being spoken, I knew that this tenderness was real, yet as soon as I tried to consciously prolong my vision of my mother, instantly I was thrown back into my physical body and shivering once again with hypothermia amongst the rocks. But now none of my suffering mattered. I knew I'd be safe. When the morning dawned, the storm clouds lifted, and I descended safely.

As the years passed, I felt lucky to have had my out-of-body experience. It was such a personal and profound revelation that I told very few people of it. I felt singled out, charmed, protected. And bolstered by this unwarranted self-confidence, *I began to believe that I could survive virtually any climb I attempted.* Each climb I tried was harder, riskier, and more life-threatening than the last. When my mother died, I was so young—two and a half years old—that I have never had any mental recollection of her. So, logically, and I think understandably, I began to wonder whether, if I pushed myself to my utmost on other climbs as I had on the Diamond, I might see Irene again. In fact, all during my twenties, I found it impossible to suppress this wish "to visit" with her.

In the August following Lauren's death, I remembered having seen a thin crack slicing straight up the center of the Diamond when I'd soloed the face seven years earlier. I knew that this crack was unclimbed. It was a potential new route. Impulsively, I decided to attempt to climb it alone, to push myself to that next edge of possibility. A new route up the Diamond would be my tribute to Lauren, and I knew immediately what I would name it: *Bright Star.*

Death could be a serene conclusion to life—but death could also be hated, cold, ugly, and unfathomable. Death was human, yet very inhuman. For weeks and months after Lauren died, I still could not accept its irrevocable finality. I had watched and sensed Lauren's soul leave her body, and that vision lingered painfully on in every cell of memory in my brain. Why had life been torn from her grasp? I had found no answer to this question. I only knew that to sustain Lauren's memory, and to find a way to continue with my own life, I had to try to solo a new route up the Diamond. And what if I injured myself or died? Grief had pushed me beyond the brink of caring.

* * * * * * * * * * * * *

In the first week of September, 1984, three friends helped me shoulder one hundred pounds of equipment and food up the Longs Peak Trail to the Chasm View overlook, a spectacular rocky notch at 13,500 feet in elevation. Bidding good-bye to Larry, Denny, and Jan, I carefully rappelled down the five-hundred-foot cliff to the foot of the Diamond. After slowly working my way to my left across a ledge system known as Broadway, transporting my loads in stages, I set up my bivouac in a small sheltered cave beneath the towering wall.

Settling down for the night on the rock-strewn ledge at the base of the Diamond, I watched the pink hues of evening rise like vapors from Colorado's eastern plains, tinting the brush-stroke clouds upon the horizon. Lights from small ranches appeared in the dark valley below, while the evening star—alone, and first to grace the night—sparkled directly overhead. Only two and a half months had passed since Lauren's death, but already my final conversation with her felt a lifetime away. Alone on my ledge, I hugged my sleeping bag for warmth, and relished the timelessness of my solitary view.

Strong forces were at work for the next three days while I lived on the Diamond's vertical precipice. Providentially, the weather was clear and crisp, with no afternoon thunderstorms—and thin vertical cracks beckoned skyward, piercing the heart of the gold-plated granite wall. After two rope lengths of strenuous aid climbing, where I supported my weight by hanging from marginally placed pitons (knife-like blades of chrome-moly steel hammered into cracks), and tiny wedge-shaped wired nuts (slotted into the cracks), I arranged a hanging bivouac three hundred feet up the wall. Sitting comfortably on my portaledge (a suspended platform akin to a collapsible Army cot), I admired the evening quiet, sipped my tea, and contemplated nature's great symphony.

The author during his solo first ascent of Bright Star *(V 5.9, A3) on Longs Peak.*

On Day three, five rope lengths of climbing—hand and fist jamming up awkward cracks, more tricky artificial climbing, and the back-breaking manual labor of hauling my equipment—saw me arrive exhausted on the Yellow Wall bivouac ledge, a slender shelf four hundred feet below the Diamond's summit. The temperature plummeted that night as I searched the sky for the storm that I knew would probably soon threaten me. The weather had been too good for too long. I tried to direct my thoughts to Lauren; I was doing this climb for her, infusing the ageless stone with her spirit. My life had been forever altered by her death; I was no longer the person I had once been.

My brain agonized the next morning when I realized that I was irrevocably committed to finishing the climb. Retreat was now only a last-ditch option. In photographs, I recalled seeing an elegant crack splitting the gold headwall above the cliff's final overhangs; reaching this crack became my goal. Numbed with cold, I hammered pitons and wedged wired nuts into devious cracks in the stone, placing one anchor for each new body length of height. One hundred feet higher, I arranged a belay anchor below a six-foot horizontal ceiling that jutted out spectacularly over my head. Below, over fifteen hundred feet of empty, cold air separated me from the rippling waters of Chasm Lake.

Swinging spider-like past the edge of the top overhang, I looked up expectantly. I could do it! A lovely climbable crack led directly to the top—but I had to hurry. A storm had arrived, and it would soon break. Ominous gray clouds raced demonically over the jagged rocky summit, now a stone's throw above me. With adrenaline-fed urgency, I climbed rapidly toward the top.

Then, at the end of the difficulties, two college climbing friends of mine, Peter Gallagher and Russ Johnson, appeared like apparitions. Having just completed another route on the Diamond, Peter and Russ helped me haul up my equipment to the finish. Unfortunately, the threatening storm cut short our impromptu celebration. We hurried past the scene of my earlier out-of-body experience near the summit of Longs, and raced down the North Face descent. Safely back at the Chasm View overlook where I'd begun my vertical journey three days prior, my friends wished me luck and headed down a different way.

Alone once again, I stumbled downhill to the normal hiking trail at the Boulderfield. Incredulous at my luck that the weather had remained fair as long as it did, and that the route had been feasible, I could hardly believe I'd succeeded on *Bright Star.* Hoisting my gargantuan pack filled with gear and ropes onto my shoulders, grimacing and smiling simultaneously, I hobbled awkwardly down the uneven rocky trail in an endless series of knee-pounding sprints.

Longs Peak welcoming the storm, seen from the Boulderfield. The Diamond's upper half is visible.

Out of breath, I stopped to rest for the fiftieth—or the one hundredth—time. Glancing back up at the mountain, I watched in awe as a black blanket of angry clouds steamrolled up the back side of Longs and engulfed the Diamond's stark precipice in wrathful fury. I could no longer recognize the golden vertical wall that I'd spent the past three days climbing, but now it no longer mattered. I was safe, I was on the trail, and my adventure was over. Minutes later, storm clouds dropped earthward, cloaking Longs Peak and pouring pounding waves of hail from the darkened sky. Soaked to the skin in seconds, I began to shiver violently.

I could have cared less.

Propping my eighty-pound haulbag against a convenient granite boulder, I sat down and laughed and cried. Only this time, my tears flowed not from sadness, but from strength. Unseen hands—God's, Lauren's, or both—had just safeguarded me through one of the most positive experiences of my life.

Lauren had known the answer all along, that the only way to live life was as intensely and completely as possible, choosing energy over despair. I knew that I would follow her example and live my life to the fullest, but on that stormy September day on Longs Peak, I could never have fathomed where that challenging path would soon take me: to the Himalaya, to Nepal, Tibet, and China. Three times within the next four years, I would attempt to climb Mount Everest, and in 1988 I would almost lose my life climbing a new route up Everest's most perilous side, the Kangshung Face. The next four years would truly be the storm years of my strength, and of my youth—the days when I would be tested as never before.

MOUNT EVEREST · SAGARMATHA

CHOMOLUNGMA

29,035 feet / 8850 meters

South Summit

Northeast Ridge

Camp
Five

Southeast Ridge

Camp
Four
(25,500
feet)

South Col

North Ridge

Camp
Three
(23,860 feet)

LHOTS

Camp Two
(22,500 feet)

Everest's
West Shoulder

North Col

North Face

Everest's
West Shoulder

Western Cwm

Advanced
Base
Camp
(20,000 feet)

Mallory's View
Lho La Plateau

Headwall & Winch

Khumbu
Icefall

Nuptse

West Ridge
Direct Route
(Yugoslavia, 1979)

Hillary-Tenzing
South Col Route
(Swiss-British, 1952-53)

Khumbu
Base Camp
(17,500 feet)

Khumbu Glacier

Chapter 1

Beginners on Everest

*If we are facing in the right direction,
all we have to do is keep on walking.*

—Buddhist expression

Climbers love slide shows, and in October, 1984, I attended a lecture in Denver to promote an upcoming American Everest expedition. The speaker was the team's deputy leader, a prominent Colorado climber named Bill Forrest. We'd known one another for several years (coincidentally, Bill was the first to ever make a solo ascent of the Diamond on Longs Peak), and now, as Bill explained in his talk, the expedition's ambitious goal was to make the first American ascent of the *West Ridge Direct Route* up Mount Everest.

A week earlier, I'd met several of Bill's teammates at a fund-raising breakfast. Some lived in the Denver-Boulder area, while the remainder hailed mostly from California. After I wrote a newspaper article about their quest, my friendship with the Colorado contingent grew—and quite unexpectedly my name was added to a list of alternate members.

Left: *Everest.* Swiss Foundation for Alpine Research / American Alpine Club Library

After his lecture, Bill asked if we could speak in private. "Well, we've talked it over," he said matter-of-factly, "and we'd really like to have you on the team."

I thought I'd known what Bill might say, but when I heard his words, I was speechless. At first I thought he might be joking. Climb Everest—me? I had wanted to climb in the Himalaya ever since reading my first climbing book at age eleven. After recovering my composure, I told Bill that I definitely wanted to go, and we shook hands. To compound my good fortune, a week later my employer, Eastern Mountain Sports, agreed to sponsor me. I was the newest member of the 1985 American Mount Everest West Ridge Expedition.

I felt swept away by events too good to be true. Going to Everest already felt like a turning point in my life. In fact it felt predestined. But what of the timing of my invitation? Did Lauren have a premonition of our destinies— of her own death, and of my journey to Everest? I became convinced that she had. I recalled telling her of my wish to climb in the Himalaya, and her tearful reaction that she didn't want me to go, how she said that she would die before I went there. Now climbing had killed Lauren, taken her from her parents, her loved ones, and me, and had made my life a purgatory filled with guilt and heart-wrenching sadness. Yet climbing had also brought me such great gifts. It had shaped the majority of my life, given it direction and meaning, and con-stantly pushed me forward to meet new and unexpected challenges.

* * * * * * * * * * * * * *

I grew up in Lexington, Massachusetts, just west of Boston. As a restless ado-lescent, I had begun to get into some youthful troubles, nothing serious, but bothersome enough that my parents took me to a psychiatrist. His wise recom-mendation was that I needed an outdoor activity I could channel my energy into. My stepmother, Dorothea, liked to bring home books from the local library for me to read. One day she handed me a new book—about the Abominable Snowman, the Yeti. The legends about this mysterious mountain creature and the isolated, glacier-clad peaks of Nepal and Tibet, enthralled me.

My next library book inspired my lifelong love of climbing. It was *Everest Diary,* the journal-based story of Lute Jerstad, who in 1963 became one of the first Americans to climb Mount Everest. His tale of high-altitude adventure fired my young imagination like no book ever had. After devouring the remainder of the climbing books in the Lexington library, next I headed to the Appalachian Mountain Club library in Boston where I soon read all of the classic early British

My parents, Dorothea and Edward Webster, and my younger brother Mark and me.

Everest expedition books, notably *Mount Everest, The Reconnaissance, 1921,* then *The Assault on Mount Everest, 1922,* and *The Fight for Everest: 1924.*

British mountaineers George Mallory and Andrew Irvine, Edward Norton, and Noel Odell became my heroes. And, with zealous industry, I compiled my own Tibetan-Sherpa-Sanskrit-Hindi-Nepali dictionary. The words and phrases that I gleaned from various expedition books, I used quite interchangeably (the specific language didn't much matter), and I was delighted when I'd amassed enough words to assemble an entire sentence. Clearly inspired, I even wrote a fictional story, "Ang Bandar Lhamu" (The Beloved Monkey Goddess), about "a pilgrimage to riches" to Mount Kailas in Tibet. Few of the boys in my junior high school hand-lettered Buddhist prayer flags, but I did. Studiously I hand-copied *"Om mani padme hum"* (Hail the jewel in the lotus flower) in Tibetan script onto torn bedsheets, attached the prayer flags vertically to bamboo poles—in traditional Tibetan style—and proudly displayed them in my bedroom.

My parents didn't become overly alarmed about my climbing infatuation until I secretly borrowed my father's three-eighths-inch-diameter manila rope. He used the rope to lower dead tree branches; I used it to body rappel down a fifty-foot pine tree in our backyard. Sensibly, my dad bought me an instructional climbing book, and later he drove my teenage friends and me to rock climbing classes held by the Appalachian Mountain Club, the AMC, near Boston. These 1969 weekend tutorials were my first organized instruction, and I recall being ecstatic after I scaled a short, steep rock that no one else could even start.

Ed below Airation, *Cathedral Ledge, New Hampshire, 1975.* Brian Delaney

In high school I joined the Lexington Explorer Scout Troop, Post 122. With my newfound scouting friends, I began to discover the major northeastern rock climbing areas, first exploring the Quincy Quarries and Crow Hill in Massachusetts, then Cathedral and Whitehorse Ledges and Cannon Cliff in the White Mountains of New Hampshire, Ragged Mountain in Connecticut, and eventually the Shawangunks in New York state. By the age of eighteen, in 1974, I was leading 5.11 free climbs—which at the time was close to the highest degree of difficulty in American rock climbing.

Since I learned to climb in 1967, climbing has always been more than a sport to me. Over the years it has become my way of life—and the way in which I relate to the world around me. Being a climber has so engendered my positive outlook on life that, until Lauren died, I'd never once considered quitting climbing. I've always known that what I love to do most is climb—on rock, ice, or snow. And through writing, photography, lecturing, and teaching others how to climb, I've been able to earn a living— if a slender one—from my avocation.

At age twenty-eight, my climbing apprenticeship, I felt, was more or less complete. I'd climbed in many parts of America, from New Hampshire to Colorado to California, from Eldorado Canyon to El Capitan, and overseas, in England's Lake and Peak Districts, and in Chamonix and the Verdon Gorge in France. I'd ice climbed in New England, Colorado, and Scotland. The North Face of Mount Robson in Canada was my first major alpine climb. With the single exception of high-altitude mountaineering—expeditionary climbing in the Andes, Alaska, or the Himalaya—my schooling as a climber was complete.

* * * * * * * * * * * * * *

Bryan Becker and Ed Webster (top) *on the first ascent of* Super Crack *(5.10b)*
in Indian Creek Canyon, Canyonlands, Utah, in 1976. Michael Gardiner

As my teammates and I prepared for Everest, it became obvious that the hardest part of a Himalayan expedition was rounding up the necessary funds. Yet we diligently raised our $250,000 budget. Eastern Mountain Sports not only sponsored my participation on the expedition, they also supplied all of the specialized clothing and climbing gear I needed.

Several of my teammates were Coloradans. These included our expedition leader, Dave Saas, who obtained our Everest climbing permit (for only $3,000) from the Nepalese Ministry of Tourism in 1982; Bill Forrest, the team's deputy leader; Dan Larson, a local mountaineer and our expedition lawyer; George McLeod, who with his extensive Antarctic experience was our Base Camp manager; local fire fighters Jim McMillian and Brian O'Malley; Peter Athans, a seasoned Colorado Outward Bound instructor with Himalayan experience; and Scott Lankford, our Stanford-educated mountaineer. John Meyer, a sportswriter for the *Rocky Mountain News* in Denver, came as expedition journalist.

Heidi Benson from Tacoma, Washington, was our only female climber. Heidi was also the one-woman dynamo who ran the expedition's Denver office. In the four months before our departure, we organized, purchased, and packed thirty thousand pounds of food and equipment to be air-freighted to Nepal.

Our climbing leader, Jim Bridwell, lived in Lake Tahoe, California. One of the most well-known rock climbers in America, Jim is considered the godfather of modern Yosemite climbing. More recently he had transformed himself into an accomplished "super alpinist," blazing notoriously difficult, lightning-fast new routes up the world's toughest peaks.

Jim Bridwell in Yosemite Valley, California, 1979.

Other Lake Tahoe team members included Jay Smith, another rock-solid climber who ran a climbing school and guide service, and Fletcher Wilson, who was our youngest member at twenty-two, and a rock climber and speed skier.

Rounding out our expedition of twenty-one were Robert Anderson, a well-traveled mountaineer and Coloradan who currently lived in New Zealand; Kim Carpenter, a lanky rock expert from Redondo Beach, California; Randal Grandstaff, a climbing guide from Las Vegas, Nevada; Andy Politz, a mountain guide on Mount Rainier in Washington State; Kevin Swigert, an expert cross-country skier, climber, and winner of the television competition "Survival Of The Fittest," from Ketchum, Idaho; Dr. John Pelner, who practiced medicine in Kansas, and Greg Sapp, a mountaineer and real estate broker from Phoenix, Arizona. In Nepal, expatriate climber Rodney Korich would handle logistics.

On paper, our expedition was traditionally organized and reasonably well qualified. But our goal, Everest's *West Ridge Direct,* was one of the mountain's longest and hardest routes. First ascended by a fifty-man Yugoslavian national expedition in May, 1979, the climb had only been repeated once by an equally large, well-equipped Bulgarian national team in 1984. A dozen more expeditions to the route had failed, including American attempts in 1981 and 1983. Given the climb's great difficulty and tremendous horizontal distance—as the crow flies, Everest's summit is five miles distant from Khumbu Base Camp, and over two miles higher—to succeed, we would need exceptional individual perform-ances and excellent weather. The route's crux was reputed to be difficult rock climbing between twenty-seven thousand feet and the 29,028-foot summit.

Yet Dave Saas had insisted on an unusual stipulation, that none of our team should have previous Everest experience. Theoretically, such equal foot-ing gave everyone a fairer chance of summiting. "We've got guys who haven't been above fourteen thousand feet, but that's not necessarily a liability," Dave said. "Who we do have are people who will give this climb their all, to prove they can climb at altitude."

Bridwell was more of a realist when it came to measuring our capabilities. "Our greatest strength comes from not having any prima donnas," Jim said, "but we've got to keep *the lambs* out of harm's way. There's no point giving fate *too much* of a chance."

Our West Ridge expedition was an odd coupling: a devout Mormon, Saas, teamed with a hard-drinking, cigarette-smoking Yosemite superstar, Bridwell, leading a crew of "slang-slinging" hip Californians and mellow Colorado moun-tain men. Few expedition members had previously attained an altitude of

Training for Everest: Ed leading pitch one of The Yellow Spur *(5.9) in plastic boots on a cold November day. Eldorado Canyon, Colorado, 1984.* Chester Dreiman

twenty thousand feet, the usual prerequisite for a Himalayan expedition; and only Athans, Bridwell, and Sapp could claim prior Himalayan experience (on Makalu, Pumori, and Annapurna III, respectively). Were we unreasonably optimistic in hoping to vanquish one of Everest's longest and hardest routes? Would our potpourri of experience and attitudes gel to achieve such a lofty goal, or had we too been swept away by Everest-mania?

I took the positive approach, assuming that we could and would work well together. As Bridwell put it, we would climb Everest's West Ridge because we had the will to succeed. I was merely glad to have been invited and cared little that I was now a cog on a large and occasionally impersonal expedition wheel. Group dynamics had never been my strong suit; on Everest I hoped to roll with the punches.

My obvious downfall was in high-altitude climbing experience. I had none. My altitude "record" before going to Everest was a paltry 14,420 feet, the summit of Mount Harvard, *third-highest* of Colorado's many fourteen-thousand-foot peaks. But the plus side of such a large, sponsored expedition like ours was that it gave aspiring climbers like myself that crucial first-time opportunity to climb in the Himalaya. We altitude novices felt lucky to finally test ourselves. And in hindsight, I think the investment proved to be quite worthwhile. Six of the West Ridge team became active Himalayan mountaineers in subsequent years. Yet our first-ever high-altitude expedition was bound to throw some of us for a few knocks. "Beginners on Everest" was Bridwell's half-facetious appraisal of our skill level.

A dozen Sherpas from Mountain Travel, Kathmandu's oldest and largest trekking agency, would climb with us. Their job was to help carry the food, supplies, and other equipment we would use to stock five preplanned campsites. The best Sherpas might also be chosen for a summit bid. Thirty oxygen bottles would improve everyone's chances of reaching the top, while thirty thousand feet of fixed rope—a thousand feet more than the height of Everest!—would create a "rope highway" up the mountain, linking one camp to the next.

* * * * * * * * * * * * * *

On February 15, 1985, I left Denver for Nepal with Grandstaff, Larson, McLeod, "Mac" McMillian, Pelner, and Saas. That night we met the rest of the team at Heidi's mother's house in Tacoma, Washington—except for Robert Anderson who flew to Kathmandu from New Zealand. After the weeks and

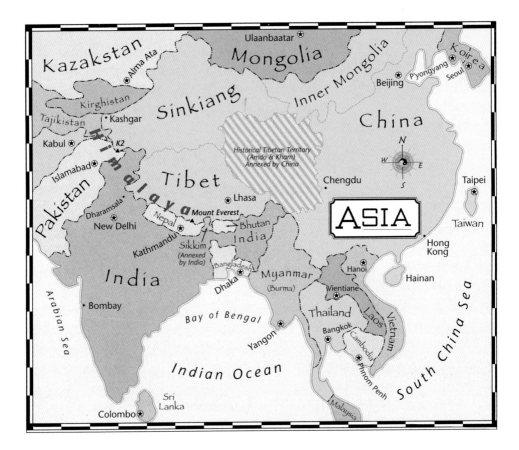

months of daily chaos and long hours, there was a tired but tangible euphoria at our rendezvous. Finally we could concentrate on what we did best in life: climb! However, there was also regret because at the last moment Bill Forrest couldn't come because of business tie-ups. I'd been really looking forward to climbing with Bill, particularly as he'd invited me on the team. We were sorry, more sorry than we knew at the time, to lose his wise counsel.

The following afternoon I walked through the international departure gate at Seattle's Sea-Tac Airport. I felt little emotion besides expectancy. I shed no tears, I had no loved ones near, no wife, children, or girlfriend with whom to share precious last few moments. The head cold I'd caught lent a surreal feeling to the proceedings: Heidi with tear-stained cheeks hugging her brother and mother farewell; Fletcher quietly reading a Louis L'Amour novel; Bridwell play-acting in pantomime; and Kim, the California hardman, casually clad in a black muscle shirt, flexing his biceps, smoking a cigarette.

Every cell in my body tingled in anticipation of our Everest adventure. As the Thai Airways jet took off for Bangkok, I had the clear sensation that my many years of climbing had paved the way for this new life chapter.

Jim Bridwell, Dave Saas, and Kim Carpenter arrive in Kathmandu.

After a two-day, halfway-around-the-world flight with brief stops in Japan and Thailand, we landed in Kathmandu, Nepal's capital. Few of us had been to Asia, and the sights and sounds of Kathmandu bombarded our senses with new ways of living, new ways of being, and new ways of dying. The next ten days were an enchanting time of personal exploration and cultural readjustment as I underwent an awakening to Hindu and Buddhist beliefs, and gained insights into a world view beyond my western concepts. Unfortunately, my head cold had almost predictably worsened, and stepping out into the noisy, chaotic streets of Kathmandu, it took me several days to regain my balance.

We arrived on February 18, the start of *Losar,* the week celebrating the Sherpa and Tibetan New Year—now the Year of the Wood Ox. There was plenty of work to do before we reached Base Camp. Forays were made in search of climbing gear in the shops of Thamel, Kathmandu's trekking shop district; expedition clothing was tried on to make sure it fit; and hundreds of loads were repacked at the dusty Mountain Travel courtyard. At night we made merry with our teammates and foreign mountaineers, including the Norwegian Everest expedition and Britain's Chris Bonington, our future neighbors on the Khumbu Glacier. It was also then that Brian O'Malley met Carrie Fisher of *Star Wars* movie fame, but that's a story I'm not qualified to tell.

At another of our evening socials, I met Karen Fellerhoff, an American trekking leader with ambitions of working for Dick Bass, the wealthy Texas mountaineer who would also be attempting Everest that spring. Karen and I biked around Kathmandu the next day, clinking our handlebar bells to alert pedestrians, cars, and sacred cows of our presence. Bodhnath, our first destination, was the capital's largest Buddhist temple. Throngs of dirt-poor hill folk circumambulated clockwise around the massive *stupa,* gaily decorated with long

The author arriving in Nepal at the start of the Everest West Ridge expedition.

fluttering strings of prayer flags to celebrate the new year. Karen explained that walking the wrong way (counterclockwise) around sacred Buddhist objects and structures—prayer wheels, a *stupa, chortens,* prayer walls, or even a temple— brought bad luck, which then required considerable self-sacrifice to repair.

After visiting the nearby Sherpa Cultural Center—and watching a New Year's blessing ceremony where, in something like reverse communion, the Sherpas blessed the monks by tossing barley flour into their faces—we headed to Pashupatinath, Nepal's most revered Hindu temple, on the banks of the holy Bagmati River. Being non-Hindu prevented us from entering the temple complex proper, so we walked through a colorful market and gazed at the distant *ghats,* the ritual cremation sites alongside the riverbank. Destruction, creation, and renewed destruction are the underlying tenets of Hinduism, Karen told me, and each day brings a new test to the precarious balance of good and evil.

"There is a saying in Kathmandu. Hindus celebrate with blood, and the Sherpas with *chang*," Karen elaborated. Hindus, she said, prefer to placate their gods by sacrificing animals—slitting their throats, or cutting off their heads—while Buddhist Sherpas were more likely to pray, and then throw a party.

"Hinduism is just too fatalistic and bloody for me," Karen admitted.

From a hilltop above the river, we stared at the *ghats*. "There may be bodies burning," Karen warned. "You don't have to look if you don't want to."

But I had seen death. I did not avert my eyes from the *ghats*. I looked at the fires, the glowing human embers and smoking piles of wood with the certain knowledge that life truly ends in death—and yet life, in all its wondrous forms and resiliency, goes on.

An elderly Hindu man approached us. "Truth is beauty, beauty is death, death is truth," he said in a calm, declarative voice while pointing toward the human ashes an attendant was sweeping into the Bagmati River's dark, rushing water.

* * * * * * * * * * * * * *

On February 22, I joined my teammates at two blessing ceremonies (or *pujas*) being held for the success of our expedition. Each was conducted at Bodhnath by the reincarnate head lamas, or *Rinpoches,* of the two largest monasteries near Everest, at Pangboche and Tengboche. At birth a *Rinpoche* is believed able to identify objects from their previous life and the children are usually singled out for identification by their parents because of their precocious behavior. Once recognized, the reincarnate typically advances quickly to become a lama. The reason that they excel is simple: they have "retained knowledge" from their former existences.

First we met the Drew *Rinpoche,* the reincarnate lama of Pangboche, the home town of our *Sirdar* or head Sherpa, Ang Zangbu. The Drew *Rinpoche* was a balding, gray-haired man of seventy, who wore black-rim glasses, dressed in a simple orange robe, and sat comfortably on a pillowed couch. Two nuns served him.

We filed into the small room one at a time, then knelt, presenting him with a cash donation wrapped inside a white *kata,* or greeting scarf. Dave Saas gave a one-thousand-rupee note, which was about forty dollars. The rest of us offered ten or twenty rupees each. In return, we received red cotton blessing cords, which we tied around our necks for good luck on the climb. Afterwards, as the Drew *Rinpoche* talked with Ang Zangbu, several times I heard them mention Chomolungma, the Sherpa and Tibetan name for Mount Everest. It made me wonder how many times brave mountaineers, women and men from around the world, had knelt before this lama, asking for his prayers and good luck before heading to Chomolungma?

That afternoon we met the Tengboche *Rinpoche*, Ngawang Tenzin Zangbu. Born in 1935, he is believed to be the reincarnation of Lama Gulu, the lama who founded Tengboche Monastery in 1916. When Lama Gulu died in 1933—on the very night that Tengboche was destroyed by an earthquake—he was reborn in Namche Bazaar as an ordinary villager, and named Passang Tenzin. Later, he was discovered to be Tengboche's reincarnate lama, or *tulku*, by the head lama of Rongbuk Monastery in Tibet, the Dzatrul *Rinpoche*, who gave him his new name, and the monastery at Tengboche was rebuilt.

(A popular destination for climbers and trekkers, Tengboche Monastery was destroyed a second time, by fire, on the evening of January 19, 1989. An electric spaceheater started the blaze. The monastery was rebuilt with assistance from Sir Edmund Hillary's Himalayan Trust, the American Himalayan Foundation, and other concerned international aid groups and individuals. After a concerted rebuilding effort, Tengboche was rededicated in September, 1993.)

We couldn't wait to leave Kathmandu for the mountains, but stormy weather was conspiring against us. After one flight to the Lukla air strip was canceled, we attempted a second dawn departure. Our bags were all over-weight, but it wasn't anything a lot of loud shouting couldn't resolve. Finally came the expected bad news: "All flights canceled due to weather."

That evening Karen and I walked to Swayambhunath, the Monkey Temple, on top of a prominent hill rising to the west of Thamel. A lengthy stone stair-way led through a *Wizard of Oz*-like forest. Gnarled trees loomed skyward in haunting silhouette, while agile monkeys swung from branch to branch and scurried in the underbrush. In the setting sunlight, the view from the temple's sacred summit was breathtaking. In spite of Kathmandu's seeming complexity, its labyrinthine chaos of back streets and alleys, from this vantage point the city appeared quite contained. Checkered green fields and thatched homes lay just beyond downtown Thamel's hustle and bustle.

We walked clockwise round the whitewashed *stupa,* spun prayer wheels, and stopped before the open doorway of a shrine. The serene gaze of a twenty-foot-tall gold Buddha pulled us inside.

As we stood by a table of burning yak butter candles at the Buddha's feet, Karen mentioned that Buddhists do not revere the actual statues. "Their wor-

Kathmandu's Monkey Temple is a revered and popular destination.

ship isn't materially bound in any way. The significance of the statues lies in what they represent, the knowledge that human beings—each of us—have the innate potential to achieve perfection and a balanced harmony, no matter what religion or background we might hail from.

"What I find appealing about Buddhism is its emphasis on the creation of goodness in the world. Buddhists believe that the underlying fabric of the universe is good and loving and full of hope. So I always pray before the Buddha because I'm in reverence of that potential, for mankind's inner perfection."

Buddhists believe that goodness and merit on earth can be created in a multitude of ways: by chanting prayers, twirling prayer wheels, stringing up prayer flags to flutter in the wind, carving a prayer into a rock face—or simply by doing good deeds for others.

"Just remember," Karen added, "whenever you encounter a tricky problem or a potential confrontation in Asia, just smile. Then everything will always turn out for the best."

Karen had gotten the job of Base Camp manager for Dick Bass's Everest attempt, so we spun a ten-foot prayer wheel to pray that our respective teams would both meet with success—and watched the fire-orange sun drop behind snow-capped, black-shadowed Himalayan peaks.

* * * * * * * * * * * * *

As we snaked and bounced through Kathmandu's back streets to Tribhuvan International Airport for the third time in almost as many days, Kim Carpenter exclaimed, "Man, this place makes Camp Four"—the legendary climber's campground in Yosemite Valley—"look like Beverly Hills!" The weather still had not cleared, and after a week, Kathmandu's excess of air pollution, dust, haze, filth, and animal and human excrement was beginning to take a predictable toll on our health. Colds, scratchy sore throats, plugged ears, or worse—violently upset stomachs and diarrhea—were common complaints.

Fortunately, this morning our luck appeared to be changing. America's ambassador to Nepal, Leon Weil, and his party of trekkers also were waiting for a Lukla flight. Ang Zangbu paced the floor with palpable agitation, occasionally glancing out the windows at the two Twin Otters parked on the tarmac.

"Fog in Lukla," he told me dourly. "Very bad if we don't fly today." Then, as if a magic wand were waved, a Royal Nepal Airlines pilot opened the cockpit door of one plane. Zangbu shot me an enthusiastic thumbs-up: "I think we go!"

Duffels of climbing gear, canned goods, crates of eggs, and twelve nervously expectant passengers crammed with equal billing inside the plane. I sat beside an elderly Sherpa; his wife sat across from us. As the engines throttled to full power and we mad-dashed down the runway, the old Sherpa clamped his eyes shut, prayed furiously, and fingered a string of prayer beads at lightning speed. For the next hour we rested in God's hands. As I peered out the window, Everest's singular pyramid suddenly soared high above the lowland clouds. I shuddered. The black, rocky, wind-blasted summit was bare of snow.

Following the Dudh Kosi ("Milk River") drainage upstream into the foothills of the Himalaya, at last we began our final approach to the Lukla airfield at nine thousand feet. Built in 1964 to help ferry in supplies to construct Sir Edmund Hillary's schools in the high Sherpa villages, Lukla's sloped dirt runway is located at the end of a narrow U-shaped valley crowded by twenty-thousand-foot-high peaks. When I caught a glimpse of the airstrip out the plane's front window, it looked like an elongated potato patch. Nearby, the crumpled fuselage of a crashed plane testified that, as rumor had it, we would indeed only get one try at landing. Across from me, the Sherpani grandmother began retching into a paper bag. Then her husband began chanting loudly and with great conviction.

We must be getting close. When the fog parted, the pilot eased down the plane's nose again, and the landing strip screamed upward toward us. Colliding with Mother Earth, we bounced crazily up the rutted, uphill-tilted runway, and all onboard—the Sherpa grandparents included—cheered wildly with relief.

Happy to be again on terra firma, I thought for a moment or two that I'd traveled backward in time. Wood and stone houses with slate roofs dotted the hillside; a throng of smiling, dirty-faced villagers crowded around us. Breaks in the clouds revealed swathes of snow, ice, and rock floating as high as heaven. So this was the Himalaya, a destination of sublime beauty and mystery, a landscape dominated by eternally snow-fed glaciers, and punctuated by soaring peaks of fantastic height; a place where tradition joined the people in a rhythmic seasonal union with nature—and a place where the unexpected often came true.

We left Lukla for our next stop, Namche Bazaar, on the morning of March 1. I relished the time to hike, to relax and to think. My muscles enjoyed being stretched and tested; the clean air refreshed my lungs. Sherpa homes sprouted organically along the trail, while spectacular vistas at every turn drew me on ahead. And I'd thought the French Alps and Canadian Rockies were impressive! That day the Himalayan scenes I read about as a boy came alive.

Robert Anderson entering Namche Bazaar.

The Sherpa capital of Namche Bazaar. The Kwangde peaks rise behind.

Countless numbers of porters labored along the dirt trail. In the mountains of Nepal, all burdens move by foot, either human or yak. Fortunately, approaching caravans containing up to fifteen yaks could always be heard ahead of time, as the yak drivers whistled and hooted to encourage their lumbering beasts.

I quickly learned that preplanning my location when a yak train passed by me could be a life saver. The uphill side of the trail was best, well away from a cliff edge or a stone fence. Otherwise you risked being gored by swaying horns, or forced overboard—right off the trail.

As Robert Anderson and I passed through the entrance to Sagarmatha National Park, we entered the preserved parkland surrounding Everest, and started up the switchbacks of the infamous Namche Bazaar hill. Our pace dropped to a crawl as we noticed the increasing altitude one boot step at a time up the dust-covered trail. The majority of footprints were left by barefooted men, the porters who rested their heavy loads on a wooden crutch at the end of each switchback. Some carried double loads, weighing up to 175 pounds.

At 10,300 feet, Namche Bazaar was where we began to acclimate to the Himalaya's rarefied air. Nestled in a natural horseshoe-shaped amphitheater below the towering peaks of Kwangde and Tamserku, and home to over a thousand Sherpas, Namche lords over the Khumbu Valley as its unofficial capital.

Given the village's ideal location and altitude as an acclimatization lay-over en route to Everest Base Camp, we noticed several new lodges being built to house the ever-increasing numbers of foreign trekkers.

For better or worse, our expedition was now split in half. Arriving in Namche the day before, the "advance group," consisting of Jim Bridwell, Fletcher, Randy, Greg, and Kevin had, under Jim's leadership, chosen to continue on to Base Camp, ignoring the need to acclimatize. Knowing Bridwell's love of action, we speculated that they would probably have fixed ropes up the two-thousand-foot-high Lho La rock headwall—our climb's first technically difficult section—before we caught up to them.

This dividing up of the expedition definitely ruffled some feathers in the "B Team." Kim Carpenter and Jay Smith were noticeably upset that Jim had left without them, while Andy Politz was angry that "they would clean up on all the leading." Even Dave Saas saw his fears confirmed, that Bridwell would run ahead of the group. I noted that Pete Athans, our most experienced Himalayan climber, took the controversy in stride.

"You can't put the cart before the horse," Pete said bluntly.

There was no doubt Jim Bridwell was a driven man, but it was for precisely this reason that he'd been chosen as climbing leader, the one in charge of making decisions on the mountain. I found the bickering and jealousy tedious. The leadership vacuum—or lack of communication—had commenced. Dave Saas freely acknowledged that he wasn't a technical climbing expert, and Bill Forrest, our respected deputy leader, wasn't with us. That left Bridwell, whose best ascents had all been accomplished with teams of fewer than six climbers, as our effective leader. Everest's West Ridge was Jim's first (and to this day his last) foray into large-scale expedition climbing. It was to prove to be a very different kettle of fish from what he was used to.

Dave's plan for every member to have an equal chance of summiting, however well intended, was a statistical impossibility. No twenty-member team could possibly have enough resources and manpower to support every climber in a try for the top. The majority of members had to assume a supportive role, and only the very strongest climbers would get a crack at the summit.

About this time I began to feel I'd had enough of Everest logistics. For the umpteenth time we had to reorganize and repack all of our loads, this time for the yaks to carry to Base Camp. I'd had more than my fill of packing loads in Denver; furthermore, I was still trying to shake my head cold. Let the other guys pull their weight for a change, I thought.

At our evening meeting, Saas spoke first. "All I've heard for the last three years are superstar climbers saying, 'That's not how you organize an Everest expedition.' Well, they never thought we'd get out of the U.S.—and here we are in Namche! How many of you guys really thought you'd be here on your way to Everest?"

"Probably none of us, and after this expedition, we'll never want to go on another!" Jay answered to spontaneous laughter. Clearly the logistical night-mare of repacking had gotten to everyone.

Then George said he thought we should "air concerns." Catching Dan's eye, I knew I was in for trouble. Our clean cut, up-and-coming lawyer had assumed the unenviable job of tracking each load's contents. His extreme punctuality and authoritatively voiced commands had caused me to avoid him recently.

"Several people have felt Ed hasn't been pulling his weight the last few days. You've got to change that," Dan said staring at me. "And be more punctual, too."

I was on the spot. "Dan, you're always ordering me to hurry up, pack this, do that," I responded. "I need my own time, too, to write in my journal, to be alone, to think. I wish you'd quit ordering everyone around and relax a little."

"Two things can make us a success," Scott interjected. "One, give 110 per-cent effort every day. Two, think of the other guy first."

"We're all a little new to this game," Dave Saas admitted, "but if we can't work together and make this expedition a success, there are going to be a lot of people saying 'I told you so.' "

After some silence, Jay said firmly, "We've got to do it. We all have to stay focused on the goal, the summit." Everyone cheered.

I met Dan outside afterward. "Ed, you've really been out of it recently. What happened to the Ed Webster I knew who always pitched in and helped?"

I agreed I hadn't been myself. I promised I'd try harder to do my share, but inwardly, I was worried. What if I wasn't cut out for big expeditions? Like Bridwell, I'd also done almost all of my hardest climbs with one or two part-ners, usually with good friends. Now I was about to embark on the hardest climb of my life, in a foreign country, with two dozen people I barely knew. I tried to keep an open mind, to view this expedition as a learning experience, a sort of high-altitude sociology study, but inside I desperately wished a close climbing friend or two were here, people I could talk to—and trust with my life.

* * * * * * * * * * * * *

My first view of Everest—and the plume. Ama Dablam is on the right. Scott Lankford

We left Namche Bazaar for Tengboche on March 6, minus Brian O'Malley, who'd taken ill and decided to return home. That afternoon our column of yaks, climbers, porters, and Sherpas headed up and down the steep hillsides to the famous monastery, eventually becoming enshrouded in a thick, cloaking mist. It suited me well, this shuffling pace behind a yak train. The secret mountain splendors that I knew were soaring—and hiding—all around us would have to wait until the weather cleared the next morning.

Innumerable young children were hauling wood up the trail to the village of Khumjung atop a nearby hillside. Vibrant smiles plastered their faces. *"Namaste! Namaste!"* they shouted in chorused greeting. How many times does a person say *"namaste"* in one day in Nepal? It was as though every person walking down a busy city street took the time to stop, smile, and greet their fellow passersby.

Tengboche Monastery at sunrise.

Everest West Ridge expedition members at Tengboche. (Left - Right) Standing: *Lopsang Sherpa, George McLeod, Scott Lankford, Kim Carpenter, Peter Athans, Heidi Benson, John Meyer, Dave Saas, Jim McMillian, and Udab Prasad Dhungama, our Liaison Officer.* Kneeling, Front Row: *Dr. John Pelner, Jay Smith, Ed Webster, and Dan Larson.*

Ama Dablam—one of the world's most beautiful mountains.

I followed patiently behind the footsteps of a young Sherpa girl carrying a monstrous bale of hay on her back—her yak's dinner. Emerging from the misty forest at 12,600 feet, we passed through a narrow painted archway, built to ward off evil spirits, and entered the grassy compound of Tengboche Monastery.

I was thrilled to be here. After eating dinner in a smoky lodge, Heidi, Dan, and I stepped outside to get some air. Pausing on the sacred stone steps of the Sherpas' most important monastery, we watched the full moon being born amongst a swirling sea of silver clouds, with the mountains Tamserku and Kangtega glowing like cosmic apparitions. Then, higher still, much higher than imagination dared possible, Ama Dablam's luminous fang appeared. I'd read about these mountains for years, since childhood, but never had I thought I would see them with my own eyes—which moments later welled with tears.

During our trek to Base Camp, I was realizing how important it was for me to approach Everest in an honorable way. I had no desire to be part of another foreign expedition that came to Nepal, climbed, conquered, and departed without paying reverence to local beliefs and customs. Maybe I was feeling guilty for the tremendous material wealth we were transporting through the poor stone and wood Sherpa villages. If we as mountaineers didn't possess a genuine reverence for these peaks and for Sherpa culture, then our expedition became just another gross imposition of western technology upon the world's tallest mountain. Had our team traveled halfway around the world merely to lay siege to Everest—and take product endorsement photos? Or, as pilgrims journeying to a holy site, could we experience the sacred realm of the Himalaya in harmony with the people who lived here? Everest, for me, was just such a revered destination.

Passing through rhododendron forests replete with silver birch and hanging moss, the following morning we hiked to Pangboche, a sunny cluster of houses with a monastery tucked cozily into a juniper grove above the Dudh Kosi river. Here we attended yet another blessing ceremony, my fourth! Cymbals, drums, horns, and bells made a surprisingly agreeable cacophony. That evening, camped in Pheriche, we received two notes. One was from Bridwell; the other, while anonymous, was clearly written by Andy. Base Camp was established, and Bridwell planned to fix ropes up the start of our route to the Lho La plateau.

The next day Dan and I went for an acclimatization hike over the scenic pass of the Kongma La, an 18,160-foot saddle in the ridgeline separating the trekking peaks of Kongma Tse and Pokalde. It was a personal altitude record for us both. And although Everest remained hidden behind the rocky Nuptse wall, Lhotse's massive South Face, plus Makalu, Baruntse, and lovely Ama Dablam all were visible. The following day, however, my head cold made a comeback, and I gobbled down whole garlic cloves in my oatmeal to fight it off. The only member of the team who had managed to stay completely healthy so far was Robert.

Dan Larson atop the Kongma La. Makalu on far left.

Just prior to reaching the dusty and forlorn outpost of Lobuche (16,168 feet), I got a thrill seeing the Lho La plateau—the Tibetan border—off in the far distance. We decided to acclimatize at Lobuche for an extra day; the members of "the bullfrog club" needed to regain their voices. After writing letters and updating diaries, Robert and I went for a walk. Then, while jointly solving a 5.10 boulder problem, we decided to be Base Camp neighbors. Dark-haired and blue-eyed, Robert was also tall, strong, confident, and had a good-natured laugh. I liked his low key, low stress, yet motivated approach to life. As we encouraged each other up the boulder problem, we discovered that we'd climbed in many of the same parts of America and Britain. And our friendship began to grow.

Sign near Gorak Shep. The triangular summit is Everest's West Shoulder; the glacial saddle is the Lho La Plateau. Above this col is Changtse, the North Peak of Everest.

On March 13, Robert and I arrived at the Gorak Shep tea house, the last human habitation before the Khumbu Glacier's lower stony wastes. Revived by two cups of lemon tea, we crossed a sandy hollow below Kala Pattar (an 18,200-foot-high "hill" and the most popular destination for Everest trekkers), to the Everest Memorial rock.

The Everest Memorial rock in 1985. Many more names have been added since.

Carved on the face of a flat granite boulder beside the trail were the names of many of the mountaineers who had died on Everest. These included the American Jake Breitenbach, who died in 1963, Major Harsh Bahuguna, an Indian who perished on the 1971 International Everest Expedition, and the Bulgarian, Kristo Prodanov, who reached Everest's summit alone and without oxygen via the *West Ridge Direct* in 1984, but died in a severe storm on the descent. It was a haunting feeling to walk by these memorials, knowing that those and up to sixty more had hiked past this very same spot, never to return.

Continuing up the rubble of the lower Khumbu Glacier, we got lost in a forest-like maze of *névé pénitants*—spiny ice needles created by differential melting—that stuck through the glacier's surface layer of rocks and boulders. Meandering toward Base Camp, we saw Lingtren, a towering rock peak, then the snow dome of Pumori, and half a mile east, the tumbling and splintered dazzling chaos of the Khumbu Icefall.

"My god!" exclaimed Robert. "Base Camp looks like a beehive!"

Sherpa masons had built three adjoining stone huts—a cooking shelter, communal dining area, and Sherpa mess—on top of the rock-strewn glacial ice. One- and two-man tents sprouted like multi-colored weeds around the camp's periphery, and climbers swarmed everywhere beneath the flags of America and Nepal. After a warm reunion with the advance team, Robert and I pitched our own tents toward the Norwegian Base Camp, also under construction. Everest Khumbu Base Camp, one of the most overused, trashed-out mountain campsites in the world, would be our home for the next two months.

I was soon at work organizing the "fish boxes," the tough corrugated waxed boxes in which we'd shipped our food and supplies. Designed for packing fish, most of the boxes had barely survived their ordeal-by-yak. And, the new recruits, like me, were being seriously affected by the debilitating 17,500-foot altitude. George and Dan barked orders to the worker bees, and as tempers flared, I switched to sorting climbing hardware and fixed rope, an area more in my expertise. The Sherpas, meanwhile, finished roofing our stone dwellings, stretching tarps and plastic sheeting over the wood pole rafters.

Advanced Base Camp (or ABC), our Camp One, would be located on the Lho La plateau, a massive glacial shelf at twenty thousand feet. Mount Everest's West Ridge doesn't actually extend all the way down to Base Camp. The ridge's lowest section—the West Shoulder—rises out of the Lho La ice plateau. And, down at Base Camp, we were separated from Everest's West Shoulder by an initial two-thousand-foot-high rock buttress. The job of fixing ropes up to the Lho La had fallen to Jim, Pete, Kevin, Jay, and Randy. Although it was, in general, fairly easy climbing, the buttress possessed lethal quantities of loose rock. One day, Bridwell had nearly been killed there by falling rock. "I wasn't expecting to be with you tonight," he quipped, "but obviously someone up there likes me."

On March 15, the entire team dressed in their matching Gerry climbing suits for the traditional Base Camp blessing ceremony, without which the Sherpas would not begin climbing. A lama from Pangboche officiated. The stone altar was laden with trays of offerings: nuts, M&M's, Snickers bars, hard candy, lemon drops, and cookies. While the lama recited his incantations, green juniper boughs were burned, producing a fragrant, thick white smoke, and strings of colorful prayer flags were hoisted skyward, tied to a central maypole. The lama later confided that this was his fifth Everest Base Camp *puja*. All the teams, he told us, had reached the summit—and, even better, no one had been killed.

This was excellent news, which we celebrated with the Sherpas by drinking whiskey and rum. I was amazed to discover how little alcohol it took to get seriously drunk at 17,500 feet. Not much! Bridwell, revved and well-tanked by dinner, began barking orders like a drill sergeant. Kevin and Jay were assigned to climb to a bivouac platform—nicknamed Camp Point-Five—below the Lho La's upper rock headwall. Then, once they gained the metal, tripod-like winch tower at the headwall's crest, they were to set up our motorized hauling system. (Following the example of earlier expeditions, we planned to haul loads up a five-hundred-foot in-situ steel cable that the Yugoslavian expedition had

Jim Bridwell at our puja blessing ceremony at Everest Khumbu Base Camp.

installed up the vertical headwall during their first ascent of the *West Ridge Direct* in 1979.) A gas-powered Honda motor would raise loads clipped into a continuous thousand-foot-long loop of heavy nylon rope, easily winching one-hundred-pound-plus loads up the steel high wire, and would enable us to quickly stock Advanced Base Camp on the plateau.

The next day, Kim, Fletcher, Pete and I instructed our lesser-experienced Sherpas in ice climbing, jumaring (using clamp-on ascenders to climb a fixed rope), and rappelling (rope-descending) techniques. Since we planned to fix rope not only up the vertical rock walls to the Lho La, but also up another four thousand feet of forty- to sixty-degree snow and ice slopes leading to the West Shoulder, all of our Sherpa staff had to know safe methods for ascending and descending these lengthy sections of fixed rope. Class was held on a nearby ice pinnacle, where we arranged several practice ropes.

Pete and I coached Dawa, one of our cooks. He finally got the knack for jumaring up the rope, shifting his weight from one clamp to the other, and was doing a classic job of rappelling—until he let go of the rope and fell twenty feet before Pete stopped him five feet above the ground! Typical of the Sherpas, Dawa grinned broadly as though his fall had been great fun. My conclusion was that although the Sherpas had a natural talent for climbing, their rope handling needed a little work. Back at Base, I bumped into Bridwell at his tent.

"What I'd like to see," Jim said, bringing up tactics, "are several cohesive groups within the expedition who'll take care of themselves and develop their own morale and momentum."

"Won't we all become fragmented?" I asked.

"No, because it's important to feel comfortable with a certain group of partners. You have to develop a deep trust, not just of your own abilities, but of how you and your partners work together as a unit. Who would you like to climb with?"

I wasn't sure yet. I told him I'd think about it.

"We'll be successful if only one of us reaches the summit, but I think we've got what it takes to get a lot of guys up there," Jim continued. "Obviously I'd like to be one of them, but if I'm working to establish Camp Five, and I'm too tired to make it, and you and your partner make it instead, then we've still been successful."

Somehow in the next month and a half, we had to find a way to climb as a team, to work together, to achieve our common goal.

Could we?

Turtles and Hares

Group dynamics is a bit like skiing moguls.
You've just gotta bend your knees
and let the bumps glide by.

—Scott Lankford

n March 17, Kim, Mac, and I helped ferry loads up the mountain, one of the necessary grinds of expedition climbing. It was a grueling two-thousand-foot pull, ascending fixed ropes up a craggy outcropping toward the Lho La ice plateau at twenty thousand feet. Topping the buttress was a five-hundred-foot-tall vertical rock headwall, graded an intermediate difficulty of 5.8, A2. Several days earlier Bridwell & Co. had neatly avoided this section by front-pointing up the glacial ice wall just to the right of the headwall; then, after walking west a short distance across the plateau, they rappelled down the rock buttress, stringing a handrail of fixed ropes from above.

Getting out of Base Camp was invigorating and exciting. The views of the nearby Khumbu peaks, Pumori and Nuptse, along with the emerging West Shoulder of Everest, plus Cholatse and Taweche in the distance, were all unforgettably spectacular. To our right, we also enjoyed a bird's eye view of the chaotically fractured Khumbu Icefall. The Norwegians, bolstered by their

Left: *Rinsing Sherpa climbs up to the Lho La Plateau on the Nepal-Tibet border.*

TIBET

Lingtren
22,142'/6749m

International Border

Khumbuts
21,867'-6665

Pumori
21,867'/6665m

Changri Shar Glacier

Khumbu
Base Camp
17,500'/5300m

Khumb
Icefal

KalaPattar
18,222'/5554m

Khumbu Glacier

Gorak
Shep

N
W   E
S

Kongma Tse
19,085'/5817m

Lobuche

To Pheriche and
Namche Bazaar

Kongma La
✗

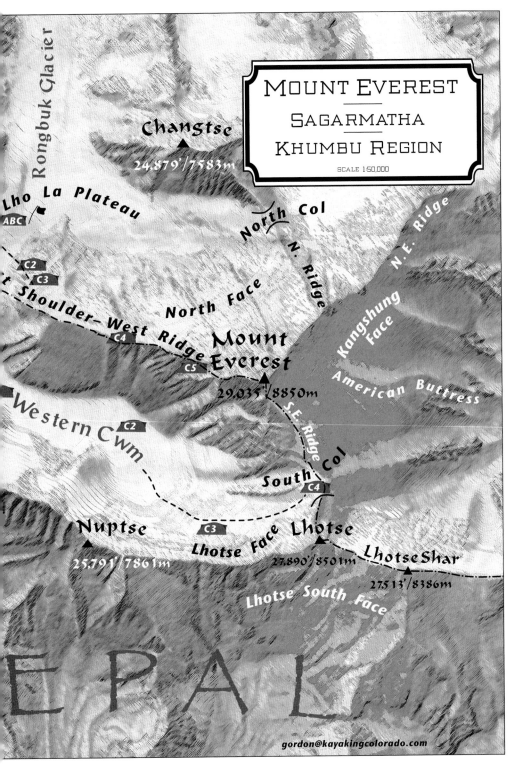

MOUNT EVEREST

SAGARMATHA

KHUMBU REGION

SCALE 1:50,000

Rongbuk Glacier

Changtse
24,879'/7583m

Lho La Plateau

ABC

North Col

N. Ridge

N.E. Ridge

C2

C3

North Face

Kangshung Face

t Shoulder–West Ridge

C4

C5

Mount Everest
29,035'/8850m

American Buttress

S.E. Ridge

Western Cwm

C2

South Col

C4

Nuptse
25,791'/7861m

C3

Lhotse Face

Lhotse
27,890'/8501m

Lhotse Shar
27,513'/8386m

Lhotse South Face

EPAL

gordon@kayakingcolorado.com

47

Everest Base Camp is immediately below the Khumbu Icefall. Lho La at top left.

platoon of able-bodied Sherpas, and Chris Bonington, were busy constructing a route in-between its yawning crevasses and tottering ice walls.

The greatest danger on our route up the buttress was from falling rock. Stones and blocks randomly whistled down the precipices, crashing into two immense gullies we nicknamed the Bowling Alleys. Unaccustomed to such high odds of being hit by rockfall, that first day we scurried like scared mice past the most lethal sections. Anchoring our fixed ropes every one hundred to one hundred and fifty feet, were odd-looking, tent-peg-like pitons of Bulgarian and Yugoslavian extraction. Between each anchor the rope was tied with ten or fifteen feet of slack. This allowed us to angle around and bypass any loose sections by leaning sideways on the rope, and after we'd carted up our loads, to clip our descenders into the fixed lines and easily rappel off.

Although we were equipped with the most technologically advanced equipment and clothing, our Everest attempt was being conducted in 1950s and '60s-style: as a traditional Himalayan siege climb, a type of climbing popular in those decades. By establishing stocked campsites linked with continuous lengths of fixed rope, we could climb up and down the mountain virtually at will, even in storms. After building a solid pyramid of supplies and support in the lower and middle camps, our top camp would be placed as close to the summit as possible. From that single tent, we would launch two, or possibly three, summit bids.

Back at Base Camp on my rest day, I was relatively astonished to notice that several of our Sherpas—Ang Zangbu included—were having trouble fitting crampons onto their boots, so I pitched in and helped them. But it did seem ludicrous to be adjusting crampons for someone who'd already climbed Everest! Zangbu had reached the fabled top in 1979 with Alaskan Ray Genet, Hannelore Schmatz, the wife of the German expedition leader, and Sungdare Sherpa. After summiting late in the day, they were caught in the dark descending the summit ridge. Only Zangbu and Sungdare survived. Genet simply disappeared, but for six years now, Mrs. Schmatz's body had been frozen in place where she died below the South Summit—a grisly reminder of Mount Everest's human toll. Rumor had it that she was still there, her sun-bleached hair blowing in the wind.

At dinner, Bridwell asked Fletcher and me to install four aluminum ladders up the Lho La rock headwall. These ladders plus several flexible cable caving ladders would simplify passage up the vertical rock face. "You're someone I can count on to rig them right," Jim told me, adding, "You know, sometimes I think people think we're here on vacation! Our job is to climb the mountain."

Moti Lal load-carrying on the Lho La Headwall.

Our base of operations for the next three days was Camp Point-Five at 19,500 feet, one rope length below the winch cable strung up the Lho La headwall. Fletcher, Bridwell, and I arrived just before a heavily-laden group of Sherpas who seemed to enjoy displaying their "boy's club" good humor—and a surprisingly casual attitude toward danger. Several of the Sherpas, I noted, rarely used a jumar to clip into the fixed lines, preferring instead to grasp the rope barehanded—or to climb completely unroped. If their safety standards were somewhat below par, their stamina was nothing short of Herculean.

Team Sherpa on the Lho La Plateau (in Tibet) at 20,000 feet. Pumori rises behind.

Only when carting a sixty-pound load were they even slightly out of breath. To descend, they either wrist- or shoulder-rappelled, but seldom used a figure-of-eight descender, the safest descent method.

Of our dozen climbing Sherpas, Ang Zangbu and Lhakpa Dorje had already summited Everest, which among the Sherpas (as among Westerners) was a well-respected accomplishment, and a springboard to fame and fortune. Moti Lal and Penzo were strong mountaineers, but the remainder of our Sherpa staff, in general, were fairly inexperienced. It wasn't entirely clear how Sherpas rose through the ranks, but Dave Saas's feeling was that their inexperience, in our case, might prove a plus, because they'd work hard to prove themselves on such a hard climb as the *West Ridge Direct.*

The Norwegians had hired a considerably more seasoned Sherpa corps. Pertemba, their *Sirdar,* was Peter Boardman's summit partner on the British first ascent of Everest's *Southwest Face* in 1975. And with their twenty-five climbing Sherpas, they could transport more equipment, faster, up the mountain. Although they were climbing Everest "the easy way" (up what was sometimes derisively called "the Yak Route"), via the South Col, their team also had a much larger oxygen supply than we: 110 bottles to our forty. Well-organized, well-equipped, well-staffed, and nordically efficient, the 1985 Norwegian Mount Everest Expedition was taking no chances in their quest for the summit.

After returning from anchoring ladders, tonight was my highest altitude to date. Only a mere ten thousand vertical feet to go, but what brutal mileage!

"Got to start toughening up the boys," Bridwell said.

Perched at our camp, fifteen hundred feet above the Khumbu Glacier, it was hard to believe I was actually—and finally—climbing on Mount Everest. What process had taken me here? For much of my life, I'd had a nagging feeling that many of my climbing adventures and my life in general were composed of experiences that *happened* to me—as opposed to being experiences that I *actively created*. Frequently I felt all too passive, a passenger instead of the driver grabbing and steering the wheel of life. Although I felt I "lived life" fully and exuberantly, I rarely if ever saw any "big picture" of what I hoped to achieve. And since Lauren's death, my life-attitude had hardened into realistic fatalism— "what will be, will be." At this point, my emotional pendulum had swung so radically between happiness and tragedy that I was content to see where fate would lead me. Still, inexplicable good luck often delivered me unusual and sometimes golden opportunities. Climbing on Mount Everest was one such example, and represented for me a long-imagined, now tangible threshold: my crossing over into a new life as a Himalayan mountaineer.

For the next two days, Fletcher and I pounded in pitons, hauled frame and cable ladders up the granite precipices, and securely strapped them all in place. Here, on this vertical rock wall, I was in my element. I couldn't have been happier. Fletcher and I got on well, too. Another native New Englander, he'd grown up and climbed a lot in New Hampshire's White Mountains.

March 21, our second day on the headwall, was my twenty-ninth birthday. I wanted to celebrate it by attaining the magical elevation (for mountaineers) of twenty thousand feet for the first time, but three days at 19,500 feet was starting to wear me out. I was constantly out of breath from the lack of oxygen, and was tiring easily. Climbing at high altitude was, as Kim said, "like running a marathon while wearing a plastic bag over your head." Leaving camp, I began ascending the upper rock headwall, the "Black Rain," which was given its name because it was where Bridwell had nearly been killed by rockfall.

Our Honda technical expert, "Mac" McMillian, had little experience with jumars, so I stopped to help him get his two ascender clamps rigged properly. The Honda gas-powered engine had been laboriously hauled up the winch cable with a hand crank the day before, and it now sat beside the metal tower atop the Lho La buttress. It was Mac's job to get the motor—and the winch system—up and running.

Kim Carpenter climbs the caving ladder up the Lho La's "Black Rain" rock headwall.

I continued up the fixed ropes toward the ice cliffs of the Lho La plateau. Panting for breath, struggling to get out of oxygen debt, I finally crossed the twenty-thousand-foot mark. I stared in awe across the empty glacial plateau into mysterious Tibet, then let my gaze trace the icy sweep of Everest's West Shoulder, high into the azure sky. It was the most desolate sight I'd ever seen, but for me, it was a rapture-producing desolation.

Tomorrow, I knew, we'd begin moving climbers up the ropes and ladders to Advanced Base Camp, and winching our loads up the "Black Rain" headwall, with the Honda engine, in less than a minute. Feeling today less concerned with the style points of our expedition, I felt that at last I was a part of our endeavor and part of the team. I'd made a good contribution rigging the ladders, and—knock on wood—so far I was adjusting well to the increasingly high altitude.

Jim and Robert visited Fletcher's and my tent that evening at Camp Point-Five. Ang Tsering, our Base Camp cook, had sent up a cranberry nut birthday cake! We passed several pleasant hours sipping tea, gobbling cake, and telling stories. Bridwell spun several entertaining climbing yarns of his most famous ascents, of El Capitan in Yosemite Valley, Kitchatna Spire in Alaska, and Cerro Torre in Patagonia. His career as a professional climber-adventurer had taken him to many exotic parts of the world.

"Yeah, I've had some pretty offbeat locations for birthdays, too," he added. "Which would you prefer, the Antarctic Icecap or Central Borneo?"

* * * * * * * * * * * * *

Kim, Dan, Heidi, and Dave arrived to replace us, but when Kim began to complain about being teamed up with Dan, I wondered if he was really cut out to be on a big expedition. What sort of person makes a good Himalayan or expedition climber? One with considerable mountaineering savvy, but also someone who possesses complete selflessness—an unflagging willingness to always work for the team's benefit. Many climbers dream of scaling Everest, but the world's tallest mountain is clearly no place for egocentric behavior, misguided machismo, or any shortcoming of climbing ability.

At the relatively low altitude of 17,500 feet, Base Camp was home while we regained strength between forays on the mountain. Invariably, it was here that we saw teammates who'd also descended for a rest, or glimpsed others heading back up to carry loads—or, if they were lucky (and healthy, and strong), to lead the route's next section. Naturally, everyone aspired to be out in front, but so far only Bridwell, Robert, Pete, Jay, Kevin, and Randy had had their chance to savor the limelight, stringing our fixed ropes higher up the mountain. For the past several days, Randy and Jay had worked at the winch top. Back at Base, it didn't take long for them to vent their frustration.

"There seems to be some misunderstanding that we're doing all the fun climbing," Randy began. "Not so! We're busting our butts hand-winching loads up to the Lho La."

"It's all work," Jay commented dryly.

"Listen, there's no division of labor," Jim countered sharply, sensing an approaching conflict. "Everyone works together. There's no prima donna team."

"Dancing their way up the mountain in their tutus," Kevin added.

Everest Base Camp might seem an exciting place to live, but the thrill was fleeting. The unending cold, the complete lack of privacy, half-burned mounds of trash near camp, and the nightly howling of dogs prowling the garbage quickly made me wish I was back on the mountain. Slumping into a daily routine, we ate the same food day after day, and fielded the same jokes with our logistics man, Rodney Korich, and Udab Prasad Dhungama, our Nepalese government Liaison Officer. Then there was illness. George, Greg, and John were recovering down in Pheriche, while Andy had returned to Base following a week of low-altitude R&R. And I still hadn't completely licked my head cold.

The 7 P.M. radio call revealed progress. Mac had gotten the Honda up and going, a dozen loads had flown up the winch, tents were erected at Advanced Base—and insufficiently cooked freeze-dried food had created near lethal indigestion and gas. "Help us, please!" Pete pleaded over the radio.

Tomorrow would be a rest day for the Sherpas, a day devoted to gambling, their other favorite occupation. In the three weeks since we'd left Kathmandu, poor Lhakpa had already lost more than five thousand rupees, over two hundred dollars. "Won any back?" I asked him. He wouldn't tell.

Inside my tent at 9 P.M., I noticed my water bottle of herb tea (boiling hot not twenty minutes ago), and my partially filled pee bottle—those two Himalayan nocturnal essentials that you must never accidentally mix up—each were already starting to freeze in the sub-zero temperature. Ice crystals danced on the tent fabric as I sank deeper inside my sleeping bag to read Paul Theroux's *The Old Patagonian Express* by headlamp—and mentally transport myself to warmer climes.

Radio transmissions were often jocular. From Base Camp the next morning, Kevin engaged Mac at Advanced Base in some high-altitude repartee:

Kevin: "Base Camp calling Lho La. Do you read me?"

Mac: "Lho La Moving and Storage here. Over."

    (Mac and several others had been ferrying loads across the flat, half-mile stretch of glacier between the winch top and Advanced Base Camp.)

Kevin: "How was the night?"

Mac: "Fine, except a Yeti ran off with most of our food. Over."

Kevin: "Did you get the license plate number?"

Mac: "No, we think it was one of Pete Athans' old girlfriends."

Kevin: *(Laughter)* "Okay, Roger. Anything else?"

Mac: "We just decided to change our name to Lho La Storage."

Kevin: "Do you have a permit to do that?"

Mac: "You don't need one when you're in Tibet. Over."

    Bridwell, Fletcher, Kevin, Jay, Randy, John Meyer, a visiting Finn named Petri, and I all carried loads to the winch base. As I started photographing the group, Randy said, "Webster's always got his bloody camera in your face." Lingering behind, I took more photos and climbed with John and Petri, who were going the slowest. Randy still seemed peeved when he descended the ropes past me. While the others raced the clock and each other back to Base Camp, John, Petri, and I determinedly reached the winch, dumped our loads, and immediately turned around as it began to snow.

Jim Bridwell & the Hares: Jay Smith, Randal Grandstaff, Bridwell, and Kevin Swigert.

Conditions rapidly deteriorated. Soon a slick layer of snow coated the rocks, and our pace dropped to a crawl. Neither Petri nor John had jumared or rappelled more than a few times, and although both nearly slipped and fell down the slippery rocks, we managed to navigate the thousand feet of rope back to Base Camp without incident. Sitting in the mess tent after dinner, I told Bridwell I wanted to say something.

"I'm feeling very frustrated by the competitive attitude of some of my teammates," I began. "Too much emphasis is being placed on speed, how fast you can climb up and down the fixed ropes. Since the experience level of our team varies greatly, it seems to me that the experienced climbers should slow down and look out for their less experienced partners. I could've gone faster today, but I was helping John and Petri descend. Fortunately, no one was hurt."

I hadn't anticipated the response. Randy loudly proclaimed that he wasn't about to wait for anybody, and then Andy—his voice forceful with emotion—pointed out that on the 1971 International Everest Expedition, this precise attitude had led to the death of Harsh Bahuguna. A moderately experienced Indian climber, Bahuguna had died of exposure after being trapped halfway across an ice slope in a sudden snow squall when one of his crampons came unclipped—and he couldn't fix it. Thinking that Bahuguna was all right, his teammate had simply continued on ahead, and descended to the next camp.

At Andy's rebuttal, Randy stormed out of the mess tent.

Finally Kevin spoke: "I go my own speed, and I happen to like to go fast. The only person I look out for on the mountain is me."

I was appalled by such selfishness! But Kevin wasn't done. He turned to face me. "And I'm really pissed off at your accusation, Ed, that we abandoned those two guys," he continued.

"I didn't accuse anyone of abandoning anyone," I told him. "I was just suggesting that the veteran climbers keep an eye on our less-skilled members. We've got several climbers plus some Sherpas who've done very little jumaring or rappelling. This is a steep, technical route with thousands of feet of fixed rope. Either you climb quickly, without a care for your slower companions, or you pace yourself and keep an eye out for them. You can't do both."

Bridwell at this point said he thought we were making a mountain out of a molehill—and the issue went unresolved, an unfortunate, and (I thought) a totally predictable outcome.

Left: *A load flies up the winch cable on the Lho La Headwall. Khumbu Glacier on left.*

Two nights later we congregated in the mess tent around the propane space heater. Tension was still running high. "Boy, I could use a drink," Jay said before reappearing minutes later with a bottle of duty free Hennessey cognac. Slowly the bottle made the rounds. I was tipsy in seconds—then Jim Bridwell, speaking with unusual eloquence, commenced an inspired oration.

"Life isn't that difficult to figure out," he began. "Mankind is motivated by three primary forces—sex, fame, and money. In all of life's great pursuits, men and women have had to rise above these three primal impulses. So it is with life, so it is with climbing, and so it will be with Mount Everest. We will succeed where others have failed because of the power of our minds. Because we have the strength to deny the three base forces of sex, fame, and money. Climbing Everest is a simple case of mind over matter, mind over hardship, and mind over danger. We will show ourselves what is truly possible, and the result will be a triumph on the grandest scale. I know this will probably be my only chance to summit on Everest. I want to get there, but I also want to come away from this expedition being friends for life."

After my differences with Randy and Kevin, I wondered if long-term friendship was still an attainable goal. Jim insisted that it was. Long after the cognac bottle had been drained and our companions had retired to the warmth of their sleeping bags, Bridwell and I stumbled bleary-eyed through the frozen night to his tent. Jim crawled in, and I zipped closed the flap. Given my weak tolerance of alcohol, I knew it would never happen again, but for one memorable night I'd matched drinks with the consummate hard-drinking hardman, Jim Bridwell.

Suffering from an Everest-size hangover, and late for breakfast, the next morning I entered the mess tent to my teammates' collective taunts. Dan even had the gall to photograph me. "Your team portrait," he suggested. Then Rodney handed me two twenty-pound oxygen bottles to carry up to the winch base with Greg and Andy. Later, as Andy clipped the loads into the winch rope, he said he'd send every load up even if he had to descend to Base Camp in the dark. Such was Andy's intention to work for the good of all.

I'd just collapsed back inside the mess when a bearded individual in a red suit burst through the door, shouting, "It's the British invasion!" It was none other than Chris Bonington, Britain's most renowned mountaineer. As a teenager, I'd virtually memorized his first autobiography, *I Chose To Climb*. Chris had led Everest expeditions in 1972, 1975, and 1982, yet he had still not reached the summit. Everyone hoped his fourth try would be the lucky one.

Chris Bonington at Everest Base Camp, 1985.

Bonington sat down to join us for afternoon tea served American-style—with peanut butter and jam on crackers.

"Oh, marvelous! I just love peanut butter!" he enthused. Chris assured us that you could buy peanut butter in Great Britain, but on the Continent, well, it was still very hard to find. I asked him how they had been progressing, and Chris explained that they'd established their Camp One today at the crest of the Khumbu Icefall, and they hoped to have all the loads ferried there in another four days. Then Fletcher asked about the condition of the icefall this year.

"The worst I've seen it," Chris replied with a shudder. "I'm not relishing going through it many more times. The ice moves nearly every day. But in two days, I'm going on up into the Western Cwm. Well, I must be off. Radio call in fifteen minutes. Cheerio!"

* * * * * * * * * * * * * *

I climbed to Advanced Base on the Lho La plateau for the first time on March 28. We left like a marching band: Jim, Kim, Greg, Fletcher, Dan, and me. George, our Base Camp manager, recently back from Pheriche, came too, just to see and photograph the spectacular scenery, the ice-draped North Face of Nuptse and the ice-cream-scoop summit of Pumori.

Kim Carpenter and Jim Bridwell ascend the Lho La Headwall at 19,500 feet.

I could hardly believe it, but Kim and Bridwell began smoking cigarettes while climbing the aluminum ladders up the Lho La's "Black Rain" headwall! Above, we navigated the so called "Potato Chip Traverse" using several creaky granite flakes as a handrail, then cramponed up hard crystalline snow to the winch tower on the edge of the Lho La. The ice plateau, I saw, was many square miles in size. Hemmed in by the ice and rock of Everest's West Shoulder to the east, and by snowy Khumbutse to the west, it fed the central Rongbuk Glacier to the north. Although you could not see Mount Everest's actual summit from Khumbu Base Camp, seen from this vast glacial plateau, our goal now rose preeminent, its lofty pinnacle soaring nearly nine thousand vertical feet above us.

From the Lho La, we had an unusual bird's eye view of the notorious Khumbu Icefall.

Heidi Benson runs the Honda winching system atop the Lho La at 20,000 feet.

Advanced Base resembled an Arab sheik's camp dropped in the middle of a frozen white desert. Fifteen climbers jammed inside the Hanson Weatherport— a large modular tent originally designed to house Alaska pipeline workers—for our communal meal. The route across the glacier to the base of the West Shoulder, I soon learned, was easy and safely marked with bamboo wands. Everyone regularly traveled this section unroped. That day, Andy had chopped a tremendous line of steps up the West Shoulder's opalescent, thousand-foot lower icefield. The route then continued up a narrow vertical ice gully that for-tuitously bisected a difficult-looking rock cliff. Back on snow and ice above, Jay, Kevin, Pete, and Robert had fixed ropes nearly to the rumored site of a snow cave, our Camp Two.

The next morning I took photographs of Andy stacking loads as they came up the winch cable. Taking pictures was my self-appointed job.

"Too bad I've run out of film to take any more photos," Andy commented.

"Oh, I've got an extra roll you can have," I said.

"But you see, it's just that I'm *working* too hard to reload my camera."

A lone Sherpa approaches Advanced Base Camp (Camp One) on the Lho La, Tibet.

I got the message and humped a huge load back to ABC. Later, we had mail call. Letters from home had been sent up the winch! I received eight, including one from Lauren's ninety-year-old grandmother, Marmere, who wrote that Lauren's headstone had finally arrived. The image of her gravestone overpowered me, and overcome with grief and guilt, I clutched at Lauren's scarf that I wore around my neck.

On March 30, I knew I needed a dose of solitude. I also wanted to make my first load carry to Camp Two. Rising early, I headed across the glacial plateau to the bergschrund below the first icefield. It was cold in the shade, but to the north, in Tibet, a splash of bright sunshine touched a distant brown hillock. (Technically, I was already in Tibet too—by about half a mile—since the edge of the Lho La forms the international border with Nepal.)

The ice, tilted to forty-five degrees, was iron-hard, and glass-smooth. Clipping my ascender into the fixed rope, I stepped up, pushed up the clamp, and began following Andy's footsteps in the ice. Another dot started across the glacier. I felt relieved. Maybe it wasn't wise to be climbing all alone, for the first time, to twenty-two-thousand feet. But the air seemed thicker with oxygen, strangely, than it had at nineteen thousand feet, and I was able to maintain a good pace—six or seven hard deep breaths, then a half dozen steps, or two breaths, two steps, and then a quick rest. Stopping halfway up the ice gully splitting the West Shoulder's rock cliffs, I looked down and recognized Andy's wide grin flashing in the sun.

"Good pace!" he declared, joining me. "You know, don't let the others influence you. I worry about them. Haven't they ever heard of burnout?"

Currently, three of our jackrabbits were sick. Jay was spitting blood, Randy felt nauseated, and Kevin was lethargic. I'd rather be a tortoise and win the race, I thought. Climbing at high altitude was a new game with unknown rules. I thought it wise to gauge my progress one day at a time. The knack seemed to be to have the mental toughness not to give up, to push yourself hard, but never to exhaustion. How high could I go: twenty-four thousand? Twenty-seven thousand? To the summit: 29,028 feet?

The wind had risen when I noticed two more climbers below. Since the price stickers were still affixed to their sunglasses, they had to be Sherpas! (Goods with their original sales tags and stickers fetched a higher resale price in Kathmandu after the expedition.) Moti and Prithi blazed past me, and the sight of them waltzing up the final—for me, agonizing—rope lengths up the snowfields inspired me to keep going.

Grateful to be out of the wind, I collapsed inside the Camp Two snow cave at 22,500 feet. After shaking hands on our new altitude record, Andy and I excavated the cave's walls and roof, then shoveled out the debris. Leaving at 4 P.M., in two hours we had rappelled the twenty-five hundred feet to the Lho La. Robert greeted us with hot tea. I swore it had been the toughest day of my life—but didn't it feel terrific, to be so tired and to have climbed so high?

I awoke the next morning to a pounding headache, and hoped that I could descend to Base Camp to rest. Not yet. Kim and I operated the winch in a high wind, hauling loads carried by Dave, John Meyer, and four Sherpas who were heading up. Standing a mere twenty feet from the top edge of the twenty-five-hundred-foot Lho La buttress, Kim calmly yanked the generator's starter cord, gave it some gas, and warmed up the engine. The winch's speed and efficiency made the Sherpas marvel. A fifty-pound load took twenty seconds to travel five hundred vertical feet!

Back at the Weatherport, Jim gave the order. Tomorrow several of us could descend. I was completely wasted after one load carry to Camp Two. Would I ever be able to push myself and live and work at high altitude for more than a few days at a time?

Andy Politz climbing to Camp Two. The tents at Advanced Base Camp are circled.

* * * * * * * * * * * * * *

The next evening, David Breashears, Karen Fellerhoff, and two Norwegian climbers joined us for dinner at Base Camp. It was the first time I'd seen David in several years. A well-known rock climber in the mid-1970s, he'd led some of Colorado's hardest and most dangerous free climbs, including one appropriately named route called *Perilous Journey*. David had since become an award-winning mountaineering filmmaker. On May 7, 1983, he filmed the first-ever microwave video transmission from Everest's summit, a feat for which he received a National Sports Emmy for innovative technical achievement. Earlier, he'd won his first Emmy for filming the 1981 American Everest East Face Expedition for ABC's *American Sportsman*.

Back in 1983, David and Rodney were teammates on Everest. They celebrated their reunion tonight by sharing a bottle of duty-free liquor. At radio call, Kevin informed us that our illustrious leader, Dave Saas, had failed to return to the Lho La from Camp Two, and Bridwell (who'd decided to stay high) had sent out a search party. With reggae music booming from Rodney's tape deck, the atmosphere in the mess tent had all the makings of a tragicomedy should anything have happened to Saas. Fortunately he reappeared after having gotten temporarily lost—only now the search party was lost! Eventually they returned too, and the Base Camp merriment continued unabated.

I paid a call to Breashears at Dick Bass's camp the following morning and asked him for advice on climbing Everest.

"Everest is probably the most macho climb in the world, but you can't be the least bit macho about it," David said. "You've got to suffer incredibly, endure the cold, deprivation, and altitude—but you've also got to know when to turn back if you get too extended. Remember, high altitude is the great equalizer. Take your time, go slowly, and don't battle the altitude. If you stay healthy, you just might make it. Are you planning to use bottled oxygen?"

"All of us are, except Andy Politz, who wants to try for the top without it."

"The doctors I've talked to think you risk quite a lot by trying to climb Everest without oxygen," David said. "You know, the risks are just too great: up to a year of short-term memory loss, the loss of finger dexterity,"—he tapped his fingers piano-style for emphasis—"and the loss of creative powers, like word formulation, for instance."

I winced. The combination didn't sound appealing.

"Face it, climbing Everest without oxygen is an athletic achievement. It's appropriate for quick alpine-style ascents of moderate Himalayan climbs, but since you're siege-climbing up a difficult route, why not use bottled oxygen?"

I had every intention of using oxygen if and when I reached our Camp Four at 25,500 feet on the *West Ridge Direct*. If I were to stand a chance of reaching Everest's summit, I knew I needed every possible advantage.

On April 3, continuing our upward momentum, Andy and Fletcher discovered the site of Camp Three, a snow-roofed crevasse. Unfortunately, that same day Jim Bridwell left Base Camp and descended to Pheriche to let his health recover. With Jim gone, two de facto leaders emerged, Kevin at Base, and Pete at Advanced Base. Our most experienced Himalayan veteran, Pete was a natural choice. Kevin, on the other hand, just wanted the job—and it was his so-called "rotation schedule," detailing which pairs of climbers would proceed to the front lines, that was implemented. Thus:

Pete and Andy would establish Camp Three, then work on the route across the two-mile-long snow ridge to Camp Four. Robert and Randy would establish Camp Four; Jay and Kevin would rotate up and push on to Camp Five, and then be followed by Fletcher and me. It all sounded so easy! Fletcher was thrilled; he insisted that we could be the first summit pair. I told him it was wasted energy to speculate. Camps Four and Five weren't even established yet.

Pete and Andy, however, did establish Camp Three on April 6, erecting three tents inside a large crevasse at 23,800 feet. Although the tents were sheltered from the wind, the crevasse's interior temperature was icebox frigid. Next, Andy and Pete headed across the long exposed snow ridge toward Everest's rocky summit pyramid. It was hard work, and dangerous.

Said Andy: "I started small avalanches with each step. There was five feet of windslab snow on the ridge's north side. But what a feeling to be up that high! I was so happy and it was so cold that tears were running down my cheeks and freezing in place."

I was lugging two oxygen bottles up to the winch base when Jay and Kevin—with colorful Jimi Hendrix-style paisley silk bandannas tied fashionably around their heads—ran past me, without loads, en route to ABC and the Lho La. Fletcher had strained his knee, they told me; maybe I should team up with Dan.

At dinner in Base Camp, I noticed something essential within us as a group had changed. Conversation no longer dwelled on the glories of past climbs, or on our success on Everest's West Ridge. Instead, the exact date when we would leave Base Camp, how much gear we could ship home, and where people were stopping off, were the new topics of discussion. The most popular homeward destinations were Thai beaches, but any warm climate would do—as long as it was as far removed as possible from the snow and cold and suffering of Everest.

On April 8, Jim Bridwell returned to Base Camp, arriving with the legendary Texas mountaineer, Dick Bass, owner of the Snowbird ski resort in Utah. To date, Bass had nearly completed his four-year quest to become the first person to climb the highest mountain on each of the seven continents— the so-called Seven Summits. Everest was Dick's remaining nemesis, and this was his fourth attempt to vanquish it. As on previous trips, Dick had bought his way onto an Everest permit (in this case, the Norwegian's), and David Breashears came along as his climbing partner, guide, and cameraman.

Bass's colorful, talkative reputation preceded him. Speaking in prolonged bursts of first-person narrative, Dick rarely let others get a word in edgewise, yet he was pleasant, friendly, respected, and very well liked. It was obvious that here was a man who, once committed, threw himself into a project with total Texas zeal. Somehow, some day, Mount Everest would yield to Dick Bass's desire to reach her summit.

Meanwhile, our team was slowly advancing. Robert and Randy were at Camp Two intent on establishing Camp Four, Jay and Kevin were at Advanced Base, ready to move up, and Dan and I had decided to climb together.

"It's the same old story of the tortoise and the hare," quipped Bridwell. "But remember, it's the tortoise that *always* wins. No hare is going to take first in this race."

* * * * * * * * * * * * * *

Kim, Dan, and I climbed back to the Lho La on April 9, while John Meyer and Greg Sapp carried loads to the winch. For someone who hadn't climbed much beforehand, John Meyer, our team journalist, was showing considerable pluck, and stamina. Not satisfied with sending his weekly reports back to the *Rocky Mountain News* in Denver, John cheerfully hauled forty-pound loads up to the winch base—and I could see him scheming to go higher still.

I met George McLeod while he was rappelling down from the Lho La. Danger had certainly caused everyone on the expedition to wonder why they were here on Everest, but after having been sick quite a bit of the trip, George was particularly disillusioned. "Maybe a fifty-eight-year-old isn't meant to go high," he said with obvious resignation, and a week later, he went home.

John Meyer,
our expedition
journalist, checks
out the sports
pages at
Base Camp.

We awoke on April 10 to only our third day lost to bad weather. Along with snow and high winds, the low pressure system also sunk our spirits, and we lay marooned in our tents, reading, sleeping, and catching up in diaries. At evening radio call, you could hear fatigue in the many dry, raspy throats. Robert was particularly cryptic. "Didn't do much today. Enlarged Camp Three," he croaked. "We'll stay up tomorrow or come down. Over."

Yet the next morning was radiantly beautiful. Dan, Kim, and I left early for Camp Two. I caught up to Kim at the rock band; it was his highest yet, but he elected to dump his load and descend. I tried to catch Dan, couldn't, then was surprised to see our lead pair, Robert and Randy, quickly descending. "Eat and drink as much as possible," encouraged Robert, who looked robust. Randy, meanwhile, stumbled past me in a daze, his eyes glassy and unfocused.

After nine and a half hours of lung-bursting labor, I reached Camp Two. I was too late for radio call, but I caught a magnificent sunset instead, watching the orange sun sink behind Pumori. Dan melted snow and ice chunks in two hanging stoves suspended from the ice cave roof. Following a good meal, we melted several more quarts of water to drink during the night—my first at this altitude: 22,500 feet.

It was a comparatively short climb (thirteen hundred vertical feet) to reach Camp Three. And it was a good thing, too. The next morning, Dan and I were on empty. I noticed that I was out of breath even when sitting still, a rather frightening sensation. To accomplish virtually anything: sit up, put boots on, cut snow chunks to melt for water, light the stove for breakfast—and especially, to eat—required a gargantuan force of will. Everest's thin air was slowly strangling us.

Although we had little in common, Dan and I got on reasonably well. But his replies to my questions—except to how he met his girlfriend, Debbie—were naggingly short. Was it the sheer dullness of my inquiries, I wondered, or was oxygen deprivation deactivating our numbed brains? Dan was cheerfully halfway through his "How-I-Met-Debbie" monologue (four years earlier, in a Safeway grocery store in Chicago, while he was paralyzed with a hangover) before I realized he'd already told me the story before.

At least the weather was fine as we left camp. Sucking in long slow breaths of cold air, I concentrated on pulling as much oxygen as possible into my hungry lungs until the next rest. The slope was forty-five degrees, not steep, but it felt endless. Occasionally there were treacherous ice patches. A continuous leftward diagonal along the fixed ropes threw my rhythm off sync, and I began to yawn profusely, sucking in additional oxygen. Each step required five to ten inhalations.

A commonly used rule for safe acclimatization is to "climb high and sleep low." In four days, I'd ascended from Base Camp (17,500 feet) to Camp Three at 23,800 feet. I decided to drop my load and return to Camp Two for the night, to "sleep low." Jay, Kevin, and Dan thought my decision was ridiculous.

"This is Everest!" Jay exclaimed. "You've got to tough it out, man!"

At radio call, I informed Bridwell of my descent.

"Layton, I told you that stove was hot," Jim replied in a fatherly tone of voice, making an oblique reference to his young son.

I returned to Camp Three the next morning, but now Jay and Kevin, exhausted from excavating old fixed ropes across the ridge toward Camp Four, had decided to descend. Then, as I melted snow for tea, Dan showed up.

Tibetan Folk Tales in Tibet. Ed reading in the storm at Advanced Base. Heidi Benson

He'd carried a load up onto the ridge with Sherpas Ang Danu and Lopsang. I handed him a brew. Without a word of thanks, he asked me if I'd enlarged the new tent platform. When I said I'd only been in camp for an hour, he shot back: "Well, if you can't get anything done, you should get up earlier!"

That night, the temperature inside our crevasse-walled campsite plummeted to minus twenty-degrees Fahrenheit. Even my tentmate, Lopsang, said, "Too cold in here!" And when a Sherpa complained, you knew it was bad. Then, when I tried to write in my journal, my pen froze. I thawed the ink over the stove. The cold was virtually unbearable. I was clad in two layers of polypropylene underwear, a pile jacket, pile pants, down-insulated climbing bibs, two layers of socks, aveolite bootliners, and a balaclava—yet I shivered all night long inside my five-inch-loft, five-hundred-dollar Everest-insulated sleeping bag.

Lopsang and Ang Danu left at 9 A.M. for Camp Four, but returned only minutes later. "Too much wind. We go Lho La." I decided to stay at camp to see if the weather would improve tomorrow. It was the first and only time on the expedition that I was at the front, in a position to lead the climb's next section—but the weather wasn't cooperating. Then Dan also decided to head down. He made tea, didn't offer me any, and left. I wasn't sad to see him go.

That afternoon, Ang Zangbu, Passang Gyalchen—"PG"—and Ang Tsering arrived. At radio call, Zangbu asked for two things to be sent up: beef jerky and cigarettes! Zangbu liked to boast that he'd smoked a cigarette on top of Everest in 1979. When the Sherpas' evening prayers were over, the strains of Radio Nepal sung out from the transistor radio inside Zangbu's tent.

Tenting inside the crevasse at Camp Three was The Deep Freeze, a degree of cold and suffering beyond anything I had previously known. Here, Hell really had frozen over! How my psyche yearned to embrace a tree, a flower, or a green lawn. Everest meant three months of endlessly cold fingers and toes. Sure, the Himalaya were the most spectacular mountains on Earth. And climbing Everest was like reaching out and touching Heaven—but to get there, you first had to suffer in a subzero Hell.

The night became a sleepless agony. Oxygen deprivation seized my brain. Was I getting cerebral edema; was my brain swelling inside of my skull? Ghost images danced among the ice crystals coating the tent roof. Then, in the middle of the night, Zangbu shouted my name. I bolted upright, and yelled back "Hello!" Later, Zangbu told me he hadn't said a word. At daybreak, my stomach seized up. I thought I'd vomit in thirty seconds. I couldn't escape from the tent; the zipper was frozen solid! Somehow I held everything down.

"I'm descending, Pete. Feel awful. Horrible night. Zangbu and the Sherpas will try for Camp Four. Over."

Down at Camp Two, feeling somewhat better, I encountered Bridwell and Fletcher. "Did you know Dan is trying to usurp my position as climbing leader?" Bridwell asked me. Yes, I did think that some of his comments made it seem so.

"Dan's the one member of the team I can't call a friend," Jim said, exasperated. "He's always trying to one-up me. Why? We all know Dan is strong."

Then Bridwell floored me: "Randy's out; he's finished. He might have cerebral edema. He's gone to Pheriche to be monitored at the high-altitude clinic."

"It *does* appear that the hares are losing," I answered.

* * * * * * * * * * * * *

The Norwegian Base Camp was a quarter mile down the glacier from us, and Dick Bass's tents were pitched beside the Norwegians'. One evening, Dick invited me to stay for some gambling with Chris Bonington and two of the Norwegians. No sooner had we begun than Dick launched into a recitation of his Seven Summits odyssey to climb the Vinson Massif, Antarctica's tallest peak.

*Gambling at 17,000 feet with millionaires.
Chris Bonington pays off his poker debt.*

In 1983, Bonington had guided Dick and his cohort, Disney executive Frank Wells, up the peak. Something that I thought added greatly to Bass's credibility was how freely and good-naturedly he admitted that he and Wells had been partnered up the mountain by their "hired guns."

Poker was on the social calendar the following evening as Dan and I challenged Dick, Karen, Chris, and Arne Næss, the Norwegian Expedition's leader. Næss, like Bass, was also a business tycoon—a shipping magnate. High-altitude gambling with multimillionaires was an unusual challenge. Arne took the game especially seriously, slapping down the cards, then boisterously shouting out the good—or the bad—news. Chris was also feeling quite jolly, and clearly relished the "high stakes." Yet Karen was the evening's sharpest card shark, and pocketed twelve hundred rupees, about fifty dollars. Dick and Arne were immeasurably impressed. Bonington and I lost, but Chris maintained his well-known cheerful positivism. In two days' time, he, two Norwegians, Odd Eliassen and Bjørn Myrer-Lund, and three Sherpas, including Pertemba, would be attempting Everest's summit.

As April progressed, we became increasingly preoccupied with logistics, planning the push to Camps Four and Five, plus determining who'd be chosen for our summit team. Zangbu said he'd never seen an expedition where everyone just did as they wanted, heading up or down the mountain almost at will. That's the democratic American way, we replied. It had also become obvious that certain people had appointed themselves to be on a summit attempt, whether Bridwell agreed or not. Robert reacted strongly to this "self-anointing."

A lone climber ascends fixed ropes up the icefield on Everest's West Shoulder.

Ang Zangbu and Jim Bridwell at ABC on the Lho La. Everest's North Face behind.

Scott Lankford jugs the icefield.   *Dan Larson at Advanced Base Camp.*

"I met Kevin and Jay descending from the Lho La. You know where they were heading? To Pheriche, for a rest," Robert said. "When I saw Kevin's rotation schedule, I thought, 'Now here's the Kevin Swigert-Get-Me-On-Top-First-Schedule.' That's all these guys are concerned with: when their time's up on the chart. As though a climb like Everest can be scheduled weeks in advance! Who's going to erect the camps? Who's going to do the grunt work? I'm just going to plug in when the fallout occurs, when people get sick or exhausted."

* * * * * * * * * * * * * *

Pete, Andy, and two Sherpas finally established Camp Four (25,500 feet), at the base of Everest's upper 4,500-foot-tall rock pyramid, on April 18. The next afternoon, Bridwell was back in Base Camp planning our first summit bid.

Ang Zangbu favored a four-man attempt. "Your mind very different above eight thousand meters," Zangbu warned from experience. "Anything happen. Rope of two, one climber sick, all effort wasted. Rope of four, stronger, safer."

"We're talking about one of the hardest and longest routes up the world's tallest mountain," Jim said. "All the jet stream has to do is descend a few thousand feet, and you're fighting for your life. People can die up there in minutes."

Everyone appeared to have a better idea of how to climb Everest than Bridwell. When Dan insisted, "I think we should—" Jim finally slammed down his fist and exclaimed: "Look, I make the decisions, and I'm going to wait on my decision for the moment!"

But Kevin still hadn't had his say. "I just feel like nothing gets done when Jay and I are away," he began. "We fixed the ropes almost to Camp Two, but only another rope length was put in after we descended."

"We had bad weather,"—Fletcher protested—"so not much got done."

"Okay," Kevin said defensively, "but I still feel that psychologically I have been carrying the entire weight of this expedition."

At hearing that, Bridwell looked more frustrated than ever, while Dan, the lawyer, jumped into the ring to arbitrate:

"That's not true, Kevin. Pete and Andy have been pushing out the route, so has Robert, so has...." Dan said.

"I've never heard people talk so selfishly!" Bridwell shouted before he walked out of the mess tent.

On April 21, I climbed back to the Lho La. Pete and Andy had returned to Advanced Base after establishing Camp Four. Pete's eyes were sunken and his face was ashen gray. Andy had coughed up blood and needed some codeine to soothe his throat. After overhearing a remark that they hadn't stayed "up high" long enough, both were thoroughly disgusted.

"I want to straighten some things out," Pete told Jim at radio call. I'd never seen Pete so upset before. "Andy and I not only dug out platforms and set up the tents, but we had to pick up all the loads people had dropped here and there along the ridge. We were not sitting up there with our thumbs up our asses."

To which Bridwell replied from Base Camp: "I didn't copy that last part. Can you repeat. Over?" Pete groaned. "Hey, I just like to be appreciated," he said.

"We've never been united as a group," Heidi observed. "There's no honest communication, that's our problem."

Dan suggested that Pete should become actively involved in planning and leadership, since he'd been on six previous Himalayan expeditions, but Kim defended Bridwell as our climbing leader. "Jim's been on the cutting edge of rock climbing for a decade. His routes in Yosemite speak for themselves. And now he's taken world alpinism to a new level."

"Bridwell's always drunk everyone else under the table and succeeded on the hardest climbs," Scott added with noticeable admiration.

Meanwhile, the Norwegian team, bolstered by their legions of able-bodied Sherpas, had progressed up the *South Col Route* with considerable ease. Over the radio that evening came the thrilling news that Chris Bonington, the Norwegians Odd Eliassen and Bjørn Myrer-Lund, and the Sherpas Pertemba, Ang Lhakpa, and Dawa Nuru had all summited that day.

Bonington's lifelong desire to climb Mount Everest had at last been fulfilled.

* * * * * * * * * * * * * *

Two days later, I ferried an oxygen bottle and two food bags to Camp Two in my best time yet, six hours. Three hours later, I was back on the Lho La. Maybe I was finally getting fully acclimatized. Kevin and Jay, unfortunately, were both sick. I was shocked when Kevin proclaimed, "I don't know if anyone else is feeling like me, but I just want to get someone—anyone—to the top and go home." Perhaps because of Kevin's statement, the mood became one of "first and goal." Robert, Ang Danu, Ang Tsering, and Lopsang moved up to Camp Four.

"Just one white boy up here," Robert observed at radio call, "and three shorter, but much smarter friends. We're feeling great, Jim, and we're ready to fix ropes to Camp Five tomorrow."

"Great news, Robert. Are you sleeping on oxygen tonight?"

"Ten-four. It's already set up."

"Keep up the good work. We're gonna do it!" said Bridwell.

Peering into the Weatherport, Ang Zangbu seemed confused by the sudden shouting and enthusiasm.

"What happen?" he asked curiously.

"Oh, nothing," said Jim. "It's how Americans build their morale."

On April 26, in high winds, Robert, Ang Danu, Ang Tsering, and Lopsang fixed fifteen hundred feet of rope above Camp Four. It was an impressive performance. Robert thought the old Bulgarian and Yugoslavian ropes strung through the rock bands might speed our progress to Camp Five. At evening radio call, Fletcher was a live wire.

"This is the Skull, come in," he said, using his new nickname for the Camp Two snow cave. "You know, life isn't too bad when you sleep on four liters of oxygen per minute. What's on for tomorrow?"

"Water polo at eight, piano lessons at ten, a short break for lunch, then the afternoon Jacuzzi, over," Pete responded from ABC.

"That's exactly what I thought we were doing," Fletch said.

On April 27, Pete and I returned to Camp Two. Pete soon distanced me on the fixed ropes and disappeared into the clouds. By afternoon, it was snowing hard. Then Heidi and Dan rappelled past me, descending. Each had carted a load across the two-mile snow ridge to Camp Four.

"It was horrendous," moaned Dan. I asked Heidi if she'd heard the rumor that she'd been picked for a summit team.

"Right!" she laughed. "Who asked me? Sometimes I really enjoy this climb, other times I have to ask myself, 'What the hell do I think I'm doing here?' All I honestly want is to relax, eat a good meal, and take a hot shower."

Seven Sherpas welcomed me into the Camp Two ice cave, but there was one minor problem. We were one sleeping bag short, and I was the odd man out! Luckily I found Saas's extra parka and Bridwell's extra climbing suit to sleep in.

The next morning, I left for Camp Three carrying two oxygen bottles—twenty pounds apiece—and my camera gear. If I wanted to be on a summit team, I needed to prove that I could go high and carry a heavy load. As I toiled upward, Robert emerged from the clouds and extended a snowy mitten. "Ah, one of the healthy ones," he cracked, still blessed with his infectious good humor. A week of climbing above twenty-four thousand feet hadn't slowed him one bit.

"How was it up there?"

At 23,000 feet on the West Shoulder, Robert was suitably attired—and healthy.

"Some of the best climbing I've ever done. Not hard, but what a view!"

"Is Kevin coming down?"

"He's ten minutes behind. He kept wanting to climb on oxygen. Up there you've got to be willing to put all the chips on the table. I burned out each day we spent fixing rope above Camp Four, but so what? That's life at high altitude. You burn out, you recover, and then you do it all over again."

Several minutes later, Kevin stumble-stepped past me. His spark was out. He was descending, he said, because the expedition had turned into a job, and the sooner we left for home, the better. I didn't agree. If only I could romp up these thirty-degree snow slopes! If only I could be paired up with Robert! I dropped the two oxygen bottles when I arrived at camp and immediately turned around. Jay and Andy were ascending to Camp Three from the Lho La—a 3,500-foot one-day push—to assume their place in line.

"I've got enough gas left for a few more carries to Four, then I'm done," Andy coughed. "We've got to get Robert to the top of this mountain, that's what we've got to do."

Sherpa brothers Rinsing and Passang Gyalchen, "PG" in the Camp Two ice cave.

I lodged with a gang of Sherpas at Camp Two. While settling myself in, I asked Moti how long he thought it'd take me to climb from Camp Three to Four.

"One week!" he laughed.

"I'll show you," I answered. "For me, five minutes. I'll grow wings and fly!"

"No, you do same as me, seven hours. My time today. Only I sick!" Moti added with a snort. We laughed again. The Sherpas were such a hard-working, good-natured group. Sometimes I thought they'd been born with permanent smiles. Ang Tsering explained their life in simple terms. "Sherpas have no money, but we need no money. We never rich, but life is good to us."

I labored slowly to Camp Three in a swirling snowstorm the following afternoon. The unusual midday halo around the sun, the Sherpas said, foretold an early monsoon. The daily snowfall had doubled in the last two weeks. After two rope lengths, I thought of Lauren and burst into tears. Remembrances of her hadn't hit me often during the climb, but suddenly I was completely overcome with emotion. I hung limp from the fixed rope, crying. The landscape was a blank white sheet except for the sun burning a pin hole of bright light through the clouds. I couldn't stop crying. The tears burned icy cold against my cheeks.

Finally my mind cleared. I began climbing again. Then the summit pyramid burst through the clouds. Three tiny black specks—Jay, Andy, and Penzo en route to Camp Four—stood out against the West Shoulder's endlessly long snow ridge. We were established on the mountain's upper slopes! I felt my resolve increase at the sight of my companions, but at the evening radio call, Bridwell was openly candid about the possibility of failure.

"The Sherpas are losing steam. If the afternoon snow keeps up, we could be finished," he said. "We've got to make a summit bid soon. Once we've established Camp Five, we're going to keep ferrying up members and loads. Those who are strong will have a chance to prove themselves."

At Camp Three, I tented with Penzo, our most religious Sherpa. His parents were very poor, he said. Penzo had never learned to write, but when I showed him my journal, he beamed with pride and happily told me: "We have a Hillary school in my village, and both my younger brother and sister go there."

I surprised myself by getting up at 5 A.M. on April 30, early enough to see a pink sunrise spread over Tibet, and for nearby Pumori to catch the first warming rays of sun. After my good start, I attained a new personal altitude record with every upward step I took. But I wondered when I'd hit the physiological "wall" at around twenty-four thousand feet that had stopped most of my teammates cold in their tracks. Less than half of our twenty-man expedition had

Storm clouds stream over Everest's summit pyramid, viewed along the West Ridge.

reached Camp Four, at 25,500 feet. Could I? Andy and Jay passed me with ease, unburdened, aiming to pick up oxygen bottles cached along the ridge.

"Use the rest step," Andy advised helpfully, pausing to demonstrate the technique for me. "Make your steps even every time."

Up here, conservation of energy was paramount. My throat was parched; lozenges no longer relieved the dryness. I coughed a dry high-altitude cough, and occasionally spat up green phlegm, a sign of trouble to come. I trudged onward, following the well-trod track along the ridgecrest. Penzo had continued ahead, on his own. Soon it was noon and I began to doubt that I could reach Camp Four. If I wasn't almost there by three, I'd have to turn back.

At 24,500 feet, I sat down on a rock to rest, and almost instantly slipped into a dazed stupor. I was shocked to realize where I was when I revived. So this was the "wall"! The thin air contained half the density of oxygen found at sea level. I turned around at 3:30 P.M., having traversed only two-thirds of the ridge. I felt like a failure; I hadn't even been able to carry a load to Camp Four. Andy and Jay caught me up on their return. By the time we reached Camp Three, I knew I couldn't endure another night inside the frozen hell of that crevasse. I told Jay I was heading down to Camp Two.

"You gonna be okay?" Jay asked with concern. "Man, you look wasted."

Rappelling carefully, I reached the snow cave at dusk. Luckily, Scott and Penzo were there. "Take off your boots and harness and get into your sleeping bag," mothered Scott. At last I was warm and dry. I ate meagerly, soup and crackers, but it tasted divine. On May 1, I continued my descent. I met Jim and Heidi on their way up. I told Bridwell I wasn't sure if altitude and I mixed after all.

"Lots of people's summit aspirations are premature," he said bluntly.

Exhausted, I descended all the way to Base Camp. By evening I had a sinus infection. Doctor John put me on antibiotics. For consolation, Rodney and I walked over to Bass's camp. Karen Fellerhoff had David Breashears on their radio, up at Camp Two in the Western Cwm. His voice sounded feeble, but he and Dick Bass had indeed reached the summit of Mount Everest the day before!

"It was horrendously dangerous," David related. "You can't begin to imagine how big Everest is until you crawl on top of it. Ang Phurba was snowblind, then Dick ran out of oxygen just before the summit, so I gave him my bottle. After fifteen minutes on top, we left. How Dick kept going on that last stretch is beyond me. The guy's a phenomenon." They climbed unroped their entire summit day.

Dick Bass had, in fact, achieved two unique goals. He'd become the first person to climb the highest summit of each of the seven continents; and at

Robert Anderson and Pete Athans at Base Camp.

fifty-five, he also became the oldest person to scale Everest—stealing the title from Bonington who, at fifty, had climbed the peak only the week before!

When David inquired about our progress, Pete took the radio. "Robert and I are making our first summit bid in a few days."

"Have plenty of oxygen for the climb," David said, "plus more in reserve at your high camp for your descent. I can't emphasize it enough. Climbing without oxygen is just too debilitating. Remember: Everest is just a big pile of rocks."

Bridwell had given the nod to Pete and Robert to make our first summit attempt for the simple reason that they, along with Jay, had consistently been our strongest members. My summit chances were finished. My personal best would be 24,500 feet.

On May 3, Bass and Breashears, Bonington, and the Norwegians all left for home. Their Base Camps were dismantled and personal gear chaotically sorted into loads for the yaks and porters. In half a day they were gone, and Base Camp became depressingly desolate without them.

* * * * * * * * * * * * * *

Jim Bridwell and Greg Sapp ferried loads to Camp Four on May 4, but arrived late. Greg returned to Camp Three, but Jim was too tired and decided to stay at Camp Four—without a sleeping bag! Then, after surviving a bitterly cold night, Jim discovered the next morning that the Sherpas had mistakenly set the flow rate on their oxygen regulators at eight liters—instead of one—per minute. They had wasted three entire bottles.

The North Face of Mount Everest at sunset from the Lho La Plateau, Tibet.

It was just more bad news. Not only were our oxygen reserves at Camp Four now jeopardized, but all the climbers who'd been selected to support Pete and Robert's summit bid had been forced to descend because of poor health. In a risky move, Robert and Pete decided to make their attempt on the summit with no support climbers at Camps Two, Three, or Four. And, if they got into trouble above Camp Five, at twenty-seven thousand feet or higher, well, realistically, who could help them anyway? Once they'd entered the Death Zone (any elevation above twenty-six thousand feet), the only real rescue was self-rescue.

Bridwell and Saas decided to mount only one follow-up summit attempt. I was crestfallen. I'd hoped Fletcher and I might compose a third summit bid, but Dave soon set me straight: "I'm sorry, Ed. We're going to begin clearing the mountain on May 9, on the day of our second attempt. We don't have enough oxygen bottles, or the manpower to carry them up, for another try."

Of course he was right; we didn't have much drive left. But I couldn't understand the decision to start evacuating the mountain *on the same day* as our second attempt, when the summit pair would be in their most vulnerable position. It seemed unconscionably risky, not to mention defeatist, for us to be abandoning the expedition just as our lead climbers were striving for the top. Yet that was indeed what happened.

But had Pete and Robert established Camp Five? That evening, Kevin worked the radio at Camp One (Advanced Base). At Base Camp, all ears strained toward the radio Rodney held in his hands.

"Camp Five, this is Camp One. Do you read? Over."

There was no answer. Kevin tried again.

"Roger, Camp One. This is Camp Five. We copy, over."

A huge cheer erupted. Pete and Robert had reached 27,200 feet!

"That's great news, Camp Five. Any problems?" asked Kevin.

"We were a bit late because of picking up some oxygen bottles cached between Camps Four and Five," Pete answered, "but no, everything's fine. With the exception that we're tenting on a thirty-degree slope. There's some tent fabric here; I think we're on top of the old Bulgarian camp."

Since Pete and Robert hadn't fixed any ropes above Camp Five, tomorrow their plan was, in Pete's words, "to fix ropes up what we have to, then go for it."

Every face in Base was grinning a smile a mile wide. This was what we'd broken our backs to accomplish, to give two of our teammates the chance to aim for the top of the world.

"Go for it, guys! Reckless abandon!" Bridwell yelled from ABC.

"Well, Jim, the way things look up above, we won't have any choice," Robert answered.

I awoke early on May 6, my blood tingling with excitement. Prithi was already burning juniper boughs at the Base Camp altar. A few clouds floated lazily on the horizon; otherwise it looked like a perfect day. But word came of Robert and Pete's defeat at 10 A.M. Little was clear due to the fracturing of their radio transmission. Evidently, after being slowed by a steep rock cliff, they had decided they didn't have enough fixed ropes to risk going higher. Robert had also had trouble with his regulator and oxygen bottle.

My sunken spirits were lifted by the timely arrival of a support trek that included two friends of mine from Colorado, Ellie Caulkins and Eve Nott. Our huge supply of Snickers bars soon compensated them for the rigors of their journey to Base Camp. That evening I realized that if I wanted to do any more climbing—and to leave some of Lauren's belongings high on Everest, as I had planned to, I'd better return to the Lho La the next day.

It was now or never.

* * * * * * * * * * * * * *

After saying good-bye to Eve and Ellie, I reclimbed the ropes to Advanced Base on May 7. On my way up, I met Bridwell descending the mountain for the last time. After admitting he'd never been so sick in his life as on this trip, Jim speculated that "for my first time leading an expedition of this size, I think I did pretty well. We've been a David and Goliath story right from the start. But Jay's a star! If anyone can climb the West Ridge Direct, *he can,*" Jim predicted confidently. "The verdict will soon be known."

Originally, Jay and Andy had been our second summit team (supported by Dan and Kevin), but Kevin had taken sick again, and Dan and Robert exchanged places at the last minute.

An overnight snowstorm and high winds on May 8 delayed their attempt, and everyone stayed at their respective camps. I doubted that I had enough energy to reach the West Shoulder again, but I was adamant that I had to try. John Meyer was aiming for the magical altitude of twenty-four thousand feet, and he wanted to come too. The expedition would be over in several days. No one could understand why I wanted to go back up.

"You couldn't pay me enough to go up there! Let the Sherpas bring down the gear," Fletcher exclaimed.

LONGS PEAK (14,255 feet)
Rocky Mountain National Park, Colorado

Bright Star V 5.9 A3
Ed Webster, solo
September 3 - 6, 1984

—for Lauren—

Lauren Husted   Colorado, Summer, 1983

Swayambhunath, the Monkey Temple.

Market scene, Kathmandu.

Sagarmatha
from
Kala Pattar.

Dan Larson, Bill Forrest, Jim Bridwell, and David Saas in Denver, 1984

*Barry Bishop and Lute Jerstad celebrate the 30th Anniversary
of their ascent of Mount Everest. Tengboche, Nepal, 1993*

1985 American Everest West Ridge Expedition

at Khumbu Base Camp, Nepal

Back Row, Standing: *David Saas, Ed Webster, Jay Smith*
(with purple bandanna), Kim Carpenter
Jim Bridwell, Randal Grandstaff (hat)
Dr. John Pelner

Middle Row, Standing: *Rodney Korich (on far left), Kevin Swigert*
John Meyer, Heidi Benson, Dan Larson
Fletcher Wilson, George McLeod

Front Row, Kneeling: *Jim McMillian, Scott Lankford*
Robert Anderson, Andy Politz, Peter Athans

Shrouded corpse on the banks
of the Vishnumati River, Kathmandu.

Clockwise from Top:

The versatile, obedient Yak.

A Sherpani girl carries
her yak's dinner—a bale of hay.

Tengboche Monastery, in 1985.

Sorting loads in Namche Bazaar,
with the Kwangde peaks behind.

The venerable Tengboche Rinpoche, Ngawang Tenzin Zangbu.

Ang Zangbu Sherpa, our expedition Sirdar, and a lama from Pangboche at the puja blessing ceremony for the 1985 Everest West Ridge Expedition. Behind: Robert Anderson, Heidi Benson, Jay Smith, and Randal Grandstaff

Ed Webster on glacier. Fletcher Wilson

Heidi Benson on the Lho La Plateau.

Peter Athans.

Scott Lankford and Apple Computer's Apple IIc.

Karen Fellerhoff, Dick Bass, and David Breashears at Khumbu Base Camp.

David Breashears, future Everest IMAX filmmaker.

Fletcher Wilson gazes at the Khumbu Icefall, with Taweche and Cholatse rising in the distance.

Chris Bonington contemplates his next move.

Dick Bass contemplates successfully reaching his Seventh Summit, Mount Everest

Kim Carpenter admires Mallory's View
of the Khumbu Icefall and Nuptse.

Kim Carpenter ascends the Lho La Headwall.

Climbing fixed ropes through spindrift at 21,000 feet, up Everest's West Shoulder.

Sunset on the North Face of Mount Everest from the Lho La Plateau, Tibet.

Team Sherpa ascends Everest's West Shoulder.

Rinsing Sherpa flashes a smile while carrying to Camp Two on the West Ridge Direct. Lho La Plateau and Pumori behind.

Two fashionably-dressed Sherpas—Lhakpa and Mingma—model their Casio wrist watch.

Penzo departs Camp Three at 23,500 feet on the West Ridge Direct. Tibet beyond.

John Meyer attains Everest's West Shoulder at 24,000 feet, with summit above.

Jay Smith and Andy Politz on the snow arête of Everest's West Ridge Direct.

Sunset on Mount Everest's West Ridge, and on Lhotse, from Pumori. Peter Athans

Above: *Ed, Billy, and the helicopter.*

Right: *Billy Squier hanging out.*

Background: *God's rays and Everest, from 20,000 feet in the helicopter.*

A team of Sherpas ascend ropes up Everest's West Shoulder to clear the top camps.

"I'm not going up to retrieve equipment," I said. "I've got my own reasons."

"Then just go and do it," Scott said firmly. He and Heidi were the only ones to whom I'd told the truth.

John and I left early on one of the finest weather days of the entire trip, but, unfortunately, Jay, Andy, and Robert were only climbing up to Camp Five that day. Then seven Sherpas blasted effortlessly by us, their job to retrieve all of the salvageable equipment from the upper camps.

*Ed trying to
warm his fingers
in a snowstorm
at 23,000 feet.*
Robert Anderson

After two months of effort, the climb was ending. I felt a panging mix of emotions. We'd been distilled into two groups: one totally dedicated to reaching Everest's summit, and the other, burned out, ragged, finished, their sole desire to find a warm beach or to fly home to America as quickly as possible. Like several other members, I didn't think that this very democratic expedition should have concluded without a group vote deciding whether to end our efforts or not. And it seemed unwarranted and unwise to begin dismantling any of the camps before we knew the fate of the second summit team.

After a cozy night in the Camp Two ice cave, John Meyer and I ascended to Camp Three on the morning of May 10, while Robert and Jay were heading toward the summit. (We'd learned at the previous night's radio call that Andy thought Robert was going stronger, so they too traded places.) The Sherpas had already emptied Camp Three. John and I headed upward toward the crest of the West Shoulder, and reached it at 1 P.M. Looking up, we saw the summit of Mount Everest rising infinitely higher still, fresh snow sprinkled on the black rock, the mountain set against an oatmeal-gray sky.

*We'd given it our best:
Jay Smith and Andy Politz
descend along the crest
of the West Shoulder
at 24,500 feet.*

John had learned to climb only six months earlier. He gamely posed for victory pictures at his new altitude record of twenty-four thousand feet. Then we watched two tiny dots grow to human proportions as they approached us. Ang Danu and Ang Tsering were carrying immense loads of gear down from Camp Four. Had Jay and Robert reached the top?

"No summit," Ang Danu said unemotionally. "They down already, and now coming to Camp Four."

The expedition was over. Jay and Robert had turned back. I knew that we'd done our best, but I couldn't help feeling emotional. At the root of my feelings was neither profound disappointment nor wrenching sadness, but the realization of what climbing on Everest now meant to me—a very great deal. I was a changed person, and on the whole, the experience had been extremely positive.

I told John I wanted to be alone; he started back down. Then I walked ahead thirty feet into the virgin snow. After sinking to my knees, in a moment I was sobbing. It felt like the holiest place on Earth. The highest peaks on the planet and Tibet's brown plateau peeped in and out of the thick clouds. Carefully I untied Lauren's scarf from my neck, placed three snapshots of us inside her favorite book, John Gardner's *The Art of Living*, and tied up the bundle in the scarf.

The mists wrapped around me like a soundproof curtain, cutting me off from the rest of the world as my crying continued like another force of nature. Between sobs, I spoke out loud to Lauren about the last year of my life. I told her that I had done the best I could on this expedition. I was happy, too, that I had brought some of her to Mount Everest. Placing the book in the snow, I wiped away my tears, then turned to descend. There was nothing else to say or do.

* * * * * * * * * * * * * *

Penzo summed up everyone's feelings when he exclaimed, "Very good climb! No one hurt, good weather, and good Lho La disco." The Sherpas, you see, had made steady use of a ghetto blaster at Advanced Base. We'd gotten higher on the route than the two previous American attempts. And by jumaring up old Bulgarian fixed ropes, Robert and Jay nearly reached the top of the Yellow Band, at 28,200 feet. But it was nervy climbing. The ropes were very frayed. Sometimes just one piton was discovered to be the surviving anchor. The cold, too, had been particularly intense. Robert said he was still freezing even though he wore *nine* layers of clothing!

Once again, faulty oxygen apparatus had ruined Robert's chances. The regulator valve's threads wouldn't mesh with the threads of the full bottle that he needed to change to. Oxygen hissed out wastefully. Although it was only 10 A.M. when they reached their high point, Robert and Jay calculated that they didn't have enough of a safety margin of remaining oxygen to reach the summit and descend, before Robert's now half-empty bottle ran out. And running out of oxygen on the descent meant high odds for being killed.

Of the two teams that have successfully climbed Everest's *West Ridge Direct*, the Yugoslavians chose to descend the neighboring *Hornbein Couloir* after pre-fixing it with rope and a high camp, and the Bulgarian team traversed over the summit and descended via the *South Col Route*. No expedition has yet climbed up the *West Ridge Direct*—and managed to come safely back down it.

Top: *Base Camp; Taweche and Cholatse beyond.* Bottom: *Rodney Korich celebrates.*

After two months of laboring like worker ants, everyone on the team wanted to get back to Kathmandu. Some had unsatiable cravings for Big Macs. Some were headed to the white sand tropical beaches of southern Thailand. Still others just needed to go home and back to work.

"The Turtle." That was the affectionate nickname Fletcher gave me in honor of my halting, contemplative gait. The whole question of pacing oneself at high altitude had been a key element of discussion and strategy throughout our entire expedition. Was it better to climb light and fast—like a hare—or to plod steadily along like a tortoise? I was in the latter camp. I liked to smell the roses, but I had also thought that I might just win the race.

In the end, the riddle went unsolved. Neither hare nor turtle summited Everest's *West Ridge Direct.* On May 15, we broke Base Camp and hastened downhill, away from the frozen realm of white, gray, and blue to the green world waiting below. Upon reaching Tengboche monastery four days later, Robert and I decided to spend the night there, while the rest of the team descended to Namche Bazaar. The next morning, Robert left early to beat the heat, but I lingered on, taking photographs in the crisp bright light.

Tengboche is among the most beautiful places in the world in which to awake. Birds chirp merrily, yak bells tinkle, and Tibetan horns sound. But on this particular morning, a jarring noise intruded upon my mountain reverie—the steady drone of a helicopter. Everyone, from colorfully robed monks to a few foreign trekkers, spilled out to welcome its arrival. The helicopter had already landed when I approached. A Nepalese man whom I thought I knew emerged from the crowd. He walked up to me, and extended his right hand.

"Ed Webster, am I right? You have been on Mount Everest," he said in perfect English. "I am Fabian; we met at a party in Kathmandu two months ago." I had to admit, Fabian was a hard name to forget, especially for a Nepali. After shaking hands, I motioned toward the helicopter sitting beside us.

"Ah, yes!" he responded. "I am the tour guide for Billy Squier, the American rock 'n' roll star. Do you know him?" I knew Billy's brand of heavy metal guitar.

"Billy wants to fly up to Everest in this helicopter," Fabian continued. "You know the Himalaya, so you must now be Billy's guide! You must show him the mountains." A quart of adrenaline dumped directly into my veins. Me? Fly back *up* to Everest, *in a helicopter?* I was momentarily dumbfounded. Of course, yes, I would love to go! After grabbing my cameras, I leapt into the back seat.

Billy looked like a rock 'n' roll star: agile, athletic, and slightly detached from the rest of the world. He hopped onto the front seat, turned around, and said, "Hi, I'm Billy Squier. How's it going?" After introducing myself, we shook hands. "Okay, let's get this show on the road," Billy declared.

"Do you want to use oxygen?" the pilot inquired as he slipped on his own oxygen mask. I didn't need it; I'd just spent two months on Everest. But Billy?

He also declined. His highly aerobic diet of live rock 'n' roll appeared to have preconditioned him. When the helicopter engines roared, we lifted skyward, and Tengboche's golden rooftops fell away beneath us.

The pilot charted a beeline up the valley past Pheriche and Gorak Shep to Everest Base Camp. Unfortunately, clouds obscured the summits of Taweche, Cholatse, and Pumori, but luckily the Big Three—Everest, Lhotse, and Nuptse—were clear and unswaddled and bathed in sunshine.

The Khumbu Glacier and Everest Base Camp were now directly beneath us. Every few seconds I pried myself away from my camera's viewfinder to stare out the Plexiglas window, my eyes frozen upon the austere yet awe-inspiring beauty. The reality that this was actually happening needed constant reinforcement. A helicopter ride to Everest! Only four days earlier I'd walked away from Chomolungma; now, from my aerial vantage point, I could study her every feature in minute detail. And

The view out the helicopter's front window.

just there was the summit itself, the magical meeting place of Heaven and Earth.

As we spiraled above Base Camp to gain height, the entire helicopter began to shudder with increasing complaint as the engine strained to keep us aloft in the rarefied air. Our altitude was nearly twenty-one thousand feet because I could look straight across the twenty-thousand-foot Lho La plateau into Tibet. The awful loud vibrating continued. Well, if we crash, what a hell of a way to go, I thought. Sitting up in front, occasionally leaning out his fully opened side window, Billy snapped pictures like this was just another everyday scenic ride.

Turning, the helicopter crested Nuptse's West Ridge, then began traversing the massive South Face of Lhotse—one of the largest mountain escarpments on earth—ten thousand vertical feet of black castle walls laced with snow and

Webster and Squier and the helicopter at Tengboche. As the inventor of "helicopter mountaineering," Billy counted the Matterhorn and Mount Fuji among his ascents.

ice frosting. I tried to absorb this astounding panorama, but I could not. It was incomprehensible. These were the biggest mountains on Earth. And what were we in God's great scheme? Nothing but an off-course dragonfly waiting to be swatted like an objectionable nuisance. Luckily for us, God's fly swatter was off target this particular morning.

As we at last dropped in altitude, the helicopter's engine relaxed. After cruising past 20,253-foot-high Island Peak, we whizzed below Ama Dablam's clouded summit and all too soon landed back in Tengboche, where we were instantly deluged by a mob. The entire magical flight had taken twenty minutes.

When Billy informed me that there was an extra seat if I wanted to fly back to Kathmandu, I wondered what the rest of my teammates would say when they found out I'd beaten them back to civilization! I dispatched a trekking friend to carry the news of my unexpected departure down to Namche Bazaar.

On the return flight to Kathmandu, Billy explained to me how the whole crazy idea of helicoptering up to Everest had originated. The previous week he had trekked along the Annapurna circuit, and he'd decided that since he was in Nepal, it would be a shame not to see Everest, too. But he had only a day or two left, so he had asked Fabian if there were any helicopters for rent.

Fabian said: "There are no helicopters."

There had to be a helicopter somewhere, Billy claimed. Fabian returned an hour later and said, "Yes, there is one helicopter—but it belongs to the Prince."

"Okay," Billy replied, "then go to the Palace and tell the Prince that I want to rent it." An agreement was struck, money paid, and Billy got the Prince's helicopter for half a day. But, in secret, Billy had dreamt up a considerably more outlandish plan: to try to land the helicopter on the summit of Everest!

"Yeah, I offered $10,000 in cash to a couple of pilots, but they both turned me down," he told me, still sounding dejected as we buzzed back toward Kathmandu in our rented mechanical insect. I gathered that Billy thought that his "landing on top" idea had been totally sane, as well as practical.

"Helicoptering to the top of Everest, it's never been done, has it?" Billy asked.

I shook my head sideways. "Ummm, no, I don't think so."

We landed at noon at Tribhuvan International Airport. A Mercedes Benz—probably also the only one in Nepal—chauffeured us to the Yak & Yeti Hotel. In the top-floor presidential suite where Billy was lodging, I melted under my first real hot shower in three months. Later, lunching and having drinks under an umbrella at poolside, we talked about climbing, the Himalaya, and my Everest expedition. Billy was well-informed and genuinely interested in mountaineering. He was reading Chris Bonington's *Annapurna South Face*.

Then, as we walked into the hotel lobby from the pool, Billy was summoned to the front desk. A clerk politely handed him a telegram.

"He found me; I can't believe it!" Billy raved.

The message was from his manager in New York City.

Civilization had indeed found Billy, and I had found civilization. Billy's Everest experience had taken less than four hours, from getting up and having a cup of coffee, to helicoptering up to Everest in an hour and a half, and returning to the hotel by lunch. Today had been just another ordinary day in the life of a rock 'n' roll star; Billy's next destination was scuba diving in Sri Lanka. Reflecting back upon my own three months of hard-won Himalayan experiences, I compared the physical and mental vicissitudes of my Everest journey with his. And, I had to admit, however vicarious my participation had been in this morning's wild aerial adventure, I wouldn't have missed my helicopter ride with Billy for anything!

Walking back into the sun toward the hotel swimming pool, I thought of my teammates back up in Namche Bazaar, and I laughed—well, at least a little.

The tortoise *had* won.

Chapter 3

Journey To Tibet

What would a season in the Himalaya be without death?
These are the highest mountains in the world.
Without death they would not be the mountains that they are:
dangerous mountains which deserve our utmost respect.
Every climber who comes here knows the game—and the rules.

—Roger Marshall

S peeding along Beijing's haunted tree-lined avenues at 2 A.M., a shiny new tour bus whisked us past multitudes of drab concrete buildings into the center of the sleeping city. Turning onto a broad boulevard, we passed by the Workers' Stadium, then drove out into the immense expanse of the People's Square, Tiananmen. Out of the dusty black night loomed the rectangular silhouette of Mao Zedong's stone mausoleum, and as we crossed Tiananmen Square, I felt we were traversing the age-worn heart of Communist China.

Left: *Prayer flags flutter in front of Mount Everest, Rongbuk Base Camp, Tibet.*

At forty-four, British-born, now resident-Canadian mountaineer Roger Marshall was the leader of this miniexpedition to China and Tibet. A maverick on the Himalayan climbing scene, Roger (on paper) was also the expedition's only climber. Just ten months after my return from Nepal, Roger invited me to go back to Everest, to its northern, Tibetan side, to be his photographer during his attempt to solo the world's tallest mountain. Since Roger would be climbing alone and unsupported, I wouldn't actually accompany him, but would photograph him from a distance. And naturally I hoped I'd do a bit of climbing on my own. All together we were a team of four: Roger, his girlfriend Ruth De Cew, my new girlfriend Kristina Kearney, and me.

Roger Marshall.

Kristina and I met at a party in Colorado a week after I returned from Everest's West Ridge. I liked her down-to-earth, fun way of being, and felt comfortable in the fact—which she candidly admitted—that she had absolutely no interest in climbing, or even in learning how to climb. Unlike my relationship with Lauren, with Kristina, there was virtually no pressure or expectation of going rock climbing together. Climbing was not the basis for our relationship— and yet it felt quite ironic that I was invited to go on this, my second Everest expedition, in large part because I had a non-climbing girlfriend who Ruth liked, and furthermore, who Ruth thought would be a good female traveling companion. As for my climbing ambitions while we were in Tibet, I told Kristina that I wouldn't climb "much," and that of course I would be very careful.

In the select and rarefied world of professional, sponsored mountaineers, Roger's rugged good looks and supreme self-confidence helped set him apart. The reddish-blond hair and beard, chiseled features, quick British humor and accent fortuitously endowed Roger with the heroic image that the public associates with Himalayan climbers. Trained as a newspaper journalist, he could rattle off quotable quotes and expertly manipulated the media ropes of self-promotion. Roger also possessed first-class mountaineering credentials. His 1984 solo ascent of Kanchenjunga, the world's third-highest mountain, had catapulted Roger into an élite group. Only three mountaineers had soloed an eight-thousand-meter peak—Reinhold Messner, Pierre Béghin, and Roger—so his current goal of climbing Everest alone was not entirely unrealistic.

Years ago Roger emigrated with his wife and two sons from the English Lake District to Vancouver, Canada. After his sons had grown up, Roger and his wife separated. More recently, Roger had moved to Boulder, Colorado, where he was living with Ruth, planning for Everest, and training and climbing in the Rocky Mountains. My Everest teammate Pete Athans—another Boulder resident in a city filled with climbers and outdoor folk—introduced me to the pair.

Roger Marshall's Everest fascination, like mine, was long standing, but his journey to Chomolungma had been circuitous—and jarring. While living in Vancouver, Roger obtained an Everest permit from the Nepalese Ministry of Tourism for the post-monsoon climbing season of 1982, but eventually he relinquished the expedition leadership to George Kinnear. Then, after Kinnear was injured, Bill March was chosen to lead what had evolved into the 1982 Canadian Mount Everest Expedition, with Roger onboard as a member of the climbing team. Unfortunately—or fortunately, depending on your perspective—Roger's complete disregard for authority culminated in several embarrassing "incidents" involving "impolite language" mixed with alcohol. When March decided Roger's behavior reflected poorly on their nationally sponsored effort, he was unceremoniously kicked off the expedition in Namche Bazaar—within sight of Everest.

In hindsight, getting the boot from the Canadian Everest expedition (which did place the first Canadians atop Everest—at the extremely high cost of six lives) was probably the best thing that ever happened to Roger Marshall.

Roger, in his impetuous, nonconformist way, decided to do things differently. Renouncing traditional expedition climbing altogether, he embarked on a solo Himalayan career. In 1983, he attempted Lhotse Shar (27,513 feet) in Nepal, and reached twenty-six thousand feet without bottled oxygen. Then, in October, 1984, he completed his daring solo ascent of Kanchenjunga. In 1985, Pete Athans joined Roger on an expedition to Ama Dablam, one of Nepal's most beautiful peaks, and Cho Oyu (26,906 feet), the world's sixth-tallest mountain. After Pete and Roger both successfully soloed Ama Dablam, even their most determined efforts to scale Cho Oyu in winter failed just short of the prize.

Undeterred by slightly frostbitten fingers and a short-lived bout with cerebral edema on Cho Oyu, Roger next fixed his sights on soloing Mount Everest, again without using bottled oxygen. Only one climber, the daring and famed South Tyrolean mountaineer Reinhold Messner, from Italy, had accomplished this harrowing ascent. Over four days in August of 1980, Messner climbed Everest—without breathing bottled oxygen and completely alone from bottom to top, and back down again; "by fair means," as Messner put it. Roger desperately wanted to repeat this accomplishment, and then to surpass it—to become the first person to climb the world's five highest mountains (Mount Everest, K2, Kanchenjunga, Lhotse, and Makalu) alone, without oxygen.

The scheme was pure Roger Marshall, audacious, ambitious, intriguing, and highly marketable. It would also prove to be undeniably dangerous. Everest stood next in line in Roger's plan to solo the five highest 8,000ers, and the CMA, the Chinese Mountaineering Association, had granted him a permit to attempt Everest's North Face in Tibet during the 1986 summer monsoon season.

Not long after Roger invited me along as his photographer, I got a letter from New Zealand from Robert Anderson, another of my West Ridge partners. Also eager to return to Everest, Robert had just bought his own permit from the CMA to climb the mountain from Tibet. But Robert's projected ascent in the spring of 1988 would be up the little known East, or Kangshung, Face. Did I want to come?

Yes, I did, I thought—although everything I'd ever heard or read about the heavily glaciated, two-mile-high precipice made it sound like one colossal death trap. Still, my own growing fascination with Everest made me prepared to entertain extreme risks, and I wrote back expressing my interest. I also asked Robert if he intended to repeat the 1983 *American Buttress*—to date the only established line up the face—or was he thinking of venturing onto new ground? I ended my letter by noting that this year, although I probably wouldn't go any higher than the North Col or up on Everest's North Peak, Changtse, my upcoming expedition with Roger Marshall would give me the opportunity to visit Tibet, gain more high-altitude experience, and make a reconnaissance for future trips, like the Kangshung Face expedition.

* * * * * * * * * * * * * *

A dingy and peeling caravanserai of unknown vintage, the Bei Wei Hotel welcomed us from the Beijing airport. Since China reopened Tibet to climbing in 1980, the CMA has housed foreign mountaineering expeditions at the

A face in Beijing.   Dragon staircase, the Forbidden City.

Bei Wei. Our interpreter, Mr. Fu Yide (pronounced *"Foo E-da"*) and our Liaison
Officer, Mr. Li Chen Xiang (pronounced *"Zi-ang"*), had warned us that the Bei
Wei wouldn't be the best of accommodations, and they were right. However,
after our twelve-hour airborne incarceration, anything closely resembling a
bed was as good as sleeping at the Ritz.

Our first full day in China, June 17, began early. Roger was briefed by several CMA officials, while Mr. Yide took Kristina, Ruth, and me sightseeing at the
Temple of Heaven in a popular nearby park. That afternoon we toured the
Forbidden City. A thirty-foot-high red brick wall and a towering portrait of Mao
guarded the entrance. Beyond, one spacious brick-and-stone courtyard after
another led us closer and closer to the innermost sanctuary. Here, secluded in
their royal gardens and private apartments, the Chinese emperors spent their
entire lives, perhaps never once venturing beyond the tall, sheltering walls to
mingle with their subjects.

Kristina Kearney, Ruth De Cew, and Roger Marshall atop the Great Wall.

The following day, we visited the Great Wall, an hour's drive northwest of Beijing. Nearly two thousand miles long and built sixteen centuries ago, much of the wall is in disrepair, yet small portions have been reconstructed for the benefit of foreign tourists. As we rounded a bend in the road, I glimpsed a strong gray stone mass muscling its way up valleys and over mountains—a masonry serpent winding and stretching from one horizon to the other.

We paid our admission fee and merged with the international throng promenading along the stepped and ramparted crest.

An estimated four hundred thousand workers died during the wall's construction. "Now that many thousands of tourists come to the Great Wall each year, and because China is able to earn hundreds of thousands of dollars in foreign currency from them, the people of China thank the emperors who built it," beamed Mr. Yide, our interpreter. After soaking up the view from on top of one of the wall's many watchtowers, we purchased the obligatory tourist T-shirts emblazoned with the slogan, "I Climbed the Great Wall."

That afternoon we had to hurry to catch our train at Beijing's central station. Although it would have been quicker to fly to Chengdu, the capital of the Sichuan province—our next destination—Roger opted for a two-day train ride, thinking that it would be a more scenic introduction to China. With four bunk berths per room, rest and wash rooms at either end of the car, and a companion dining car, the overnight, steam-powered sleeper to Chengdu already seemed like a pleasant alternative.

By 6 A.M. farmers were hoeing the land as we click-clack-click-clacked across an infinite expanse of yellow earth, past homes carved into dirt cliffs beside the tracks, and endless fields of corn, wheat, beans, squash, and countless other crops.

"Yet we must still import food each year from Canada and the United States to feed ourselves," Mr. Yide observed.

Later, as he and I stood looking out the train window, I asked Mr. Yide how he felt about America and about the late-sixties Cultural Revolution in China. At first, he seemed noticeably disinclined to discuss either topic, but finally he answered me in a hushed voice, wary that we might be overheard.

"I can honestly say that fifteen years ago, I thought America was China's number one enemy. During the Vietnam war, propaganda was thick. In those days I never could have imagined what Americans were truly like, nor could I have expected to meet an American, like you, in person during my lifetime.

"Now I can say that Americans are a good people, very friendly, and that they are willing to help China. Perhaps in many ways, we are very backwards in China. The only way we will learn to help ourselves is with western technology. This the U. S. A. and our other western friends will provide."

"Could you please tell me about China's Cultural Revolution?" I was interested in this period of Chinese history, and how it had adversely affected Tibet.

"For about five years, there was a cultural revolution in China. We now know that it was a great step backwards, for our nation, and for our peoples. Nothing positive was accomplished. Teachers did not teach, students did not learn, workers did not work, and farmers did not farm. This was very bad. Most Chinese would like to forget this period, it was so terrible. We wish it had never happened."

That evening we dined on carp, and ate a fish that appeared to be of such antiquity, we speculated that it had been preserved since the Ming dynasty. When we told this to Mr. Yide, he translated it for Mr. Li, our Liaison Officer, who found the joke immensely funny. Mr. Li's boyish face warmed even more when Roger, still joking, poured most of a bottle of vinegar over his own bowl of rice and ate it with zeal. Later, Mr. Li and Mr. Yide advised us about local foodstuffs we could purchase in Chengdu and Lhasa.

We arrived in Chengdu in a dreary morning rain that made the lifeless gray city skyline of apartment complexes even more depressing. We had missed our hotel breakfast, so we went to a local restaurant instead. The floor was slippery with slime, and the plastic-covered tables were layered with accumulated grease. The food tasted rancid. I opted for the safe Asian meal of a bottled orange soda, but Roger bravely ate his breakfast, claiming he had to keep up his weight for the climb.

Life couldn't have been a whole lot worse. All of our baggage was missing (inexplicably, it hadn't been placed on the train in Beijing), and Roger and Ruth were in the midst of a serious row. When Ruth accused Roger of being manipulative, he stated flatly that she could go home if she felt that way. Ruth sat alone, in tears, at a separate table. I walked over and gave her a hug. Expedition life wasn't always roses. As romantic as it sounded only a week ago, being in China was starting to grate on us. Kristina, on the other hand, was still relatively wide-eyed, enjoying her first trip to Asia, and holding up bravely.

After another squalid meal at the hotel, we realized that food in China bore virtually no resemblance to American-style Chinese food. Now everyone was complaining: Kristina about the filth, Ruth and I about the food, and Roger about the bill. Like everything else we required in China—plane tickets, ground transportation, lodging—our hotel meals had also been paid for in advance, before we left the United States. It was no use grumbling now; the Chinese had cashed the check months ago! So we sat in envy, watching the hotel patrons around us eat consistently more nutritious-looking meals.

That afternoon we went on a shopping spree, buying plastic cooking and washing bowls, black beans, forty rolls of toilet paper, and straw mats for Base Camp relaxing. Roger, Ruth, and Kristina made an incongruous sight, three blond heads adrift in a sea of black hair. Material goods and customers seemed equally plentiful in the colorful downtown free market, and my photography kept me at my customary turtle's distance behind the others.

We flew from Chengdu to Lhasa on June 21, the summer solstice. At 6 A.M. we traveled through Chengdu past hundreds of early morning joggers to the equally crowded airport. Our hosts sped us through ticketing and the security check, then Roger and the polyester-clad CMA men discussed our upcoming three-day jeep ride to Everest Rongbuk Base Camp.

"There will be absolutely no smoking in the jeep," Roger insisted. "I'm paying three thousand dollars for this jeep, so no smoking!"

Left: *Train stop en route to Chengdu.*

The Great Corrugations from the air, on the Chinese-Tibetan border.

"But the driver will fall asleep!" protested the CMA man. "Many drivers in Tibet smoke opium to stay awake," he added.

"Okay, then," Roger said, "he can smoke as long as it's opium!" We all laughed. Roger and Ruth were adamantly antismoking. To climb Mount Everest without oxygen, clear air and clean living were of primary importance. Roger, the native Englishman, had even taken the unthinkably drastic step of quitting alcohol.

An aging Boeing 707 lifted us gently into the air toward Lhasa, Tibet's capital, eight hundred air miles to the west. I didn't realize how mountainous the Chinese-Tibetan frontier was until I saw the so-called Great Corrugations, a dramatic uplift of several extensive and parallel mountain ranges. The highest mountain in this remote Himalayan region was the ice-clad Namcha Barwa (25,532 feet) of which we enjoyed an excellent view to the south.

Those with a passion for mountaineering history might be interested to know that in 1986, Namcha Barwa was the world's highest unclimbed mountain. Guarded by near-impenetrable terrain, the glacier-clad peak rises near the great bend of the Tsangpo-Brahmaputra River in eastern Tibet, close to the Myanmar (Burma) border. After joint Chinese-Japanese Alpine Club attempts in

1990 and 1991, Namcha Barwa was finally scaled on October 30, 1992 by yet another logistically massive and expensive Chinese-Japanese expedition. The Japanese had sweetened the deal by promising to give the expedition's twenty-five four-wheel-drive vehicles to the CMA at the trip's conclusion. Eleven climbers summited on one day. At present, the world's tallest unclimbed peak is Shartse I (also called Peak 38) at 24,902 feet, between Shartse II (Junction Peak) and Lhotse Shar on the Lhotse Wall Ridge on the Nepal-Tibet border.

We began our slow descent over Tibet's Tsangpo River valley. The engines strained as we glided above the river's braided gravel banks. Then the plane began bouncing so unnervingly that Kristina, who was not overly fond of flying, clenched my hand in a vise-like grip until my knuckles turned white. After a safe landing at the Chinese military airport some forty miles from Lhasa, we walked out onto the tarmac in bright morning sunshine, breathed in draughts of cold mountain air, and felt Chengdu's dreary tropical veil finally lift.

My well-being, sadly, was temporary. A foreign tour group, and then a cluster of unwashed Tibetans, crowded onto our bus. The potholed road was incredibly bumpy; the bus's shocks were incredibly old. And the driver's breakneck pace, swinging curveball-wide around each bend of the road, was typical of Asia.

"Where'd this guy get his license—Sears?" asked Kristina moments before we barely avoided crashing into an oncoming bus that swerved into our lane to avoid a bicyclist.

The Tibetans pushed up against us. The stench of sweat, dirt, and rancid yak butter was overpowering. The bus bounced jarringly—and with unerring accuracy—from one large pothole to the next. Five consecutive days of travel were catching up to me. Feeling increasingly nauseated, I simultaneously began falling asleep and getting hot flashes. Saliva had collected in my mouth, too, and realizing that I was about to retch, I began searching for a suitable receptacle when, in the distance, I spotted a towering white and red fortress crowning the top of a distant hill in the center of a broadening green valley.

This dream-like dwelling was the Potala, former home of the Dalai Lamas, Tibet's spiritual and secular rulers. In 1950, soldiers of the People's Liberation Army (the PLA) overwhelmed the two-thousand-member Tibetan army, and arrived below the Potala to "peacefully liberate the peasants from serfdom." When a 1959 revolt against the Chinese invasion force failed, His Holiness the fourteenth Dalai Lama, Tenzin Gyatso, fled into exile with eighty thousand followers—and eventually set up the Tibetan government in exile in the hill town of Dharamsala in the northern Indian state of Himachal Pradesh.

Lhasa on the midsummer solstice, seen from the main steps of the Potala.

Roger, Kristina, and Ed in front of the Potala. Ruth De Cew

Fortunately, my first view of Tibet's most well-known structure distracted me sufficiently from my misery to effect a last minute cosmic *retchus interruptus.* Upon entering the city of Lhasa proper, the geographical goal of many a diehard explorer from Sven Hedin to Heinrich Harrer, I swallowed my built-up saliva with a degree of smug satisfaction. I had reached fabled Lhasa, "the Place of the Gods," Buddhist crucible of legend, mystery, and more recently, ethnic oppression.

I noted all too soon that the Chinese preference for monotonous, massively ugly cement architecture had utterly overwhelmed the Tibetans' colorful, quaintly painted homes. With its new and unsightly "modern" concrete, brick, and corrugated-steel-roof backdrop, even the splendid Potala palace appeared out of place, a tarnished relic from a bygone glorious past.

We acclimatized for two days in Lhasa—at 11,800 feet, one of the world's highest capitals—at the Lhasa Holiday Inn, a four-hundred-room, western-style domicile catering to well-heeled tourists (like us) flushed with hard currency.

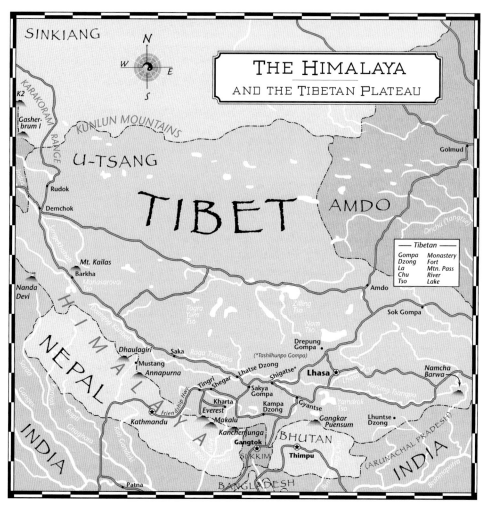

The Tibetan people have been ruthlessly persecuted by the Chinese, who militarily conquered Tibet in 1950. Over 99% of Tibet's once estimated 6,000 monasteries, including Khampa Dzong (below) and the monastery at Shekar (on right) have been destroyed since the Chinese take-over. 1924 Photographs by Noel Odell

As a young teenager, I'd read the accounts of the first British Mount Everest expeditions of the 1920s and '30s. Visiting the Potala had been a lifelong goal, and it was well worth the wait. The next morning, we toured the Potala on a festival day—the day after the summer solstice—and a horde of wide-eyed, wild-looking nomads from Tibet's western steppes gave the palace a lively yet immensely religious air. Mr. Yide accompanied us, along with a largely silent Tibetan woman, and a brash Chinese soldier whose presence I found offensive.

Although it boasts over a thousand rooms, thirteen stories, a reputed ten thousand shrines, and two hundred thousand statues, only small sections of the white-washed, gold-roofed building are open to the public. Considering it was built between 1645 and 1694, the impression that the Potala's gargantuan seven-hundred-foot-high size makes is utterly fantastic. Entering into the dimly lit interior, we passed through a columned court into the burial room containing the remains of several previous Dalai Lamas. The sixty-foot-tall, gold-leaf-covered *chorten,* or burial repository, for the salt-dried body of "the Great Fifth" Dalai Lama (Ngawang Lobsang Gyatso; 1617-1682, who ordered and also supervised the Potala's construction) was by far the largest. The *chorten* of the much less revered twelfth Dalai Lama (Trinle Gyatso; 1856-1875) seemed diminutive.

Long lines of Tibetan faithful toured the Dalai Lamas' home with us. Proceeding in small family groups, they intoned a constant stream of prayers, nimbly fingered strings of prayer beads, and made offerings of coins and *kata* scarves to the various Buddhas whom they wished to propitiate. Pausing beside two-foot-diameter butter lamps, they would pour off the excess of melted yak butter from their own small candle, and say yet another prayer. Smoke-filled rooms reverberated with steady murmuring and the shuffling of leather-clad feet upon the earthen and wooden floors. And when my eyes met theirs, wide, gracious smiles were the predictable result.

For only fifty dollars in cash (payable, of course, to a Chinese attendant), we were told that you could photograph either, but not more than: one room of the Potala, one gold Buddha, or one colorful mural. Our continually arrogant Chinese soldier *cum* tour guide took great pleasure in force-feeding us propaganda upholding the righteousness of China's "liberation" of Tibet. I quickly grew weary of hearing his repeated drivel of how virtually all of the Dalai Lamas had traveled to Peking to pay obsequious homage to the Chinese emperors, so Kristina and I purposefully lagged behind to stay out of earshot.

The highlight of the day was walking through the Dalai Lamas' private rooftop quarters, through the thirteenth and fourteenth Dalai Lamas' receiving

The main entrance of the Potala.

The Barkhor market.

Happy Chinese soldiers in Lhasa.

and prayer rooms, their private sitting room, and the dining room. The bedroom was off limits, but you did get the sense that at least these rooms had been preserved almost as they had been left in 1959 when His Holiness the fourteenth Dalai Lama was forced to flee into exile.

Many Tibetans devoutly prostrated themselves on the floor before the Dalai Lama's vacant throne in his official receiving room. Several of the pilgrims appeared to have traveled great distances to have reached the Potala, and their faith in the Dalai Lama seemed not in the least diminished by his absence. Buddhism permeated every aspect of a Tibetan's daily life in Lhasa, and the more time I spent in the city, the sharper and more clearly defined became the division and derision between the Chinese occupiers and the Tibetan people. When we visited outdoor markets that afternoon, the Chinese soldiers stood out in their drab green uniforms and caps. Tibet is an occupied nation.

Walking through the Barkhor, Lhasa's central marketplace, we followed the circular promenade around the city's second most revered destination, the Jokhang Temple. (In 1987 and 1988, the Barkhor and the Jokhang Temple were the scenes of brutal repression and the killings of Tibetan freedom protesters and monks by Chinese police and soldiers.) Joining into the clockwise human flow, we paced around the Jokhang, but sadly didn't have time to enter it. Even as we were harangued by traders selling everything from turquoise to prayer flags to bronze Buddhas, we found the majority of Tibetans to be very friendly.

As Roger was paying the expedition traveling expenses for the four of us, plus Mr. Li and Mr. Yide, at eighty-five dollars per person per night, the daily lodging tab totalled $510. When Roger discovered that the hotel charged walk-in guests a modest 100 yuan (about thirty-one dollars) a night, he threw a fit. Where was the extra fifty-four dollars per person going? To our very good friends at the Chinese Mountaineering Association in Beijing, of course!

We'd heard tales of exorbitant prices mountaineering expeditions were obligated to pay in Tibet, so it came as no surprise that Roger was feeling taken for the privilege of climbing here. Considering the large sum of money ($50,000) he'd paid up front to the CMA before the Chinese embassy even issued us visas, I thought Roger would explode when Mr. Yide informed him of an extra four-yuan-per-person fee to purchase a special border permit.

Roger's favorite subject for ridicule and complaint—other than the CMA—was the wastefulness of large, nationally sponsored Himalayan expeditions. His disastrous experiences on the 1982 Canadian Everest Expedition had forced his unyielding conclusion that big expeditions were no longer acceptable.

Yamdrok Tso from the crest of the Khamba La.

"Traditional expeditions spoil it for everybody," he claimed. "They absorb the sponsorship money smaller expeditions could use, plus with their enormous logistics, they overwhelm the local villages and cultures of the countries they visit. The Canadian Everest Expedition's budget was $400,000. I could have climbed on that money for the rest of my life!"

We were supposed to leave for Shigatse, Tibet's second-largest city, the next day—a bumpy two-hundred-mile drive on dirt roads—but of course we didn't. After yet another round of China's national sport, of "hurry up, and wait," Roger went to the Lhasa CMA office to investigate. First he was told a jeep wasn't available. Then it turned out that our eight duffels hadn't arrived yet from Chengdu. After being promised our baggage would soon appear, we amused ourselves writing postcards and mailing them at the Lhasa post office using seventy-fen stamps depicting Everest's North Face.

The Chinese Army truck carrying our errant baggage left an hour before seven of us piled into a four-wheel-drive jeep for the eight-hour ride to Shigatse. Driving out of Lhasa heading southwest, we traveled a paved road for a short distance (rumored to be the only segment of its kind in Tibet) along the banks of the Lhasa River, the Kyi Chu ("River of Happiness") to the main bridge over the Tsangpo Chenpo—"the Great River." On the riverbank, soldiers were building a pontoon bridge, while machine-gun-toting guards stood alertly in sentry boxes.

We took the panoramic southern route to Shigatse, headed over the 16,500-foot-high Khamba La pass, then traced the banks of the sacred turquoise lake, Yamdrok Tso. Passing numerous fortified Chinese army barracks, we also saw multitudes of ruined monasteries which had all been reduced to piles of hilltop rubble. The cruel disparity between the pious Tibetans and the militaristic Han Chinese turned my stomach. It was grimly evident that one deadly machine gun burst by the Chinese would swiftly curtail any attempted Tibetan insurrection. Was it even right, I asked myself, that we were here in this fascist state, paying our dollars to the CMA in Beijing, in order to climb mountains in Tibet?

Atop the Khamba La, we admired the crystal blue waters of Yamdrok Tso, a lake so large that it resembled an inland sea. Later, as we circumnavigated the shoreline, I was surprised to see afloat a gaily painted, Tibetan houseboat. Turning uphill away from the lake, we ascended an increasingly narrow river gorge. Our driver gnashed gears and bounced across washouts until we topped out at seventeen thousand feet on the Kharo La: the "wide-mouthed pass." A much smoother dirt road led to Shigatse, with its forty thousand residents.

We lodged in another poorly built, western-style hotel near the town center. Many books on Tibet, I now realized, showed only the preserved parts of Tibetan culture, what predated or had somehow survived the Red Guard's furor. The modern Chinese influence of cinder block buildings with corrugated tin roofs was boringly sterile, and the not-so-silent heaps of rubble of Samdup-tse *Dzong*, a Tibetan government building and fort bombed and destroyed during the late-1960s Cultural Revolution, only amplified my growing anti-Chinese feelings. Greenback-spending Western tourists *had bought*—quite literally—the 1980s Chinese "make-over" of Tibet. A surprising number of Westerners were in town.

"Excuse me, but are you in the trekking group?" a dapper American tourist in the hotel lobby made the mistake of asking Roger.

"No, vee are Chinese," he said, pulling his eyes sideways into narrow slits.

Later, at dinner, Roger asked, "Can you imagine spending a couple of weeks driving around Tibet, spending thousands, and eating this awful food? It amazes me that the people who invented the wheel are still eating with wooden sticks."

Roger—who was highly opinionated, rough around the edges, and a person who embraced climbing for the sheer pleasure and renegade fun of it—was the embodiment of "the climber's climber." At times he could be surprisingly formal, but to reach Tibet as a solo mountaineer you had to have polish and dash. Roger had each. The few times I'd seen him speak to reporters, he maintained a strictly professional image. He had to, to survive. But once he was on the road he was playful, irresponsible (at least he liked to pretend to be), forgetful, and even somewhat unorganized. In other words, Roger was having the time of his life.

"Ever fallen into a crevasse?" I asked him.

"Once, up to my armpits," he answered. "I don't think about the danger when I'm soloing in the mountains. Once you've been on the climb for a few days, there's no more danger or fear. I'm never afraid when I solo."

I looked at him hard, but his poker face was too good. It was impossible to tell if Roger was telling the truth—or not.

Circumambulating Tashilhünpo Monastery, Shigatse.

The following morning, Kristina and I walked along the dirt path encircling the Tashilhünpo Monastery. Built in 1447, two centuries later the monastery became home to the Panchen Lama, Tibet's second most powerful spiritual and temporal leader. Although he was never more than a regional head, the Chinese government nonetheless backed the Panchen Lama as Tibet's pre-eminent ruler after the Fourteenth Dalai Lama set up his government in exile in India.

The track was narrow, well-worn, and wound up the steep hillside behind the monastery's stone-walled perimeter. Colorfully painted Buddhas adorned many rock outcrops, and a steady stream of Tibetans shuffled past us—in the opposite direction. I finally realized, to my considerable chagrin, that we were walking counterclockwise around the monastery, "unwinding" our future lives!

A celestial figure watches over Shigatse, with the ruins of Samdup-tse Dzong behind.

1924: Shekar Dzong, the monastery of the White Crystal. Photograph by Noel Odell

On June 26, we drove west to Shekar, switchbacking over two high passes of fifteen thousand and seventeen thousand feet. Just below the top of the second pass we encountered a solitary bicyclist grinding up the lonely incline.

"Got to be a Brit," Roger declared. Sure enough, a GB sticker adorned the bike's rear fender. Fifteen minutes later, we met the solitary adventurer atop the barren windblown pass. The cyclist's olive-green windjacket was coated with a fine red dust. Mark Skinner of Leicester, England, had embarked on this round-the-world bicycle trip two years earlier with his girlfriend, Jenny Clare, to raise money for charity. A year later, Mark later explained, after the unbearable heat and crowds in Egypt, Jenny dropped out. He had persisted.

"Only a Brit would bicycle alone across China and Tibet, or try to solo Everest," Roger said, introducing himself. Another crazy Englishman, I thought.

"I hope there's a shower in Shekar," Mark said.

As we bounced around the road's millionth bend, ahead we saw the ruins of the now-destroyed "White Crystal Fort," Shekar *Dzong,* protruding from the angular backbone of a distant hill. Pictures in prewar Everest expedition books depict a massive monastery-fort climbing the precipitous hillside in a series of

1986: The ruins and partially rebuilt monastery of Shekar Dzong.

stepped buildings. Shekar Monastery, consecrated in 1385, had also fallen victim to the insanity and terror of Mao Zedong's late-1960s Cultural Revolution. The fort was dismantled stone by stone by Red Guards and coerced local villagers. The roofs were gone, the walls were destroyed, the stone steps had eroded.

We lodged in the Chinese-run, military-style barracks near Shekar's center. The accommodations were sparse, and the food was atrocious—worse than in Shigatse and Chengdu. Although it would be three thousand feet higher than our present altitude of 14,400 feet, with our snug tents, warm sleeping bags, and American food, Rongbuk Base Camp was going to be a considerable relief.

That afternoon, we hiked up through the ruins of Shekar *Dzong* with our newest expedition member, our Sherpa *Sirdar,* Pasang Norbu. Forty-two, and hailing from Namche Bazaar in Nepal, Pasang was typical of the industrious Sherpas. He ran two trekking lodges year-round with his wife and family. He also worked as a cook and headman on treks and expeditions in the spring and fall climbing seasons. And, although just under five feet in height, Pasang commanded a boundless energy. He jumped eagerly from task to task and smiled merrily. It was obvious he'd be a cheerful companion; I liked him immediately.

Narrow alleyways led us to some buildings at the monastery-fort's base. Here, we saw Tibetans being allowed to rebuild one of their sacred structures. Young men carried heavy juniper timbers on their backs up the dirt track to the monastery entrance. Several of the buildings had, in fact, already been rebuilt. Since 1981, Beijing had generally become more tolerant of Tibetan Buddhism and religious worship; yet these monastery rebuilding projects were primarily cosmetic, a way of "beautifying" Tibet in order to promote it to well-heeled, package-touring western tourists—to keep Chinese coffers full.

The devastated *Dzong* thrust its skeleton skyward. Climbing over unstable mounds of slate and limestone at 15,000 feet was tough exercise for our first high-altitude workout. I turtled along, breathing heavily, remembering the effort and agony of exerting oneself in the high, thin air. The trail ended just below the fort's summit, where a masonry wall blocked our progress; below loomed a three-hundred-foot drop. Sensibly, we stopped, but Roger decided he had to reach the top. Tricky 5.8 moves up loose blocks didn't bother him one bit.

"He's a mountaineer, he can't help himself," I told Pasang. "He has to get to the summit no matter what."

The panorama surrounding us was a picture of peace. The Shekar Valley was remote enough and so sparsely settled that you thought maybe, just maybe, you were back in old Tibet. As they caught a patchwork of dappled sunlight, the hills to the east strengthened this effect. Their earthy tones of dusty gold and brown were unlike any colors I'd ever seen.

It was frigid in the morning twilight when we left Shekar for Base Camp. No one had slept a wink because of barking dogs. I'd even gotten out of bed and lobbed a few stones over a nearby rock wall at the howling beasts. However, we now had another problem. Our interpreter, Mr. Yide, had been unwell since Lhasa. The day before, he'd been checked over at a local hospital by a Tibetan doctor who pronounced that Yide had appendicitis and should return home immediately. A second opinion, from a Chinese doctor, said he was fine.

"I don't want him coming to Base Camp if he's going to be sick, or die," said Roger, adding, "but we do need him."

Mr. Yide decided to come. Seven of us crammed into the Nissan Rover. Ten miles out of Shekar, we turned left up an unobvious side valley, south of the Friendship Highway linking Shekar with the Tibet-Nepal border. We weren't alone. A westerner carting a huge backpack tried to thumb a free ride.

"Some people pay for transportation, others don't," deadpanned Roger.

Left: *Approaching the monastery and the ruins of Shekar Dzong.*

George Mallory, Andrew Irvine, and two Sherpas inspect Mount Everest (on left)
from atop the Pang La on April 26, 1924. Gyachung Kang and Cho Oyu on the right.
Photograph by Noel Odell, courtesy of Peter Odell

Atop the Pang La, a prominent 17,200-foot pass, a feeling of great remoteness enveloped me. Some thirty-seven miles distant rose the chain of the Himalayan giants: Everest in the center, easily identified by the large snow plume blowing from its summit; Makalu, the world's fifth-highest peak, on the far left; and Cho Oyu, the sixth-tallest peak, on the right. I slapped Roger on the back in congratulations. It had taken a lot of dedication for him to make it here.

The road to Base Camp continued down the far side of the Pang La, then up a twisting valley through scattered villages. We'd been told that the river, the Dzakar Chu, that drained Everest's North Face and the Rongbuk Glacier, had to be at low ebb for vehicles to safely ford it. It was already noon; would the river be swollen with midday glacial meltwater? It was. We waited for the Army truck carrying our equipment to arrive, then transferred our gear and ourselves into the back of the truck to attempt the harrowing river crossing.

The Dzakar Chu was turbulent, fast-running, and of unknown depth. When we were halfway across it, our driver turned the truck downstream. Moments later we were stuck in the center of the raging torrent. Roger spared no words cursing the truck driver, the Chinese, and the CMA. For an hour it looked like the entire expedition might drown. Our jeep driver, Dawa, who'd remained on the river bank with the jeep, tried pointlessly to pull us out with a length of manila rope, which predictably broke. A crowd of villagers gathered to watch the spectacle. An hour later, a big cheer erupted as a communally owned tractor with six-foot-diameter tires hauled us out with a steel cable.

Back on dry land, Roger tried to convince the recalcitrant Dawa, Mr. Yide, and Mr. Li to drive back to the last village to inquire about renting another tractor to help us ford the flood. Dawa declined. The way he acted, you'd have thought he owned the jeep, though he didn't.

"Who's side is he on, anyway?" demanded Roger, staring holes through Dawa. I asked Mr. Yide why Dawa wouldn't help us.

"You Americans always think you should have everything done your own way! But you are not in America. You are in China!" Mr. Yide suddenly exclaimed with surprising animation.

"Yes, but in America, if we pay someone to do a job, as we have paid Dawa's salary through the CMA, then we expect that person to help us," I replied calmly.

"You think you have paid for these services, but you have not always paid," Mr. Yide answered.

"But we have paid Dawa to help us!" I protested.

"Dawa is paid five yuan per day," said Mr. Yide.

"But we pay the CMA twenty-six yuan a day for him!"

"His pay is only five," corrected Mr. Yide.

"Then the Chinese are screwing the Chinese!" Kristina shouted.

"No!" Mr. Yide answered angrily. "The Chinese do not screw the Chinese or anyone else!"

I seriously questioned the veracity of his statement. When Roger returned several hours later from his village visit, I was relieved to see him grinning.

"Prepare yourselves for a small change in plan," he said. "We're staying here for two nights, then taking yaks the rest of the way to Base Camp."

After our jaws recovered, we began to look forward to the slow approach by yak caravan. Instead of two hours in a truck, reaching Base Camp would now take two days on foot—a pale emulation of the three-month overland treks from Darjeeling, India, to Everest Rongbuk Base Camp made by all of the pre-WWII British expeditions. But even this short walk would prove beneficial to us since moderate exercise speeds the acclimatization process. Meanwhile, Mr. Yide, who was still ill, no longer wanted to come if we had to walk. In less than a minute, he said good-bye and left for Lhasa with Dawa.

It took a full day's work to make all of our loads yak-worthy. As we repacked, Roger and I discussed how bad events in life often become blessings in disguise. I mentioned his transformational firing from the Canadian Everest expedition.

"I used to go with the crowd, using Sherpas, oxygen, and big teams," Roger said, "before I saw how incredibly wasteful traditional expeditions are."

"But how'd you feel when you were kicked off the team?"

"Crushed—my life's dream was gone. I was standing in Namche Bazaar. *I could see Everest*. I was shattered. But in retrospect, my life was thrown into a new and positive direction. I knew I wanted to come climb the high peaks with small expeditions, or entirely alone. I guess you need some traumatic experiences or your life stagnates. A shock can actually prove very beneficial."

On June 29, Pasang persisted through four hours of verbal price and weight negotiations with the local village yak drivers. Our loads were finally strapped on, and we headed up the trail toward the legendary Rongbuk Monastery. However, just as our yaks were fording the Dzakar Chu, in a moment of supreme irony, a jeep full of Japanese tourists successfully drove across the river!

Roger was beside himself. "If that doesn't take the cake. Five days wasted!"

We hiked along a trail on the river's left bank. The going was easy, but not for Mr. Li, whose high-heeled loafers—all the rage in Beijing—were utterly useless for hiking. Soon he was limping with horrible blisters and, much to Roger's delight, he rode a yak the remaining distance to Base Camp. That night we tented on a hillside at 15,300 feet, overlooking a wide bend in the Dzakar Chu.

It had been desperately hot at midday, but the hike was good toughening medicine for us. Kristina, who wasn't an avid climber, was showing her mettle. We were at last getting close to our goal. When I asked the Tibetans where Chomolungma was, they nodded in the affirmative, then drew a wide arc in the air with one hand. Everest, I gathered, was just around the corner.

First light saw the drivers round up the yaks from the hillsides and tether them near the campfires. Breakfast for Tibetans and yaks was identical: a nice doughy ball of *tsampa*—barley flour moistened with salt tea and water. After the Tibetans finished their own meal, they moistened additional *tsampa* and fed it ceremoniously to the yaks, who gobbled up their gluey barley balls in huge hungry gulps.

Roger and Ruth ran ahead to locate Base Camp while Kristina and I settled in with Mr. Li behind the last yaks. "Keep a watchful eye on the Tibetans," Roger told me with a note of seriousness in his voice. He was worried about theft.

The stupa at Rongbuk Monastery, and Chomolungma.

The drivers sang their sing-song harmonies and yelled at the yaks to keep them moving, tossing occasional stones at their hindquarters for emphasis. When we passed a Buddhist prayer wall, the yaks and Mr. Li walked to the right, counterclockwise, and the yak drivers, Kristina, and I walked to the left, clockwise. The yak men winked at us, then scowled at Mr. Li, obviously a heathen.

Framing the valley's head, the North Face of Mount Everest suddenly overwhelmed our view ahead. A surge of exhilaration ran through my body, and I hugged Kristina. But it was so strange and disorienting, seeing Everest's opposite, flip side. Everest in 1985 had been such a learning experience; I wondered, pondering all of the intangibles, what would Everest 1986 be like?

The road became endless, the sun blazing and merciless, and the thinning air and dearth of oxygen increasingly noticeable. Finally, ahead we saw the yaks pastured on a meadow at Rongbuk Monastery where we lunched. Afterward, I photographed the monastery ruins, the crumbling stone and plaster walls, and faded Buddhist imagery left exposed to the weather. Artillery or dynamite must have been used to blow apart the walls; piles of rusting tin cans—the remains of soldiers' meals?—filled the hollows of the rubble-strewn floors.

Sherpas and Tibetans crowd into the courtyard of Rongbuk Monastery in 1924.
Photograph by Noel Odell, courtesy of Peter Odell

The ruins of Rongbuk Monastery, 1986.

Wandering amongst the tattered walls, I felt that I was a foreigner trespassing on holy ground, yet even worse, I sensed that a tremendous and palpable evil still lingered in the air. In this place of reverence and worship, crimes against humanity had been committed by Chinese troops. I felt compassion for the monks and nuns who had been tortured, and had died here—and disbelief at the monastery's near-complete devastation as I walked below the bullet-riddled, pockmarked, peeling murals of Buddhas in their terrestrial and celestial forms.

Back at the main entrance, I found Pasang printing prayer flags with one of our yak drivers and two elderly nuns who lived at Rongbuk. One nun, her head closely shaved, helped Pasang ink the carved stone dyes, press the cotton fabric into place, and pat the ink onto the cloth. Everyone was in a jovial mood, gossiping as they worked. Pasang said he was making plans for our expedition blessing ceremony before Roger began climbing.

Two hours later when Kristina and I arrived at a grassy, trash-covered glen beside two small ponds, Roger, Ruth, Mr. Li, and Pasang were nowhere to be seen. This was indeed the Base Camp site of the early Everest expeditions of the 1920s and '30s *(see photograph on page 133),* and the yak drivers had already untied the loads, freeing the yaks to cavort in the water. Eventually Li reappeared and attempted to explain to Kristina and me, in Chinese, what was going on. As storm clouds gathered and blackened the sky, Roger and Ruth returned, but the clouds were benevolent compared to Roger's mood.

"He doesn't know a damn thing!" Roger bellowed. "We've scouted out a good site for Base Camp up ahead, but Li called back the yaks."

Further upstream were several better camping sites, Roger said, including a small knoll in the center of the gravel plain below the Rongbuk Glacier's terminal moraine. This site was close to water, and even better, completely clean. Falling rain and now snow forced us to camp where we were tonight, but when the weather cleared at noon the following day, Roger and the yak drivers agreed on a thirty dollar "moving fee."

"We go Base Camp. You come too, Mr. Li," Roger gestured. Li mentioned Beijing. At that, matters disintegrated. Fortunately a yak driver who spoke Tibetan and Chinese intervened. Li spoke to him in Chinese, the yak driver passed the message in Tibetan to Pasang, and Pasang translated into English for Roger. In the end, Mr. Li was given two tents so he could camp at "the yak ponds" by himself.

"Our" Base Camp was fifteen minutes farther up valley, near the foot of the Rongbuk Glacier's terminal moraine. We erected seven tents: a large Coleman

Everest Rongbuk Base Camp, 1986.

that doubled for Pasang's kitchen and a dining area; two small Coleman dome tents (one for Pasang, another for storing extra equipment and food); two North Face VE 24s (for Roger and Ruth, and Kristina and me); a Sierra Designs for additional storage; and a Sierra Designs King Dome—with a hole cut in the floor—for showering. Some Italian trekkers later observed, "We heard you were an expedition of only four, but you have so many tents!"

The date was July 1, 1986. We were established at Rongbuk Base Camp at seventeen thousand feet, several miles to the north of Mount Everest's North Face. After enduring three weeks of bland Chinese food, we celebrated with the first of Pasang's excellent meals and settled into our new home.

* * * * * * * * * * * * * *

Although China is over three thousand miles wide, the Chinese use only one time zone. Not surprisingly, this is "Beijing time." Instead of rising at 10:30 A.M. "Beijing time," we decided to move our watches ahead by three hours, so that "Rongbuk Base Camp time" corresponded more closely to the times of the day we were used to at home in Colorado.

Everest Rongbuk Base Camp, 1924. Note Noel Odell's photo caption on left edge.
Photograph by Noel Odell, courtesy of Peter Odell

Foreign mountaineering expeditions were only allowed back into Tibet by the Chinese government in 1980, but it wasn't until 1986 that China granted individual travel visas to foreigners for Tibet. As a result, that summer large numbers of trekkers and adventure seekers from around the globe were wandering freely around the Tibetan countryside for the first time ever. Invariably many of these hardy souls were intent on reaching Mount Everest's historic northern Base Camp—and would wander up to our tents. Today, a Belgian appeared.

"Aren't you the Everest expedition that is sponsored by Freddie's Hot Dogs?" Frank, the Belgian, asked. Earlier, Mark Skinner, the British solo cyclist, had informed Frank that Roger's expedition was financed, in part, by Freddie's Hot Dogs of Boulder, Colorado—which was actually true. After Roger produced a plastic hot dog with "Freddie's" written in fake yellow mustard (brought along specifically for the necessary promotional photos), eventually the truth was divulged. Freddie Snalam, a friend of Roger's, was a one-man hot dog vendor!

"I did think it was strange for a hot dog company to sponsor an entire Mount Everest expedition," Frank quipped.

The next day, Mark Skinner doggedly limped into camp in bicycling shoes, his only footwear. "All done with the climb, Rog?" he asked.

"Yup—actually, we were just getting ready to leave for Hawaii," Roger answered. Typical Brits, I thought.

"Well, I didn't know if I should take you seriously," Mark replied. "Soloing Everest in three days—and sponsored by a hot dog company!" Although he was now "only" a year behind schedule, Mark said he would be cycling through Colorado the following summer. We promised to buy him lunch at Freddie's.

I never got tired of looking at Everest from the north. Elegant and pyramid-shaped, the great mountain dominated the relatively smaller peaks to its east and west that flanked each side of the Rongbuk Glacier closer to our camp. To our west rose the rock massif of Ri-Ring, first climbed in 1921 by George Mallory and Guy Bullock. Farther east, hidden from Base Camp, was a jagged wall of peaks. Highest was the prominent Kellas Rock Peak named for Dr. Alexander Kellas, a member of the 1921 British Everest expedition, who died unexpectedly of heart failure on the approach. It was first climbed by Eric Shipton, H.W. Tilman, and Edmund Wigram. And nearby was Kharta Changri, ascended by Edwin Kempson and Charles Warren. Both these two peaks were climbed during the 1935 British Mount Everest Reconnaissance Expedition.

Interestingly, this same British team was the first to be joined by an amiable, energetic young man—Tenzing Bhotia, later known as Tenzing Norgay—who would go on to participate on seven Mount Everest expeditions in his lifetime.

The view from Tilman's Lake: Changtse (left) is the North Peak of Mount Everest.

Of all the mountains neighboring Everest's northern flank, the most famed, and the highest, is Changtse. Named by George Mallory in 1921, Changtse means "north peak" in Tibetan. Although the mountain tends to blend in with Everest when viewed from Rongbuk Base Camp, this 24,879-foot rock-and-snow monolith is nonetheless a formidable objective. The first attempt on the peak by Eric Shipton, H.W. Tilman, and party was defeated by deep snow in August, 1935. Surprisingly, Changtse was not ascended until October 14, 1982 when, in a solo effort, Udo Zehetleitner (a member of a German Everest team) reached the summit. The peak's other ascent—that I knew of—was also done alone, by Gino Casassa from Chile on May 14, 1983. I didn't know if it had been climbed since.

Changtse had fascinated me since the age of thirteen, when I had read accounts of the early British climbers ascending to the fabled North Col, the high snow saddle that separates Mount Everest and Changtse. As Roger was permitted to ascend to the North Col and then up Everest's North Ridge, I planned to climb to the Col to photograph his progress, but I would go no higher as Roger's ascent of Everest would be done strictly solo. In the back of my mind, though, I was already wondering if after fulfilling my photographic duties I might try and climb Changtse.

That afternoon, Kristina and I visited the memorial cairns atop a small hill near our Base Camp. The stone tablet dedicated to the British mountaineers Joe Tasker and Peter Boardman affected me the most. I'd met Boardman in 1978 at a lecture he gave in North Wales; afterwards, we'd gone pub-crawling until we couldn't see straight. In 1982, Boardman, Tasker, Chris Bonington, and Dick Renshaw had attempted the first ascent of Everest's Northeast Ridge, without bottled oxygen or Sherpas, in admirably lightweight style. Bonington last saw Boardman and Tasker through a telescope on May 17, as the pair disappeared behind the Second Pinnacle, moving between the spiky rock outcrops at 26,900 feet. They were never seen again, their fate a puzzling mystery.

(Peter Boardman's body was discovered by three Kazakh mountaineers on May 15, 1992 near the top of the Second Pinnacle. Chris Bonington verified Boardman's identity after seeing a photograph of his corpse. I later also saw the picture; it was definitely Boardman. Tasker's body has never been located. His fate and the cause of their deaths remains one of the most baffling and poignant of Everest's many unexplained fatalities. Boardman and Tasker, each prolific mountaineering writers, penned several outstanding books, and the Boardman-Tasker Award—named in their honor and presented yearly in London—is mountaineering literature's most prestigious award.)

When I mentioned to Kristina that Roger had told me that I could climb "anything except Everest," tears immediately welled in her eyes.

"I thought you said you were just here to photograph," she answered in a high-strung voice. "I should have known that you had some climbing plans up your sleeve!"

Although I certainly enjoyed her companionship, I was increasingly feeling that having Kristina on the expedition was presenting numerous emotional complications that I hadn't had to face on Everest's West Ridge. Each day I had to answer to her need to constantly know where I was, what my plans were, plus details of the more ambitious climbing goals I was fermenting. And, no matter how calmly or confidently I expressed my hopes and plans, perhaps because she was not a climber, her responses were inevitably more emotion- and worry-filled than I would have liked. And this, I felt, caused unnecessary tension between us. I thought that I might be capable of soloing Changtse, and if I did attempt Changtse, I would stay within safe limits. And yet if I mentioned this desire of mine to solo Changtse to Kristina, I knew the predictable result. She would worry that I would get hurt, or even more probably, get killed.

Although we had just arrived at Base Camp, Roger wanted to establish our Advanced Base below the North Col as soon as possible. Establishing this high camp would speed acclimatization, plus keep him fit for an August summit bid. Roger also wanted to get a close-up view of the route, and inspect snow conditions. Accordingly, the yak drivers and yaks returned to Base Camp on July 5 to transport our food and equipment to Advanced Base Camp.

An unexpected stowaway arrived with them. "Life at the yak ponds is very lonely," Mr. Li pantomimed, so we helped him move his tent to our site.

"Hurry up and wait" proved to be a phrase that Tibetan villagers understood as well (or actually even better!) than the Chinese. The yak drivers delayed their departure for an entire day, sorting, weighing, and re-sorting loads until it grew so late that we decided not to start until the next morning.

"Any other country in the world, they wouldn't have a job," Roger moaned.

Kristina was feeling under the weather with a nagging cold, so Roger, Ruth, Pasang, and I went for a training hike.

"Look!" Pasang exclaimed joyfully, pointing his finger at two abandoned stone dwellings. "Chinese miss these!"

Though dilapidated, both structures had withstood the ravages of time. Pasang explained that they were hermitages occupied by monks from Rongbuk Monastery. The meditation chamber of the first hermitage was still gaily painted in red, blue, and yellow. Small wall niches probably once held statuary; the remains of the hermit's yak-hair mattress covered the floor. In the second hermitage, a narrow doorway led to a tiny cell whose floor was still lined with dry straw. Two portals fitted with wooden bars let in parallel shafts of dusty sunlight.

"Head lama meditate here," whispered Pasang reverently as we sat inside the Lilliputian apartment. "This room very, very holy."

The strong presence of a mortal attempting to achieve enlightenment served to calm my mind. But I wondered if the hermits attained Nirvana within Everest's shadow—or had Chinese soldiers and the Red Guards thwarted their efforts? Only the wooden rafters and crumbling walls knew the answer. But something, a gut feeling, told me that the Chinese had won—at least temporarily. And what had China gained by its violent conquest of Tibet? A secure border with Nepal, India, and Pakistan, untold mineral and oil reserves, land to annex into Chinese provinces, and, it was rumored, a nuclear testing ground.

Pasang had visited Rongbuk monastery in 1956, over a decade prior to Rongbuk's destruction, on a Tibetan pilgrimage with his stepfather when he was just thirteen. I asked Pasang if he thought the Tibetan people would ever be free of the Chinese. He shook his head sideways.

"I not think so. Tibetan children, they have change of mind toward the Chinese," Pasang said, inverting the palm of his hand for emphasis. Was materialism winning the minds of the people in what, for centuries, had been one of the world's most spiritual of nations?

* * * * * * * * * * * * *

We left Base Camp on July 7 for the long hike up the East Rongbuk Glacier to the North Col camp, the site mountaineers have used since the British first explored the approaches to Everest in the early 1920s. Roger, Ruth, and Pasang ran ahead to catch up to the yaks and our loads, while Kristina, still sniffling and coughing, and I followed. Loose stones, gravel, stream crossings, and small crevasses to jump made for arduous going. Most expeditions navigate this fatiguing section with one or two intermediate camps, but Roger planned on walking the entire distance—ten stony, torturous miles, rising from seventeen thousand feet to just over twenty thousand feet—in one day.

Politely I suggested to Kristina she should turn back before we'd gone too far, but she'd made up her mind to come. On our first stream crossing, she fell in and drenched a boot. Tears. At another dangerous section we had to run

Névé pénitants (ice needles created by differential melting) on East Rongbuk Glacier.

across the scattered debris of fresh rockfall whose source was a hanging glacier a thousand feet higher. Then, while dashing across a loose slope of boulders perched above a swift-running glacial stream, a television-sized boulder careened past us, only thirty feet away. Terrified, Kristina hesitated, and then froze. "Come on!" I yelled at her frantically—and she ran ahead and made it.

The trail became increasingly difficult to follow. Hoof prints, yak droppings, and tiny cairns gave us occasional clues. Leaving the left moraine, we crossed over onto the glacier's center, to a medial moraine, a No-Man's-Land of slaty rock and gravel sandwiched between the East Rongbuk and Changtse Glaciers. This section of the approach to the North Col, trapped between parallel rivers of ice, is so unusual that mountaineers refer to it as the "Miracle Highway."

Kristina had never been on a glacier. What must she be thinking? She was too exhausted from the altitude and the coughing fits to tell me. The hike became an endless and grueling nightmare. One o'clock became three o'clock became five o'clock, and still there was no sign of camp. "Surely they're just over the next hill," I encouraged. We plodded along the elevated gravel walkway beside a sea of spiky ice teeth. The mists descended; snow fell lightly. At last, footprints in the mud. "Yaks!" We reached camp, just over the twenty-thousand-foot mark in elevation, after an eleven-hour marathon. Ruth walked out to greet us, knowing Kristina must be exhausted, and they embraced tearfully. It was Kristina's highest altitude.

No one slept much because of the increased height, and our resulting insomnia made the day's hike, in retrospect, seem even worse. I had also been concerned that during the night Kristina might develop high-altitude sickness, but luckily she did not. A somber morning grayed. Two inches of new snow blanketed the ground while low vapors hung around the ice pinnacles. Ruth, Kristina, and Pasang decided to descend while Roger, the yak men, and I would continue to our "official" Advanced Base Camp below the North Col.

"So this is what Himalayan climbing is all about," Kristina coughed before leaving. "Remind me to stay at Base next time."

Dusted by a light snow that fell all day, the yak drivers led the yaks, neck bells tinkling, off into the mist. Then, in a strange twist, the yak men turned on the speed and easily out distanced Roger and me. The Tibetans seemed to be taking sport in showing us how unfazed they were by the high altitude. Finally, up ahead I heard yelling and confusion.

"A crevasse. A bad one," Roger said. The fissure was black, bottomless, and had no easy bypass. Roger waved his arms, and the loads dropped into the snow. The Tibetans assured us that Chomolungma lay just ahead, said their farewells to us, "*tashi delai*," and turned for home.

We erected two tents and prepared for another long night of misery. I tossed and turned while Roger snored. I decided I wasn't sleeping well because of our rapid elevation gain, ascending in two days from Base Camp at seventeen thousand feet to Advanced Base at 21,200 feet. But, as Fritz Wiessner once had told me, for unexplained physiological reasons high-altitude mountaineers often don't need much sleep. And, true enough, the next morning found me feeling unusually invigorated, even after two nights with virtually no sleep. So far, I noted happily, my body was adapting better to altitude this year.

We went to investigate the traditional Advanced Base Camp site, which was only ten minutes beyond our crevasse. Waist-high stone fences marked previous living quarters; piles of half-burned trash and tin cans marred the landscape. The Madrid Everest Expedition had ruined the campsite by burning their waste and cans inside several of the enclosures. Didn't it ever occur to them that other climbers might want to camp here? The mess sickened us.

Roger at ABC below the North Col. Everest's summit at top center.

We also had our first view of the original British *Mallory Route* ascending to the snowy saddle of the North Col. Changtse was now on our right, and Everest rose to the left. The East Rongbuk Glacier below the Col was actually a large basin of relatively flat snow, but telltale surface ripples marked numerous hidden crevasses. Rising in front of us, the two-thousand-foot-high snow slopes of the North Col sparkled, while farther right rose a bastion of rocky outcrops forming Changtse's East Face. And to our left loomed Everest's monolithic Northeast Ridge, a towering spine of windswept rock decorated by a spider's web of snow. Most prominent were the jagged Pinnacles, the three rock spurs that formed the ridge's crux. Everest's summit lay behind and considerably to the right of the Pinnacles, and actually appeared lower due to foreshortening.

Gladdened that the route to the Col didn't appear as fearsome as we'd imagined, we returned to camp and basked in some welcome sunshine.

"You know, when you start Himalayan climbing as late as I did, you've really got to go for it," Roger said. "If I don't make it up Everest, I might be washed up, but on the other hand, if I solo Everest, I'll be the new spokesperson for Dupont Thermax."

As the sunset colors faded from the mountaintops surrounding us, we continued our freewheeling talk. "Don't you ever worry about getting too old for Himalayan climbing?" I asked. "Old" in Roger's case was a relative term. He was a very in-shape forty-four!

"I do worry some. I know I can't keep on climbing eight-thousand-meter peaks forever, and doing the big peaks is what's important for sponsorship. You can succeed on hundreds of harder, smaller mountains, but fail on the eight-thousanders and the general public will never know your name. You've got to climb the big Himalayan peaks if you want to make a living at this game. Soloing Kanchenjunga was my big break, otherwise I'd still be an unknown, one of the many."

I could tell Roger was winding up his "devil-may-care" attitude, preparing to commit himself mentally and physically to attempt his solo ascent of Everest. Participating in the high risk game of Himalayan mountaineering was a deadly serious business.

The next day was beautiful, but we headed back down to Base Camp. Kristina assured me that her descent of the East Rongbuk had gone well, if arduously, and even Mr. Li seemed glad to see us, as he smiled and poked his head out of the cook tent. It was time to rest and gather strength.

* * * * * * * * * * * * * *

In the lazy days that followed, two trekkers from Boston, Thea and Yurick, and a German trekker named Peter, appeared and kindly volunteered to post our mail, so we set to work writing a stack of postcards and letters. This was our only way to communicate with the outside world. Thea and Yurick, like a Swiss couple we'd met earlier, had also been teaching conversational English in China, an apparently popular method of financing Asian travels.

We had several lively discourses together, and one evening discussed the number of Tibetans who were killed during and immediately after the mid-1960s Cultural Revolution. Yurick estimated that when the Chinese authorities forced Tibetans to grow wheat instead of barley (their traditional staple crop), that a million people perished in the ensuing famine. Roger claimed he believed the Han Chinese historical view, that the Chinese had overthrown a religiously dominated feudal society, and liberated the Tibetan people, primarily the landless serfs. The Chinese takeover of Tibet, Roger forcefully continued, was a People's Revolution, and it was the Tibetans themselves who tore down the bricks and walls of the monasteries. I didn't buy Roger's explanation.

Peter, the German trekker, painted a much less endearing picture of the gentle, religious Tibetans. His voice wavered with fear.

"Yesterday, I was very frightened," he told us. "I met three yak men coming down the valley toward me. When they motioned toward my two water bottles, I resisted, so they threw stones at me. I gave them one bottle before they left me alone."

The yak drivers, of course, were ours, the same men who'd just helped us establish our Advanced Base Camp! Roger lapsed into silence, conjuring up some sort of fitting punishment. "Really unforgivable behavior," he muttered.

At dinner another night, Roger told us about his childhood, growing up in Kendal in the English Lake District, where he was born in 1941. At sixteen, he left school to work in the local slate quarry. At seventeen, he started as a newspaper journalist, but was fired for writing only stories that interested him.

"My life has always been full of changes. I immigrated to Canada at the age of twenty-five with a wife, two kids, and two hundred dollars in my pocket. I know how to survive."

Besides working as a journalist in Vancouver, Roger also worked in the Canadian Rockies on rigging and carpentry jobs, in mines, building dams, and blasting railway tunnels. He'd run a logging company and a mountaineering company. A jack-of-all-trades, Roger was a true adventurer. Eventually he grew tired of life at home, but his ex-wife, Dorothy, still lived in Golden, British Columbia, in their original log cabin homestead.

"I'd raised my family, I'd been a good husband, and my two sons had left home," Roger explained. "Then there was the Himalaya. Five years ago I made the choice to climb here, and I've never regretted the life I've chosen for a single moment."

Pasang, Mr. Li, Kristina, and I walked downvalley to Rongbuk Monastery on July 14 for the blessing ceremony that would officially "start" our expedition. Roger and Ruth, however, chose not to attend.

"You know I don't believe in that rubbish," Roger declared, somewhat predictably. "They're just tricks used to extort money."

After hiking for two hours in a light drizzle, we arrived at Rongbuk and entered the newly rebuilt prayer room amidst the broken walls and rubble. Four nuns, two monks, and two apprentice monks sat inside, chanting.

Rongbuk Monastery's Head Lama, the Dzatrul Rinpoche, hands out kata scarves at the 1924 Everest puja ceremony. Photograph by Noel Odell, courtesy Peter Odell

Tibetan prayer books—stacks of loose-leaf paper sandwiched between two rectangular wooden covers—lay open atop low wooden tables set at their knees. Each nun and monk sat cross-legged upon greasy black cushions, which looked like they might have been purple several centuries ago. We sat on our own cushions against one wall.

"Sheb, sheb" ("more, more"), urged Pasang as he pressed cups of warm, rancid butter-flavored Tibetan salt tea into our hands. My stomach almost retched at the sight of the gray liquid with milky, floating globs of yak butter, but we took several bird-sized sips to honor our hosts. I tried my best to thwart the eager young apprentice whose job it was to refill our cups, hiding my cup where it was hard to see, shaking my head "no," wincing in feigned pain, and pointing abjectly at my stomach.

In a moment of superstitious weakness, Roger had given Pasang the sum of two hundred yuan (about sixty dollars) to donate to the nuns and monks. Kristina and I made smaller gifts. Some of the money was accepted as payment for the prayers to Chomolungma for the expedition's success, while the remainder was allocated to the monastery's rebuilding fund.

Geoffrey Bruce, George Mallory, and Edward Norton attend their blessing ceremony

at Rongbuk Monastery on May 15, 1924. Photograph by Noel Odell

The main shrine we sat inside appeared new and recently painted. Local villagers had begun restoring the monastery in 1982, and one day, the nuns told us, they hoped to have rebuilt the entire Rongbuk complex. Contributions were being solicited from passing expeditions and trekkers. Pasang told us that what the nuns really wanted was a new gold Buddha.

After a lull, the chants began slowly increasing in volume and fervor.

"Now they pray to Chomolungma, and for Kristina's cold to get better," Pasang whispered. And in a motherly moment, one of the nuns, a woman of perhaps sixty, later told Kristina an age-old Tibetan cold remedy: "drink hot lemon."

When the prayers ended, I asked Pasang to see if the nuns had any blessing cords. They carried out a fistful of gold cords fresh from Dharamsala, India, which, they said, had been blessed by His Holiness the Dalai Lama. With a new blessing cord tied securely around her neck, I'd never seen Kristina looking happier. But our day wasn't over. Mr. Li departed for Base Camp, and Pasang said quietly that he had a secret to show us. Eventually we came to a small room.

"This my surprise," cried Pasang exuberantly, as though he were unveiling a many-centuries-lost treasure. "This cave. Come on!"

After Pasang lowered himself into a narrow hole, then disappeared, we carefully climbed down a ladder of polished stones and followed him into the murk. The cave's opening let in just enough light for us to see we were inside a recess some twenty feet in diameter. Wooden shelves lined the walls and held a collection of bottles filled with mustard-seed oil. But none of us had any matches! Luckily, Pasang chanced on a pack hidden inside of a tin box. In a jiffy he'd made six wicks out of grass stems wrapped with fingerfuls of cotton. Reverently, we placed three burning candles beside an altar holding two statues of the Buddha.

"When I was boy in Namche Bazaar," Pasang whispered to us, "this cave then even famous place to come and pray."

Back outside, we noticed many clumps of hair, seemingly both human and yak, littering the ground surrounding a ten-foot-tall stone-and-mud monument. Piles of ashes and bone chips filled most of a shallow hollow in the ground.

"Many people burned here," Pasang explained matter-of-factly, answering our puzzled looks. Then, nearby, we found dozens of pressed-clay tablets—palm-sized representations of the Buddha, *chortens,* and other Buddhist iconography—randomly arranged beneath jutting rocks to keep them dry. What were they? And why were there so many? Kristina wanted one as a souvenir.

"When person dies in Tibet, his body, her body, their flesh is fed to birds. But if no wood, there can be no fire," explained Pasang. "Other places, body is

The final resting place of Rongbuk Monastery's monks and nuns.

first burned some, then flesh cut off and fed to birds. Soul is free of body, of life vehicle. Then soul can hurry to rebirth. Sometimes bones can be left over. They get ground up, mixed with mud, and made like the Buddha," he added.

"Then ... these statues are made from human bones?" Kristina asked. When Pasang nodded in the affirmative, I wasn't at all surprised when Kristina set the small human-bone-and-clay tablet she'd been holding back down on the ground.

Pasang was eager to show us other new things. He soon located patches of a stinging green nettle, a plant whose leaves, he assured us, were good to eat and tasted like spinach. "This Milarepa's food. Milarepa was poet of all Tibet. He was hermit. He eat just this—called *sa thukpa*—for many years." We picked the tender spiny leaves using homemade wooden prongs, keeping our fingers well away from the nettles, which stung something awful if you brushed against them by mistake. A dinner of mashed potatoes mixed with *tsampa*, grilled soy burgers, and boiled *sa thukpa* made for a wonderful end to our blessing day.

Now Roger could climb, if only the monsoon weather would cooperate.

Chapter 4

Changtse Solo

That man is the richest whose pleasures are the cheapest.

—Henry David Thoreau

D uring a week of continuous rain and snow, Everest vanished upward into the heavens, becoming at least temporarily an abstract concept. I had faith we'd soon return to the fray, but inside I was becoming increasingly frustrated. I enjoyed taking photos for Roger, but as the days slipped by, I realized I wasn't doing much to challenge myself. *I wasn't doing any climbing.* All we did during periods of bad weather was sleep, eat, read, eat, read, and sleep. I began to seriously consider attempting to climb Changtse, Everest's North Peak, alone.

Monsoon snowfalls melted into monsoon slush. We brushed the wet mush from the tents barehanded and ate our dinner leftovers for breakfast. Low mists hugged the slate-gray moraines and choked out all color. Reading

Left: *Changtse* (in left foreground) *and Mount Everest, with its Hornbein Couloir.*

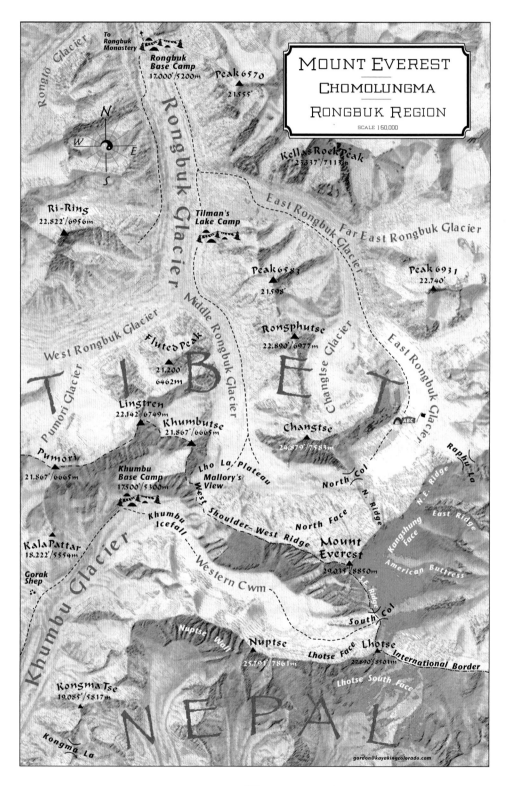

MOUNT EVEREST
CHOMOLUNGMA
RONGBUK REGION
SCALE 1:50,000

To Rongbuk Monastery

Rongié Glacier

Rongbuk Base Camp
17,000'/5200m

Peak 6570
21,555'

Kellas Rock Peak
23,337'/7113m

N
W   E
S

Ri-Ring
22,822'/6956m

Rongbuk Glacier

Tilman's Lake Camp

East Rongbuk Glacier

Far East Rongbuk Glacier

Peak 6583
21,598'

Peak 6931
22,740'

West Rongbuk Glacier

Middle Rongbuk Glacier

Fluted Peak
21,200'
6462m

Rongphutse
22,890'/6977m

Changtse Glacier

East Rongbuk Glacier

T I B E T

Pumori Glacier

Lingtren
22,142'/6749m

Khumbutse
21,867'/6665m

Changtse
24,879'/7583m

ABC

Rapha La

Pumori
21,867'/6665m

Khumbu Base Camp
17,500'/5300m

Lho La Plateau
Mallory's View

North Col

N. Ridge

N.E. Ridge

East Ridge

West Shoulder

West Ridge

North Face

Kangshung Face

American Buttress

KalaPattar
18,222'/5554m

Khumbu Icefall

Mount Everest
29,035'/8850m

S.E. Ridge

Gorak Shep

Khumbu Glacier

Western Cwm

South Col

Nuptse Wall

Nuptse
25,791'/7861m

Lhotse Face

Lhotse
27,890'/8501m

International Border

Lhotse South Face

Kongma Tse
19,085'/5817m

N E P A L

Kongma La

gordon@kayakingcolorado.com

150

Photograph by George Mallory, Courtesy of the Royal Geographical Society

Prior to 1921, no Westerner had succeeded in reaching the foot of Mount Everest, although the mountain had been photographed from some sixty miles away. The object of the 1921 British Mount Everest Reconnaissance Expedition was to make a thorough topographic, geologic, and photographic survey of the peak, and to ascertain if a feasible route to the summit existed. George Mallory and Guy Bullock first explored the upper Rongbuk Valley, and the Middle and West Rongbuk Glaciers, from June 27 to July 25, 1921. On July 5, Bullock and Mallory ascended Ri-Ring; on the 19th, reaching the Nepal border at the edge of the Lho La plateau, at "Mallory's View," they saw and named the Western Cwm (above the Khumbu Icefall). Mallory's regal photograph above, snapped on July 23 from Ri-Ring, is considered by many to be the finest "portrait" ever made of Mount Everest. Ironically, it was only taken because, on his first Lho La foray, Mallory had inserted the film backwards into his "quarter plate" camera.

A herd of gentle Nawa (Tibetan blue sheep) graze on the sparse alpine vegetation growing on the stony glacial moraine near Rongbuk Base Camp.

King Lear did little to improve my state of mind. Why were we living in this sterile, high-altitude world, placing ourselves for months on end in such cold and deprivation? Was I questing for self-knowledge, searching for a more perfect illumination of myself—or intent on reaping personal glory? Even when writing in my diary (a normally reliable form of solace), I found that words were beginning to fail me. In Himalayan solitude, the mirror reflecting a person's motives of ego and desire comes quickly face to face.

Quick! Grab a new book. *The World According to Garp* was a godsend. Gossiping over our meals about Who-is-reading-What was a sure sign of Base Camp lassitude. Even Roger blurted out, "Let's just pack up and go to Hawaii," before adding that in 1983, trying to solo the 27,500-foot peak of Lhotse Shar in Nepal, he'd endured five solid weeks of rain, sleet, and snow.

Then, on the morning of July 16, a single jeep appeared downvalley from our Base Camp. After a hand-waving figure emerged and yelled out a greeting in Chinese, Mr. Li ran full speed—a feat in high-heeled black loafers and polyester bell-bottom pants—back to the yak ponds in what was, undoubtedly, one of his life's most jubilant moments. Mr. Li's English-only solitude had ended.

The jeep belonged to the small Swiss-French Third Pole-Qomolangma Expedition led by Jean Troillet, an extremely experienced Swiss mountaineer. Among his companions were fellow Swiss climbers Erhard Loretan and Sandro Godio, plus French Himalayan ace Pierre Béghin, Pierre's wife Annie, and French mountaineer and filmmaker Jean Afanassieff. Troillet, Loretan, and Béghin were three of the world's best Himalayan mountaineers, and Afanassieff had been the first Frenchman to scale Everest. Pierre, like Roger, had soloed Kanchenjunga, while Troillet and Loretan had accomplished a phenomenal three-day round-trip ascent of K2 in Pakistan, the world's second-tallest mountain, in 1985.

Their present goal was equally—if not considerably more—audacious: to make a rapid alpine-style ascent of the "Super Couloir" on Everest's sheer, nine-thousand-foot-high North Face. The route's first half, up the continuously steep *Japanese Couloir,* was originally siege climbed by a large Japanese team in 1980 using fixed ropes. The top section, the *Hornbein Couloir,* was pioneered in 1963 by the legendary American mountaineers Tom Hornbein and Willi Unsoeld, who achieved an inspired first ascent done in lightweight style.

The Swiss-French team's translator, Mr. Chen, informed us that we'd soon be joined by four more expeditions: Chileans attempting the standard *North Col Route,* a large British team trying the redoubtable (and then unclimbed) Northeast Ridge, an American group hoping to film a new hang-gliding record

Mount Everest's Northeast Ridge (up left skyline), the route taken by George Mallory and Andrew Irvine on June 8, 1924.

POST CARD.

W. Oldroyd
"Fair View"
Bardsea
Ulverston
Lancashire
England

MT. EVEREST EXPEDITION, 1924.
Leader   -   - Gen. Hon. C. G. Bruce, C.B.

Mt. Everest from the Base Camp in the Rongbuk Valley, TIBET.

Dispatched by Postal Runner to India.

Best   Wishes -
J.B.L. Noel . Captain:
. Mt. Everest. Expedition.

The Film of this great Exploit will be shown throughout the country, commencing at the Scala Theatre, London, November, 1924.

1924 Everest expedition postcard, sent by the team's photographer, Capt. John Noel.

off Everest's West Shoulder, and another American team whose modest goals were to make the first American ascent of Everest's *North Col Route,* put the first American woman on the summit, locate the bodies of British climbers George Mallory and Andrew Irvine (who disappeared near the summit in 1924)—and film everything in the process. If they chanced upon Mallory's camera and could develop any pictures it contained, then the nagging mystery of whether Everest's summit was attained twenty-nine years *before* Edmund Hillary and Tenzing Norgay reached it in 1953 might also be solved.

Our time alone had ended, but I looked forward to greeting both of the American expeditions because I had good friends on each.

Clear skies on July 21 saw Roger peering intently through his high-powered binoculars at Everest's magnificent northern face. *Messner's Solo,* the route Roger hoped to repeat, traversed across the low-angled face's middle portion from left to right, and entered the Great, or Norton, Couloir below a steep, obvious bottleneck in the gully. Exiting this section onto the snow terraces and rocks leading to the summit was the crux. The bottleneck had been scaled only twice, by Reinhold Messner in 1980, and by the small Australian team who did the first complete ascent of the Great Couloir (via the *White Limbo Route*) in 1984.

"Looks bloody hard," Roger said seriously. I'd noticed subtle changes in Roger. Gradually he was facing up to the total commitment of the challenge he'd set for himself. There was good reason Everest had only been climbed alone once. Climbing Everest unsupported and solo *was* The Ultimate Climb.

Roger's commitment to his solo ascent of Everest was total; it had to be. But how great was my own self-confidence as a mountaineer? Did I have what it took to solo Changtse? Although I enjoyed my role as expedition photographer, it was a relatively inconsequential "job." At least I had reached Tibet; I had to try and summit at least one peak. The urge to test myself again at high altitude was impossible to quell. Over the years, I had safely soloed several long and demanding rock climbs; I knew the stringent mental and physical rigors of the soloist. And Roger had given me his blessing to climb "discreetly." So one day, hoping to embolden my confidence, I set off alone from Base Camp to explore the Middle Rongbuk Glacier's west side—to photograph Everest from the peak of Ri-Ring.

My initial challenge was to ford the Dzakar Chu's icy torrent just downstream from where it burst from the Rongbuk Glacier's icy mouth. The one-hundred-yard-wide river of glacial melt water had braided itself into several swift-flowing branches. As I crossed it, I stepped into an unexpectedly deep hollow and nearly got swept away before throwing myself frantically onto the far bank. Then, after exchanging wet Nikes for dry Nikes, I scrambled to the top of a stony hill and traversed left across tedious loose scree. Eventually, I was able to head straight up into the entrance of one of Ri-Ring's side valleys.

My pace remained steady. I wasn't becoming lightheaded like I had on my first trip to Advanced Base, and this boosted my assuredness. My main worry was injuring myself in the loose, unstable rocks. Finally, at about nineteen thousand feet, I reached a small level terrace and sat down, now quite winded, to finish my pint of water, eat an energy bar, and take a few photographs.

Reinhold Messner reaches the summit of Everest, alone and without using bottled oxygen, on August 20, 1980, accomplishing the purest ascent ever of Earth's tallest peak.

Photograph courtesy of Reinhold Messner

Note: On the summit is the survey tripod left there by Chinese climbers in 1975.

Sometimes being alone is good. Time spent apart from others can give you the often much-needed chance to reassert your independence in nature, to develop your inner strengths, set your spirit free—and become truly alive. But being alone, depending on the circumstances, can also be desperately frightening. On this day, for several long minutes as I sat and rested, my aloneness was anything but peaceful. My earlier self-assurance, worn down perhaps by the strenuousness of my exertions and hours of rock-scrambling, had fled.

As I caught my breath, I began to realize that I was now many miles from Base Camp and partway up an obscure cleft in the mountainside. If anything unfortunate happened to me—a sprained ankle, for instance—no one would ever find me here. Realizing this, not just hypothetically, but as an acutely genuine fact, I began to feel tremendously vulnerable. As these primitive fears took hold, they overwhelmed my otherwise rational thoughts, and I began to breathe irregularly and to hyperventilate. I could do nothing to stop my irrational panic; it fed voraciously upon its own momentum and grew rapidly, uncontrollably, until adrenaline was coursing through my brain, limbs, and body. I knew now, with horrifying certainty, that I could easily die in these gray, sterile rocks. As my nervous system continued to accelerate out of control, the lifeless eternity of death gripped me to the core, strangling me, dragging me to the edge of that gruesome and empty abyss—and now, in the very next second, I knew that my life was going to end in a cold eternal death, that no force on earth could stop death from happening to me—and maybe IT WAS HAPPENING RIGHT NOW.

My fingertips tingled and burned; my breathing was fearful and rapid. My eyes watered. When my vision blurred, I stood up, quite wobbly-legged, and tried to loosen the panic's murderous chokehold by swinging my arms in demented spirals—and, at last, these gyrations broke my fear mechanism. Gasping in oxygen, I eventually managed to calm myself with deep regular breaths, and very gradually my world returned to peace. After quickly snapping some pictures of Everest, I headed back toward Base Camp.

As I descended and recrossed the scree slopes, I pondered what I had just experienced. Many seasoned mountaineers have died for no apparent reason at high altitude. What had happened to me back there? I could think of no logical explanation. Still feeling considerably unhinged and chastened, I tried to fathom what it would be like climbing alone, and at a much higher altitude—up to 24,879 feet—on Changtse. Could I handle it? I now had serious doubts. And why did I want to solo such a big peak any way? Several years after this episode, I became all too familiar with panic attacks. But at that time, on that hike, I was unfamiliar with the term, the terrifyingly real experience of having one, and of the accumulated trauma that they strew in their destructive wake.

Returning to Base Camp, I found Roger anxious to return to Advanced Base, and to establish his route to the North Col. Jean Troillet, Roger had just learned, was also planning to solo Everest, and this had turned up the heat. Currently, the Europeans were shifting their Base Camp up to the traditional jumping-off place for expeditions to Everest's North Face: Tilman's Lake, a tarn and green oasis at 18,260 feet, alongside the upper Middle Rongbuk Glacier. So the next day found me hoofing the ten miles back up the East Rongbuk to our tents. Events were speeding up, but fortunately so was I. I clocked the hike in just under ten hours. By 7 P.M., Roger, Ruth, and Pasang and me were snug in our sleeping bags, satiated by dinner, numerous cups of tea, and every high-altitude mountaineer's favorite dessert: four extra-strength Tylenol.

The next morning, snow pattered on the tent roof while Pasang snored beside me. We wouldn't be going anywhere soon. I read T.E. Lawrence's beautifully exact prose in *The Seven Pillars of Wisdom,* and delighted in the vivid contrast between his descriptions of Arab sheiks riding camelback across sun-baked deserts, and my gloriously frozen, white glacial view out the tent door.

Roger shoveling snow at Rongbuk Base Camp.

Roger preparing to leave for Advanced Base, with Ruth (left), Pasang, and Kristina.

The weather remained stormy all day long, and on into the following day. Despite the socked-in conditions, the next afternoon Roger and I decided to thwart "tent fever" by helping out Pasang with a little pet project of his. Two weeks before, on our first trip to Advanced Base, Roger and I had found fifteen abandoned propane bottles. Two were even full. When we'd told Pasang about them, his eyes had instantaneously flashed with rupees, and he made plans to take the bottles all the way to Kathmandu, get them refilled, then have them portered the several days journey back up to his home in Namche Bazaar. He expected to earn a bundle renting them to trekkers and expeditions.

So that afternoon we did the yak work, helping Pasang transport all of the heavy, awkward-to-carry cylinders the short distance back down to our campsite. Grunting as I picked up two cylinders at once, I shouted to Roger:

"Now this is finally starting to feel like an expedition!"

Pasang was catapulted into heaven—or Nirvana—at this unexpected and unusual swapping of roles between Sherpa and Sahib. "As long as I live, I never forget you and Roger carrying propane for me!" he exclaimed, laughing uproariously, slapping his knees and guffawing so hard that tears flowed from his eyes.

"Amazing how Pasang's energy picked right up as soon as he smelled a profit coming," Roger observed dryly.

The snow persisted. Lying in our tents, we made the best of things. It is this forced inactivity on Himalayan climbs that demands incredible patience. Many climbers can't handle it. In twenty years of rock climbing, I'd encountered many situations where my inner fortitude was tested to the breaking point: by bad weather, heat and cold, by getting benighted (stranded on some obscure crag or mountainside after dark), and occasionally just by the overwhelming isolation and commitment of a challenging climb. Because of our learned ability to withstand suffering, I'd been convinced that rock climbers were amongst the most durable of people—but after two Himalayan expeditions, I knew better. Rock climbing, in fact, had barely begun to prepare and harden me for the numerous deprivations involved in climbing the world's tallest mountains.

Roger was of the opinion that no other sport demanded as much of an individual as high-altitude climbing, although he allowed that long-distance ocean sailing was a close equivalent. (It was Ernest Hemingway who claimed that, in fact, there were only three "real" sports: bull fighting, race car driving, and mountaineering.) When I pointed out that sailing actually had a greater number of additional material buffers to protect you from hardship and the environment than did climbing, Roger readily conceded that point.

"No sport except mountaineering calls for such patience, exertion, and the ability to withstand suffering," he had continued. "You know, I've often heard people compare marathoning with Himalayan climbing. But that's ridiculous! A marathon ends in three hours—in only a fraction of a single day. A Himalayan climb means months of daily living in the cold, plus coping with changeable situations that are stressful and dangerous, and frequently life-threatening."

As the hours of waiting out bad weather dragged on into days, I had plenty of time to consider the truth of Roger's claim. Yet, even while tentbound, I was finally beginning to feel reasonably strong. Constantly breathing fresh air—and sleeping outside on the ground—plus miles of arduous hiking, had at last boosted my fitness. And, after four weeks of acclimatizing, I could now notice a sublime physiological difference. I hadn't forgotten about the "episode" on my recent training hike, but after several days back above twenty thousand feet, I felt freshly transformed. I was now living this climb, actively feeling the pulse of the mountains surrounding me—and excited to have reached a state of coexistence, or at least sympathy, with the elements.

"Roger will solo Everest, and I will climb Changtse. The trappings have all been shed," I wrote in my journal.

The next morning, though, it was *still* snowing. Ruth had been sick and hardly had ventured outside their tent in two days. She was weak and disappointed. After giving Roger a kiss, she left for Base Camp with Pasang.

"I hate worrying about women on expeditions, but what can you do?" Roger confided to me after they'd left. "They're never satisfied staying at Base, and who can blame them? They want to participate."

There is absolutely nothing wrong with women doing a climb with male partners. Difficulties arise when it is your girlfriend who is your climbing partner. That partnership—when the man is the "teacher," and the woman is "the student"—often, at least in my experience, gives rise to an unhealthy dynamic, emotional outbursts, rifts, even tragedy. Since Lauren's death, I'd climbed with a few women climbers, but in general I found that, emotionally, I could no longer bear what I felt to be an overwhelming responsibility for a female climbing partner. For that reason, I shied away from climbing with women, and I still do.

Ruth was something of a climber, though—plus adventurous and tough-skinned—so Roger was placed more in a defensive position, of having to say, "I know you want to come, but you can't." Kristina was not a climber *per se,* although she'd done a few beginning rock routes. She made no pretense of wanting to climb, but I knew that she worried about me while I was climbing.

Yaks carrying the Chilean team's loads head up the East Rongbuk Glacier.

Kristina had already expressed to me her fear of my desire to solo a mountain while Roger was soloing Everest. And so as I mulled over my own climbing dreams and plotted to turn them into reality, I was not at all looking forward to telling Kristina that I was also going to attempt a solo ascent.

The snow fell thicker throughout the day. No climbing, no pictures, no North Col, no progress. "Maybe we should have left for Base, too," Roger said glumly. Our muscle tone deteriorated with each passing day that we remained inactive above twenty thousand feet. Knowing that he could eat better at Base Camp, and thus maintain his strength and weight, was a constant worry to Roger.

Finding myself in a rare poetic mood, I wrote in my diary:

> White flakes of snow blow across black hard rock
> We sit, we dream, we think—
> Who knows when the storm will stop?
> The world is quiet except for falling snow on the tent roof,
> and the sliding roar of avalanches in the mist.

July 27. More snow. The monsoon showed no signs of quitting. "No bloody point in staying here!" Roger shouted at 6:30 A.M. We stowed our valuable gear into duffels, then shut and padlocked the tent door zippers to curtail the reach of inquisitive fingers. A yak train was due up with the Chileans' provisions.

"We can't sit here in the snow waiting for the yak drivers, just to see if they'll rip us off. They'll have to knife the tents to get anything," Roger said grimly. I shuffled along the moraine's loose stones using ski poles for extra balance—and watched Roger disappear down the glacier like a rabbit on the run.

* * * * * * * * * * * * * *

Of course, we could have predicted it. The next day the weather at Base Camp was perfect! The trick was gauging the weather twelve miles away at Advanced Base. The two campsites were so far apart, and differed in elevation by nearly three thousand feet, that they seemed to be influenced by completely separate weather patterns. At Base, it was impossible to know with any degree of certainty whether it was snowing—or sunny—on the North Col slopes.

When the weather again dawned perfect on July 29, Roger's anxiety surged. Perhaps I'd have felt the same if I'd placed my Himalayan climbing career on the line—and $50,000 of my sponsor's hard cash—betting on a single climb.

Roger Marshall waiting and watching at Rongbuk Base Camp—inspecting Everest.

The Swiss-French team had briefly returned to Base Camp, however, and one evening they came over for dinner. Although Roger saw Jean Troillet as the competition, he was also noticeably impressed by Troillet's audacious plan for his own solo attempt on Everest. Jean, you see, had decided to dispense with such seemingly essential items as a tent and a sleeping bag, and the only food he planned to carry was what he could fit into his jacket pockets or in a small day pack. By starting to climb at night, and wearing his down suit for warmth, he expected to be able to ascend six thousand vertical feet before the next morning. After bivouacing and resting during the day—in the warmth of the sun—at the top of the *Japanese Couloir,* he would continue up the *Hornbein Couloir* the following night, and reach the summit on the morning of his second day on the mountain. The entire descent could then be made that same day, in daylight, in one long push. That was Troillet's game plan.

"Jean has really got me thinking," Roger confessed to me later, somewhat in awe of his rival. I could see the cogs whirling inside Roger's brain.

"Everest, with style," that was what Troillet called it. Polish mountaineer Voytek Kurtyka, who'd also successfully used this technique in the Himalaya, termed it "night-naked climbing." And indeed, you were climbing virtually naked. Since you had no tent, no sleeping bag—not even a climbing rope—there was precious little room for error, illness, or bad weather. It was stylish methodology, but it was high-altitude Russian roulette nonetheless.

I wondered if Roger was at all worried about dying on Everest? Somehow I didn't think so. Roger was a great believer in Providence, but more importantly, in the virtue of self-will. At times, he struck me as keenly aware of the dangers of an Everest solo. Other times, he seemed blissfully ignorant, or at least uncaring.

"God has a lot more in store for me," he once declared to me with swaggering certainty. "He won't kill *me* yet."

I was now actively plotting my own solo schemes. Sometimes I wanted to rush headlong into this game of high-stakes, high-altitude climbing, but then, I would remind myself: what was the point of hurrying? On Himalayan peaks, there is usually no sudden showdown between the mountaineer and the mountain. And although Troillet's game plan called for a rapid, two-day blast, this would be preceded by a month of careful training and acclimatization. In the Himalaya, human endurance and mental willpower are pitted against mountains of seemingly infinite size. To succeed, "to summit," one simply had to persevere, learn to live amongst the almost unfathomable scale of these peaks, aim for the top, and keep putting one boot in front of the other.

Yet safety in numbers in the mountains is also an enduring myth. Our small team purposefully lacked the "security" of a large expedition (such as on my Everest West Ridge trip) in order to more fully activate, and experience, the realities of man meeting mountain. Opting instead for safety in competence and safety in speed—we moved lightly, quickly, cautiously, calculatedly. Divorced from the security of climbing with big teams employing thousands of feet of fixed rope, the solo mountaineer faces the mountain's challenges with a new vision. He (or she) must patiently mark their days, knowing that when a clear day of weather does come, they must climb on impulse, with agile quickness and supreme self-reliance. There is, I believe, no other human endeavor like soloing a high Himalayan peak, except perhaps a deep ocean dive, a polar crossing, or a solitary walk in space. Nowhere else on earth than upon a high Himalayan summit is one so utterly cut off from the world of the living.

And the solo mountaineer feels this separation acutely. Beyond the reach of rescue—by both man and helicopter—at the highest altitudes there exists only competence and self-help, raw human courage, and the indomitable will to live. On the world's tallest peaks, all other preconceptions are foolishness, and any misguided or unfounded confidence, or egotistical bravado, usually prove fatal.

A heroic challenge indeed, but alongside my own mountaineering aspirations came not a little self-doubt. I wasn't quite as certain as Roger that "God won't kill me yet." I still asked myself if I could maintain my health and strength at over twenty-four thousand feet—and could I handle this level of challenge alone on Changtse? The next three weeks would tell.

In the meantime, some members of our support team managed to find their own life-threatening adventures at Base Camp. Our interpreter Mr. Yide's affliction had indeed turned out to be appendicitis, and his replacement, a boy-faced college student named Ma Qian Li, now arrived at camp. Like our Liaison Officer, Mr. Li, Mr. Ma also had no climbing nor even outdoor experience. One evening, Ma (as we came to call him) decided to visit his Chinese friends at the Chilean Base Camp downvalley. He left about 8 P.M., after dark. While crossing the river he was swept away, lost his prescription glasses, his umbrella—and more seriously—his high-heeled loafers. Luckily, he managed to crawl ashore, barefoot, blinded, and soaking wet. After crisscrossing the gravel flats for more than two hours, he finally stumbled upon the Chilean camp.

A few days later, Ma still looked the worse for wear. His face was bloated and his gaze was sullen. He obviously needed some cheering up. Kristina happened to ask Pasang if he knew how to swim. "Sherpas only swim during the day," Pasang answered, waiting for the words to register on Ma's face. "Chinese like to swim at night while Sherpas sleep. Then, in day time, Sherpas swim while Chinese sleep!" Luckily, Mr. Ma laughed as hard as we all did.

However, our staff from the Chinese Mountaineering Association, notably our Liaison Officer, Mr Li, was continuing the time-honored CMA tradition of being less than helpful. Mr. Li had lived at the Chilean Base Camp with the Chilean's L.O. and translator since they'd arrived. Roger was paying both Li and Ma's salary, but when he asked them to watch Base Camp so we could all four take a ski trip onto the Lho La plateau, they refused. And then, when Roger wanted to hire some of the Chilean's yaks to carry our skiis and gear, Li informed Roger that he would have to pay the CMA-stipulated two-hundred-yuan "gear and clothing fee" for the yak drivers—again. Roger had already paid the fee once, and the Chileans had, too. It was pure extortion, and Roger was steaming.

"You're just a bunch of crooks!" he shouted at them, after complaining that Li was putting his efforts into hindering rather than helping our expedition.

"If this was America," Roger continued, "you'd all be in jail!"

The Chileans themselves were turning out to be the best of neighbors. University club climbers from Santiago, they'd trained for Everest for five years on mountains like Aconcagua and Denali. While the team's average age was only twenty-five (young for Everest), what they lacked in years they made up for with humor and pluck. Plying us with hot chocolate and cookies, the Chileans would

Chilean Everest team: Claudio Lucero Martínez (left); *Rodrigo Jordan Fuchs* (right).

often regale us with stories of exotic climbing in the Towers of Paine and Patagonia in South America. When Roger asked Claudio Lucero, their leader, if he might climb the same route they intended to do (a query guaranteed to raise the hackles of virtually any Himalayan mountaineer), Claudio replied openly, "We are climbers. We must help each other." Later, when we asked if we might use their fixed ropes to ascend to the North Col, Juan Andrés Marambio Smith, their doctor, was quick to answer.

"Of course," he said with a warm smile. "We are here to help!"

On August 4, Roger and Ruth departed on their ski trip to the Lho La plateau, while it was decided that Pasang, Kristina, and I would stay in Base Camp and mind the store. Some new visitors also arrived, American trekkers Chris and Eriko, who shared stories of their own faraway travels, and brightened our days. Roger and Ruth, meanwhile, found cloudier conditions. The skiing was good, but it was a long hike to the snowfields. They made it all the way to Mallory's View at the southern edge of the Lho La, above the drop-off to the Khumbu Glacier and Nepal—only to have monsoon clouds obscure the vista.

On August 7 and 8, while Ruth and Roger rested up after their return, Kristina and I visited Tilman's Lake Camp, which was a veritable Garden of Eden

Jean Troillet.   Jean Afanassieff.

compared to Rongbuk Base's gravel desolation. Green blades of grass, a natural spring, and fantastic campsites surrounded the tranquil pond on the elevated east bank of the Middle Rongbuk Glacier. Jean Troillet and his Swiss partner, Sandro Godio, were preparing for a midnight training climb of a six-thousand-meter mountain over on the west side of the Middle Rongbuk Glacier. Erhard Loretan had already soloed the same peak, an impressive performance considering that a week before, he'd crashed his parapente and torn an ankle ligament.

Troillet was a gregarious, friendly man whose face sported a contagiously enthusiastic grin, and whose arms and legs bulged with Popeye-sized muscles. Jean delighted in showing me some of his specially designed, ultralight gear: step-in, clip-on crampons, two ice axes riddled with holes to reduce weight, and a Bluet propane-butane cartridge stove with a hanging pot set. On their training climb up Fluted Peak they planned to wantonly splurge on weight— by wearing harnesses and belaying each other with a six-millimeter rope!

"In America there is not this competition for lightness and speed that exists in Europe," Jean observed. "I have tried to shave all possible weight off of our equipment."

Jean Afanassieff told me it took five hours to reach Mallory's View at the edge of the Lho La, and four hours to return. Kristina and I left by 6:30 A.M. the next morning, but the weather worsened as we boulder-hopped up the glacier's edge. When it began to snow heavily, we opted for retreat. But by climbing at night, Sandro and Jean had finished their ascent of Fluted Peak's North Face before the weather broke. Back at camp, Jean happily rubbed his hands together.

"Now we are really itching to climb Everest!" he said, adding cautiously: "But maybe we will have to wait just a little bit longer."

Hiking back to Base, Kristina and I crested the final moraines—and saw *two* new groups of tents. The British Everest Northeast Ridge Expedition and a group of trekkers had invaded our sanctuary. But among the Brits I had several old friends, including Pete Long and Paul Moores, who I was very glad to see. The Brits, however, were soon humoring us, and could be seen marching off on "training exercises," carrying monstrously large, heavy-looking backpacks, whilst daintily holding aloft their ubiquitous black umbrellas in one hand.

Roger, however, was edgy. We'd leave for ABC in the morning. If the snow conditions and the weather cooperated, this could be it—his solo of Everest.

* * * * * * * * * * * * * *

Yak drivers.

A quick eight hours and twelve brutal miles later, I walked into Advanced Base Camp on August 11. "Brace yourself," Roger spoke in a tense, barely controlled voice.

"The Tibetans knifed my tent."

I was shocked, but I wasn't overly surprised. I immediately checked my own tent, quickly cataloging my camera gear, clothing, boots, crampons, and ice axes.

"What'd they get?" I asked Roger.

"Looks like they took our eating utensils, cups, and a few other odds and ends. The bastards lifted the tent up and knifed the tent floor so it wouldn't be obvious from the outside."

So much for the Chilean team and their Sherpas guarding our campsite, but at least they loaned us cups and spoons so we could eat.

After dinner came the real shock. "They stole my good inner boots!" Roger exclaimed after further inventorying his gear. Fortunately, he was able to fit a spare pair of liners into his Asolo plastic boot shells. The climb could continue.

In changeable weather the following morning, we decided to climb to the North Col. "You always *ought* to get up and climb," Roger moaned, "but how the Swiss and French get up at midnight and go all night is beyond me."

That not-so-hidden rivalry! Roger claimed he wasn't contending with Jean, but it was his unwillingness to admit to having a competitive streak that really bothered me. Roger Marshall was the most competitive mountaineer I'd ever met. He was endlessly comparing himself yard-for-yard, hour-for-hour, and climb-for-climb with Messner, Troillet, and Béghin. Mountaineering had started out (after a scientific phase) as a sport of honor, of man and woman against mountain, and nothing more. But in these days of sponsored, professional, paid climbers, the fun of ascending mountains seemed increasingly to have degenerated into a contest of man-versus-man, woman-versus-woman, and hype.

Standing below two thousand feet of forty-five to fifty-five-degree snow slopes leading up to the North Col, Roger encountered a brief ethical dilemma. Should he use the Chilean's fixed ropes up the slopes—or would that tarnish the purity of his solo? Messner hadn't used any ropes on his solo ascent. But the Chileans had chosen the easiest and most natural line of ascent to the col. Reluctantly, Roger began following their footsteps—but without touching their ropes. I, fortunately, had no need of such high morals. I happily clipped into their ropes with a jumar and a sling attached to my harness, and started up.

The day was scorchingly hot, and I'd forgotten what hard work it is to climb at over twenty thousand feet. Although I felt slightly lightheaded, I discovered I could climb for thirty to forty feet at a stretch before resting. Soon the afternoon mists thickened, and separated us into our private worlds. The final hundred-foot slope to the Col steepened to nearly seventy degrees—then abruptly turned horizontal. I was on Everest's North Col (23,183 feet), a place of mountaineering legend, and the launching point for every summit attempt by the pioneering British climbers—Mallory and Irvine included—of the 1920s and '30s. It was here on June 6, 1924 that Noel Odell snapped the last picture of the pair alive.

I followed the Chileans' ropes and emerged onto a wide snow saddle. When the mists cleared, Roger appeared, too, and I framed him with Everest's singular summit soaring six thousand feet higher behind him. Roger was gloating; he'd beaten Messner's time to the Col by half an hour! I wondered what difference it made, since Roger had ascended in someone else's footsteps. Messner hadn't.

Roger on the North Col, with Everest's summit and the Great Couloir on right.

And people say climbing isn't competitive?

When minutes later the clouds re-enveloped us, it was time to descend.

"I think I'll just rappel down the ropes," I said, fumbling for the carabiners I'd brought for that purpose.

Suddenly, Roger's tone of voice completely changed. *"You're what?"* he scolded, as though rappelling down fixed ropes in this particular situation was totally against the rules. "This is the Himalaya, Ed. Speed! This is modern climbing. You can walk down that snow slope!" Roger ridiculed.

Caught off guard, I nearly lost my composure. And, before I could reply, Roger turned and walked away. I didn't want his sermon to ruin my first trip to the North Col. The views across Everest's vast North Face to the Great Couloir, and beyond to the West Ridge, were spectacular. High above, I could also discern the First and Second Steps on the upper Northeast Ridge, where Mallory and Irvine had disappeared in 1924. I tried to forget Roger's berating, but found that I couldn't as I rappelled methodically back down the ropes.

Below, I stopped to chat with the Chileans, who were heading up. Víctor Hugo Trujillo, only twenty-two, the youngest member of their expedition, approached me. Just then the sun burned through the clouds and, for a moment, it was so terrifically hot that I thought I might pass out. How could Víctor Hugo be wearing long underwear, three shirts, and Gore-tex bibs? Roger and I, by comparison, wore only long underwear and light wind pants. In broken English, Víctor Hugo explained that he wanted to stay covered up since he'd been badly sunburned. Well, that much was obvious!

Back at camp, Roger smiled warmly at me, his fickleness fled. Drained by two hard days in a row, I let my anger go. I didn't want to argue, not now. For the moment, we were confronted by another all-too-familiar problem. Would the weather improve, or should we retreat again to Base? With deep monsoon snow blanketing the mountain, climbing conditions were still very poor.

I asked Roger how he would feel if he reached the eight-thousand-meter-level, and then got bogged down in the snow. Given the near-continuous daily snowfall we'd been having, such a scenario was entirely plausible, and it could easily result in Roger being too tired to give Everest another try later on.

After a moment's pause, Roger conceded the logic of my implied suggestion. "Okay, we'll go down to Base. Forget Jean climbing at night to get the hard snow—we'll give it another week to settle."

After enjoying the Base Camp breakfast fare the next morning, Roger quipped, "It's amazing how far you'll walk for a good meal." Yet, despite these stabs at good humor, it was obvious the strain of the climb was getting to both Ruth and Roger. In the last week, especially, Kristina and I had both felt a palpable tension building. Either Roger or Ruth seemed capable of lashing out at us at any time, for any violation, real or imagined, and the next occasion would surely arrive soon enough.

Predictably, it rained that afternoon. Tentbound, I heard a voice outside.

"Anyone alive?" it asked.

I stuck my head out the tent door—and found myself inadvertently mistaken for Roger by Ronald Faux, a reporter for the London newspaper, *The Times*, and the author of the only biography of South Tyrolean mountaineering legend Reinhold Messner. I introduced myself and directed Faux over to Roger's tent, but he explained that he'd already tried it, and had gotten no response.

"Do you think he's asleep?" When I shrugged, Ronnie said he'd return later.

I was positive Roger had heard him, but that he hadn't wanted to be bothered. A former journalist himself, Roger had a deep-seated mistrust of the media. And when I later mentioned that Ronnie Faux had stopped by, Roger replied, somewhat irritated, "Yes, I heard him calling outside my tent. I've already been in the *New York Times;* so why do I need the London *Times?*"

It was appearing to be one of those days. Kristina and I both felt low. Clouds rolled annoyingly over Everest's Northeast Ridge while we washed our laundry in freezing meltwater and verbally ragged on Roger and Ruth. Something was coming to a head.

When Faux returned the next day, he and Roger spoke in the cook tent for over an hour. When I stepped in to make some tea, I introduced myself again—it seemed harmless enough. Five minutes later, Roger got up and left. I figured he was sick of talking to Faux since he'd shown so little interest the previous day; I soon discovered otherwise.

Desperate to give my sagging psyche a boost, I'd decided to try soloing Peak 6570, a twenty-one-thousand-foot summit just above Base Camp, the following day. I was in the process of searching through our storage tent for my extra crampons when Ruth and Roger cornered me.

"What the hell did you think you were doing, barging in and interrupting my interview like that?" Roger stormed.

Before I could respond, Ruth interjected a similar complaint. I said I honestly had thought the interview was over—but there was no stopping their wrath.

"And then you went on and on about the bloody West Ridge, which was a total disaster!" Roger fumed. "You didn't get anywhere, certainly not to the top!"

"Well then, if we're being so open, there's something that I'd like to get off my chest, too," I shot back. "Remember when we were up on the North Col and you gave me a hard time about rappelling down the Chilean ropes?" I said, pointing my finger at him, and feeling my nervousness showing.

"I know that I haven't been on as many expeditions as you have, Roger," I said trembling, "but don't ever lecture me again about how to climb."

Roger nodded affirmatively, surprised I think by the vehemence of my anger, but he did not speak. Ruth turned and left.

"If I want to use fixed ropes, that's my decision." My voice quaked; I could not believe I was lecturing Roger—of all people—on the importance of individual freedom in the sport of climbing. "Climbing gives us personal freedom— but I've also seen someone die climbing. I know what *this game* is all about."

Living for a prolonged time at high altitude, I knew, often makes climbers very emotional, but I was still taken aback by the strength of my words and feelings. Roger, however, responded with grace, apologized to me, and said that his words on the Col had been uncalled for. And I in turn apologized to him for intruding on his interview. In the spirit of reconciliation, I added that I wanted to do a good job taking pictures for him.

"So? Do we understand each other?" he asked. Then, with a smile, he added, "You know, it really felt good to yell at you and get rid of all that anger."

"Yeah, things are fine," I said. "Just don't ever lecture me about my climbing again." I realized too late how poorly chosen my parting words were, but Roger apologized a second time, and we shook hands. Our first blood feud was over.

Later, I told Roger of my decision to solo Peak 6570 east of Base Camp.

"I have to climb something while I'm in Tibet," I said.

"Just don't go and kill yourself," was his reply.

* * * * * * * * * * * * * *

On August 15, I left Base Camp before dawn. After two and a half hours of scrambling up an endless ridge of loose rocks and scree, I was at last able to strap on crampons and begin zigzagging up the cold crusty snow of Peak 6570. Far below, I noticed four dots leave the British Base Camp and follow after me.

A large gray disk of cloud spun overhead, while morning mist clogged the valley floor. Soon we'd be returning to Advanced Base—Everest for Roger, and hopefully Changtse for me. If I succeed today, I told myself, maybe I could pull off a 7,500-meter peak. Wary of a careless slip, I watched my crampons carefully, climbing up the easy-angled, yet dangerously-inclined-enough snow.

After much fatiguing cramponing, I reached the lower summit. It was nameless and only 6,343 meters (or 20,810 feet) high, but it was still my first real Himalayan top. A metal Chinese surveying tripod graced the snow dome's crest. I considered continuing up to the highest summit on the ridge, of Peak 6570. Why not? I needed more practice on corniced snow arêtes with giddy exposure.

The snow was softening, and it soon began balling up under my crampon points. I navigated past two rock outcrops, then proceeded up the final seventy-degree snow ridge. The drop-off below my boots was now well over two thousand feet. One false step would be your last. Staying alert, monitoring my breathing, I tried to maintain an even pace, kept a tight grip on my ice ax, and plodded the last few steps to the top of Peak 6570—to the 21,555-foot crown.

The summits of Everest, Changtse, Pumori, and Gyachung Kang were blanketed by thick cloud, but still, what a thrill! My shortness of breath ended once

My first Himalayan summit—Peak 6570, Tibet.

I stopped. Replacing it came a keen exhilaration and a wondrous enjoyment of my solitary view. At last I'd done something I could write home about!

Ten minutes later, I heard a British-accented voice shout out: "Thanks for the steps, mate!" It was Trevor Pilling, one of the youngest and fittest of the English climbers. He arrived alone; evidently his three companions had turned back. Besides being something of a daredevil—he loved parasailing—Trevor had climbed extensively in the Alps and Asia. I immediately liked his *joie de vivre* and warm manner. Then, while we ate a quick lunch, Trevor exclaimed:

"I thought we'd lost you, Ed! Didn't you hear that monster avalanche cut loose just to the left of the summit?" I hadn't.

"It was a big one," said Trev. "And I thought you were in it!"

Then we glissaded, sliding down a thousand or more feet of perfect sun-softened snow, whooping and hollering like two truant schoolboys negotiating the world's best sled run.

* * * * * * * * * * * * * *

Kristina was absent upon my return. "She's at the British camp," Ruth said. When Kristina returned, she admonished: "They're party animals, drinking beer and hundred-proof rum, smoking cigars and cigarettes! You'd think they might be training for Everest a bit more."

"Actually, they *are* training," I explained. "That's how the Brits prepare themselves for high altitude, by simulating brain cell destruction with massive self-administered doses of alcohol and nicotine."

"Oh, so that's how they do it," Kristina said.

We often socialized over at the British Base Camp. Tea time could last for several hours, and in proper English fashion, liquid consumption was by no means limited to tea. Small talk was frequently punctuated by jaw-breaking laughter, and covered every conceivable subject from Argentina's sinking of Her Majesty's warship *Sheffield* in the Falkland Islands War, to the British TV show, *Spitting Image* (a Monty Pythonesque satire that used puppets to mock leading political figures), to the best ways to proposition French girls at the legendary climber's hangout, the Bar Nationale, in Chamonix.

The 1986 British Everest Northeast Ridge Expedition was an eclectic crew, both young and old, and their camaraderie was terrific. One day I asked their leader, Brummie Stokes (himself an Everest summiter—now minus the obligatory frostbitten toes, all ten, in fact), how he'd selected such a fine team.

"First, no prima donnas, but I had to have read about them in the climbing mags. I had to know they could climb. Second, they had to sit and listen more than they talked—"

"How'd Mo Anthoine get on then?" someone shouted.

"Third, they had to be the ones staggering out of the pubs at closing time!"

Only the dedicated, if aging, core of British mountaineering had gotten invites. The team included Joe Brown, Mo Anthoine, Paul Nunn, and Paul Moores.

Earlier, Moores, whom I'd first met several years earlier while ice climbing in Scotland, dropped a bombshell. "Keep it quiet," he whispered in my ear, "but apparently one of the Chileans got the chop yesterday. Someone fell through the North Col cornice and down the Col's east side."

The drop of nearly two thousand feet had been fatal. For the rest of the afternoon I felt a sick knot in my stomach. I laughed at the jokes and gags of the British—this was life. Then I thought of the Chilean climber, now cold as glacial ice. That was death.

At dinner that evening, we celebrated Roger's forty-fifth birthday. Following beer, *mo-mos* (steamed vegetable and meat-filled pastries), and fruitcake, Pasang presented Roger with a *kata* blessing scarf for luck and Ruth with a pair of turquoise earrings. Roger proclaimed that it was the best birthday he'd had in years. But outside, the snow kept falling.

Our Chinese Mountaineering Association staff, however, were becoming impatient. September 4—our Base Camp departure date for Beijing—was approaching. With a considerable volume of new snow decking the slopes of Everest, the ominous vertical streaks of new avalanche tracks were everywhere.

"Roger is a very, very patient man," sighed Mr. Ma.

The Chinese confirmed that a Chilean climber had died, but that wasn't the only tragedy. BBC World Service radio announced that British mountaineers Alan Rouse and Julie Tullis had reached the summit of K2, but perished in a storm on the descent. Two Poles had also died. It was the worst possible news to hear before we returned to the mountain, yet Roger didn't appear the least bit upset. Still, I wished Kristina hadn't been within earshot.

Nattily dressed in a pair of pink and purple lycra tights, Roger set out for Advanced Base Camp early on August 19. Ruth walked him partway. On her return, she looked exhausted.

"These deaths are starting to get to me," she said. But which Chilean died? No one knew. "How will they get his body home?" Kristina asked.

"More than likely he'll be buried in a crevasse," I answered.

She shuddered. "Oh, that's awful."

Pasang then explained how climbers who die on the Nepalese side of Mount Everest are usually cremated on a hilltop above the village of Lobuche.

"The view from that hill is very good," Pasang said.

I followed Roger the next day back up to Advanced Base. Kristina was also growing weary of the comings and goings of expedition life, but seemed happy as we walked along the trail. I'd told her I'd probably be attempting Changtse.

"Be careful," she said. I knew she'd say it; she always did. I told her I would.

As I reached the British camp halfway up the East Rongbuk Glacier, I heard the New Zealander Paddy Freaney urgently yell out, "Put the kettle on, put the kettle on!" Over mugs of hot coffee, I listened to them aim at any and all targets.

"Roger hasn't run out of protein powder yet, has he?" Paddy asked gently.

"Well, we are a bit short of Spam," I replied. "It's Roger's favorite."

"We'll have to get him a tin then, won't we?" Paddy promised, rummaging through their food boxes.

"How 'bout curried chicken?" Joe Brown queried. "He'd love that."

"Of course, good for keeping your sleeping bag warm at night!" Paddy said.

When I finally met up with Roger he'd just visited the Chileans' camp. There was no dissuading them from going home. They'd voted, and their expedition was over. I could see where the North Col cornice had broken, and below, a gigantic horizontal fracture marked where the avalanche began.

"It was Víctor Hugo," Roger said unemotionally. "He was warned not to go too close to the cornice. He didn't listen."

Víctor Hugo was one of the Chileans whom I'd gotten to know and like. After he broke his neck in the fall on August 16, his teammates buried him below the rock cliffs of Changtse.

"The Chileans told me something very interesting yesterday," Roger mentioned the next morning, as we sorted gear and food for his next attempt. "Before soloing Everest, Messner studied the monsoon weather patterns very carefully. And apparently he discovered that each year in late August there's usually a clear calm spell—and he decided that was when to climb."

Messner attained the summit of Mount Everest, alone, on August 20, 1980.

Time was dwindling, yet Roger appeared in no rush. Decisions that other mountaineers would have made months earlier, he was still making. Which pair of boots to wear? Should he bring two ice axes, or only one? I was dumbfounded when Roger casually told me that actually he'd never climbed with any of this gear before. It had all been given to him by the manufacturers.

He hoisted his rucksack. "Here goes," Roger said and left. It was August 22. I wished him luck.

Víctor Hugo would not have wanted his teammates to call off their climb, but their hearts were gone. The Chileans dismantled their camp—and the Brits took their place. Joe Brown came trudging up the trail and sat down on my stone doorstep to chat. We could see Roger climbing toward the North Col. Joe truly hoped Roger would make it. Over the years, Joe had reached several very noteworthy summits himself, making the first ascent of Kanchenjunga in 1955, and a year later, the spectacular Karakoram rock tooth, the Mustagh Tower.

"It's always better coming home with a peak in yer pocket," Joe said.

I'd delivered Pasang his cup of tea the next morning—taking great pride in loudly shouting "Bed tea!" while he was still asleep—when we noticed the weather. As Pasang put it, "downside" was blue, but "upside," toward Everest it was black, cloudy, and ominous looking.

Roger had said he'd descend if all systems weren't go. Shortly thereafter we spied a tiny speck descending from the Col. And two hours later, Roger entered camp like an apparition, exhausted, foul-tempered, and fed up.

Roger approaches the North Col (on far right), *while the summit bathes in sunshine.*

"Eight inches of snow fell last night," he said in disgust, "and the snow was already knee deep."

It was snowing hard now, and the wind, too, was picking up. I really didn't want to descend to Base Camp again. My acclimatization appeared to be at its optimum, and I felt I'd reached the psychological crux where it was better to stay up here at ABC until the expedition ended. At least at Advanced Base Camp you could see the weather firsthand. Unfortunately, Roger's climbing permit expired August 31, so he would soon have to switch to a different route. "The Body Snatchers" expedition (as Roger called them), who hoped to locate George Mallory's body and camera, held the North Col permit for the autumn, post-monsoon climbing season which began September 1.

All permit changes had to be negotiated with the Chinese—at Base Camp. After a quick good-bye, Roger and Pasang vanished downside into the storm.

* * * * * * * * * * * * * *

The British wasted no time reconnoitering their route up the Northeast Ridge. On August 24, Paddy Freaney and Bill Barker were preparing to cross the East Rongbuk Glacier's white expanse. Could I tag along? We roped up and started across the undulating surface. There were a few crevasses, all small enough to avoid or jump across. Bill scouted, I came second. Every five minutes Paddy yelled "Hold up!" and marked our path with a five-foot-tall bamboo wand.

We rested below a rock buttress—Bill's Buttress, Bill decided to name it, oddly enough—and admired the view. The Raphu La, the pass situated at the base of the Northeast Ridge, was still a ways off to our east, but already midday clouds were surging through the gap. Rumor had it that from the edge of the Raphu La you could see the little-known eastern side of Everest, and Makalu.

Changtse, tallest of Everest's northern satellite peaks, was visible off to our right. Examining it, I realized that it'd be easier to climb Changtse's East Face and Northeast Ridge rather than the mountain's Southeast Ridge, which rose up precipitously from the North Col. On the East Face itself, I noted two fairly obvious lines of ascent: a narrow, vertical snow gully bordered by rock buttresses in the center of the face, or a series of snow ramps half a mile to the right. Both routes finished up Changtse's moderate-looking, low-angled Northeast Ridge.

That afternoon, I hiked up below the North Col to inspect the two routes. The right-hand line appeared easier, but I couldn't be sure because the central gully was hidden by clouds. I thought hard about soloing Changtse, what it

Bill Barker and Paddy Freaney below Everest's Northeast Ridge. Changtse on far right.

would involve. I felt mentally ready, and also physically strong. The snow was freezing hard at night, the timing felt good, and Roger hadn't returned from Base Camp. I decided to attempt the easier right-hand line.

Walking back to camp, I stopped at Víctor Hugo's grave, and stood beside the small mound of stones piled at the base of a towering, cathedral-like rock cliff. The simple wooden cross seemed to move slightly in the wind. I knew that Víctor Hugo had died doing what he loved, but the bleak finality of his death haunted me. I added several stones to the pile and said a prayer for him.

The next day, I marked the approach across the glacier to the start of my proposed route, inserting several bamboo wands so that I could find my way in the dark, then I cramponed up the first few hundred feet to get a feel for the climbing. When Roger still hadn't returned by the afternoon, I decided to try Changtse that night. After saying my good-byes to the Chileans, I told Paddy and Bill where I was going.

* * * * * * * * * * * * * *

August 26. The starry midnight sky beckoned, while a three-quarter moon bathed the high, crystalline peaks in a pure, white light. When I turned off my headlamp, I found that I could still see quite well, so I left it switched off. Then I arrived at Víctor Hugo's grave, stopped, and closed my eyes.

"You died with honor," I said aloud. "You died doing what you loved."

After clipping on my crampons, I felt buoyant and ready to dance on this mountain. I gained height quickly, moving up the forty-five-degree incline with cat-like efficiency, alternately daggering my crampons and sixty-centimeter ice ax into the Styrofoam-like snow slope. Protruding rocks let me rest on their tops, and the bright moonlight showed me where to go next. But because of the unusual and almost otherworldly moon glow, the mountain's features kept popping out in front of me, with each portion of the snow slope being far bigger than it had looked from below. Occasionally, I needed a breather, stopped, turned my headlamp on, drank, and adjusted my clothing so I didn't overheat.

Over my left shoulder, Everest rose to meet the heavens. I could pick out the great mountain's every feature in the soft moonlight. There wasn't a breath of wind. But what was I doing, climbing Changtse, Mallory's North Peak, alone, at night? I was summoning my childhood dreams and making them come true.

The terrain didn't feel dangerous until I reached a point just below the Northeast Ridge. I took out my second ice ax for greater security and moved up a sixty-degree runnel of sugar snow plastered over loose shale. The exposure loomed greater with every upward step, and climbing unroped at twenty-three thousand feet, I knew I was treading dangerous ground. The final twenty feet to the ridge was too dicey, so I downclimbed, traversed left and tried in three different places to gain the ridge. I couldn't do it. As soon as the sun rose, the temperature soared and the snow softened; in a few hours, the snow would melt and become too unstable. Defeated—but alive to return another day—I retraced my steps to camp. By 7 A.M., I was at the British tents. Joe Brown had a brew on.

"Well, did you do it?" he demanded. I explained what had happened.

"Ah, y'did the right thing," Joe answered. "You would've 'ad to downclimb that section if y'd got up it. That's the real test on a mountain—whether y'can get down the bugger."

"Yer here, yer alive," Mo Anthoine added. "That's success enough."

I'd gotten within a stone's throw of the summit ridge, but I couldn't quite pull it off. On the way down, however, I made a short detour and had a productive look at the left-hand alternative: the snow gully running up the center of Changtse's East Face. That had to be the way!

Joe Brown.

* * * * * * * * * * * * * *

Rodrigo Jordan Fuchs was the last of the Chileans to leave for home. He'd made a quick visit to the Raphu La, the pass overlooking the mysterious Kama Valley below Everest's Kangshung Face. "What a view!" he exclaimed. I decided I had to see it for myself. So rather than resting, I joined Joe and Mo on their load carry over to Bill's Buttress, to the base of their route. Joe casually tied into the climbing rope, picked up his one really important piece of equipment—a black umbrella to shade himself from the sun—and shouldered his rucksack.

Mo Anthoine and Joe Brown on the East Rongbuk Glacier. Khartaphu on left.

"Ummm, where's yer ice ax?" Mo demanded.

"What do I need an ice ax for?" Joe shot back.

"In case I fall into a bloody crevasse, that's why!"

"Well, I'm going first, so I'll be the one doing the falling in."

"Listen, I *could* fall into a crevasse," Mo replied. "Y'know, it's been known to 'appen to the second man."

"Okay—well if you do, I'll run back to camp, fetch Brummie, and 'e'll 'aul you out!" Joe answered. "Come on then, let's get going."

"You mean I don't have time to smoke one more fag?" Mo queried.

"No, you can have your cigarette on the trail. Let's go."

Below Bill's Buttress, I untied from Joe and Mo and followed Rodrigo's footsteps to the Raphu La, keeping the magnificent snow peak of Khartaphu on my left. I stood at the edge of the Raphu La at 9 A.M., but sadly, monsoon clouds already had obscured the panorama. Instead, I absorbed the atmosphere of Everest's Kangshung Face through my ears, listening to the roar of avalanches thundering through the mist like clockwork, in regular thirty-second intervals. Which gave me pause to question Robert Anderson's sanity, his prior climbing invitation to me—and why anyone would want to climb the East Face of Everest.

Back at the British ABC, I joined Brummie, their leader, for tea and biscuits. A career soldier, a real man's man, this was Brummie's third time on Everest. Four of his companions, however, he related to me in a somber voice, had died on his previous Everest expeditions.

"Just a bloody shame about the Chileans," Brummie continued. "It 'appens, though. People die here. But just look at this place! I do love these mountains."

Setting down my cup of tea on a rock, I soaked up some more of the sparkling, sunny, king-sized Himalayan view surrounding us.

"They really grow on you, these mountains, don't they?" Brummie said in continuation of his earlier thought whilst happily chomping away on another biscuit and nodding affirmatively.

Yes, I had to agree with him. These mountains really did grow on you.

* * * * * * * * * * * * * *

August 27. Who can sleep before a climb like this? I couldn't. I left camp under clear skies at 9 P.M. A headlamp blinked on as I tip-toed past the British Advanced Base tents. It was Trevor Pilling's light.

"I'm off to try Changtse again," I said.

"Well, good luck. I was wondering what daft bugger would be wandering about at this time of night. I should have known it was you!"

Crossing the moraines felt interminable. I wondered, did I have more—or less—energy than the previous night? It felt like less. I passed Víctor Hugo's grave for the third time.

"I'm going to do it tonight," I told him quietly.

Out on the glacier, my headlamp threw a small yellow circle of light onto the snow. Like a grazing cow, I swung my head from side to side searching for telltale signs of hidden crevasses, for faint dark furrows in the snowy white carpet. I was scared to death of falling into a crevasse, of vanishing forever into an icy tomb! Then I stopped, switched off my headlamp—and was plunged into the inky depths of a moonless Himalayan night.

Slowly, very slowly, my eyes readjusted to the darkness. Up ahead, I could discern two shadowy rock buttresses. A narrow white gash, a snow gully, sliced vertically between them. I headed toward my intended route up the gully with an ice ax gripped in each of my hands like a gunslinger's pistol, the muscles of my upper torso tensed and expectant, ready to throw myself forward to try and save my life at the instant I felt my boot break into a hidden crevasse. In the moon's eerie half light, I stealthily crossed the snow-filled amphitheater, Changtse before me, and Everest and the North Col to my left.

Recent wet-slab avalanches down my intended line of ascent had deposited a scattering of two- to three-foot in diameter bowling balls of rock-hard frozen snow. This odd-shaped debris, looking like a giant's marble collection, demanded extra concentration. Wearing my newly-sharpened crampons, stepping on top of the balls actually did make for easier, if slightly precarious, walking. And fortunately, the bergschrund—the horizontal tension fracture breaking the foot of the gully I was entering—was narrow and had mostly been filled in by the marbles. I easily stepped across it and began an endless procession of back and forth zigzags up the gully's forty-five-degree incline of hard snow.

I was incredibly relieved to be off the glacier which, because of lurking crevasses, was probably the climb's most dangerous section. The remainder of the route I expected to be reasonably safe, but I also had a time limit. I had to be finished and back down the gully by midday tomorrow at the very latest—before the sun could warm the snow and trigger more wet-snow avalanches. By day, this gully was a death trap. My educated bet was that I could climb Changtse in less than twenty-four hours—scale the gully at night, summit by dawn, and complete my descent before the morning was over.

Ed, a member of "the white hats," flies to China. Roger Marshall

Above:

The Forbidden City, Beijing.

Left:

Street scene, Chengdu.

Right:

The Great Wall.

Chinese soldiers polish their jeep below the ruins of Shigatse Dzong, Tibet.

Yaks and yak drivers cross the Dzakar Chu below Rongbuk Monastery.

Praying at the Jokhang Temple.   Roger Marshall in front of the Potala, Lhasa.

Soldier at
the Potala.

Checkpost
near Shekar.

The North Face of Mount Everest in moonlight, from Rongbuk Base Camp.

Ruth De Cew, Roger Marshall, Kristina Kearney, and Ed Webster celebrate Marshall's 45th birthday.

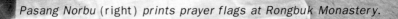
Pasang Norbu (right) *prints prayer flags at Rongbuk Monastery.*

Our *Sirdar,* Pasang Norbu Sherpa, at Rongbuk Base Camp, with Everest behind.

Pierre Béghin, Marshall, and Jean Troillet.   *Roger Marshall.*

Chomolungma, the Goddess Mother of the World.

*Northeast Ridge up left skyline, Great Couloir in center;
Hornbein Couloir on far right, Changtse in foreground.*

East Rongbuk Glacier, Tibet.

Roger hikes up "the Miracle Highway," East Rongbuk Glacier.

Roger Marshall on the North Col of Everest; Great Couloir on left.

Joe Brown and Mo Anthoine.

Roger, the Himalayan Soloist.

Bill Barker approaches Everest's Northeast Ridge, with the Pinnacles above.

Sunrise on the North Col of Mount Everest from Changtse.

Sunrise from 22,500 feet on Changtse; Raphu La and Kanchenjunga on right.

The North Face of Mount Everest from Changtse.

Above: *The view to the north.*
Left: *Ed Webster on top of Changtse.*

Above: *Hornbein Couloir at sunset.*
Left: *Swiss mountaineer Jean Troillet.*
Below: *Troillet with his Everest certificate.*

Fritz Wiessner's last climb, at age 86:
Wind Ridge, *Eldorado Canyon, Colorado.*

Robert Anderson

Ed Webster

Norbu Tenzing Norgay

Billy Squier

Mimi Zieman

Joe Blackburn

Paul Teare & Tsering Dolkar

Kasang Tsering

Stephen Venables & Pasang Norbu Sherpa

Blessing ceremony, Bodhnath, Kathmandu

FACES OF KATHMANDU

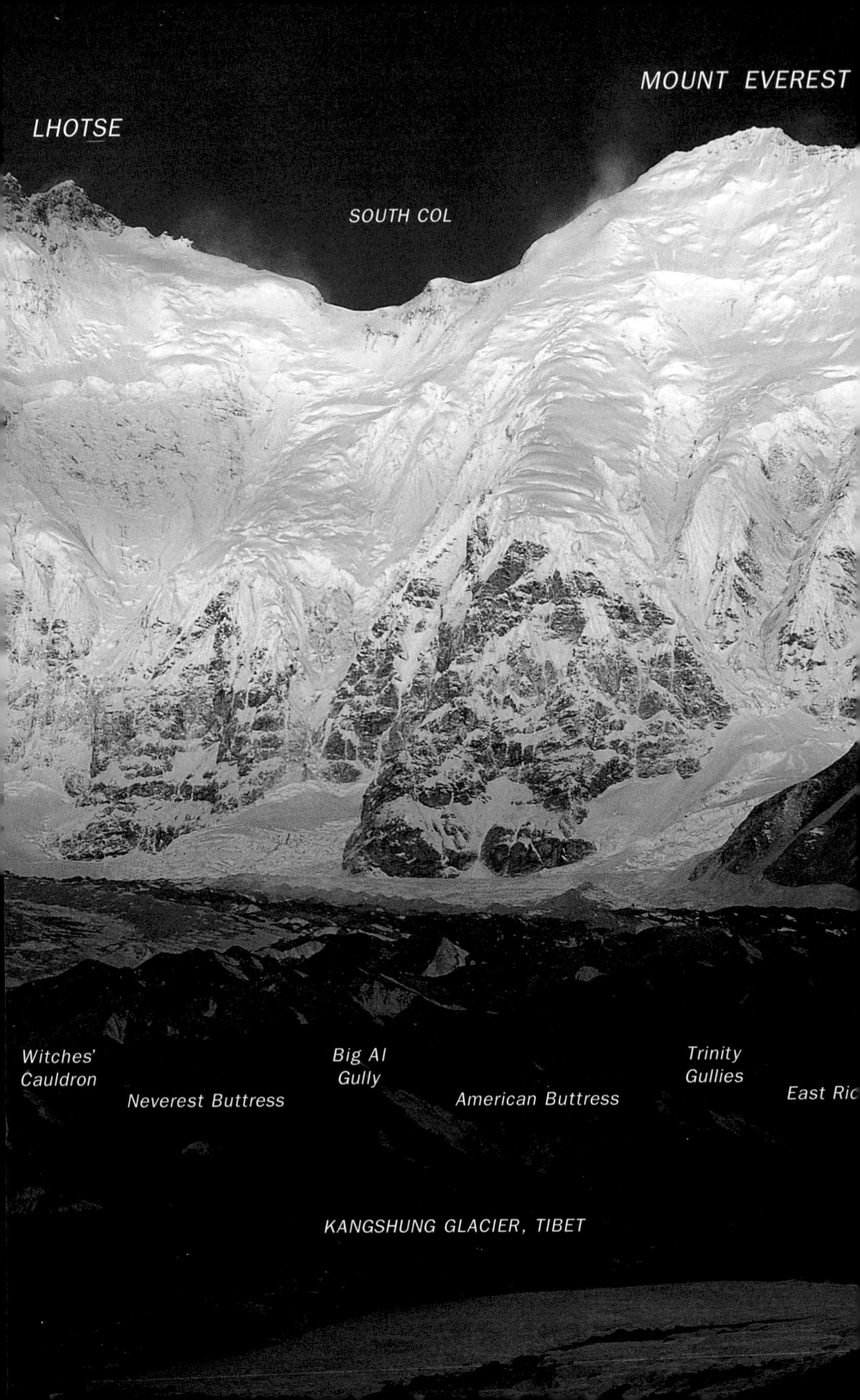

LHOTSE

MOUNT EVEREST

SOUTH COL

Witches'
Cauldron

Big Al
Gully

Trinity
Gullies

Neverest Buttress

American Buttress

East Rid

KANGSHUNG GLACIER, TIBET

My zigs and zags shortened as the snow steepened and the gully narrowed. And my gasps for air deepened as I gained altitude. Keep it steady, I told myself. Don't rush; you'll get there. Overhead, the stars twinkled against the black tapestry of midnight. I was glad that I'd gotten such an early start. In fact, I'd never begun a climb so early. At 1 or 2 A.M., sure, but never at 9 P.M. !

The gully tilted upward again. Higher, I noticed that it split into two branches, and each one disappeared into the blackness. I hadn't noticed that the gully forked. Damn! Now which way should I go? Was one branch a dead end? This was the high price of night climbing: temporary blindness. You had to have thoroughly investigated your route in advance, have a homing pigeon's sense of direction—and be lucky. I picked the lower-angled left-hand branch, hoping that it'd be full of snow. It was.

Now I was deep inside a claustrophobic cleft, sandwiched between darkly brooding rock walls. Nervously, I climbed higher up the narrowing gully. Then, up ahead, a black cliff—a vertical rock step—blocked my way. A long and time-consuming leftward detour might circumvent it, but then, with considerable relief, I noticed a snow and ice ribbon hanging down the rock barrier on the right. It looked short, hard, and possible. I headed toward it.

Each of my ax picks sunk securely into the frozen, snow-covered curtain, biting into a solid layer of hidden ice. Swinging my axes and kicking in the sharp front points of my crampons, I quickly climbed the thirty-foot-tall snow swatch. My movements felt effortless and oddly rehearsed. At the final vertical bulge, I paused, hung back from my axes, and took an extra deep breath. Suddenly I was struck with the full magnitude of my situation, and wondered, "What the hell am I doing in a situation like this at twenty-two thousand feet in the Himalaya?" When my calf muscles started to burn, I remembered the answer—the chance to turn my youthful dreams into reality—lurched my left crampon points up as high as possible, speared them into the ice, and muscled through the crux.

Perhaps because of this success, ten feet higher I slipped unexpectedly—teetering out of balance uncontrollably backwards for a split second—before fate and a spontaneous muscle reaction fortuitously reeled me back in. Hyperventilating like crazy for several minutes, I vowed to be more careful.

I now stood at the base of an endless snowfield sprinkled with occasional jagged black rocks. Dimly visible above on the skyline was my final objective: Changtse's Northeast Ridge. The snow slope I climbed by rote movements, first angling one way, then back the other, feeling light-footed and sure on my feet. But the underlying mountain bedrock, as I had feared, was only thinly covered

Dawn from 23,000 feet on Changtse. On right, beyond the Raphu La, is Kanchenjunga.

by a mask of snow. First I tried a narrow snow chute, but was turned back a mere twenty feet below the ridge by more sugar snow over rock. Feeling very frustrated, I decided to traverse farther right, and discovered to my considerable relief a slightly wider snow-filled depression leading up toward the ridge.

At every step I prayed my ax pick wouldn't penetrate through the inches-thick snow-covering and hit rock. If it did, I might be defeated. Climbing at night, unroped, without a partner or a belay, and now with nearly three thousand feet of exposure licking at my heels, I knew I couldn't push the odds much further. After thirty precarious feet of climbing up the fragile snow layer, I had passed the crux. The angle relented. Not only was the summit ridge just ahead, but of equal importance, I knew I could safely reverse what I'd just ascended.

It was still pitch dark when I gained the ridge at 2 A.M. I was considerably higher than the nearby North Col. It had taken me five hours to climb three thousand vertical feet. But Changtse's Northeast Ridge—instead of being a flat, easy walk as I had hoped—was tilted at a sharp, church-roof-like angle.

Sunrise on Mount Everest and the North Col from Changtse (on first attempt).

But at least it wasn't corniced. Although the summit itself didn't look all that far away, in actuality, it was over half a mile, a respectable distance at twenty-three thousand feet. Had I known this I might have descended, but an inner voice kept pushing me forward, urging me not to turn around until I had reached my first major Himalayan summit. I would not descend in defeat.

I began the heavy labor of plowing my way to the top. I excavated a trench up the ridge crest with three or four kicks of my right leg. I soon tired. It was slow, laborious work, but I sensed progress. I just hoped I'd be near the summit when the sun rose and the temperature soared. A quick glance over my shoulder revealed only a velvet black horizon and the dim silhouette of distant peaks.

In my right hand I held a ski pole; in my left, my ice ax. As the summit grew faintly closer, the eastern sky flowed blood-red above a row of jagged, sharp-toothed peaks, including Kanchenjunga and Jannu. My confidence grew.

Then the sun was up, and bathed these highest mountains on Earth in molten silver and gold. And I was here, a lone human, savoring this seldom-seen delight of color and form, seeing the Himalaya come alive with the new day! Mount Everest appeared so close I felt like I could reach over and touch it. And this highest summit of all caught the heavenly sunlight and held it for me to admire. Would I ever stand on that lofty point, I wondered?

Reaching a flat portion of the final ridge, I put down my pack, ate, drank, and set up my small tripod to take some self-portraits. Then I set off for the top, carrying only my sixty-centimeter ice ax, a ski pole, and my Nikon.

Unbelievably, the early morning sun was burning hot, and the last sixty-degree snow slope became grueling. Could the snow avalanche

Self-portrait, with Changtse's summit ridge.

and sweep me four thousand feet into the abyss? Probing the slope with my ax, I felt the snow to be fairly well-anchored, so I continued, but this new nagging fear of an avalanche wouldn't leave me. I was so close to the top. I pulled up, moving forward on my knees.... A false summit! Changtse's real crown appeared to rise one hundred yards in the distance and another sixty feet higher.

I stood up, gasping in the thin air, my mind and body reeling from the many continuous hours of concentration and exertion. Just the physical effort of gasping for oxygen seemed to make me even more breathless. I had to succeed; I'd come so far. No one else would ever know if I didn't reach the top—but I would. It was pride. I left the ski pole behind and began crawling forward on my hands and knees through the deep feathery snow. My throat was utterly parched. My chest shuddered as each lungful of air was inhaled, utilized, and quickly discarded. Foot-by-foot, I gained height. I could taste success.

Ed almost on top of Changtse. The true summit rises on the left.

A three-by-four-foot snow dollop was my reward, and abruptly the mountain fell away in front of me, dropping with alarming verticality several thousand feet to the Lho La plateau. It was 8 A.M. on August 28, 1986. I glanced toward Base Camp, six miles distant and seven thousand vertical feet lower. Beyond me, thirty yards along Changtse's near-horizontal summit ridge, another cock's comb snow lump rose some forty or fifty feet higher, but getting to it without a roped belay looked somewhat precarious. I also considered that I had made this climb without a permit; additionally I recalled the sanctity of these rarefied summits, as I panted and caught my breath. Although I wasn't standing on Changtse's absolute highest point, I realized that I'd come as far as I wanted, so I sat down on my summit—and left the gods theirs, untrod. After a wave to Base Camp, I then thanked Khumbila, the Sherpa god of the Everest region, for getting me here. I couldn't believe my eyes when I looked at the view; I felt that I was sitting at the center of a great and wondrous wheel, and arrayed around me were many of the tallest mountains on the planet.

Mount Everest's majestic North Face rose a mere mile away, while to the east and west reared two more eight-thousand-meter peaks, Kanchenjunga and Cho Oyu. I sat relishing my bird's eye view of Everest; Himalayan climbing was what I loved! And the route that I'd climbed up Changtse's East Face, to the best of

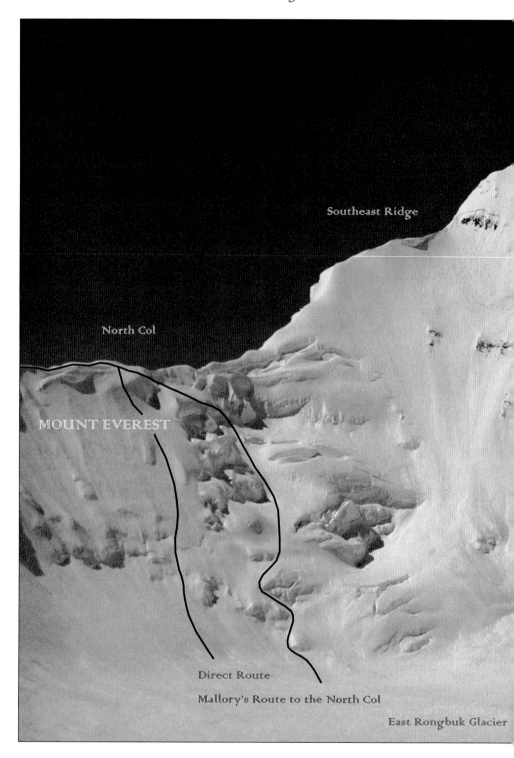

Southeast Ridge

North Col

MOUNT EVEREST

Direct Route

Mallory's Route to the North Col

East Rongbuk Glacier

Changtse (24,879 feet) — Everest's North Peak

Northeast Ridge

East Face

Webster's Solo

First Attempt

Changtse's East Face from Everest's Northeast Ridge. Photograph by Trevor Pilling

Top: *Changtse's Northeast Ridge, with Ed's footsteps. Mount Everest's Northeast Ridge is in profile on the right, with Kanchenjunga beyond. The Raphu La is the pass at the ridge's base*

Above: *Ed returns to Advanced Base Camp after his fifteen and a half hour solo ascent of Changtse. Everest North Col on left.* Bill Barker

Right: *Changtse's East Face from the Raphu La. Víctor Hugo Trujillo's grave is below the rocks at the bottom right-hand corner of the picture.*

my knowledge, was new. It was indeed a picture perfect day—sunny, relatively warm, and without any wind. The gods had indeed smiled on my endeavor, and although I felt incredibly small sitting on Changtse's summit ridge, I'd never felt in greater harmony with the spirits and forces of nature. The uncertainties and risks of my solo climb had dramatically opened me to life's endless possibilities, and contemplating this thought, wondering what my future held, I perched quietly on top for another twenty minutes, delightedly savoring each sublime moment, and photographing each absolutely stunning view.

Gravity assisted me on my descent. I'd tasted victory, but I knew I couldn't let down my guard. Facing uphill into the slope, I carefully backtracked down from the summit, retrieved my ski pole and pack, then headed back along the crest of the Northeast Ridge. The weather remained glorious. As long as the snow didn't soften too much, I'd be fine.

At the top of the upper snowfield, I again turned uphill to face the mountain, and gingerly kicked my way back down the shallow snow chute. The sun was relentlessly hot; I felt like a fly in the center of a three-thousand-foot-tall reflective oven. Feeling machine-like, reverting to well-learned mountaineering skills, I trusted my reflexes, forgot the danger and the sweat, and ever so carefully reversed each step back down Changtse's entire four-thousand-vertical-foot East Face. A long, easy leftward traverse took me around the crux rock band and ice curtain, then I descended the lower snow gully, sliding in my boots at every step through inches of mushy snow. After fifteen hours of climbing and a last terrifying dash across the dangerously sun-softened glacial snowfield, I reached the main trail and bamboo wands below the North Col. I'd made it!

Resting at last, sitting on top of my pack, I was completely numbed by my efforts. I could not eat. Nor could I move. I began to hallucinate. Some tents were nearby, and other climbers, too. Hmmm, maybe I should go see who they were. I stood up, quite shakily, and began walking toward them. Oh, of course: they were glaciologists taking ice core samples from the glacier!

I continued stumbling downhill in the direction of Advanced Base Camp. Then I passed Víctor Hugo Trujillo's grave, marked by its simple wooden cross. *"Hola! Hola!"* a voice called out to me. I turned around to see who it was.

Víctor Hugo was standing fifty feet away from me in the white glare of midday. He was waving his hat. "Congratulations," he said in English. "You did it!"

"Hola! Hola, Víctor Hugo!" I shouted out joyously, thanking him.

Moments later—after he had melted back into a pile of stones—I paused again to accept his congratulations and to enjoy our friendship.

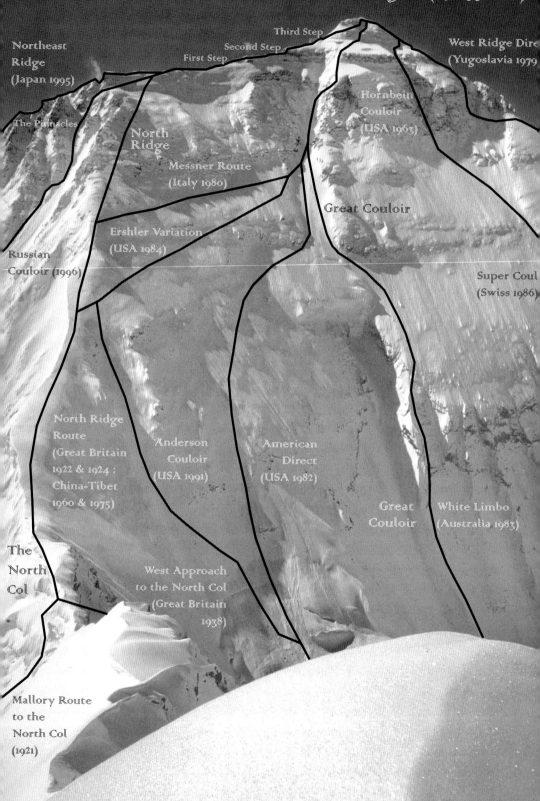

Mount Everest - Chomolungma (29,035 feet)

Third Step
Second Step
First Step

Northeast
Ridge
(Japan 1995)

West Ridge Dire
(Yugoslavia 1979

Hornbein
Couloir
(USA 1963)

The Pinnacles

North
Ridge

Messner Route
(Italy 1980)

Great Couloir

Ershler Variation
(USA 1984)

Russian
Couloir (1996)

Super Coul
(Swiss 1986)

North Ridge
Route
(Great Britain
1922 & 1924 ;
China-Tibet
1960 & 1975)

Anderson
Couloir
(USA 1991)

American
Direct
(USA 1982)

Great
Couloir

White Limbo
(Australia 1983)

The
North
Col

West Approach
to the North Col
(Great Britain
1938)

Mallory Route
to the
North Col
(1921)

One hundred yards from the British camp, I flashed Bill Barker the thumbs up. Focusing his camera on me, Bill answered in his best Texas accent: "Well, wha'dya know. I guess some congratulations are in order."

"Yup," I grinned. "The peak is in the pocket."

* * * * * * * * * * * * *

Two days later, the Swiss-French team made their bid to climb Everest "with style." Troillet, Loretan, Godio, and Béghin left an advanced camp on the Middle Rongbuk Glacier on skis, then started up the *Japanese Couloir* at 11 P.M. on August 28. Unfortunately, soon afterwards Godio was struck by falling ice. Although not seriously hurt, he wisely descended. By 11 A.M. the next morning, the remaining three had attained a height of 25,750 feet. Then, after digging out a platform in the snow, they spent the daylight hours brewing drinks on a small stove to rehydrate their parched and exhausted bodies. By climbing mostly at night, and carrying a minimum of food and cooking gear, Troillet, Loretan, and Béghin hoped to ascend Everest without oxygen, radios, ropes—or even tents. One lightweight sleeping bag apiece was their sole luxury.

After sunset, as the temperature plummeted, they began climbing again to generate body heat. Unfortunately, in the middle of the night, Béghin could not stay awake and was forced to turn back from halfway up the *Hornbein Couloir.* Loretan and Troillet somehow persevered, stopping only for several hours during the coldest part of the night. As dawn's first blush tinted the sky, they continued on with their final push. At 2:30 P.M. on August 30, the pair stood atop Mount Everest, having made the fastest, and arguably one of the most stylish ascents ever, of the world's highest mountain.

Even more remarkable was their subsequent four and one-half hour descent of the peak, down a total of nine thousand vertical feet! Asked later how they managed to descend so quickly, Troillet explained that, finding near-perfect snow conditions, they decided to sit down and glissade—and slid on their backsides most of the way.

"It was insane," Troillet said, twirling his forefinger beside his head for emphasis, as if any was really needed. "Up there, you know, at those altitudes you do not think very well. On the way down, we were sitting side-by-side, glissading down the mountain, looking at each other, digging our ice axes into the snow for control, flying along. Absolutely crazy!"

Left: *Everest's magnificent North Face from Changtse. Various routes are marked.*

When asked if they had used a secret new fabric—"speed Gore-tex"—on their climbing suits (a popular running joke at Base Camp), Troillet chuckled.

"I also hallucinated a marching band on the way down, as we glissaded," he said seriously, "and musicians playing their instruments, which I could hear."

"Plus skiers skiing next to us, carving lovely turns," he added matter-of-factly.

Troillet and Loretan's well-planned success on Everest was stunning, almost unbelievable—yet their margin for error had been slender. Only a single day after they were safely off the mountain, a gigantic avalanche swept their entire route.

Roger waiting for better snow conditions at ABC below the North Col.

*   *   *   *   *   *   *   *   *   *   *   *   *   *

Roger returned to our Advanced Base Camp on the second-to-last day of the good weather, on August 29. Realizing he was about to miss the summer's best weather spell, in one day he climbed from Base Camp all the way up onto the North Col. I met him there, lying in his tent, the following afternoon. All morning long he'd jealously watched Loretan and Troillet climb the *Hornbein Couloir* to the summit. Unlike their route—an avalanche track periodically swept clean of laborious-to-climb deep snow—the snowpack on the North Col and the face above was soft, fresh, and unstable. The weather was also changing, and typically, for the worse. When a lenticular storm cloud hovered over Everest's summit on August 31, Roger descended empty-handed again.

I'd told Roger that Kristina and I needed to return home to America no later than mid-September. Our departure date was nearing, yet Roger still had not made a serious attempt on the summit. I wanted to get some good climbing photographs of him, but I couldn't stay on indefinitely. I felt bad that he hadn't capitalized on the good weather during the last week of August, but for a variety of reasons he'd stayed at Base Camp until it was too late.

After Roger was instructed by the Chinese officials to switch to a different route after September 1, he decided to attempt the *Super Couloir* instead. Ruth would stay in support and take telephoto pictures of his ascent, so we were free to leave for home. Wishing Roger and Ruth good luck, Kristina and I left Rongbuk Base Camp for Lhasa on September 8 in a jeep with members of the British Everest Northeast Ridge Expedition. Our traveling companions were Ronnie Faux, Loel Guinness of the brewing and financing family, and Nigel Goldsack, production supervisor of the expedition's movie crew. In mere seconds, we were transported physically and spiritually away from Base Camp, away from Everest, and into the laughing, jovial care of the Brits.

*   *   *   *   *   *   *   *   *   *   *   *   *

None of the expeditions attempting Everest's northern side in the autumn post-monsoon climbing season of 1986 succeeded. Roger Marshall attempted the *Super Couloir* on September 19. He reached a high point of 25,300 feet, but was unable to locate the start of the *Hornbein Couloir*, so he said, because of the mountain's severe foreshortening. Roger's prolonged stay at high altitude—

Jean Troillet mails off several hundred Everest expedition postcards in Beijing.

Everest historian and author Audrey Salkeld holds a 1922 British Everest expedition oxygen bottle found near Advanced Base Camp below the North Col in 1986.

three months living between seventeen thousand and twenty-three thousand feet—also no doubt contributed to his decision to descend.

Pilot and climber Steve McKinney launched his hang glider from 20,500 feet off of Everest's West Shoulder after strong winds prevented a higher take-off. And the Mallory and Irvine Expedition reached 25,500 feet on the mountain's North Ridge before storms and snow curtailed their efforts. Tragically, one of their most experienced Sherpas, Dawa Nuru, was killed in an avalanche below the North Col during the closing days. The team was also unable to locate the final resting places of George Herbert Leigh Mallory and Andrew Comyn "Sandy" Irvine. And, due to deep snow and bad weather, the British Northeast Ridge Expedition also failed to accomplish its goal of vanquishing the Pinnacles.

(Following two more unsuccessful British attempts on Everest's Northeast Ridge, in 1986 and 1987, the Pinnacles were at last climbed in their entirety by New Zealander Russell Brice and British mountaineer Harry Taylor in August, 1988. Caught in worsening weather, the pair wisely gave up the summit and safely descended the *North Col Route*. A large, well-equipped Japanese expedition finally accomplished the coveted first complete ascent of Everest's Northeast Ridge. Relying upon four thousand feet of fixed rope, bottled oxygen, plus a team of twenty-three Sherpas, Kiyoshi Furuno, Shigeki Imoto, and the Sherpas Lhakpa Nuru, Dawa Tsering, Nima Dorje, and Pasang Kami, attained Everest's summit on May 11, 1995—and they too descended the mountain via the North Col.)

Above: *The Pinnacles, the crux of Everest's Northeast Ridge, seen from the east.*

Chapter 5

Four Against
the Kangshung

"Four against the Kangshung Face? You're mad.
Go and climb a smaller mountain!"

—*Dr. Charles Houston*

En route home, in Beijing, by surprise I had bumped into Robert Anderson, who was there signing the protocol for his Everest East Face trip, set for the spring of 1988. Again, Robert invited me to come. His timing was horrible. I'd been on Everest for the past two months; I needed to go to the beach! But after some serious reflection, I wrote him and accepted. Summiting on Everest, perhaps without bottled oxygen, felt like a more realistic goal after my solo success on Changtse, plus I very much wanted to return to the Himalaya and to Tibet. And luckily, as of yet, I still hadn't actually *seen* the Kangshung Face. Robert, I think, always knew that I would say yes. His reply from his home in New Zealand was simple and understated. In other words, it was typical Robert:

Left: *Everest's East Face was first photographed in 1921.* A.F.R. Wollaston / RGS

"It's great you're coming. We'll make a good team, and I think your recent experiences in China and Tibet will help us."

The type and size of our expedition was defined early on. Robert and I only wanted to climb Everest with a small team. We'd already experienced the petty rivalries and impersonality of large scale Everest expeditioning, and the logistical nightmare of "freight-handling" food, equipment, and oxygen bottles that often overwhelms the beauty of the mountains. Our Himalayan heroes— Eric Shipton, H.W. Tilman, Fritz Wiessner, and Reinhold Messner—advocated four- to six-person expeditions emphasizing camaraderie, friendship, and low impact on native cultures. Any expedition worth going on, as Tilman once famously claimed, could be planned on the back of an envelope.

While we didn't exactly plan our Kangshung Face expedition on a piece of scrap paper, Robert and I wanted to break new ground on Everest, especially in how we visualized our eventual climb. Our primary goal was to keep suspense and challenge high, and, by our definition, have a genuine adventure. This meant that intrinsically there had to be a very high degree of risk, and certainly no guarantee (and even very little likelihood) of success. In that respect, the East Face of Mount Everest was the perfect objective! Struggle, danger, and uncertainty would be our daily climbing companions on the mountain. Facing straight ahead into the unknown with a small team of friends was the only way that we wanted to climb Everest.

That said, we faced numerous immediate, and major, problems. Who would we invite to climb with us? Should we repeat the only known route up the Kangshung Face, the 1983 *American Buttress,* or try a new line, if there was one? Then there was the money. China and Tibet are amongst the most expensive places in the world to climb; our estimated budget was a quarter of a million dollars. How would we find sponsors to believe in our wild dream— and fund us with the necessary backing?

Robert flew to Colorado over the 1986 Christmas holidays and we met at his father's house in Lakewood, a Denver suburb. His dad, Mads Anderson, would be our expedition treasurer. Robert informed me that we were now a team of five: he and I, Bill Forrest and Dan Larson from the West Ridge team, and Peter Hillary, Sir Edmund Hillary's son, who Robert knew from New Zealand. More of Robert's friends, Tom Hinds and Karen Murgolo, were heading our fund raising effort. Radiating enthusiasm, Robert had no doubt we'd soon be on our way, fully sponsored, to Tibet. Our official moniker was the 1988 American–New Zealand Mount Everest Expedition.

At this stage, we desperately needed more information about Everest's East or Kangshung Face, and to inspect pictures of it. Conveniently, one of the successful summiters from the 1983 American Kangshung Face expedition, George Lowe, lived in Denver. One winter night, we listened to him narrate slides of their epic ascent. Between listening to George's vivid descriptions and brushing up on my "Everest reading," I soon learned why only three expeditions had ever approached the peak from this side.

Known as Everest's "Forgotten Face," the mysterious Kangshung Face on the Tibetan (east-facing) side of Chomolungma presents the mountain's most dangerous aspect. George Mallory and Guy Bullock were the first Europeans to sight and closely inspect the face during the 1921 British Mount Everest reconnaissance—the first-ever expedition to Everest. In a prescient observation, Mallory later wrote that, "other men, less wise, would attempt this way if they would, but, emphatically, it was not for us."

Given Mallory's negative pronouncement, the face's geographic remoteness, and the dearth of any detailed photographs of it, the Kangshung Face lapsed into obscurity and became widely accepted among mountaineers as unclimbable. This neglect lasted some sixty years, until 1980 when American mountaineer Andrew Harvard arrived in the Kama Valley to reinspect the precipices. His findings were surprisingly hopeful. Using big-wall rock climbing techniques, Harvard believed that the massive face—although an extremely daunting and dangerous proposition—was, in fact, climbable. The most obvious and safest route appeared to be up the prominent central rock buttress.

The first American attempt on Everest's Kangshung Face was led by Richard Blum during the 1981 post-monsoon season. The team of nineteen included George Lowe and John Roskelley, America's two best Himalayan mountaineers. No Sherpa climbers were employed. The extremely technical climbing up the initial four-thousand-foot rock buttress rapidly lived up to Harvard's predictions.

Discord among the members, however, added to the team's difficulties. Declaring the climb too dangerous, Roskelley departed early. The remaining climbers persisted. After two months of backbreaking effort, they climbed and fixed ropes up the entire *Lowe Buttress* (as they named their climb), with Lowe, Sue Giller, Gary Bocarde, Dan Reid, Eric Perlman, Geoff Tabin, and Lou Reichardt leading key portions of the route. Some sections featured strenuous, overhanging direct aid climbing on dubious quality rock. The terrain was technically as difficult—or harder—than any previous Himalayan climb, plus subject to great uncontrollable dangers from falling rock and ice.

The route's features and campsites were given names, appropriately, having a "bowling" theme. These included the Bowling Alley and Pinsetter Camp. Helmet Camp at 22,000 feet was situated on the buttress crest. And although several members wanted to push on for the summit, the team had limited reserves after the successful siege of the buttress. With avalanche danger on the upper slopes running high, climbing leader Reichardt called off the attempt.

The follow-up American expedition to Everest's Kangshung Face arrived in the autumn of 1983. Led by James Morrissey, composed of thirteen climbers, this better-organized effort featured a greater concentration of will than the first team. This second expedition also had the advantage of having fixed ropes already strung up the entire *Lowe Buttress*. The hard climbing, essentially, had been done. The remaining labor was to transport enough supplies up to Helmet Camp, establish several higher campsites, and then attempt the summit.

The nightmare of load-carrying up the four-thousand-foot buttress was lessened (but made considerably more complicated) by the team's construction of two elaborate winching systems. Rocket launchers—the same type that fire ropes between ships at sea—were used to string the hauling ropes. John Boyle engineered a motorized pulley system (powered by a five-horse-power gas engine) that hauled eighty-pound loads up the first thousand feet. Higher, on the final eight-hundred-foot vertical rock headwall, a gravity-powered system, using a counterweight of haulbags filled with snow, hauled up more than half a ton of gear and food. Radio communication coordinated the complex logistical movement of climbers and supplies.

Helmet Camp was stocked by September 28. As of October 4, three higher camps were established, at 23,500 feet, 25,000 feet, and 26,000 feet. Finally, on October 8, Carlos Buhler, Kim Momb, and Louis Reichardt, breathing bottled oxygen and climbing through deep snow, reached the lofty 29,028-foot summit, the first climbers to do so via Everest's Kangshung Face. The following day, George Lowe, Jay Cassell, and Dan Reid repeated the ascent, also using bottled oxygen, with Lowe making his ascent virtually alone, far ahead of Cassell and Reid. After a planned third summit attempt was thwarted by storm, the expedition withdrew safely from the mountain—a great success.

Sixty-two years after George Mallory's first sighting of it, Everest's last unclimbed face had been scaled by an American expedition that was, from all accounts, unusually harmonious. Lowe would later write that, "we were lucky having such a cohesive team. Everyone involved reached almost 25,000 feet. In fact, ours has been the only really good big expedition that I know about."

MOUNT EVEREST

KARTSE
(21,490 feet)

Helmet
Camp

1983 American Buttress

The view north across Everest's Kangshung Face, with the profile of the American or Lowe Buttress *on the right* (marked) *and Kartse, climbed by Mallory in 1921, beyond.*

After Tom Hornbein and Willi Unsoeld's 1963 first ascent of the mountain's West Ridge, this was only the second American new route up Mount Everest.

Sitting on a sofa in George Lowe's warm living room, we stared in awe at his all-too-cold and all-too-real photographs. Robert and I were alternately enthralled and terrified by images of thunderous avalanches, overhanging rock cliffs, and teetering ice walls. The twelve-thousand-foot Kangshung Face looked like your worst Gothic nightmare. How could we ever hope to climb this two-mile-high precipice with just a small team, a minimal amount of fixed rope—and without the typical expedition crutches of bottled oxygen, radios, and Sherpa support? "By fair means," as Reinhold Messner always advocated?

Were we certifiably crazy—or might there be another route up the face more suited to the style we envisioned? George clicked the next slide onto the screen. There, in a close-up photo, I thought I saw the answer. Just to the left of the *Lowe Buttress* protruded another buttress, somewhat smaller in size. Although it, too, appeared extremely difficult, I had an immediate hunch "it would go," and that maybe, just maybe, it could be climbed by a small team. I walked up to the screen to have a better look.

"What about this buttress, over on the left?" I asked.

"We didn't give it much consideration," George said. "The avalanches coming down the gully beside it were HUGE." However, I then considered that both of George's Kangshung Face expeditions had taken place during the post-monsoon, or autumn, climbing season. Each summer, monsoon storms deposit a heavy snowpack in the Nepal Himalaya, which exponentially increases the size and danger of subsequent avalanches. Might we find safer conditions on the mountain *during the pre-monsoon season, in the spring,* I wondered, directly after winter's powerful jet stream winds had stripped Everest of excess snow?

I was convinced that the left-hand buttress was our climb. When I explained my reasoning to Robert, he answered that, fortuitously, he'd secured his Everest permit for April and May. The climb's toughest section up the initial rock and ice buttress, I continued, would be concentrated at relatively low altitudes, between nineteen thousand and twenty-three thousand feet. This portion could be fixed with rope for safe passage. The long midsection up a low-angled snowy buttress—although crevasse riddled and, in places, avalanche prone—also looked feasible. Above, once on the South Col, we'd follow the Southeast Ridge and the standard *Hillary-Tenzing Route,* the easiest and most popular way to the summit. And this top section had already been climbed without bottled oxygen!

An avalanche roars down Lhotse's North Face. "Our buttress" and the Kangshung Face are on the right, and the South Col is barely visible at top right. Stephen Venables

Yet I couldn't help but notice that George was shaking his head sideways and whistling under his breath. He clearly thought I was out of my mind. But I really believed—I had a strong gut feeling—that the left-hand buttress could be climbed. I drove home that night to Boulder absolutely elated, and 99.9 percent positive that we'd just stumbled upon a new route up Mount Everest.

The climb's seriousness hit home hard with Dan and Bill. Each were soon to be married. The following morning, they phoned Robert and dropped out. A new route up Everest without the benefit of oxygen or Sherpas was not a project for married men. Most Himalayan expeditions go through personnel changes, so we weren't overly worried. Others would surely want to come.

Robert then invited Jay Smith, another West Ridge alum. One of America's best young alpinists, in 1986, Jay had made the first ascent of the impressive Northeast Ridge of Kangtega (21,932 feet) near Everest. One of Jay's Kangtega partners was a Canadian, Paul Teare. A carpenter, Paul, like Jay, also lived in

Lake Tahoe, California. Each were talented ice climbers, having mastered several of the Canadian Rockies' hardest waterfall ice routes. And Paul had recently soloed the difficult Yosemite Valley ice climb, *The Silver Strand*, unroped.

Although neither Robert nor I knew Paul, we immediately accepted him. A friend of Jay's was a friend of ours. Paul additionally had previous Himalayan experience, on Gangapurna in Nepal. Again, we were five.

To have any hope of climbing a new route up Everest, we obviously needed the strongest possible team. We felt that six climbers would be our optimum number; we also needed a team doctor. Robert invited Miriam Zieman, a medical student from New York City, who we'd met in 1985 when she was trekking to Everest Base Camp. With her adventurous spirit, it didn't take long for Mimi to say she wanted to come with us. Then our fundraisers, Tom and Karen, dropped out, but recommended a friend, Wendy Davis, to take over. A savvy New Yorker, Wendy became our one-woman fundraiser and PR firm. And Joe Blackburn, a professional New York–based photographer became our expedition photographer. A former student of the legendary Ansel Adams, Joe had already been the official photographer of Yosemite National Park.

Our "support team" also grew. These were people who would travel to Base Camp with us, and the list now included: Miklos Pinther, the United Nations head of cartography, who was interested in surveying Everest using satellite measuring technology; rock star Billy Squier (my old helicopter buddy); and Norbu Tenzing Norgay, the eldest son of Tenzing Norgay, Hillary's partner on the first ascent of Everest. I met them all in New York in June, 1987.

While I was in New York City, Kristina phoned from Colorado.

"Oh Ed, I don't know how to say this," she began. Something in her voice sounded very wrong. After a pause, she added: "I just found out about it this morning." Her voice betrayed how upset she was, and I knew it was going to be some terrible news.

"Roger Marshall was killed on Everest last week."

I was speechless. I knew Roger and Ruth had returned to Tibet so that he could again try to solo Everest's North Face. But—Roger dead? I felt a profound mixture of emotions: loss, sadness, and anger. After our 1986 expedition, my relationship with Roger had completely soured. To put it plainly, he was jealous. I had summited; he hadn't. He wouldn't talk to me or give me any of the photos I'd taken. I never told Roger I was returning to Everest in 1988. Now I could only remember the good times that we'd shared, and what Roger had taught me: that climbing alone or in small teams at altitude is possible, but extremely risky.

Although Kristina and I comforted each other, and Ruth, during Roger's memorial service a month later in Colorado, the combined stresses of Kristina's and my own struggle to earn a living, my imminent return to Everest, and my inability to completely commit to her in marriage were all factors fraying at our relationship. By autumn, we'd split up. My single-minded drive to climb as much as possible—and scale Everest—had claimed another relationship.

The Kangshung Face trip, however, seemed to be gaining some momentum. Several publicity ploys were generating interest in our endeavor. The eldest sons of Sir Edmund Hillary and Tenzing Norgay were both on our team—and by a happy coincidence, our Everest climb would occur on the thirty-fifth anniversary of the mountain's first ascent. Accordingly, Robert and Wendy asked John Hunt in England, leader of the 1953 British Everest expedition, to be our honorary leader. This Lord Hunt generously agreed to do—with a small stipulation.

"Since what you are attempting is an anniversary ascent of Everest, which was, after all, a British climb, wouldn't it be more fitting," he politely suggested, "if you had a British mountaineer on your team?"

Of course, he was right, plus we still needed our sixth climber. Luckily, Lord Hunt had just the right fellow in mind. Stephen Venables was a widely experienced Himalayan veteran with impeccable expedition and alpine climbing credentials. Robert phoned Stephen in London and invited him to join us, but for Stephen, it wasn't such an easy decision.

Although lured by the adventure of doing a new route up Everest, a mountain that he had long dreamt of climbing, Stephen had serious reservations about embarking on such a dangerous climb with climbers whom he didn't know. But, as luck would have it, I had rock climbed previously with two of Stephen's regular partners, Dick Renshaw and Choe Brooks. After they assured him that I was "a nice bloke" (coincidentally I'm also half English; my father was born in London), Stephen took the gamble. He joined the expedition in December, 1987, a scant three months before our departure for Asia.

Wendy phoned me almost daily to relate the latest news of impending sponsorship that would catapult us halfway around the world to Tibet. Although she knew relatively little about mountaineering, Wendy was one diligent fundraiser. Still, the money was slow in coming. Then she had an imaginative idea: invite the original sponsors of the 1953 British Mount Everest Expedition to sponsor us. Three companies accepted and became our principal sponsors: Eastman Kodak, Rolex Watch USA, and Burroughs Wellcome Pharmaceuticals. As "Everest '88," we were also the "35th Anniversary Ascent."

And, somewhat humorously, I thought, now that we had a Canadian and a British climber each on board the team, the American–New Zealand Mount Everest Expedition had evolved into a complete misnomer.

But at last it appeared we had a strong enough team. Then the bubble burst in late December. After hints of disillusionment, Jay said he couldn't come because of work obligations. How were we going to climb a new route up Everest with five climbers? Finally we got the really bad news. Peter Hillary also dropped out.

I was shell-shocked. We'd raised our budget, but now we didn't have enough climbers! Peter Athans, also temporarily on the team, had jumped ship to go to K2. And our invites to John Roskelley, David Breashears, Todd Bibler, Mark Hesse, and Tom Dickey were each declined. Their replies began to have a predictable and familiar refrain. The route was "too dangerous," the ava-lanches down the Kangshung Face were "too big," the team was "too small."

"If you survive, give me a call when you get home," Breashears said encouragingly. Another conversation, during a rather somber phone call with Robert, summed things up quite well.

"It looks like we'll just have to go with the four of us: you and I, and Stephen and Paul," he said quietly.

I tried to forestall my growing fears. At the core, I knew that we still had a very good team, but the fundamental question was whether we could stave off the burn-out, illness, and injury that are standard fare on virtually every Himalayan expedition. In the face of such overwhelmingly poor-looking odds, Robert maintained that we could still be successful.

"Lord Hunt told me that if we were going to succeed on Everest, I needed to do three things. Pick people who were experts in their field: good on rock, good on ice, and good at high altitude; assign them their various duties before the expedition began: to organize the food, climbing equipment, and logistics; and finally, above all other considerations, make sure we got along well together."

But that, quite honestly, we had no way of knowing. We'd never all met, let alone climbed together. I'd rock climbed once with Paul in Eldorado Canyon, near Boulder, in September, 1987. On a crystalline autumn day, we ascended the *Yellow Spur,* my favorite Eldorado climb, and one fact had quickly become clear. Paul was about the funniest person I'd ever met. With Paul on the team, we could be assured of laughter even during our darkest moments.

But: Robert had never climbed with Paul, and none of us had ever roped up with Stephen! In January, 1988, Stephen flew over to attend an expedition

Which mountain is highest ? Makalu is on the right; Everest's Kangshung Face (with cloud) rises in the center. Das Studio / American Alpine Club Library

press conference in New York City, where he met Robert, Wendy, Mimi, Joe, Miklos, and Norbu. In what was perhaps Wendy's finest hour, she orchestrated a dizzying series of press and photo sessions: the climbers receiving their watches from the president of Rolex; the team holding the United Nations flag at Rockefeller Center; then a visit to the Explorers Club headquarters. To top off the week, Robert and Norbu appeared on *The Today Show* with Jane Pauley.

In retrospect, although our planned Everest ascent was shaping up as an extreme endeavor (and *an extremely stupid one,* most people thought), I honestly don't think we were completely crazy. Behind our hair-brained scheme lay a modicum of reasoning and sanity. We each had previous Himalayan experience, plus our individual climbing skills meshed perfectly. Stephen was our versatile Himalayan expert, veteran of a dozen expeditions. Robert's strength was his yak-like, bullheaded ability to plow up endless Himalayan snowfields, what he termed "high-altitude wallowing." Paul, our ice man, could hang suspended from vertical ice for hours on end. And I was the rock technician, the big wall specialist equipped with rurps, bashies, skyhooks, and the knowledge of how to use these gadgets. I don't think Robert necessarily knew it at the time, but he'd picked a team that perfectly fit Lord Hunt's success model.

After back-to-back Everest trips, I was sure my third trip to the mountain would etch the year 1988 in stone. As we prepared to leave for Tibet, each of us, I think, felt this sentiment quite keenly, that our Kangshung Face expedition could be the one climb to mark our entire lives—provided, as David Breashears had said, we survived it.

Thankfully the months of effort and organizing drew to a close. With Rob Dorival, our nutritional expert, I packed enough food to feed eight people for four months, plus ropes, tents, and other expedition equipment, into seventy identical blue plastic barrels. (A twenty-page computer list kept the contents straight.) The barrels were then airfreighted to Beijing by Lindblad Travel, Norbu's employer. The night before leaving Boulder, I ritually sorted rock and ice climbing gear, cameras, lenses, batteries, street clothes, climbing clothes, nutritional and vitamin supplements, medical supplies, a Sony Walkman and cassettes, blank diaries, paperbacks, passport, traveler's checks, and plane tickets into neat piles on the floor. Then I stowed the whole lot—all the possessions I'd need for four months—into two large duffel bags.

Two months previously, I'd begun to date a woman I'd met where I worked, at an indoor rock climbing wall in a local recreation center. Randa Hessel loved to hike, but she was not a climber, which to me was actually a plus. We'd known each other only a relatively short time, and as yet I hadn't mustered the courage to broach the subjects of how dangerous, and possibly fatal, climbing could be. I could see no feasible, gentle way to tell Randa about Lauren's death; moreover, if Randa had known about that tragedy, she would have been deathly afraid for me as I prepared to embark on my Kangshung Face expedition. So, it was due in part to her lack of knowledge about climbing and mountaineering that Randa, I think, gave me her willing and loving support. And I, not without sensitivity, felt caught in a painful dilemma and weighed down by my tragic past. I felt guilty for not telling Randa about Lauren and her death, and caddish for purposefully not informing Randa of the life-and-death nature of our expedition to Everest.

I was going to Tibet to attempt a new route up Mount Everest with three partners and no bottled oxygen. Oh.

Randa's curiosity finally got the better of her about an hour before I left for the airport in Denver. "What happens if you break your arm or leg?" she asked. After an awkward silence, I assured her that there was a hospital nearby— a considerable stretching of the truth.

"Well, I know you have to go. This climb is important," she replied.

It was of great importance to me. I was returning to Everest because I loved the high mountains. Climbing was my life. Ever since returning from Tibet a year and a half earlier, I'd been craving an adventure of the same or preferably an even greater magnitude. Himalayan vistas and mountains were lodged in my soul, and aspirations of vertical rock climbs no longer satisfied me. I wanted more high-altitude mountaineering, and most of all, to live and experience a "pure" adventure—a challenge whose outcome I could not predict.

A new route up Everest with a team of four. What could possibly be more adventurous and challenging than that? Not very much; perhaps going to the moon? Randa and I said our good-byes, and planned (rather optimistically, again denying the danger) to meet in Hawaii after the climb was over.

* * * * * * * * * * * * * *

My sister Susan and my parents met me in Boston. The next morning, I dropped my father at the train station on his way to work. It was the last time I'd see him before I left for Asia. Standing beside the train tracks in a light drizzle, we had an upbeat talk about achieving goals, *attaining and fulfilling ambitions in life other than climbing,* and about coming home in one piece. That was also important! Then we hugged, and Dad wished me luck.

Although my father once admonished me in a letter that he didn't want his son to be "a playboy living in the shadow of the mountains," I now appreciated how incredibly supportive he and my stepmother Dorothea had been of my climbing ambitions over the years. First as a teenager, then in college, and more recently as I'd tried to earn a living from climbing, they had always been there for me. The road hadn't been an easy one. At thirty-one years old, I was unmarried, of slender resources, and had opted for the uncertain life of a mountaineer and rock climber. I had no regrets about my path, however, because doing what I loved to earn a living consistently overshadowed my desire just to earn money.

Everest the mountain and Everest the symbol had worked its magic not only on me, but interestingly, also on my parents. Ever since I'd gone on my first Everest expedition, my relationship with them had steadily improved. Climbing in the Himalaya had somehow legitimized all the wayward, wandering years of my early twenties, when I rock climbed across the United States and Europe, hitchhiking from one cliff to the next, sleeping in fields and on friend's floors, climbing nonstop, living life on the edge. The fact that I had now climbed on Mount Everest had miraculously and tangibly altered my parent's view of my life. I was no longer a climbing bum; I was a mountaineer.

Fritz Wiessner in the Elbsandsteingebirge, Dresden, East Germany, 1973.
Photograph by Steve Roper

Later that day I drove to Stowe, Vermont, to visit an elderly man who had greatly inspired me. Now nearly eighty-eight, Fritz Wiessner was a German-American rock climber and mountaineer. He was also the first man in history to climb for an extended period above eight thousand meters (26,247 feet) without bottled oxygen—for four days and nights—a feat he accomplished on K2 in 1939. Since then, Fritz had staunchly advocated man's ability to climb at high altitude without large cumbersome expeditions and the aid of oxygen.

Fritz and I had become friends during the past several years. I frequently asked his advice on Himalayan climbing and training. We had also rock climbed together, first when Fritz was eighty-five years old at his beloved Shawangunks in New York, then a year later in Eldorado Canyon in Colorado. Sadly, in the spring of 1986, he had suffered the first of several crippling strokes. Now partially paralyzed, he was confined to a wheelchair.

Sitting upstairs in his exercise room, Fritz, his wife Muriel, and I watched the Winter Olympics on television as we ate dinner. Fritz's gymnastic rings hung motionless from the ceiling. His bar bells lay silent on the closet floor. We talked, watched the ice skating, then Fritz lost interest in his meal and slumped in his chair. It seemed he'd fallen asleep, but when Kathy, his nurse, came to straighten him, he was no longer breathing.

"Fritz! Fritz!" she yelled, shaking him. Fritz's face was white and sweaty.

"Phone the hospital, Muriel! Quick, Ed. Grab his ankles!"

Panic energized me as we lifted Fritz into bed. Kathy vigorously shook him and shouted his name. Fritz's eyes popped open.

"Who am I?" Kathy demanded. Fritz twisted up his face.

"What a ridiculous question to ask me!" he bellowed, just like his old self. We all laughed, relieved that he was okay, but it had been a close call, too close.

I shook my head. Why would Fritz almost die now, for heaven's sake?

I tape-recorded Fritz twice the following day. It was hard work digging under his thick German skin. Though specific details were difficult to recall, occasionally the years fell away from his face, Fritz would warm to the occasion, and vividly recall memories of climbs he had done, often up to fifty years ago. His face would become alert, its furrowed lines of age moving happily with the pleasant recollections of his youth.

Then, at last, after much conversation, Fritz paused. For several minutes, he held his chin in one hand, and gazed silently out the window. I noticed he was watching a flock of birds fluttering amongst the tree tops. I read his thoughts. How he wished he could leave his worn-out body and join them! I asked Fritz if I might have a piece of his climbing gear for good luck on Everest. I found a piton and a carabiner. It was time to go. I was flying to New Jersey the next day.

I knelt beside Fritz in his wheelchair and I assured him that I'd try my best to climb Everest without oxygen. In the past five years, Fritz had taught me a great deal, and not just about climbing—but about living a full life, about the joys of raising a family. Beyond all his renowned exploits as a rock climber and a mountaineer, Fritz Wiessner was a man of tremendous personal integrity and inner strength. He'd never quit the struggle for excellence, and now Nature, his friend and adversary during a long and fruitful life, had nearly run her course. I hoped my teammates and I could also prove, as Fritz had on K2, what positive thought, dedication to a goal, and will power could achieve. After saying good-bye, I drove back to my parent's house in the rain. And I never saw Fritz again.

* * * * * * * * * * * * * *

At LaGuardia Airport, Paul Teare strode out of the crowd, hand extended. Ellen, Joe Blackburn's wife, drove us into "the City"—New York. Pre-expedition panic had reached full throttle. Paul and I were flying to Kathmandu via Frankfurt and New Delhi on February 20. Joe, Mimi, and the support team, Miklos, Norbu, Rob and Wendy, were flying to Beijing to rendezvous with Robert and Sandy Wylie, a New Zealander friend of Robert's. Paul and I would meet Stephen in Kathmandu, plus pick up Pasang Norbu, who was coming again this year as our *Sirdar.*

Departure. Heaving five monstrously heavy duffels into an airport limo at Joe's Connecticut home. Sharing hugs with Joe, Ellen, and their young daughter Claire. "See you guys in Tibet in a week or two," Joe said.

"Where is Daddy going, Claire?" Ellen prodded.

"Hima-waya," she answered.

The Pan Am terminal at Kennedy International was a mob scene. Paul tossed a ninety-pound duffel bag up onto the scale. The attendant's eyes bulged.

"You'll have to pay for this," she said.

"We have an authorization letter for excess baggage," we said.

"This letter is no good," she snapped. Could we see her supervisor?

Paul soon corralled him: "Hello, sir? My friend and I are members of a Mount Everest climbing expedition," Paul began politely. (Hadn't I heard this line in other airport terminals before?) "We have permission from Pan Am for excess baggage." Paul then produced the infamous "letter of authorization."

Just then Scott Morris, a Pan Am service rep, happened by. Paul repeated the monologue for his benefit, and thrust forward "the letter." It happened to be folded in thirds. Paul directed him to the pertinent lines: "Approval has been given for one extra bag, apiece. (Norbu is carrying the letter of authorization.)"

"Who's Norbu?" Mr. Morris asked predictably.

"Norbu Tenzing is the son of Tenzing Norgay, Sir Edmund Hillary's partner on the first ascent of Mount Everest," Paul beamed, quickly adding: "Norbu is a member of our expedition."

Mr. Morris's interest was peaked, so to speak.

"And your sponsors are . . . ?"

"American Express, Kodak—and Rolex," I said, flashing my new watch.

"Is Pan Am sponsoring you also?" Mr. Morris queried.

"I was told that Pan Am gave us reduced fares," I said truthfully.

"Come this way," said Mr. Morris.

Paul and I towed an oversized duffel to a scale, then loaded it and four others. Mr. Morris tagged them, and Paul and I watched like proud parents as our little bundles disappeared down the chute toward Asia. We thanked our benefactor profusely, and later, sitting in the plane, Paul casually reread "the letter."

"Oh my god, look at this!" he screamed into my ear. "I swear, it was innocent!"

The folded letter had concealed the small, but rather important fact that the passengers who were authorized to have extra baggage were, in fact, Norbu and the members of the support team, who were flying to Beijing on CAAC, the Chinese Airlines! Paul hurriedly flipped to the page detailing our itinerary. There was no permission for any extra baggage. It was an honest mistake. The folded letter, the Hillary-Tenzing connection, and the Rolexes, had won the day.

From Frankfurt, Germany, we continued on to New Delhi. Many passengers were Indian citizens returning home. Sitting amongst the consecutive rows of turbaned heads, Paul and I felt like the proverbial goldfish in the fishbowl as we prepared to reenter Asia, the land of mystery.

In New Delhi we were met by the honorable Mr. G.P. Singh from Mercury Travels. We were *only* two hours late, and it was *only* 3 A.M., yet the indefatigable Mr. Singh could hardly contain his exuberance. Everything was "sir" and excited and exclamatory: "Pleased to meet you, sir!" "Right this way, sir!"

The night air felt cool and refreshing. We jammed the duffels into and on top of a dilapidated taxi and chugged off to our hotel. Everyone in India, in fact, seemed eager and officious; the red-uniformed hotel doorman (complete with ostrich-feather-plumed hat) jumped immediately to attention and saluted us.

Paul Teare—International Man of Mystery—in Delhi.

"Good eeevening, sir! Yes, sir! How nice to see you, sir!"

Mr. Singh would return at precisely 1 P.M. We fell into bed. It was February 22 . . . wasn't it? After flying halfway around the world, west to east, crossing so many time zones, we'd lived two days in under one.

Laboriously we restarted ourselves with caffeine, while outside it was just another hot day in India. Mr. Singh brought bad news. Our Kathmandu flight was delayed till 6 P.M. because of bad weather. We taxied to Indira Gandhi International Airport. Paul assumed command at the Royal Nepal Airlines check in. Their baggage allowance was twenty kilos per passenger. We had over *two hundred* kilos! This time Paul chose the direct approach: bribery.

"How would you like to earn some extra money for you and your family?" he whispered discreetly to the attendant.

"I put it right-in-pocket," Paul continued in an exquisitely hushed voice, while with his best sleight of hand, he slipped invisible rupee notes into his breast pocket. The attendant imperceptibly shook his head no, then rolled his eyes in the direction of his supervisor who was standing nearby. But gears were spinning furiously inside the baggage man's head. This was easy money! Paul merely shrugged his shoulders, and we retreated.

Eventually we paid the baggage man a twenty-dollar "fee." Our five duffel bags were checked in; none were weighed. The supervisor was conspicuously absent. Hoisting our nearly one-hundred-pound duffels, the baggage man groaned as his eyes bulged out of their sockets. Our baggage charges came to an arbitrary fifty-seven dollars. But later, when the announcement came that we could clear customs, Paul's new friend magically reappeared. Our bags were "very, very heavy." Now it was a thirty-dollar "fee." A deal was a deal in Asia—unless you thought you could get a little more. Being good sports, we paid.

Sitting in yet another airport transit lounge, Paul observed: "Gee, it's getting dark outside. Time to wake up."

* * * * * * * * * * * * *

Peering out the plane window, I noticed clustered flecks of yellow lights signaling our proximity to Tribhuvan International Airport. The plane's engines droned. We descended through jarring turbulence, and the Himalayan earth swept up to meet us. "Welcome to Nepal" read a mahogany sign. Long forgotten scents in the night air refreshed me. At customs, Paul unzipped a duffel for a cursory inspection, and the official waved us through the exit to a clamoring throng of taxi drivers.

Mukund, our man from Mountain Travel, drove us along the pot-holed roads into sleepy Kathmandu. Faceless night people strolled dusty sidewalks; I felt like a time traveler returning home. The van's horn sounded. A figure pushed open the recalcitrant metal gate. It had been three years since I had stayed at the Tibet Guest House on my Everest West Ridge Expedition, but the same young man, Tsiting, was working the front desk. He greeted me warmly, like the proverbial lost lamb who at long last had stumbled home.

At dawn, I walked to the Guest House's rooftop terrace and was overcome by an incredibly strong feeling of deja vu. Visions of packing up for Everest in 1985 caught me completely off guard. I realized, too, that Kathmandu would never be like it was on my first visit, but I was overjoyed to have returned. To the east, the rising sun tinted the foggy clouds with pink. And overhead, black crows cawed and whirled in the gray sky of dawn. Swayambhunath's gold stupa crowned Kathmandu's western hillock, and strings of prayer flags fluttering from nearby rooftops created goodness as they fluttered in the breeze.

Paul and I had long lists of errands to run. We also hoped to locate Stephen Venables. We'd seen his picture once! In the hotel lobby we met Pasang Norbu, my friend and *Sirdar* on Roger Marshall's Everest expedition. Pasang's gold front tooth still gleamed. And when I told Pasang that he hadn't grown an inch, all four foot ten inches of him chortled heartily.

At Atlas Trekking in the heart of Thamel, Kathmandu's trekking shop district, we met the proprietor, Mr. Hari Har Acharya. Hari Har wore a pastel-colored Hindu skullcap. Mild mannered, he was nonetheless a shrewd Nepali businessman who knew the value of American hundred-dollar bills and the myriad ways to obtain them. I paid out the money we owed for Pasang to come with us, and we diligently double-checked our equipment-still-needed and food-to-buy lists.

Later, back at the Tibet Guest House, Paul announced excitedly:

"He's here!"

I guessed correctly. Venables had arrived. Without having the faintest idea of where we were lodged, or where Atlas Trekking

Pasang Norbu Sherpa was again our Sirdar.

was, Stephen had walked the streets of Thamel hoping to spot one of us. He'd been told of a good place to change money, went into a courtyard, looked up, and there it was: Atlas Trekking. After Hari Har directed him to the Tibet Guest House, Stephen literally bumped into Paul on the street—deeming him to be an American by his omnipresent baseball cap. Stephen stopped by our room several minutes later. Tall and slender, wearing wire rim glasses, and showing a trace of thinning hair, he was friendly, funny, and eminently British.

"Ronnie Faux and Dick Renshaw both send you their best," Stephen said as we shook hands. "Did you know you were even mentioned in an article in the London *Times,* 'Mr. Edward Webster'?" he chuckled with obvious amusement.

The previous week, in Bombay, India, Stephen had been a guest speaker at the sixty-fifth anniversary of the founding of the Himalayan Club. The famed American mountaineer and world expert on high-altitude human physiology, Dr. Charles Houston, also was in attendance. Stephen confided our plans.

"What? You're mad to try that!" Houston had exclaimed.

"But just look at Boardman and Tasker," Stephen answered in our defense. "When they set off to try Changabang in India in 1976, just the two of them, everyone said they were crazy. Yet they succeeded on a very difficult route. Small teams are commonplace in the Himalaya today, relatively speaking."

Like other athletes, mountaineers also have something of a penchant for trying to outperform each other. A noteworthy ascent might be a tough climb done by a small team, such as Boardman and Tasker's two-man Changabang expedition, or it might be a solo ascent, or a highly technical and challenging new route. On Everest, the longest-standing stylistic debate has surrounded the use, or non-use, of bottled oxygen. The British mountaineers who first attempted Everest in the 1920s endlessly debated the merits of using supplementary oxygen ("English air," the Sherpas called it). How high could humans survive in the Earth's rarefied atmosphere? Very high. On June 3, 1924, Major Edward F. Norton climbed to 28,126 feet without oxygen on Everest's North Face, establishing a high-altitude record that stood for twenty-eight years.

When Everest was finally scaled by Edmund Hillary and Tenzing Norgay, using bottled oxygen, on May 29, 1953, "the oxygen debate" did anything but end. Could Everest, people wondered, be climbed completely "unaided"? On May 8, 1978, South Tyrolean mountaineer Reinhold Messner and the Austrian ace Peter Habeler finally ascended Everest without supplementary oxygen, refuting once and for all many a scientist's claim that physiologically it could not be done.

Of the roughly two hundred people who had successfully reached the summit of Mount Everest by the end of 1987, only twenty had done so without breathing bottled oxygen. No British mountaineer had yet to accomplish this near-superhuman feat, and only one American, Larry Nielson, had achieved an oxygenless ascent. Nielson followed in the footsteps of his oxygen-breathing partners, yet his climb from the South Col to Everest's summit on May 7, 1983 still nearly cost him his life. Frostbitten, stumbling, and temporarily blind, he was carried partway back down to their high camp on the Col by a partner.

A commemorative expedition postcard from Messner and Habeler's first "oxygenless" ascent of Mount Everest in 1978. Author's collection

We would not bring any bottled oxygen up Everest's Kangshung Face. Our reasons for disdaining oxygen were partly aesthetic, but mostly practical. Foremost, we wanted to see if we could climb Everest unaided and in good style; it was both a personal and ethical challenge to climb without the heavy encumbrance of oxygen bottles. We also were not bringing any Sherpas to help us carry loads—standard practice on 95 percent of all expeditions to Mount Everest. Logistically, this lack of hired manpower made it virtually impossible for us to carry two twenty-pound oxygen bottles apiece (in addition to food, sleeping bags, tents, etc.) to the South Col, at twenty-six thousand feet, where most teams begin breathing bottled oxygen. But climbing a new route up the world's highest mountain with a team of only four, and without bottled oxygen, without Sherpas, and without radios? This wasn't Changabang, a twenty-two-thousand-foot peak. This was Everest, the single mountain on earth that exceeds twenty-nine thousand feet in elevation. Plainly, my teammates and I wanted to face the ultimate challenge in mountaineering: of climbing Mount Everest by a new and untried route—and "by fair means," Messner's famous dictum—even if we failed.

At the American Embassy commissary in Kathmandu, we hoped to meet my West Ridge teammate, Rodney Korich, for dinner. He wasn't there, but we gorged on air-lifted American hamburgers and Heineken beer. I was relieved when Stephen relished the cuisine. I'd selected all of our American-style food.

Next came an event which we anticipated and dreaded in equal measure. Kathmandu's Reuters correspondent and "gal-about-town" expedition historian, Elizabeth Hawley, arrived to interview us about our quest. A legendary figure in Himalayan climbing circles, the middle-aged Miss Hawley was something of a free spirit. She did, after all, drive the only yellow VW bug in Kathmandu!

Miss Hawley informed us that there would be a large-scale siege on Everest this spring. The Chinese-Japanese-Nepalese Friendship Expedition, and the Australian Bicentennial Everest Expedition would crowd the Khumbu Glacier Base Camp with over 250 people. The so-called Asian Friendship team, with its one hundred climbers, 150 support members and journalists, and a $7,000,000 budget, planned to make not only the first live video transmission from Everest's summit, but the first-ever south-to-north and north-to-south traverses of the peak. Fortunately, the team would be split in half, one group attempting the *South Col Route* in Nepal while the rest swarmed over Tibet's *North Col Route*.

"It's going to be a zoo," she lamented. "And it's the Australians I feel sorry for. I think they're in real danger of being trampled to death."

Above: Question and answer with the indomitable Liz Hawley. Right: Morning prayer.

We filled out Miss Hawley's information forms with a sense of duty and honor, entering answers to a variety of categories to be checked if appropriate, such as: Single, Single—living with girlfriend, Married, Divorced. What these had to do with climbing talent, I wasn't sure, but perhaps Miss Hawley was searching for other types of prowess—or newsworthy scandal. Next we listed our personal tally of summits reached, by year, by route, and with whom.

Then, only after carefully scanning the room for any eavesdropping bystanders, did we describe for Miss Hawley the technical difficulties of our planned-for Everest Kangshung Face route, and Paul stealthily produced our small collection of route photographs. Impressed either by our phenomenal daring or obvious stupidity, Miss Hawley wished us sincere good luck before rushing off with her freshly inked personalized dossiers.

There were always more errands—and more emergencies. Hari Har revealed that neither Stephen nor Pasang could obtain visas from Kathmandu's Chinese consulate—unless the Sports Federation in Beijing gave their approval. Hari Har had telexed Beijing with this request. Tibet had been closed to individual travel since the October, 1987, freedom demonstrations in Lhasa.

It was imperative that Stephen and Pasang be granted visas, otherwise they would not be allowed into Tibet, and the trip would be finished before it started. All Himalayan expeditions, we veterans had learned, are actually composed of a continuous string of last-minute crises. Getting steamed up about every glitch wasn't worth it. You'd run out of energy for climbing the mountain!

Meanwhile, we still needed some more gear. We found it at Tsering Dolkar's trekking shop in Thamel. Tsering, a beautiful young Tibetan woman who spoke flawless English, had an international reputation amongst mountaineers, since many had been smitten by her enchanting gaze. Paul now presented her with a gift, one of our high fashion, periwinkle-blue, Everest '88 expedition pile jackets.

"It's powder blue, not periwinkle," Tsering corrected.

With most of our shopping and packing done, I slipped out at sunrise the next morning to retrace the solitary walk I'd made in 1985 to the Bishnumati River and Swayambhunath (also commonly called the Monkey Temple). Little had changed. I lingered, taking my time, looking, absorbing, not judging, feeling the pulse of Asian life flow around me. Young girls gathered at a pump, laughing; a boy was nuzzling his puppy; a lone woman harvested cauliflower in her mist-enshrouded field. At the foot of the temple steps, three Tibetan women prostrated themselves in devotion and prayer while nearby several young men grunted and groaned and pushed their stalled car. East meets west.

Devotions, butter candles, and prayer flags at the Monkey Temple, Swayambhunath.

I walked up the stone steps to the temple courtyard. Worshippers paced reverently clockwise around Swayambhunath's white-washed, gold-crowned *stupa*. Cradling her swaddled babe, a young woman smiled warmly at me. I photographed her from a discreet distance, not wanting to break our rapport. Instead of turning, she held her baby up, as though presenting him to the world—then pulled the bright scarf off his head. The sun shone on them both.

"Namaste," I breathed, letting my camera drop, folding my hands together in a greeting of respect.

Other interesting characters peopled the Monkey Temple's courtyard: a slightly insane, elderly Tibetan man wearing plastic neon-colored sunglasses; a young girl wrapped in a dirty cotton sheet who stood below a snarling snow lion statue; and the reverent Buddhist and Hindu temple priests, lighting prayer candles, their wax-covered fingers clutching stacks of rupee notes, fees from the many oblations. I lit several candles, too, spun prayer wheels, and whispered prayers for health, good luck, and our safe return from Chomolungma.

When I later told Stephen about my visit to the Monkey Temple, he remarked, "Oh, I've got plenty of good luck charms along to keep me alive."

Paul and I returned to Tsering's shop to pay for our equipment. Tsering had visited America, and I discovered we had many mutual friends, including Roger Marshall. "Why did Roger rush back to Everest; do you know?" Tsering queried. I knew that Roger had felt driven to return to solo Everest by his own not insubstantial ego, his view of himself as a "professional mountaineer," and the prospects that his financial sponsorship would dry up if he didn't succeed. Climbing Everest alone would be the crowning achievement of any mountaineer's career, and could be parlayed with relative ease into a lifetime meal ticket—but clearly the risks were as substantial as, or greater than, the rewards. I explained this to Tsering, who nodded in understanding.

No doubt Roger had carried plenty of good luck charms, too. Yet did his fatal fall down Everest negate their efficacy? It seemed so. Roger's death made me revisit the concept that God, or life itself, was fundamentally unfair, and that Himalayan mountaineers lived and died by the slender luck of the draw. What may or may not happen to us on Everest in the coming months had a subconscious arbitrariness about it. But superstition is a hard belief to kill, so Robert, Stephen, Paul and I all carried an eclectic assortment of charms and relics. Strung around my neck were Buddhist blessing cords, a Dalai Lama pendant, and a St. Christopher medallion. You could never have too much luck—or appeal to too many religions—when your goal was a new route up Everest.

You can buy just about any type of mountaineering equipment in one of Kathmandu's many trekking shops—even bottles of oxygen.

At another shop in Thamel, I bought a single bottle of oxygen. It would be used for medical purposes only, if need be, at Advanced Base. For a variety of reasons, we had decided not to carry any bottled oxygen up on the mountain.

After dividing and packing our equipment and food into thirty-kilo porter loads, we still couldn't decide when to leave town. We didn't want to reach Shekar in Tibet, our rendezvous, too early and have to wait for Robert and the support team, who were traveling there from Beijing. Any number of delays could hamper their traverse of China and Tibet. And having already been once to Shekar, I assured Paul and Stephen that it was preferable to arrive later than early. "One, two days Shekar, okay," Pasang agreed, "four, five days, not okay!" The dust and atrocious Chinese food in Tibet made it preferable to dine well in Kathmandu, rest, and then sprint for the border.

Waiting for Pasang and Stephen's Chinese visas to arrive, we had to delay another day. Then, miraculously, Chinese officialdom relented, their passports and visas arrived, and theoretically we were clear to enter Tibet. Finally able to take a break, Paul, Stephen, and I bicycled a dozen miles to the city of Bhaktapur, inhaling so much diesel smoke along the way that we nearly ruined our lungs.

Renowned for its intricate (and sometimes erotic) wood carvings, Bhaktapur is one of the Kathmandu Valley's three ancient capitals. After drowning our thirsts with bottles of Coke, we strolled the stone courtyards until music attracted our ears. A Hindu band of drummers and a flutist were playing, and a four-year-old boy was dancing. The band encouraged Stephen and me to join in. We did, and were rewarded by the ritual placement of a *tika,* a paint dot dabbed in the middle of our foreheads, to bring us more good luck. Returning to Thamel, we raced along on our single-speed bikes, trying to burn out our legs. And in a rare streak of competitiveness amongst our merry trio, Paul won.

At the Buddhist temple of Bodhnath, we received our pre-climb blessing from the frail Drew *Rinpoche* from the Pangboche Monastery. I'd been blessed in an identical ceremony with him before Everest in 1985, but this year I found the sense of ceremony lacking. One by one, we approached the elderly man, clasping a hundred-rupee donation within a *kata.* Accepting it, he draped the scarf over our heads and gave us each another blessing cord.

Afterwards, walking down an alley to have tea with Pasang and a friend he'd bumped into, we lined up and urinated into the filthiest, rankest-smelling ditch imaginable. In Asia, such is the commonplace mixing of the sacred and the profane, the spirit and the sewer. One minute you can experience the holiest of the Holy, and the next be gagging from the stench of human and animal waste.

We sat down in a tea house not a hundred yards from the ditch. Not too smart. After watching the kitchen boy rinse four "dirty" cups out with his black fingers under a stream of "clean" water coming from a wall spigot, I was aghast

Ed biking back from Bhaktapur. Stephen Venables

when Paul and Stephen ordered tea. Paul's cup came first. Stephen's cup was still being "washed." I motioned to Paul to watch the sanitation process. His face turned gray. Unfortunately, he'd already taken a sip.

"Um, you can cancel my tea," said Stephen, ever so politely.

*   *   *   *   *   *   *   *   *   *   *   *   *

We decided to leave early on March 1. Two VW vans would take us to the Tibetan border. The excitement of our departure was tangible as one of my Colorado climbing friends, Tom Dickey, and his girlfriend Susan Mitchell gave us each *katas* for luck. Tom, Susan, kayaker Arlene Burns, and a Texas tourist who could hardly believe we were three "Everesters" saw us off. Vowing to return alive, we bid farewell to our friends, and to the staff at the Tibet Guest House.

Surprisingly, Tibet is only a one-day drive north of Kathmandu. The dusty journey traverses some of the most convoluted countryside imaginable, zigzagging up, over, and down Himalayan foothills, through villages, and past acres of terraced fields before dropping down yet another series of tortured switchbacks into the next valley. Rounding one such corner we stopped to

Departure for Everest. Would you buy a used car from one of these guys? Tom Dickey

inspect the twisted carcass of the Lucky bus, so its destination sign read. The bus had plunged off a hairpin and wrapped itself around a large pine. A local informed us it hadn't been that bad of a crash. Only three people died.

Relaxing in the VW, we blasted the Rolling Stones and the Eurythmics as loud as possible on the cassette player, while continuously praising our own driver's skill. Paul and I hadn't yet realized Stephen's aversion to rock music, but this morning, energized by our departure, he didn't seem to mind. Arriving at a fork in the road, we turned left, north toward Tibet. To reach the Kama Valley and Everest's East Face, we had to make a tremendous loop, driving north along the Friendship Highway and *across* the Himalaya, then east over the Tibetan plateau, and finally south to the secluded village of Kharta. Here we'd begin our on-foot approach to the Kama Valley and Everest's mysterious Kangshung Face.

The Chinese constructed the Friendship Highway between 1964 and 1966 to connect Lhasa with Kathmandu. For the first time it became possible to drive across Asia from Beijing to Nepal's capital. But the road had repeatedly been destroyed by landslides, and now boasted a well-deserved reputation for unreliability. Several sections were wiped out in 1987, and the Nepalese Army was

The end of the road. Two porters prepare to cross the flood ravaged Bhote Kosi River.

currently blasting a new roadbed, considerably higher than the original track, parts of which were still visible. The way I saw it, the new road just gave our VW van farther to roll before splashing into the river! There were no guard rails.

Crossing over the Sun Kosi River, we forked left toward the village of Lamosangu, following the banks of the Bhote Kosi, one of several Himalayan rivers that bisect the range, flowing south from the arid Tibetan plateau all the way to Nepal's lush lowlands. A tremendous flood of the Bhote Kosi washed out the highway on June 30, 1987, just downstream from the Nepalese town of Barabise. Although the flood claimed many lives and homes, the disaster also had a positive effect, since local porters now had to be hired to transport all loads across the washout. The once four-hour drive from Kathmandu to Kodari, the Nepalese border post, now required a full day's journey.

The vehicles halted. Thirty feet ahead, the Friendship Highway had been chewed away by the raging river. It was time to hike. Porters appeared miraculously. Pasang and Mukund kept watchful eyes on the loads while Stephen, Paul, and I interspersed ourselves amongst the porter train as we hiked single file to Barabise. It was difficult to keep track of the loads since every fifteen

Traffic in Kodari at Nepal-Tibet border: "Do it right the first time, come to Burger King."

Schoolgirls on the trail near Barabise.

minutes the porters rested at another tea house. But turtling along, last as usual, I enjoyed the marvelous scenery as we strolled through the lush and elevated green-terraced fields.

Contrarily, Barabise was without doubt the dirtiest, smelliest, foulest place I've ever been. Human and animal feces dotted the pavement, and as we stood broiling under a fierce noonday sun, the stench of urine was overpowering. Two ancient taxis arrived amidst a crush of curious locals, as did our porters, who eventually trickled in one by one. I prayed that Pasang and Mukund had the situation under control in this shifting sea of humanity and filth.

We escaped in the taxis, driving directly into a deep, V-notched gorge. Vertical stone walls loomed overhead, while higher still, unlikely hamlets balanced upon isolated earthen terraces hundreds of feet above the Bhote Kosi River. All traces of greenery thinned as we continued to head north and approached Tibet, with its characteristic dry, lunar landscape. Gold-colored grass hummocks soon dominated the hillsides.

At Kodari, the stony gorge of the Bhote Kosi is spanned by the ungainly concrete-and-steel Friendship Bridge, the port of entry into Tibet. Paul assured the officials that we were *the* American–New Zealand Mount Everest Expedition, and miraculously we expediently passed through Nepalese customs. Fortunately, no one questioned why we were one Sherpa, one Canadian, one Englishman, and one American. The Everest magic was still working.

Paul waiting to clear customs in Kodari.

Back outside in Kodari's makeshift plywood outpost, things were nothing short of surreal. First, while we'd been waiting to clear customs, we were astonished to see a Burger King semi-trailer come crawling by—evidently it had become trapped on this section of the Friendship Highway by landslides above and below the town. Then, our actual crossing into Tibet resembled some bizarre reenactment of a Cold War spy swap between East and West Berlin. Mukund approached, and loudly commanded me to go first, "and you must watch the porters and loads. Go!"

I hadn't pictured coming into Tibet in quite this manner. Halfway across the drab concrete bridge was a painted red stripe—and with one step I left the Kingdom of Nepal—and entered Chinese-controlled Tibet. I'd walked another thirty feet when a rifle-toting, teenage Chinese border guard began shouting, "Passport! Visa!" I had caught him sleeping. He scrutinized my passport, and returned it without a word. Minutes later, Paul, Stephen, and Pasang followed me across the frontier bridge. Enthusiastically displaying his most maniacal grin, Paul shot me a victorious thumbs-up before he and Stephen hurried to join the porters up ahead, while Pasang and I leisurely brought up the rear.

Stephen and Paul—and the Friendship Bridge at the Nepal-Tibet border.

The dirt road to Zhangmu and the Chinese customs checkpoint zigzagged up a steep hillside. Currently, it too was impassable because of numerous landslides. Instead of taking the road, we hiked directly up a rough trail linking one switchback to the next. Many of our porters walked barefoot. One had cut his foot; red splotches of blood dotted the way. The inevitable green and yellow globs of porter spit also caught my attention, and I averted my eyes.

After Roger's death, I hadn't been sure if an Everest invitation would interest Pasang. Then I noticed that today Pasang was wearing one of Roger's Everest Solo T-shirts, with its quotation from Goethe: "Boldness has beauty and power and vision." I asked Pasang if he'd expected me to invite him back to Everest.

"Yes, I excited," Pasang answered. I felt relieved. "I want to come back to Chomolungma. And I happy to be with you, Paul, and Stephen."

Entering Zhangmu, we walked past wood shanties perched on stilts above the Bhote Kosi ravine. A small contingent of Sherpas from the Asian Friendship Expedition passed through Chinese customs just in front of us. I waved to three Sherpas whom I'd climbed with in 1985—Moti Lal, Mingma, and Dawa—then I recognized Pertemba, one of the most famous Sherpa *Sirdars,* leading them.

Our passage through customs was nerve-wracking. We had Chinese visas and an authorization letter from the Chinese Sports Federation in Beijing, but there was no guarantee we'd be allowed into Tibet. In Kathmandu we'd heard that some expeditions had, in fact, recently been turned back from Zhangmu.

Stephen disappeared to change money and buy beer. I told the customs officer he'd gone to buy a Coke, then Stephen reappeared and set down four bottles of beer! The Chinese officer snickered disdainfully, then snorted a little laugh. Paul promptly cracked open a bottle and took a healthy swig.

"Thirsty!" he proclaimed loudly, eyeballing the customs official.

"Please Paul," I prayed, "Whatever you do, don't burp."

"Customs first, then beer!" the officer ordered, pointing at Paul, who slowly lowered the bottle, and smiled broadly like a child with his fingers clearly stuck in the proverbial cookie jar.

An Australian, Pamela Steele, stood in line in front of us. We wondered how she intended to enter Tibet, but as an employee of the Lhasa Hotel she had the necessary papers, spoke fluent Tibetan, and breezed right through.

Pasang had crossed the border several times by this route, but as we filled out the declaration forms, suddenly he looked very worried. "Ed, what I do?" he asked nervously. Earlier, Pasang told us how in 1986 he had taken his wife and mother-in-law on a long-dreamt-of pilgrimage from Kathmandu to Lhasa. His mother-in-law, however, had gotten sick in Lhasa, so Pasang hauled her back to their home in Namche Bazaar by the shortest possible route—over the heavily glaciated, eighteen-thousand–foot-high Nangpa La pass. And, as a result, his Chinese entry visa had never been canceled when he left Tibet.

The Chinese had since been cracking down on the unauthorized flow of Sherpas, Tibetan traders, and Tibetan refugees crossing the Nangpa La, the old trade route linking Tibet and Nepal. If Pasang wasn't granted entry into Tibet, we'd lose one of our most essential members. Grimly, we waited outside the customs building. At last, Pasang emerged, grinning ear to ear, waving his passport.

"I told official I very, very, very sorry for making bad mistake. But mother-in-law almost die, and it never happen once more!" he gushed.

We bypassed the exorbitantly expensive government-run Zhangmu Hotel, and Pamela brought us to the Himalayan View, a small Tibetan-run hotel. At seven yuan per night, it was over ten times cheaper and infinitely nicer. After trooping up a winding path in the dark to the hotel, we counted the loads, and only then realized that half of our fourteen propane cylinders were missing.

"Pasang, you'll be rubbing sticks together at Base Camp!" Paul admonished.

Pasang questioned the porters and told them they wouldn't be paid a cent until the valuable propane was found. Three more porters carrying cylinders arrived, then Pasang and I scurried down to customs to search for other lost souls. We found them, huddled, tired, and hungry in a dark alley. Each porter was carrying two cylinders, a double load weighing seventy pounds. All was well. Paul lined up the porters, and Pasang paid them off to relief and laughter.

It quickly became obvious that we wouldn't be leaving Zhangmu soon. The Sherpas from the Friendship Expedition roared off in Chinese Mountaineering Association jeeps while we plotted and schemed how best to reach our next destination, Shekar. A delay was to be expected. This was Asia, after all.

No trucks came south to us across the eighteen-thousand-foot pass, the Lalung La, from the direction of Shekar. Snow had fallen in Nyalam, the next town north of Zhangmu, and at higher elevations, so the road was very icy.

Tibetan Khampas in Zhangmu. The closest fellow had shot the bobcat on the right.

Drivers made the crossing at their own risk. Not surprisingly, our CMA jeep didn't arrive. Sitting idly outside of our hotel, we watched a Tibetan woman walk past carrying her groceries; half a goat's rib cage and one hoofed leg protruded from her shopping bag.

Zhangmu was an odd place: part Chinese, part Tibetan, part Mexican border town. Chinese-made, real Coca Cola cost a dollar a can, while beer sold for fifty cents. Roaming the streets were rough-looking Khampas, the warrior class of eastern Tibet, who in the late 1950s had been covertly financed by the CIA to fight the Chinese. Bright red tassels were braided into their long, greasy hair. Nearby, polyester-bell-bottom-clad Chinese teenagers played outdoor billiards on the street corner, Tibetan women peered shyly from windows and half-open doors, and a mummified bobcat hung from the eaves. The Khampa sitting below it proudly pointed a finger to the carcass, then back at himself. It was his kill.

Zhangmu indeed has a split personality. It is commonly referred to by its Nepali name, Khasa, as well as its Tibetan name, Dam. Chinese and Nepalese currencies are equally valued. Zhangmu seemed content to let business come up to it from Nepal, or down over the Lalung La from the rest of Tibet. Yet the town quivered under an uneasy truce between the Tibetans and their Chinese overseers. I half expected—as if I were in a wild west frontier town—a gang of Khampa desperadoes to come galloping down Main Street, guns ablaze.

Stephen and I went on a training hike that afternoon. Our first goal was to acclimatize to altitudes between twelve thousand and fifteen thousand feet, then, in two or three more weeks, we'd be able to push ourselves to twenty thousand feet, and start climbing.

"Gosh, I always feel so woefully out of shape early on a trip," Stephen said breathlessly as we pushed our uncooperative bodies and muscles uphill. Then, quite inadvertently, we stumbled into the courtyard of the Chinese Army barracks atop the hill behind town. A crowd of green-suited soldiers watched us in shock, astonished by our intrusion, then yelled in Chinese (it was easy to translate) for us to "proceed out the front gate." Walking briskly in that direction, Stephen jokingly faked right, prompting more shouts, and we exited in haste.

"Friendly lot, aren't they? It's probably a restricted military target, the men's dormitory," Stephen joked. Walking past some traditional Tibetan homes, we stooped to collect fistfuls of stones, ammunition with which to ward off menacing dogs. This particular morning, I'd barely escaped getting hamburgered by an immense, black Tibetan mastiff, and I was very much regretting not getting my rabies inoculation. Stopping at an earthen overlook, we sat and admired the tranquil view back down the Bhote Kosi gorge, as it disappeared south toward Kathmandu. The sun was setting and the mountain landscape was delightfully quiet. Nepal already felt very far away.

"You know, you big wall climbers are all the same," Stephen remarked, breaking the silence. "Eventually you develop an affinity for the high mountains."

I had. The transition from short rock climbs to three-thousand-foot-high big walls like El Capitan in Yosemite Valley in California had been a natural enough progression, but Everest by a new route, without using bottled oxygen, was a challenge that verged on the incomprehensible. As the team's most experienced rock climber, it looked like the lower rock buttress would be my lead.

Back at the hotel, we learned that by sheer luck, Pamela had met a representative from CITS, the China International Travel Service. Mr. Chang Bu offered to help us find transport. Paul presented him with our expedition papers, assorted telexes, CMA letters, and my expedition business card, which presumptuously read, "Everest East Face, A New Route, Alpine-style."

"Please describe your travels," Mr. Bu asked. "Who is leader?"

"The leader of this expedition?" I asked, momentarily confused. "Robert Anderson is our leader, but he is in Beijing at the moment."

"I think what Chang Bu is saying," Stephen softly interjected with discreet British diplomacy, "is that one of us should be the leader of this group."

"I gave him your card," Paul remonstrated. "You be the leader."

With newfound pride, I wrote out our travel itinerary, then proudly signed it, "Ed Webster, leader."

"That's the first time I've ever written that," I said, adding quickly: "You chaps sign down below, here!"

"Yes, yes, yes," Chang Bu enthused. "Everyone must sign!"

Although apparently no one in Chinese officialdom cared that we were here in Tibet, with Chang Bu's assistance we might soon be en route to Shekar.

That evening, we dined home-style. The walls of our host's living room were decorated with an eclectic assortment of photographs, of the Dalai Lama, Mao Zedong, and Chou En Lai. I wondered if the photos of the Chinese premiers were displayed out of reverence or obligation. Pamela, who ate with us, had been in Lhasa during the 1987 freedom protests.

"There was no warning of what was about to occur," she said, explaining that a group of monks had chosen to march around the Barkhor, Lhasa's central marketplace, on the thirty-fifth anniversary of China Independence Day. The Chinese authorities didn't find their actions patriotic. They arrested them.

"Tibetan women began throwing rocks when the monks were arrested. The Chinese countered by blocking off the Barkhor with vehicles, which the Tibetans set ablaze. Then they torched the police station where the monks had been jailed. It was unbelievable violence. I'd gotten off work, so I went to have a look. Chinese soldiers had fired from the rooftops. Nineteen people were killed outright; sixty were wounded. I saw many of the dead lying where they had fallen."

It was hard to fathom such violence occurring just in front of the Jokhang Temple, one of Tibet's most sacred religious sites. When Pamela's story ended, the tape-recorded strains of guitar and song drifted to our ears from the next room. "Song from Dalai Lama," someone said.

We moved to the kitchen. Sitting round the wood stove, we listened to the cassette tape from Dharamsala. One person narrated the song for us, using dramatic facial gestures and sign language. Guns shooting, people dying, people crying. Pam elaborated: "This land was ours, then the Chinese came and took it away. Please go and let us live in peace again."

Four friends linked arms over shoulders and began a Tibetan folk dance, a *shabdro,* singing and moving backwards, forwards, then sideways. Cries of *"Shu! Shu! Shu!"* were accompanied by rhythmic stomping on the wood floor. A friend played a *dranyen,* six-stringed guitar with an elongated neck. All were sweating heavily; it was an athletic performance. Finally, giving thanks, we walked home through the darkened village under a canopy of stars.

Next morning, two jeeps pulled up outside our lodge. A truck was located and our gear loaded. It wasn't clear how our transportation would be paid for, but I had no doubt that a vastly inflated bill would eventually find its way to Robert. At the last moment, Pamela wasn't allowed to accompany us. A Sherpa from the Asian Friendship team appeared. Since he was "expedition," Chang Bu explained, and Pamela was "not expedition," our jeep driver wouldn't let her come. We were incensed. The jeep drivers acted as petty dictators, extorting high fees from passengers who had no choice but to pay.

"Tell the driver he is a very bad man," Pamela scolded Chang Bu, who just shrugged his shoulders. Then, as we drove away, she waved and cheerfully shouted after us: "Don't worry about me. I'll get a lift!"

*   *   *   *   *   *   *   *   *   *   *   *   *   *

We bounced across a huge landslide on the outskirts of Zhangmu, then headed north on the Friendship Highway, following the precipitous left bank of

The Friendship Highway north of Zhangmu, in the gorge of the Bhote Kosi River.

the Bhote Kosi gorge. For fifteen miles we crept along a narrow roadbed blast-ed out of vertical rock cliffs. The raging river had carved this dramatic canyon as it descended in elevation an astounding five hundred feet per mile. Legend had it that nineteenth century traders traversed the gorge along a path of two-foot-wide stone slabs set on iron rods driven into the precipices, directly above a heart-stoppingly sheer, fifteen-hundred-foot drop.

At the Lalung La's eighteen-thousand-foot summit, beside a tremendous flut-tering bouquet of prayer flags, we stopped to admire the unobstructed view of Shisha Pangma (26,397 feet), thirteenth-highest of the fourteen eight-thousand-meter Himalayan peaks. The sight made me aware of the Himalaya's astound-ingly narrow, north-to-south width. In less than a single day's drive, we had bisected the largest mountain range on earth, beginning in Nepal's lush low-lands and ending on the windswept, arid heights of the Tibetan plateau.

An hour later, near the village of Tingri, Paul cried out, "There it is!"

It could be only one mountain. Mount Everest. Chomolungma, "the Goddess Mother of the World." The summit snow plume, carried aloft by the jet stream winds, billowed into the blue heavens. Although Everest was still over fifty miles distant, its black, wind-blasted pyramid towered unrealistically high above the closer gray-brown hills. This year, I told myself, I will do my very best to reach that summit. I will strive for my goal, but I will not be killed. I will not take foolish chances. I will climb always within my ability. And I will use the knowledge that I've learned on every other climb I've done.

I cannot deny that my pulse increased at our first sighting of Everest, nor did I find I could casually look away, or pretend that the mountain wasn't there. I could not. Everest pulled at me tenaciously—like a Tibetan mastiff who would not let go—holding on tight to my deepest emotions, ambitions, and insecurities.

Then suddenly I found that I had to take an unexpectedly deep breath, and this response wasn't only because of the higher altitude.

Ed near Tingri in Tibet, with Chomolungma on the far right. Stephen Venables

Chapter 6

Shekar to Kharta

The use of travelling is to regulate imagination by reality,
and instead of thinking how things may be, to see them as they are.

—Samuel Johnson

The two halves of our expedition, having voyaged halfway around the world in opposite directions, were reunited in the unlikely outpost of Shekar, Tibet. Upon entering the "Everest Hotl Restau-rant" on the evening of March 3, I quickly scanned the room and saw—huddled in down jackets around a table at the far end of the room—the rest of the team. It was a marvelous morale booster to be together again. Bad stomachs, headaches, and altitude lethargy all temporarily vanished in our warm and euphoric embraces. Everyone had suffered their own set of hardships and adventures to get here. Mimi Zieman, Miklos Pinther, Wendy Davis, and Joe Blackburn rose from the table to greet us; so did Norbu Tenzing Norgay, Rob Dorival, and Sandy Wylie.

Left: *Seen from Shekar Dzong, Everest rises dramatically above the Tibetan hills.*

Robert Anderson was conspicuously absent, ill from eating too much greasy food and excessive arguing with Chinese bureaucrats. When Robert did appear, he was smiling, laughing, and obviously relieved to see Paul, Stephen, Pasang, and me intact and well. Standing taller than I remembered him, Robert sported a new beard, and his piercing blue eyes looked only partially dimmed by his travails with Asian bureaucracy. Our merry little band, by contrast, was dust covered from head to toe.

We told our respective tales. The Shangri-La Hotel in Beijing was "an international palace of generic opulence." And in Lhasa, because of recent political unrest, the team had been "under relative house arrest" at the Lhasa Hotel. Our youthful translator, Mr. Shi (pronounced *"Sher"*), was described by Joe as "a mama's boy from day one." Raised at sea level in Beijing, Mr. Shi had never set foot outside of the capital and was thoroughly ill-suited for the rigors of high altitude in Tibet. And, also to be expected, our Liaison Officer, Mr. Yang, didn't speak a word of English. It was for precisely this reason that we'd employed Pasang Norbu, who spoke fluent Tibetan and could converse with the yak drivers on our way to Base Camp.

Mr. Yang's dark blue and gray Mao suit revealed him to be an old-line party conformist. Rarely did a smile break his somber visage to reveal a hint of warmth or charm. Our expedition was paying both Mr. Shi and Mr. Yang's salaries, lodging, and food expenses, and ostensibly, they were here to help us. It soon became apparent, however, that the only correct way to do anything in China—and even more tellingly, to do anything *correctly* in Tibet—was The Chinese Way. Unfortunately, we'd been raised in The Western Way, to expect reasonable service and value in return for your money.

Mr. Shi and our two drivers had left earlier in the day to search for Stephen, Paul, Pasang, and me in Zhangmu. Unknowingly, we had passed each other on the Friendship Highway.

"Shi is a total incompetent," Robert complained. "He'll probably be sitting around in Zhangmu for days before realizing you're not there anymore."

That evening, we crammed into a dingy room to listen to a cassette of our very own theme song, "Climb Everest Mountain," a catchy ditty recorded by a New Zealand pop star. We then played several louder songs written and sung by our own American rock 'n' roll idol, Billy Squier, who at the last moment hadn't been able to come on the trek to Base Camp. A bottle of Jack Daniels circled the room, warming us as we field-tested the entirely predictable effects of hard liquor at 14,400 feet.

"*The Mountaineers From Three Countries,*" (Left to Right): *Ed Webster* (USA),
Stephen Venables (UK), *Robert Anderson* (USA), *Paul Teare* (Canada).

Mr. Shi returned two days later, delaying our departure for Kharta and throwing a wrench into our rendezvous with the yak drivers. Mr. Yang agreed it was Shi's fault we were late, and said we wouldn't be charged for one day of the $450-per-day rental fee for the yaks. Robert confided that he and Sandy were keeping a diary of any budget exceptions that were the fault of the CMA.

We busied ourselves reading, writing, mending clothes, listening to music, and getting exercise walking the streets of Shekar. We also hiked to the top of Shekar Ri (Shekar Peak) and the top of the ruined White Crystal Fort, where we enjoyed excellent views to the south of Mount Everest, Makalu, and Cho Oyu.

The Asian China-Japan-Nepal Friendship Expedition to Qomolangma-Sagarmatha—or, as we called them for short: the "TV expedition"—was also staying at the Shekar compound. The contrast between our two expeditions couldn't have been greater. Their team of 250 people, including roughly one hundred climbers, was preparing to attack Everest (none too strong a description) from both Tibet and Nepal. Assuming the weather cooperated, on May 5, International Children's Day, they hoped to traverse the peak from south to north (and vice versa), plus beam a live video transmission to Japan and waiting television sets around the globe. We had full intentions of crashing the party!

Mealtimes in the dining room were packed with climbers and media from their expedition. Nationality was denoted by the color of one's parka. Red, not surprisingly, meant Chinese, orange signified the Japanese, and green designated the Nepalese, who were mostly Sherpas. Suspended on one wall of the dining hall was an immense banner reading, "Warmly Welcome the Mountaineers From Three Countries." We had a feeling that the sign wasn't meant for us, but as we represented America, Canada, and Great Britain, we posed for a team photo below it anyway.

Shekar's high altitude began to affect each of us to varying degrees. The first inclination was to laze around or sleep. Fighting lethargy was a constant battle; forced exercise was mandatory. A good hike in the hills east of town helped me considerably, but sleeping was also difficult. I was plagued by insomnia. Only later did Robert begin sharing his secret aid to high-altitude beauty rest, the magic Hypnovel sleeping pills that he'd brought along—and fortunately, he had plenty of extras! Having quickly used up our tourist destinations in town, Robert and I discussed our travel logistics with Mr. Yang and Mr. Shi, who'd be staying in Kharta for the climb's duration: approximately six to eight weeks. After reaching Base Camp with us, the support team would begin their return journey home.

"When your trekkers arrive back in Kharta, then we must know when the expedition also will return," Shi demanded.

How could we know in early March when we'd be done with the climb?

"Tell Mr. Yang that Mount Qomolangma will decide when we are finished," Robert balked, using the Han Chinese rendition of Chomolungma.

Another problem was our missing Coleman cook tent. The Sheik (its real name) had missed its plane flight to China, so we were minus a Base Camp kitchen and eating tent. We tried to obtain an extra one from the Asian Friendship Expedition, but their friendliness did not include parting with a tent.

We'd given up eating Chinese food, and began polishing off fortifying bowls of Grape-nuts cereal instead. On March 6, we loaded two Chinese army trucks and left early on the bumpy eight-hour ride to Kharta. One truck brimmed with our much-beloved blue plastic storage barrels; the back of the other truck we stacked with our duffel bags—and then sat on top of them.

Even though we wore dust masks, the dust the trucks kicked up was a choking red veil that penetrated every skin pore, hair follicle, and camera mechanism. And sitting in the back of the truck only amplified the pounding jolt of every bump in the road.

Mount Everest—and the plume—from atop the Pang La pass.

"Suffering, suffering!" Robert proclaimed loudly as our insides proceeded to get scrambled. "It helps get you ready for the climb."

The trucks labored up the switchbacks of the Pang La, the 17,200-foot-high pass en route to both Rongbuk and Kharta. Taking a rest stop, we absorbed the unparalleled panorama southward across desolate foothills to Makalu, Everest, Gyachung Kang, and Cho Oyu. The morning was brisk and clear, except for the prodigious cloud pennant streaming from Everest's summit. With a shudder, we noticed it was blowing directly over the East Face, depositing fresh snow, we speculated nervously, on the avalanche-prone slopes below the South Col.

The remainder of the ride to Kharta was nightmarish. My insides felt like they were being processed inside a blender, and the switch had accidentally been left on *purée*. The duffels shifted constantly, usually crushing some hapless soul. Dust masks, sunglasses, and hooded parkas hid our identities—except for Joe, who was unmistakable in his World War II-style gas mask.

On the road to Kharta.

The roadside cliffs grew precipitous. "This ride is as bad or worse than in the Karakoram," Stephen moaned. In all truthfulness, our driver was excellent. He even stopped periodically to let everyone stretch and relieve themselves. But when we jarred to a halt one time, Paul jumped out to see what was the matter—and watched a beer bottle whiz down the embankment.

"Our driver is drunk!" No wonder the corners had been so smooth.

Another reason we'd been stopping was because Norbu wanted to determine the names of some of the villages we were passing by. The day before at the Shekar Monastery, he and Pasang and some of the others had attended a blessing ceremony—which took a completely unexpected turn.

"One of the monks asked my name," Norbu recounted. "When I said that I was Norbu Tenzing Norgay, the son of Tenzing Norgay Sherpa, the monk became extremely excited. He said that he could not believe that I was in Tibet."

The monk told Norbu that he must visit an old man named Tsawa Emchi ("the doctor from Tsawa") who worked at the hospital in Shekar. Norbu and Pasang found him. Tsawa Emchi maintained that a man called Ngondup Tsawa was a living relative of Norbu's father, and that he resided in the village of Tsawa near Kharta. Implied was the astounding and unexpected suggestion that Norbu's father might also have once lived in the Kharta Valley.

Tenzing Norgay. Swiss Foundation For Alpine Research

"This news of my father's possible birthplace has never before surfaced," Norbu told me. "His original name, Tenzing Bhotia, was Tibetan, but for political reasons, after my father had climbed Everest he always said that he was 'born in the womb of Nepal, and grew up in the lap of India.'"

I certainly knew the story. After the 1953 first ascent of Everest, quite literally overnight, Tenzing, the Tiger of the Snows, became one of Asia's most famous men. Nepal and India each laid claim to his ancestry. Tenzing maintained that he grew up in the Sherpa village of Thame near Namche Bazaar in Nepal, however he spent his adult life in Darjeeling, India, where Norbu was born. There, Tenzing worked as the Director of Field Training (Chief Instructor) of the Himalayan Mountaineering Institute.

Like any son, Norbu was keenly interested in his father's roots. "If in fact my father was born in Kharta then this trip will mean considerably more to me than just the thirty-fifth anniversary ascent of Mount Everest. It will be a pilgrimage to where life for my family began hundreds of years ago. There were times of hardship in this valley when my father lived here, Tsawa Emchi told me. If my father emigrated over the high passes into Nepal, then this puts my whole life into a new perspective," Norbu said solemnly.

But, unable to locate the village of Tsawa, we arrived at the administrative compound in Kharta. Pasang delved into our foodstuffs, impressing everyone by cooking a superlative meal on the wood stove inside the simple stone lodge. Burning juniper logs crackled as we sat around the fire, hugging its warmth.

"We've driven halfway around the tallest mountain on earth, to one of the most remote valleys on earth," Robert observed.

"Along one of the worst roads on earth," someone else quipped. It felt tremendous to have finally arrived in Kharta, at road's end. Tomorrow, we would prepare the loads, and the next day begin our hike to Base Camp. Paul volunteered to sleep beside the trucks to ward off any adventurous thieves.

Upon awakening, I stumbled stiffly outside. My lungs brimmed with clean crisp air, and my visions were of Shangri-La. To the east rose friendly, snow-covered, dome-shaped mountains. Beyond them, distant black-toothed peaks speared higher into the cobalt-blue sky. I could also see the rocky, steep-walled gorge that swallowed up the Arun River (in Tibetan, the Bhong Chu), another of the very few Himalayan torrents that bisect the range from north to south. Next to the lodge grew several stout-waisted juniper trees. Even though it was early March, the end of winter, the Kharta Valley was surprisingly warm and verdant compared with the dusty remainder of Tibet's high plateau.

Kharta, we were told, was more of a regional name for a collection of villages than an individual town. We calculated that we were the third modern expedition to pass through Kharta en route to Everest, following in the footsteps of the 1981 and 1983 American Everest expeditions to the Kangshung Face—and we all benefited from Mallory, Bullock, and Howard-Bury's first explorations of the region during the 1921 British Everest reconnaissance. The local inhabitants had seen so few Westerners that they inquisitively clustered around us, staring openly at the brightly clad foreigners. They were also particularly covetous of our western-made gear, which we padlocked and kept watch over.

Rounding up the yaks and yak herders a second time did not make the Chinese Kharta headman feel convivial toward Mr. Yang. But astoundingly, by the early hour of 11 A.M., a steady trickle of yaks, yak drivers, and women began to gather in the compound to await their loads.

In yet another western exercise in futility, we organized our seventy sixteen-gallon blue barrels and assorted duffels into neat rows. I knew it wouldn't work. It was pointless to try to impose logical, expedient organization on a completely disorganized group of Tibetan villagers. Furthermore, it was culturally impossible to order a yak driver to carry a particular load. Although CMA regulations stipulated that a yak can carry a maximum of sixty kilos (160 pounds), the number of pieces of baggage that each yak could carry was not standardized. We'd planned on each yak carrying two barrels—one on each side—with a duffel bag slung across the middle of its back. This the drivers refused. It was two loads per animal, period, so rather than sixty yaks, we now needed eighty.

Our western patience was elastically stretched to new limits, but it was a perfect afternoon with hardly a cloud in the sky. We sat in small groups on the stone wall in front of the lodge, watching the yak men weigh and distribute

Arranging loads in the compound at Kharta.

Above: *The friendly villagers near Kharta had seen few Westerners.*
Below: *The Kharta headman, Mr. Yang, Mr. Shi, and Robert Anderson converse.*

Stephen Venables and Sandy Wylie on the approach near Kharta.

the loads as they saw fit. Finally the laden yaks headed up valley across a wide, gravel delta, and we left at intervals to keep an eye on things. We camped for the night at a restful and grassy bend of the Kharta River, or Kharta Chu.

We had signed on a new cookboy, too. Kasang Tsering was a gangly, twenty-two-year-old Kharta local from Yulog village. Said Robert: "We had to hire him. He came with a cook tent." We'd sent out a request to rent a tent, and Kasang offered us not only his tent (which closely resembled a 1920s-era British Everest expedition tent), but himself also—all for two dollars a day. Plus, Kasang claimed, he'd been to the Kangshung Base Camp as a porter in 1983. He knew the way.

On March 8, camp was broken with considerable chaos about the loads. No one was sure which load was whose. Stephen and I volunteered to go last, and while everyone finished packing, I took a bath in the river, a shocking act (Tibetans prefer to wash, not bathe) that gave the local children considerable free entertainment. Who was this all-white creature of undetermined sexuality? Laughing and pointing, the children crowded as close as they dared to my pink towel-clad body—and ran away screaming when I pretended to chase them.

Norbu and Tashi.

Stephen and I fell into line behind the last yaks, and joined Rob. Spring was making a valiant return to the valley, and the newly planted fields were greening rapidly. Up ahead, we noticed Sandy and Norbu talking with several local men. At first I thought something might be wrong. But no, everything was fine. Norbu was speaking in Tibetan to an old man about his family.

"He asked me if Tenzing Sherpa was here. I said no," Norbu told me later. "I replied that I was his son. As I was walking this morning, I kept hearing people say 'Tenzing is coming,' but I couldn't figure out why they'd be saying this.

"Then the old man approached me. He told me we were related, that he was my father's halfbrother, that they had had the same father, but a different mother. A few minutes earlier, I'd been cursing our yak drivers for being so slow, then I was shocked to discover that I might be related to them!"

I listened to Norbu converse in halting Tibetan with the old man, whose name, Norbu said, was Tashi.

Tenzing Norgay's boyhood home.

"It is good I am of my generation," Norbu explained. "Sherpas younger than I in Darjeeling do not know how to speak Tibetan. They speak Nepali, Hindi, and English, and know very little about their ancestral homeland. They care only about the latest western clothing, the American top-forty hits, and which Hollywood movies were recently released. Ask them the name of a beautiful mountain, and usually they have no reply."

Norbu's two younger brothers and sister did not learn the Tibetan language.

"But my father insisted that I, his eldest son, must learn to speak Tibetan. I studied it for two years. The Sherpa language I learned at home."

"Tashi says that my father's mother was my relative who lived in Tsawa. She later emigrated to Khumbu in Nepal, and eventually to India, but my father's paternal lineage has continued to live here in Kharta. 'Where was my father born?' I kept asking Tashi, and finally he replied, 'There is his house,' and pointed to the stone house on the far hillside," related Norbu.

Norbu points: "Was that the home of my father ?"

But had his father been born here in Kharta, or in Tsawa? "The Tibetan and Sherpa words for 'birthplace' are similar: Sherpa, *'kyeyul,'* and Tibetan, *'kyesa.'* Then I spoke of being pregnant and babies. Finally, Tashi got the picture."

I watched Tashi point vigorously again at the stone house on the hillside in the distance. It was currently inhabited by Tenzing's cousin-brother's children.

"Tashi also called my father 'king' in Nepali, and said that after he climbed Chomolungma, Tenzing had become king—but not the other fellow, Hillary," Norbu chuckled.

What really convinced Norbu of the veracity of Tashi's story was that when Tashi pointed to the house in question, he called it Gangla, then added that there was another Gangla (meaning "Snowy Pass" or "Snowy Mountain Pass") nearby. Gangla, or Ghang La, was the name Tenzing gave to his own home in Darjeeling.

A Tenzing family portrait.

Norbu's father had always told him that Gangla was also their family or clan name, and the name of his parent's home. And, Gangla was the pass where as a boy Tenzing had tended yaks below Everest, developing his dream to one day climb the mountain. Tenzing's father, Gangla Mingma, was a yak herdsman.

Tashi led us to the stone house on the hill. Several gnarled junipers grew beside it, and the view of the surrounding valley and the distant snowy peaks was majestic. As Tashi introduced him to the home's current residents—"to my relatives, I now realized," Norbu said to me—"a wave of shock and utter disbelief crossed their faces. Dressed in my western clothes, I did not appear as they had pictured their blood relative to look like. When I saw their reaction to Tashi's introduction, and when the women began to click their tongues in amazement, I knew that I had found my father's home, and my family's lost heritage."

Tenzing Norgay's house in Moyun village near Kharta.

Norbu speculated that his father, born in 1914, left the Kharta Valley in 1929, at age fifteen, traveling first to Tingri, proceeding next over the Nangpa La pass to Thame, then at last settled in Darjeeling. Although it took nearly sixty years and an additional generation, the prodigal son had finally returned home.

The house where Tenzing Norgay spent his childhood in Moyun village had partially collapsed during the fighting when the Chinese invaded the valley and destroyed the two monasteries in Kharta. It had since been rebuilt. Norbu and his many newly discovered next of kin sat in the courtyard for pictures, then Tashi ushered us to the second floor living room of his home for refreshments. His wife Sarang welcomed us round the sooty hearth, and Tashi brewed a fresh batch of Tibetan tea, furiously pounding the ingredients—tea, salt, and yak butter—with a wood mixing rod inside an elongated wooden urn. Next came *chang*. On this most auspicious of days, I drank it, and wished for good health.

Stephen produced a color print of the Dalai Lama, which Norbu gave to our hosts. Sarang reverently touched the picture to her own forehead, then to the heads of each of her three children. It was a day that would go down in history in the Kharta valley. Tashi walked with us to the edge of town, pointed us on our way toward Chomolungma, and wept openly as he bid Norbu good-bye. Other eyes in our small group were also wet.

Although we were two hours late, no one at camp had worried. I was exhausted after the emotional day. Everyone was amazed at Norbu's good fortune and congratulated him heartily. Then another discovery! Sonam Phuti, one of the "camera-girls" carrying Joe's heavy photographic equipment—one of the prettiest of the Tibetan women—was another of Norbu's long lost cousins.

That night we camped on a flat terrace above the valley floor. Robert was disappointed with our modest progress, but the villagers assured him this was the traditional camping spot. The small, inconspicuous side valley forking to our left, heading south, supposedly led to the Langma La, an eighteen-thousand-foot-high pass—and eventually to the Kama Valley and the Kangshung Base Camp. Miklos, our UN cartographer, pulled out a map and reassured us that the yak drivers' directions were indeed correct.

Finally we were in the mountains! Steep hillsides rose all around us, sporting a thick cover of azalea and rhododendron. Yaks grazed contentedly, their tinkling bells serenading us "like water" as Paul phrased it. The constellation Orion appeared overhead, but was quickly obscured by menacing clouds. Soon snow was hitting against the tent fly. Norbu was my tentmate; he was still visibly shaken by the day's events.

"If we can see Mount Everest from the Gangla, then the legend will be true," Norbu spoke reverently, "that as a boy my father saw Chomolungma from the Gangla while tending the family yaks—but here in Tibet, not in Nepal."

We had a rude awakening. When it began to snow in earnest at 9 A.M., the delay was on. I couldn't get over how much the Tibetans disliked snow, even though they lived amongst the highest mountains on earth. Robert's ordered 9:30 A.M. departure became a bad joke as noon approached and we stood around half-frozen from inactivity. This was expedition climbing at its finest—another day completely wasted. Paul shouted, screamed, and then charged at the yak drivers like a mortally wounded bull, while Stephen settled for the traditional British standby: "Come on you lazy bastards, get off your arses!"

Even Norbu was disgusted by our yak drivers' utter lack of motivation.

"No future here," Robert said. "No wonder your dad left for Nepal."

Jeremy, our nickname for the head yak driver, finally loaded up and left at 12:30 P.M. That inspired the others, and slowly we began to struggle up the small side valley toward the Langma La.

Loading the yaks took an eternity. Camp at junction of Kharta Chu and Langma La.

The day ended as disappointingly as it began. When the snow storm worsened, the drivers stopped the animals after an hour's walk and dropped their loads. There was too much snow ahead and bad visibility, they claimed. In seconds flat, tents were erected, juniper bushes uprooted, and fires started for tea. In hindsight, given the number of weeks we were eventually stuck below the Langma La, tempers flared hotter that day than they need have. Our trials and tribulations with the yak drivers were essentially a cultural confrontation. We expected them to work an eight-hour day, while they minimized their labor at every possible turn—then demanded their full daily rate. A typical day began at 10 A.M., quit at 2 or 3 P.M., and was followed by a strike for higher wages.

With the Kharta headman and Mr. Yang playing cards back in town, who was going to tell them otherwise? Had Pasang not been with us to negotiate, I doubt we'd have ever reached the mountain. For the moment, we were at the mercy of the villagers. If we had refused to pay them, or angered them, they would have turned and walked home. End of expedition.

An intestinal bug attacked me on the night of March 9. I crawled outside eight times before the agony ended. Wendy was my lucky tentmate, but she slept blissfully throughout and never heard me retching in the nearby bushes. The next morning, Mimi chastised me: "Wake me up next time. I want you to be healthy!" A young Tibetan carried my pack to our next campsite, while I took each step as a personal challenge, hobbling along the snowy trail behind Mimi. My head swum as we approached sixteen thousand feet.

We'd been told the approach from Kharta to the Kangshung Base Camp was a leisurely five-day walk. It proved to be anything but that. The high country was thigh deep with drifted winter snow. Since we were the very first expedition to attempt Everest's East Face in the pre-monsoon (or spring) climbing season, that meant we had to cross the eighteen-thousand-foot Langma La pass in late winter. Approaching Rongbuk Base Camp, by comparison, was a snap. On the Chinese road you could drive to your tent's nylon doorstep.

After getting bogged down in the deep, soft snow, we finally reached a flat campsite at 16,500 feet. The others helped me set up my tent, and listening to Sting and Springsteen, I was soon transported miles away to warmer worlds. So much for the local deities protecting me from Tashi's home-brewed *chang!*

We awoke in a winter wonderland. But the sparkling blanket of white snow decking the nearby peaks worried the Tibetans, who quickly mobilized to bring their most valuable possessions—the yaks—home. From now on, 125 porters earning five yuan ($1.50) per day would transport our 110 loads to Base Camp.

Deep snow on the Langma La soon sent the yaks back home.

Paul decided that the best way to outsmart the villagers was to act lazier than them, so out came the chairs, table, umbrellas, and the ghetto blaster. But because of the repeated delays, the support team now began to worry that they might not reach Base Camp. We hoped they'd at least get over the Langma La and see Everest's East Face, but the villagers and the weather conspired against us. One hundred villagers—twenty-five fewer than needed—streamed into camp early on March 12. Paul attempted to make them stand in line, another cultural impossibility. Shouldn't the women and children get the lightest loads, while the strongest men carried the heaviest? This also was not the Tibetan way. The men chose the light loads, and left the women and children to carry the rest! The scene grew increasingly chaotic as Joe patrolled the camp's perimeter, trying to keep the men and boys from grabbing our lightest loads, the blue barrels.

Tempers flared. Normally the most mild mannered of people, Joe suddenly began yelling, "Get back, all of you! Get back!" while brandishing a ski pole at the startled villagers, who hastily backpedaled out of reach. Not knowing how to interpret his anger (or words), they laughed, which made Joe even madder.

Pasang (with towel), *Jeremy, and Robert have a "confab."*

Pasang rushed in to assist, and things went smoother until only several monster-sized duffels remained.

More men arrived at noon, but they immediately began to complain that the light loads were already taken. Stephen and Sandy had left two hours before to break trail over the pass—ostensibly to set a good example for the porters. Wendy and Miklos had accompanied Group One halfway up the hillside above camp, while Joe and Rob sat nearby with Group Two at their tents. I stood waiting to see what would or would not happen.

There are three liquid refreshments that no Tibetan can survive for very long without: Tibetan salt tea, *chang*, and *rakshi*, a more potent potato-based spirit. These beverages may be drunk at any time of day. It now, evidently, was time for tea and *chang*, so all one hundred villagers—men, women, and children—sat down for a midday drink. Wendy bravely yelled encouragement from up above, and Joe rejoined us, his anger still potent.

An hour and a half later, a "confab" erupted between Robert, Pasang, Jeremy, and a mob of fifty porters. Tempers escalated; something had to give. "Shut up!" Robert screamed when he could no longer stand the noise. "One voice, please!"

Pasang explained the situation: "Jeremy he say no firewood at top of pass. They drop loads there, then come back."

"But there is firewood on the other side of the pass," Robert protested.

"Now he say too much snow. They go tomorrow instead."

Clearly we weren't going anywhere, and our anger dissipated as we resigned ourselves to our fate.

"Well, there's only one solution to a situation like this," Robert proclaimed: "Get drunk." A bottle of Johnny Walker appeared. Paul put a Rolling Stones cassette in the tape deck and cranked the volume. The bottle made the rounds while all the loads were returned to camp. Mimi (fashionably clad in her plastic double boots) and I began to dance, much to the confused delight of the Tibetans who gathered to watch us boogie and swing. Eventually, Jeremy bravely stepped forward to dance with Mimi, and the villagers roared when he bear-hugged her, lifting her off the ground, as heavy snow began to fall.

It snowed hard for much of the next day, too. Robert told Jeremy that the porters wouldn't be paid a cent until they reached Base Camp. The news didn't sit well. Now the porters wanted to be paid for walking here from their villages!

"Not a dime till Base Camp!" Robert retorted.

Then Paul began to get a little too physical with some of the Tibetan men, to keep them away from our belongings. Pasang grew worried.

"Paul, he not touch them! They drink, you can smell," Pasang said. "Paul touch and they maybe fight. Then very bad."

Each village clan now congregated in a huddle, linking arms to keep non-members out. Should they stay and carry loads, or return home empty handed? As tempers flared again, it occurred to me that our expedition might be remembered in Kharta not so much for Norbu's homecoming, but for our having started feuds between villages. Jeremy wanted to stay; the rest of his village wanted to leave. Eventually, almost all the porters decided to go home without pay, but to return and try again when the weather improved.

Norbu still wanted to see the Gangla, to prove or refute the family legend. Pasang and I accompanied him up toward the top of the Langma La. Bad weather, deep snow and the altitude stopped us close to, but just below, the eighteen-thousand-foot saddle. A *chorten* sprouting a bouquet of fluttering prayer flags marked the top of the pass. It was actually a relief that the porters hadn't attempted a crossing today. If they had, they'd have abandoned their loads in the snow and retreated. We needed good weather and a prepared trail for them to be able to cross the pass.

Norbu Tenzing Norgay hiking up toward the Langma La. It was still winter.

Now there was no choice: the support team had to leave for home tomorrow without reaching Base Camp, or for that matter, without even seeing the Kangshung Face. They were obviously disappointed, and Norbu was especially sad not to see the fabled Gangla firsthand. I promised him I'd track it down.

After a celebratory farewell dinner, we stood around the cook tent for a long time. We'd melded into a wonderfully harmonious group, the eleven of us, plus Pasang and Kasang, and it was with a genuine feeling of nostalgia that we were turning to go our separate ways—they back to work, home, and civilization, and we, onward to the mountain. Miklos waxed romantic while sharing the sentiment that coming to Everest had been the most exciting event in his life.

"The most frustrating part of organizing this expedition," he continued, "has been the realization that it's dealing with individual people that makes the process so difficult. Just getting here to Tibet is quite an achievement."

"Ed kept warning me, no sponsorship will be firm until six months before departure," Wendy said. "And nothing will really happen until six weeks before!"

"If you've done three-quarters of the things on your 'To Do' list before you leave home, you've done well," Stephen interjected.

"And all of your friends will call up and say, 'We should get together before you leave,' but there's no time!" Paul exclaimed.

"I'd call Stephen in London with requests for names and phone numbers and addresses, and he'd reply, 'Wendy, I'm sorry, there's no way I can possibly get these to you by next Thursday,' then he'd ring back ten minutes later and say, 'Okay, okay, here they are,'" Wendy said.

I then related the story of how after I had left Colorado, my roommates changed the message on our answering machine to: "Ed has left for Everest. He won't be back for four months, so don't bother calling."

We'd shared a lot, our merry group, but Robert wouldn't let us retreat to our tents yet. "One of the things on my list was to buy some wool socks. As you can see by these cotton socks, I never quite got around to it. So I'd really appreciate it if anyone has any extra wool socks that I could have."

* * * * * * * * * * * * *

That night I dreamt of Lauren. She had been hurt, but she was not badly injured. She lay resting in her bed in a white hospital room. We hadn't seen each other in several years. I could see her if I wished. Yes, of course I wanted to see her again. I walked into the room. Her brown hair was pulled back and she was wearing her favorite bandanna, the one she always wore when we went climbing. Our eyes met. We kissed. But why hadn't we been together? Where had Lauren been all this time?

Moments later, we were floating together and swimming in a warm pool of water. Then, coming together, we spiralled round and round, floating lazily on the water's surface. Lauren lay back comfortably against my chest while I wrapped my right arm around her waist.

"What have you been doing these past few years?" she asked me.

"I went to Mount Everest and to Nepal," I answered. "And you?"

"I also went to Nepal. I floated down a long river," Lauren said.

I began to tell her about flying to the dirt landing strip at Lukla, describing how the plane swoops down out of the sky to land on the uphill dirt runway, when suddenly I realized that the reason we'd been separated these past three and a half years wasn't because we had broken up.

We were apart because Lauren had died.

Then, as the dream ended and I gradually awoke, I remembered, with dazed disbelief, where I was.

It was still snowing outside. It had stormed hard all night long.

* * * * * * * * * * * * *

"Day two of the gentle spring snowstorm," Robert declared the next morning as he excavated the camp walkways. Digging in the snow apparently reminded him of his childhood. "Everest men aren't born, they're made by their parents," Robert continued. "They're tossed outside into weather like this. 'It's a winter wonderland! Go outside and play, and don't come back in until your fingers are frostbitten!' That's what my parents used to tell me."

"Yes, Everest men are manufactured," Stephen concurred, shouting out from inside his tent. "Skiing in Switzerland when I was young, my parents made me climb up the hill with my skis on my back for the first run of the day."

Miklos roused his crew. They had to leave today, no matter how bad the storm. To make matters worse, Rob had gotten sick during the night. The hour grew late, and Joe hurried to take our group photos—along with an Explorer's Club flag, the United Nations flag, and an American Express banner. When we had gathered into a circle, with the snow swirling about us, Norbu read several excerpts from his father's autobiography, *Tiger of the Snows*, written with James Ramsey Ullman. Tenzing's words helped us unite our diverse feelings.

"The world is too small, Everest too great, for anything but tolerance and understanding: that is the most important of all things I have learned from my climbing and traveling. Whatever the differences between East and West, they are nothing compared to our common humanity.

"What I can teach is not from books, to be sure, but from what I have learned in living my own life: from many men, many lands, many mountains, and most of all—from Everest. Some of it has to do with physical and material things. But not all of it; for I think I have learned other, and more important things as well. One is that you cannot be a good mountaineer, however great your ability, unless you are cheerful and have the spirit of comradeship. Friends are as important as achievement. Another is that teamwork is the key to success, and that selfishness only makes a man small. Still another is that no man, on a mountain or elsewhere, gets more out of anything than he puts into it. Be great. Make others great."

Norbu then gave Robert replicas of the good luck charms his father had carried to Everest's summit thirty-five years earlier: a black plastic cat for good luck, a pencil stub, and a candy. "They had different candies in 1953, but I'd like to share these with the four climbers," Norbu laughed, as he handed us each a chocolate Hershey's Kiss, which we ate in communion.

On this lofty tone we disbanded. Norbu, Wendy, Rob, Miklos, and Sandy left in the snowstorm for their homes, other travels, and the world below. Eight of us would go on. With visibility at fifty feet, hiking was slow through the drifted powder. Stephen, Robert, Paul, and I escorted them back down the trail toward Kharta. Joe decided to help Pasang reorganize camp while we were gone.

Wendy and Miklos hiked gamely, and the sparkle in their eyes told the story of the dream that they knew they were living, that they were really here, amongst the mountains of Tibet and in the Himalaya, the greatest mountain range on Earth. Rob was weak and pale, but felt better once the sun came out and five porters arrived to help carry their loads. Sandy was quiet and already looking forward to the rest of his Asian voyage, while Norbu spoke excitedly of visiting Tashi. We took more pictures, waved, and bid a fond good-bye.

Golden afternoon light illuminated the peaks as we returned into the mountain fastness that was now our home. For the first time, our nucleus of four was together, as we would be, in the coming months, on Everest. With my turtling pace, I led the way back uphill. We concentrated on our breathing, and on the rhythmic timing of each forward footstep to compensate for the lack of oxygen.

"Good pace," Paul said. "Just turn off your mind and walk."

*The moment
of triumph:*

*Tenzing Norgay
on the summit
of Mount Everest,
May 29, 1953.*

*Ed Hillary took
three summit
photographs of
Tenzing; this is
the least well
known image
of the three.*

Photograph by
Edmund Hillary,
Courtesy of
the Royal
Geographical
Society

Camp looked considerably homier. Joe and Pasang had moved the cook tent, then stacked up barrels to form a wall, and roofed everything over with a tarp to make a communal shelter. We sat down for our first meal, with Pasang cooking, and Kasang serving. Looking round the table as we ate and talked, I gauged the mood of my companions by their faces. All eyes appeared to glow with a newfound intensity. It was obvious that every one of us was here for the long haul, to do this climb, and to make the expedition a success, no matter what it took. There was nowhere else in the entire world that we'd rather be right now than out here in the middle of nowhere.

In Tibet.

Chapter 7

Langma La to Base Camp

To one who has long been in city pent;
'Tis very sweet to look into the fair
And open face of heaven.

—John Keats

A sudden glow of sunshine warmed the yellow nylon of my tent. An instant later, the air became stiflingly hot as the sun climbed above the southern ramparts that guarded our isolated valley. The sky, a peculiar looking, featureless black sheet, was magically suspended in midair, lending even more of an otherworldly appearance to the mountain scenery surrounding us. But as we were beginning to learn, not all appearances need be deceiving; these mountains would indeed prove to be of another world.

After three weeks of traveling, we needed a day to wash. I filled up three sunshowers—solar-heated, black plastic bags—with ice water from a pond just below camp. An hour later, the water was pleasingly hot.

"There's Ed, poised modestly naked behind a small rock!" Robert yelled.

Everyone turned; I waved.

Left: *At the top of the Langma La, Makalu and Chomolönzo suddenly thrust into view.*

Washing up day gave us a rare chance to clean clothes—and ourselves. Mimi on left.

"I think that I am also going to have a bath!" Paul declared in his best Queen's English.

"Odd, isn't it," he added, then snorted for effect, "I don't even have to think about my pronunciation any more!"

"We'll probably all sound quite British by the end of the climb," Robert drawled. At this Stephen began to look slightly perturbed.

"Yes, that *will* be quite an accomplishment," he said.

We washed ourselves and scrubbed laundry, read, wrote, then sorted and repacked the duffels until they conformed to the desired thirty-kilo portering weight. Each chore was executed in the slowest possible motion. I wasn't feeling energetic. Worse still, I had horrible gas, as did everyone else. Our mutual distress was traced to some fresh cabbage or improperly rehydrated freeze-dried vegetables. Carrots appeared to be the worst offenders.

Even though we were camped in the midst of indescribably beautiful mountain scenery, I began to notice in myself an odd disinclination to get out the ropes and climb. Luckily, one of my strengths has always been my ability to climb hard with very little practice: as climbers say, "off the couch." I knew I had to rest before the rigors of climbing on Everest's East Face, but I didn't want to be too rusty either.

The true test on a Himalayan peak is how well one copes, both mentally and physically, with living and climbing at extremely high altitude. To make our climb even more challenging, we'd be climbing without any Sherpa assistance. Pasang's duties were limited to his roles as cook and *Sirdar*—to smooth the logistical nightmare of getting us to Base Camp. Paul, Stephen, Robert, and I would ourselves carry up every last scrap of gear, food, and the fuel that we'd need on the mountain, along with our tents and sleeping bags. Our Everest climb resembled the unrealistic situation of a marathon runner who must first set the course, select and mark the route, and then run the entire race again, all the while hoping to still have enough remaining energy to cross the finish line. Except that our "race" would last three months.

For the present, our aim was to reach the top of the Langma La, and determine the remaining distance to Base Camp. The porters were due to return in several days, and in the meantime we had to break a trail for them through the new snow to the top of the pass. Finally, early in the afternoon of March 16, we attained the eighteen-thousand-foot crest. The weather couldn't have been finer. My anticipation grew with the last few steps; I knew Everest would be visible.

"The invincible pyramid!" Paul crowed.

To our west, horizon to horizon, was arrayed an inspiring mountain vista of craggy peaks, snaking glaciers, and wreathing cloud. The lofty trinity of Makalu, Lhotse, and Everest rose, of course, highest of all, but Chomolönzo's rocky escarpments reared closer still, and with more fearsome verticality, than its taller neighbors. Admiring this same view in 1921, George Mallory wrote to his wife Ruth, "I'm altogether beaten for words. The whole range of peaks from Makalu to Everest far exceeds any mountain scenery I ever saw." We agreed. If ever Shangri-La existed, then it could easily be nestled in the enchanting Kama Valley, the approach route to the East, or Kangshung, Face of Mount Everest.

Everest itself, some eighteen treacherously rugged and snow-covered miles away, was mostly cloaked in cloud. How were we ever going to get the porters and our loads to the mountain's base? Stephen and I decided to explore down the far side of the pass. Thick clouds moved in, obliterated all visibility, and left us stumbling through knee-deep snow in a whiteout. We could always retrace out tracks, we told ourselves, unless the falling snow covered them.

Fortuitously, just when the rock cairns we were following ended, the afternoon storm receded, and a warm and golden light flooded into the valley. The physical scale of the mountains surrounding us slowly shrank to a discernible size, and I felt less intimidated by their overwhelming bulk and height. Maybe these peaks were climbable by humans after all. The descent to the Rabkar Valley, the side valley below us that formed a T-junction with the Kama Valley— which then led west to our Base Camp—no longer looked so difficult either.

"Hard to believe that we've circled nearly all the way around Everest to get here, isn't it?" Stephen asked when we stopped to admire the vista.

"You know, I've never seen a single photograph documenting this side of Makalu and Chomolönzo before," I answered.

"Nor have I. The Kangshung Face and the Kama Valley I've always found fascinating. It's been my dream to come here."

I was very glad that Stephen was part of our team. Not only was he a solid mountaineer, he was a wonderful traveling companion, filled with an iron-willed, yet boyish enthusiasm. Furthermore, he had a great appreciation for the scenic beauty of the mountains, plus an encyclopedic knowledge of Himalayan climbing history. I felt a growing kinship with Stephen—if only I could keep up with his speedy pace! We ran back to camp, almost together, happily knowing that should the snowstorms ever end, the way to Base was possible.

That night we noticed a light off in the distance. It was Kasang, returning after accompanying the support team to Kharta. He handed Robert a note from Wendy. The Coleman cook tent had arrived. A cheer went up; there would be Base Camp luxury after all! Amazingly, the nearly forty-pound tent had traveled unescorted halfway around the world.

Paul and Stephen were keen to inspect the cliffs above camp, and to break out our climbing gear. I felt incredibly lethargic though, and wondered if I was acclimatizing properly. Acclimatization is a tricky process involving timing and patience since the human body needs several weeks to multiply its red blood cell count in order to boost oxygen absorption. With each trip to a higher altitude, your body chemistry is prodded to slowly adapt. In theory, you should feel better on each successive ascent, but it's an arduous road to reach full acclimatization. I couldn't help noticing how spry my teammates looked.

We rock climbed on the triple-tiered buttress northeast of camp. Paul led up a steep and loose 5.8 crack, then Mimi and I, with Stephen soloing beside us, climbed a 5.7 fissure to the left. It was Mimi's second day of rock climbing ever! Crag climbing was one thing, but I sincerely hoped Mimi and Joe wouldn't insist on acting out their climbing fantasies on Everest's Kangshung Face.

Stephen, meanwhile, advocated that we should report our new climbs to *Mountain,* the British mountaineering magazine. "What I like about doing routes in remote places," he explained, "is that they sound so damned impressive—the Northwest Face of this or that—when in fact most of them are just little chossy bits of snow and ice."

Earlier, I'd noticed a faint, but quite inviting vertical

Ed on the first ascent of Free Tibet (5.10b) *with the Langma La in the distance.* Stephen Venables

Ed reaches a stance after the forty-foot runout on Free Tibet. Stephen Venables

fracture breaking the second tier's central slab. I launched up it using little smears for my feet and jamming fingertips into pockets in the crack. After a strenuous 5.9 reach was rewarded with a good flake, an unprotected forty-foot runout on balancey 5.7 face climbing gained a ledge. At nearly sixteen thousand feet elevation, I was pushed to the limit. We named our new route *Free Tibet* and figured that it wouldn't be repeated for quite some time.

Writing in my diary, I reflected on the wonderful harmony of our little team. I couldn't think of one negative incident to record. This wasn't supposed to happen on a Himalayan expedition, was it? Weren't we supposed to bicker, feud, be petty and jealous, and hate each other's guts by the end of the trip? Instead, we were rapidly becoming the fastest of friends. While I knew such good feelings might not last, we were certainly off to a winning start.

Robert's plan—to be at Base Camp by March 5 and climb our route's bottom buttress by the end of March—obviously was in need of some slight readjustment. The Tibetans wouldn't be able to cross the Langma La in these cold and wintry conditions, especially with their inadequate clothing, boots, and eyewear. Now a full three weeks behind schedule, we were being held hostage below the eighteen-thousand-foot Langama La pass by the continued bad weather and snow. We were, in a word, stuck.

At Pre-Base Camp, Stephen and Robert enjoy a nice cup of tea after a day's outing.

"God I need a change of view!" I heard Mimi complain.

"Too much horizontal, not enough vertical!" Robert added.

A two-day winter blizzard struck on the evening of March 18. Burrowed deep in my sleeping bag, I devoured Tom Holzel and Audrey Salkeld's fine book, *The Mystery of Mallory & Irvine,* a fascinating chronicle about the lives and disappearance of the British Everest pioneers. Pasang, listening to Radio Nepal, told us 120-kilometer winds had wreaked havoc on Kathmandu.

"Round two!" lamented Paul as our few remaining porters fled for their villages in the heavily falling snow. Robert sent word to Kharta that when the weather cleared we wanted to hire 120 villagers to carry our loads. He also offered a bonus of an extra three and a half yuan (one dollar!) for walking up here again. We had to keep the villagers happy, or we'd never reach Base Camp. Jeremy, the villager we had developed the best rapport with, had inexplicably vanished. His replacement wore green army goggles, a wild fur hat, and grinned broadly like a Cheshire cat. Eventually, Ang Chu also became our trusted friend.

Sonam Phuti and her younger brother Pinzo Norbu arrived in camp with the Coleman Sheik cooking and dining tent. With its three separate rooms, zippered doors, mosquito netting, storm flaps, and central awning, Pasang and Kasang had never seen anything like it.

"It's a house!" Robert exclaimed. "It's a palace!" Mimi countered.

"It's Ed's birthday tent!" Paul proclaimed. My birthday was the next day. After almost a month on the trail, little luxuries like a warm place to eat began to assume a primary importance for us.

March 21 dawned sunny. The Kangshung microclimate, as Paul called it, had cleared. The first day of spring, it was also my thirty-second birthday—and hopefully the start of our better fortunes. We relaxed all day. Stephen was engrossed in *Mallory & Irvine,* and he chuckled every few minutes. "The dirt! The dirt! I love it," he enthused. When the sun dipped behind the mountains at 3:30 P.M., we scurried like mice to the warmth of our feather-insulated nests.

Knowing my love of Mexican food and picante sauce, Mimi organized a special birthday feast in the Sheik. The kerosene lantern, spicy food, and cama-raderie all warmed us. We tried to save room for Pasang's carrot cake. Pasang and Kasang carried in the cake to appropriate orchestration, and I blew out the single, extra-large candle.

"Where's the booze?" I wondered, noting the absence of liquor.

"Sandy's generous contribution!" Robert beamed, producing a bottle of Glenlivet scotch to more cheers.

My teammates helped me celebrate my thirty-second birthday in style. Mimi Zieman

Maybe it was selfish, but I'd shepherded several unopened birthday presents halfway around the world, gifts from my godmother, Judith McConnell, and Randa, my girlfriend. Judy's presents were two blank diary books, and two novels, *Fifth Business* by Robertson Davies, and *The Counterfeiters* by Andre Gide.

"They're marvelous books!" Mimi said. "I'd like to read them both."

"Well, you never know what Randa might have sent," I said. First I pulled out a cassette, *Skyscraper,* by the rock singer David Lee Roth. The album cover featured photos taken by Galen Rowell of Roth rock climbing in Yosemite Valley. Paul, our hip Californian, immediately grabbed the tape for a closer inspection.

Then my fingers felt something unusually soft inside the package. Momentarily perplexed, I pulled out the next present. A silver-blue negligée! After gasping simultaneously, we erupted in laughter.

Mimi shouted: "It's a nightie!"

"Nooo," Paul responded knowledgeably, before pronouncing in a rising voice: "It's a teddy!"

It was an ironic gift to receive in a tent in the middle of Tibet in wintry weather while wearing our bulky down jackets. Laughing with near hysteria, we gasped for breath and wiped the tears from our eyes. Was I going to wear the negligée at the South Col, Paul wanted to know—or would I fly it from my ice ax on the summit? It was a birthday present I knew I'd never live down.

As the revelry quieted, Pasang turned on the nightly 8 P.M. forecast on Radio Nepal.

"And now for the weather," the Nepali announcer intoned. "Tonight it is mostly fair throughout the Kingdom."

It was fair in our kingdom, too, on that special evening as we staggered off to our respective tents, then stopped to gaze up at Tibet's full tapestry of stars.

*   *   *   *   *   *   *   *   *   *   *   *   *   *

At breakfast, I casually remarked to Paul that my shoulders were sore. Before I could explain that I had sunburned them, he said, "Chaffed by the nightie, eh?"

I knew I could not escape my fate.

Robert decided that we should repack the trail to the Langma La for the porters. We made good time, reaching the top in two hours. Robert propped up his powerful binoculars on a convenient boulder. The morning clouds hadn't built up, so we had our first clear inspection of the Kangshung Face.

"'Thirty-foot ice cliffs at five miles,' was what I told the salesman," Robert explained. "And that's what we've got. Have a look."

Hidden behind intervening ridges, the face's lower fifteen hundred feet were not visible, nor was the cloud-covered South Col, but we could see the Cauliflower Ridge—our intended line—just to the left of the 1983 *American Buttress*. Our ridge was a blocky spine formed by four gigantic ice blocks. We noted several two-hundred-foot sections of vertical ice, and on both sides of the ridge, snow, ice, and rock faces fell precipitously to the glacier. There was a good reason why no one had ever attempted this way up Mount Everest. It bore a striking resemblance to what climbers affectionately call "a death route."

"The upper snow and ice slopes above the buttress appear solid enough," Robert speculated, "but how do we get there? The actual buttress crest looks like it's far enough away from the ice cliffs on Lhotse on the left, and from the big ice gully on the right, so that it *might* be safe from avalanches."

"Except from a big blast coming off the Lhotse wall," Stephen pointed out. This was yet another danger. Even if we weren't hit directly by an avalanche, the air blast emanating from one could still nail us. At least the upper slopes leading to the South Col didn't look too extreme. Stephen even thought they resembled the well-traveled traditional line of ascent up the Lhotse face on the Nepalese side of the Col, the side ascended by the *Hillary-Tenzing Route.*

That night I ducked into the cook tent for an overdue chat with Pasang. Our friendship, after all, was one of the reasons he was here. Conversation drifted to Everest and our intended climb.

"Staying here below Langma La very good for everybody. You think bad, we too slow, but actually it really good. Now you have health, strength. Every day, little exercise, good! We get to Base Camp, you climb right away."

He was right. After two weeks camped at sixteen thousand feet, in the summer yak-grazing grounds of Lhatse—or "Pre-Base Camp," as we'd named it—we were getting increasingly fit. Our long-delayed approach march to the mountain was an acclimatization blessing in disguise.

"Climb look good," Pasang continued. "Paul show me picture. At South Col, my Sherpa friends tell me you eat and drink—drink very important—and leave tent early, 2 A.M. Easy to summit, not too hard, only very long. Reach summit at nine or ten in morning, then down quickly. Everyone is success."

I hoped his words would come true.

"Then maybe I can go home and be finished with Everest for a while. Make a new life," I said.

"Yes, have babies!" Pasang chirped with animation. He never missed the chance to encourage both marriage and having children.

The following morning, Stephen, Joe, and I hiked back up to the top of the pass to photograph Everest at sunrise. We missed the alpenglow, but got excellent shots and a panoramic view. Joe even carted up his 4 x 5 inch view camera. Back at camp, we discussed the lack of porters.

"They were supposed to return on the second clear day," Robert said.

"I'll go down to Kharta and shake things up," Stephen volunteered. An hour later, his familiar accent returned to camp, shouting triumphantly: "I saw three dots coming up, Kasang with two others. Kasang says one hundred and twelve villagers are coming!"

All afternoon the porters came straggling in, men and *didis*—women—and fortunately, fewer children. We wanted only hardy souls who could brave the snows of the Langma La. Each porter was greeted with a hearty *"Tashi delai!"* to keep spirits running high. And Pasang delighted in spreading the rumor that everyone would receive plenty of cigarettes after we'd crossed the pass.

Kasang, our happy-go-lucky cookboy, was in good spirits after running from village to village like a Tibetan Paul Revere rallying the troops. Pasang had also taught Kasang several more English words like "rice" and "vegetables," plus another extremely useful phrase: "more tea." Kasang's vocabulary had grown substantially beyond his memorable initial greeting of *"Goo mournu!"*

Robert read us his revised game plan. By his figuring, we had thirty to forty days of hard climbing on the buttress and the upper slopes to the South Col. A slender chance remained that we could summit by the end of the first week of May. Our tentative departure date to fly home was May 20.

"Our two-week delay has made things tight, but I still think we can pull it off. This'll be a tough climb, there's no mistaking that. We've got to have completely open lines of communication to succeed, so anyone—including Joe, Mimi, and Pasang—if you've got anything to say, speak up. Everyone can put in their two cents worth on this trip.

"What's going to get us to the summit is if the climbers who are feeling strong, and who are climbing in their specialty, push on ahead. I'm not planning to lead much ice, because Paul is faster on ice than any of us."

"Another important thing to remember," Paul added, "is that all four of us are going to be involved in selecting the route."

"We also want to make sure we put Advanced Base Camp in a safe location, and also situate it as close to the base of the route as possible," Robert said.

We estimated we'd need twenty porter loads of camping and climbing equipment, rope, food, and cooking gear at Advanced Base. To get established below the climb as soon as possible, we planned to recruit the twenty strongest Tibetan men for one or two extra days of work ferrying up these loads.

A clear view of the constellation Orion setting over camp was always a sign of improving weather. The last few shreds of low cloud clinging to the valley peaks were banished by the night cold, and when we awoke, a dry wind was blowing up valley from the northeast. At last—maybe—spring had arrived.

The day was a complete contrast to our first debacle with the porters two weeks ago. This time we let Pasang handle everything. We spoke softly and dismantled camp as though we could care less whether we left today or not. Paul patrolled the fenced-off perimeter (made of parachute cord and ski poles) around our stockpile of loads, while Robert, inspecting the expectant throng of dirty watchful faces, proclaimed: "No man is an island—or as they say in Tibet—every expedition needs porters."

Miraculously, eighty porters left with their loads *before* 10 A.M. Once the caravan began moving, the pace picked up. Ang Chu's group got the first loads to the top of the Langma La by 10:30, but Stephen, unable to curb his excitement, raced ahead, leaving them unsupervised. "You'd think, being an Oxford boy, that he'd know to stay with his group," Robert moaned. After two weeks of enforced idleness, everyone was impatient. At noon, Mimi left in "sweep position," trailing the final group.

Unfortunately, thirty-four loads lay unclaimed. When twenty more villagers arrived, they claimed it was too late to cross the pass today, especially since they'd walked here from Kharta that morning. This was understandable, but then the endless bickering began. Only the heavy loads remained. Tempers flared as several of the men balked at carrying, then threatened to leave.

Paul lost his patience. "Let them go then! If they don't want to work, they can leave." Voices grew louder and hotter as Pasang tried to negotiate.

"Oh, God—to be back at my office!" Robert exclaimed longingly. "The joy of asking someone to do something, and having it actually be done!"

Standing in the center of the shouting, gesticulating cluster of angry villagers, Pasang rubbed one hand over his forehead and said simply, "I have a headache." We all did. Paul marched up to the most belligerent villager.

"You don't want to work? Then go!" Paul's eyes glared; neither Paul or the villager budged an inch.

"Go home; *we don't want you!*" Paul bellowed. The dour-faced man continued to complain how unfairly we were treating them, and egged on the others. Paul patted him on the head—a bit too firmly—and the villager swung his wooden crutch at Paul, but missed. Realizing that a peaceful solution might be better, Paul put an arm around his shoulder. The angry man pushed him away.

The porters rekindled the argument with Pasang while the Anglos retreated to cool off. Eventually, Robert capitulated to their demands. Two boys were dispatched to round up six more porters to carry the six remaining loads. And the villagers decided to carry several loads partway up the pass to get a better start tomorrow. Pasang and I left at 2 P.M. to cross the Langma La, while Paul and Robert looked forward to camping at Lhatse with their newfound friends.

Pasang and I reached camp on the far side of the pass not long after the last porters filed in. Stephen had exhorted them to go farther, but again they'd refused. This time, Pasang agreed with the villagers. "Dead porter, then what?" he asked rhetorically. I told Joe, Mimi, and Stephen tales from Lhatse, then reiterated Robert's parting words: "Press on to Base Camp no matter what."

While I set up my tent, Pasang confided to me, "Tibetans say Stephen very angry with them. They say when other expeditions here, they help, no get angry. They no steal, so why angry? Better talk softly, much better."

From the Langma La, we could see only the top half of Everest's East Face (on right).

I also thought that several of my teammates were overreacting. At dinner, I expressed my view that if we didn't all adjust ourselves to the Tibetan's slow pace of life, we were going to make things miserable, and hurt ourselves and perhaps the expedition. Considering the expedition's total cost, of what consequence were the few extra yuan we were paying the porters to appease them?

Next morning the villagers formed a long line of the "walking wounded." Most complained of partial snowblindness; Mimi administered eye drops and aspirin. Ang Chu, the Kharta villagers' new headman, was a hard worker. Pasang advocated that we employ him to help carry spare loads to Advanced Base, and to run messages back and forth to Kharta, to Mr. Yang and Mr. Shi.

As we broke camp, Stephen again became livid. This time someone had grabbed a roll of his film. He'd set it down on a rock and—*poof!* But he knew better than to leave anything lying around. We'd already lost clothes and socks to quick Tibetan fingers. I left him shouting obscenities, and started off hiking down the trail with the porters, whistling yak calls, and shouting, "Okay, *Didi!* Let's go, Chomolungma!" to urge them along.

It was a pristine day. The warm sun had melted the snow from the south-facing grass slopes of the pass, and the combination of glaciers, peaks, blue sky and blazing sun was revitalizing. My shouts and whistles seem to put the Tibetans in a happy mood, too, and soon they began to answer my hoots and hollers with their own. However, when the horde of eighty-odd sat down in unison atop a dry hillock, I quickly got the gist. They wanted us to break trail. Beyond a frozen lake called Shurim Tso, knee-deep snow still blanketed the colder lower meadows undulating toward the Rabkar Valley to our west.

Pasang, Ang Chu, Stephen, and I set off across the wintry white plateau. The snow was firm, then grew deeper and softer, but no one complained. With such a circle of famed Himalayan peaks—Makalu, Chomolönzo, Lhotse, and Everest—framing our view, it was by far the most stupendous hike any of us had ever done.

"I wouldn't trade places with anyone just now," Stephen smiled.

Pasang agreed. "Most beautiful view of mountains I ever see." For a Sherpa native of Namche Bazaar, that was saying something.

Stephen took the lead. Hiking quickly, he soon shrunk to the size of a small dot in the snowfield's center, becoming dwarfed by the towering rock walls beyond. I widened the trail for the porters. Reaching at last a dry oasis of grass, we halted for lunch. Eventually, most of the porters caught up, then Mimi arrived. She was visibly upset. A couple of the Tibetan men had grabbed her by the arm and made explicit suggestions. Furious, she'd shaken them off and yelled at them to leave her alone. Fortunately, Joe had appeared. In 1986, I'd heard similar stories from several women trekkers in Tibet. Obviously, we all felt protective of Mimi. Alarmed and angry, we agreed to keep a watch out for her safety, and to severely punish anyone we caught hassling her again.

We continued scouting the best trail, traversed a snow slope due south, and stayed well above the glacier-fed Rabkar Chu ("pure white water river") until we came to more dry meadows, and huge open tracts of pastureland. "Imagine what this must look like in summer!" Stephen shouted. We ran down a steep hillside and rested on another dry knoll. Pasang and Ang Chu began to talk.

"Before Chinese come, two monasteries here," Pasang translated. "Many yaks graze here in summer; yak herders go to monasteries. One monastery over there,"—Pasang pointed to a secluded shelf just above the Rabkar Glacier— "other one higher up, beside Kangshung Glacier."

Suddenly the thought popped into my mind. "Pasang," I said, "could you please ask Ang Chu what this place is called?"

Scale in the Himalaya is hard to grasp. Lhotse top left, Everest on right, Venables below.

"He say this Gangla," Pasang replied matter-of-factly.

The legend was true! How I wished Norbu could have been here to hear Ang Chu's words. When pressed for additional details, Ang Chu said this was where Tenzing would have come with his father to herd goats and yaks each summer. The family would have made pilgrimages to the locally renowned Gangla Monastery (called Namdag Lhe Phodang—"the perfectly pure god's palace") and enjoyed views of Chomolungma's summit from the high pastures.

In his autobiography, *Tiger of the Snows,* Tenzing states, "My family lived in Thamey, and I grew up there, but I was born in a place called Tsa–chu, near the great mountain Makalu.... Tsa-chu, which means "Hot Springs," is a holy place of many stories and legends, and my mother had gone there on a pilgrimage to the monastery of Gangla, that being also our clan or family name."

Years later, I was to learn of another locally revered destination within the Kama Valley's hidden sanctuary: the holy lake of Tshechu, the lake of "Life Water." Tucked away in a high, hanging side valley, this lake is only a few hours hike from the Gangla Monastery, and is closer still to Chomolungma's mysterious Kangshung Face. Evidence from several sources points to the shores of this watery gem, Tshechu—whose "secret surface" has revealed prophetic visions— or to the sacred spring nearby, as the actual birthplace of Tenzing Norgay.

There are intriguing clues. Also in *Tiger of the Snows,* Tenzing writes: "Near it [his birthplace] is a great rock shaped like the head of the Lord Buddha, out of which water is said to flow if a pious person touches it and prays." According to Hildegard Diemberger, "At the end of the valley [above Tshechu] a cliff pointing toward the sky indicates the spring of life water. In a broad cave at the bottom of the cliff there are a few stone huts [used as] shelters for pilgrims.... The compact rock face presents a few cracks from which there runs a thin thread of clear water, which can purge sins, heal the sick, and bestow life power.... This holy site is frequently visited by pilgrims and shepherds on the high pastures."

Was Tenzing Norgay born on the shores of the holy lake of Tshechu?

Upon hearing a loud commotion behind us, we watched eighty villagers, whooping and shouting, run down the long, grassy slope to rejoin us. Pasang said they wanted to camp here. But it was only 2 P.M., and the weather was perfect. Stephen and I looked at each other, then immediately got up and bolted ahead, yelling "Chomolungma! Chomolungma!" as we traversed a dry shoulder of ground heading south—praying that the porters would follow us.

As far as we could see, slanting up the hillsides to our left, rose acres and acres of pristine snowfields. To be hiking through this scenery, carrying light loads, was to experience the ultimate freedom of Himalayan travel, that joyously carefree feeling of trekking on foot past unimaginably beautiful mountain scenery, without having a worry in the world. To the west soared the pointed, rocky summit of Makalu, the world's fifth-highest peak, while closer loomed the brown and gold buttresses of granite-walled Chomolönzo.

Abandoning the ridge crest, we descended a precipitous embankment into thickets of bushes growing in the river bottom. River Camp was on several grassy enclaves beside the Rabkar Chu, and only a few hundred yards from the entrance to the mystical Kama Valley. Here wood was plentiful. It was a perfect site, plus the altitude was roughly thirteen thousand feet. The air tasted rich with oxygen. A red-clad figure galloped down the hill. It was Paul!

"Great to finally get out of that hole," he yelled, referring to Pre-Base Camp. "Robert's coming, too, and Joe and Mimi aren't far back."

We warmed ourselves by a fire, drying out our wet boots and socks until I managed (with predictable ease) to incinerate my best wool socks. Robert arrived next, with the news that thirty-five porters had carried over the Langma La, and were camped in the upper meadows with Kasang watching them.

"Guess what else turned up?" Paul asked us, yanking an unmistakable packet from his pack. "A Fed Ex package with the Actifed from Burroughs Wellcome!" The package from one of our sponsors had been forwarded by the CMA.

As the sun rose the next morning, I heard Paul declare, "You're ruining my personal moment!" to a group of Tibetans clustered beside his tent door. It had gotten very tiresome, I had to agree, being constantly watched by an intensely interested crowd of twenty villagers. "Don't even think of coming over here!" Mimi shouted as another villager approached her tent.

As morning waned, our porters made little effort to prepare to leave until Kasang and the B Team porters hurtled down the hill like charging cavalry.

"Oh why can't the rest of you all get up and do some work for a change?" Stephen shouted at the A Team villagers who'd accompanied us over the pass.

The main group left by 11 A.M., while we awaited several B Team stragglers. A moment of indecision occurred at the wooden bridge spanning the Rabkar Chu. After crossing it, the B Team members dropped their loads and claimed they were too tired to continue! Before a consensus was reached, we tried to shepherd them along using the "get one moving and the rest will follow" trick. It didn't work. On top of a small hill, everyone stopped again to hold another council. By the time they agreed to continue, Pasang was exhausted from arbitrating. He and Kasang would stay back to watch the villagers and the loads.

A line of porters enters the fabled Kama Valley. Stephen Venables

Turning the corner to the right, now heading west, we entered the Kama Valley, and hiked along a narrow twisting path through azalea, rhododendron, and other lush vegetation. Water trickled in rivulets across the valley floor, while billowy cotton-white clouds hid the high summits. It was these same moisture-bearing clouds flowing up the Arun River drainage from the south, from Nepal, that supported the valley's verdant growth. Looking east toward the Arun, we could see the beginnings of the juniper forests local villagers had been felling at a rapid rate to supply firewood and wood beams to Shigatse and Lhasa. (Later we saw Galen Rowell's photos documenting the lower Kama Valley's excessive deforestation, some of the worst old-growth cutting in the entire Himalaya.)

What could have been a delightful hike was ruined by yet another porter strike. One clan decided they'd walked far enough for one day. The last thing we wanted was for our loads to be scattered across the countryside, unattended, and at the mercy of sharp knives and inquisitive fingers. Then Kasang appeared. He told us that the last group was on their way—but exactly where were they?

Two of the men in the striking clan were "sick," but they'd felt plenty healthy hours earlier, well enough to argue loudly for higher wages. The weather was breaking; the daily afternoon blizzard was minutes away. The villagers, we discovered, had no tent. Pasang explained that we had tarps they could use for shelter at the next campsite up ahead, and that Mimi would tend to the sick pair, but no amount of cajoling would budge them. My patience ended.

"Pasang, please tell them that if it snows, they will freeze. They will suffer because they do not have a tent, and they won't have a doctor, and they won't get their full pay because of this delay."

We hiked another hour west up the valley. I was infuriated by the villager's refusal to continue. This particular clan was carrying both of my personal duffel bags, and if either were broken into or knifed, I didn't know what I'd do.

"These people, so difficult!" Pasang exclaimed, exasperated. "They no listen."

Paul, Stephen, and Joe had built a shelter with our barrels and a tarp at Boulder Camp. We ate dinner as the snowstorm raged; it was our third major blizzard in three weeks. "When's this snow going to bloody well give up?" Stephen complained. Not soon, evidently. Exhausted after haggling with the porters, I crept into my North Face dome tent with Stephen.

The next morning it was snowing with a vengeance. We were stranded—again. Kasang finally trooped into camp leading a group of the recalcitrant porters. Cold and tired, they asked for a tarp, which of course we provided. Then, another commotion. This time, they wanted a tent. Without one, they'd go home.

Villagers carrying loads in a snowstorm, in the Kama Valley.

"They live here," Joe said. "Why aren't they any better prepared?"

It was a mystery why this one group would set out on a six-day roundtrip in early spring over an eighteen-thousand-foot pass and not bring a tent or a tarpaulin. All the other village groups had tents. The departing porters also demanded a signed note stating that they would be paid in full, even though they hadn't carried all the way to Base Camp. For once, Robert consented. "In Lhatse we negotiated for a three-day trip to Base Camp. If the porters want to get late starts, hike three hours a day, and stop early, that's fine, but they're only going to get three days of pay."

Grabbing their signed paper, the porters disappeared downvalley into the blizzard. Then out of the storm appeared six more stragglers. My fears came true when I discovered that my two duffels and one of Paul's—all of his and my personal gear—weren't with them. I knew how other mountaineering expeditions had ended disastrously when gear had been stolen; even pad-locked tents—like Roger Marshall's—had been knifed, and the contents rifled. Robert, Joe, and I hurried after the departing clan to track down our baggage.

Ed and Robert having a rest in "full yak position." Stephen Venables

The whiteout engulfed us, and two feet of new snow had erased all landmarks. Fortunately, we still found our way to River Camp, where we discovered the errant bags quickly disappearing under a mantle of accumulating snow. "Good thing we came," Robert said, "or these duffels would've been history."

Unexpectedly, two other porters appeared; Kasang had dispatched them to assuage his guilty conscience. In sign language, we asked them to carry the bags back to Boulder Camp. No; they would not! They wanted to sleep here tonight, then carry the loads tomorrow! We were disgusted. Had this same scene occurred in Nepal, any available Sherpa would have immediately offered to carry the duffels for us without a second thought, because a Sherpa's high reputation and very livelihood depends on their readiness to work.

"Well, *we're* going now," I said angrily. The duffels weighed sixty pounds each. We carried them back ourselves, pressing on through the blizzard, halting bent over at the waist in "full yak position" every five minutes, out of breath and panting, until we could again stumble forward. By the time we reached Boulder Camp, I was thoroughly chilled and shivering; I headed straight for my

Robert immediately liked the spot. Soon, we heard a yell, and Paul, Joe, and Pasang arrived—with a long string of black dots following them—the porters! Fully a month after we had left Beijing and Kathmandu, we had at last found our Base Camp.

All ended well. The porters straggled into camp and dropped their precious cargoes. Paul erected another "fence" of ski poles and parachute cord to form an enclosure where Robert, Pasang and Ang Chu sat sorting out the finances. Finally our hand (hidden till then to everyone but Robert) was revealed: we only had enough cash to pay the Tibetans a third of the amount that we owed them. As this was translated and explained to the villagers, Robert handed out all of our remaining Chinese currency, then signed IOUs promising to pay them the remainder in Kharta upon our return. Everything was handled professionally, and there were no hard feelings. Two hours later, all but the four small groups of men who would carry loads to Advanced Base Camp had been paid and left.

Pasang pays off the porters at Base Camp.

Robert and I would recon our proposed Advanced Base Camp site and cairn the route, while the others sorted out the necessary food and gear for the Tibetan men to ferry up to ABC the next day. There was still plenty of work to do, but a celebration was also obviously in order. The Sheik cooking and dining tent was set up to house Pasang's feast, and Stephen produced a bottle of Famous Grouse whisky, with which we toasted our very long-awaited arrival. As night fell, the clouds cleared to reveal Everest and Lhotse close at hand, with the constellation Orion suspended like a jeweled pendant above the South Col.

It was a sight that we'd all waited months to see.

Chapter 8

The Cauliflower Ridge

Transformation is a journey without a final destination.

—Marilyn Ferguson

obert and I left early to look for a campsite at the base of the mountain, accompanied by two strapping Tibetans who carried four tents and some stove canisters. Ten minutes west of camp, we gained the ridge crest of the Kangshung Glacier's lateral moraine. A gravel and rock slope fell away several hundred feet into rubble-strewn chaos. We ran, zigzagging down the loose embankment, out onto the glacier's rock-covered surface. Hiking across a glacier is both unnerving and exhilarating. Hidden crevasses pose a constant danger, but fortunately, the Kangshung's glacial surface was relatively compact. Well-covered with rocks, the glacier seemed to have few concealed crevasses. While the stones were treacherously loose, their abundance made hiking relatively safe. Already, we were making good time.

Left: *Robert Anderson and two Tibetan companions set out for the Kangshung Face.*

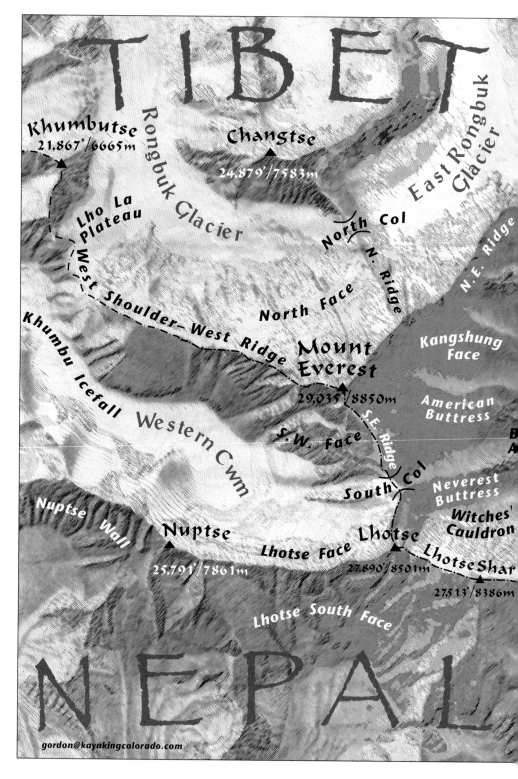

TIBET

Khumbutse
21,867'/6665m

Rongbuk Glacier

Changtse
24,879'/7583m

East Rongbuk Glacier

Lho La Plateau

North Col

N. Ridge

N.E. Ridge

West Shoulder–West Ridge

North Face

Khumbu Icefall

North Face

Mount Everest
29,035'/8850m

Kangshung Face

American Buttress

Western Cwm

S.W. Face

S.E. Ridge

South Col

Neverest Buttress

Nuptse Wall

Nuptse
25,791'/7861m

Lhotse Face

Lhotse
27,890'/8501m

Witches' Cauldron

LhotseShar
27,513'/8386m

Lhotse South Face

NEPAL

gordon@kayakingcolorado.com

304

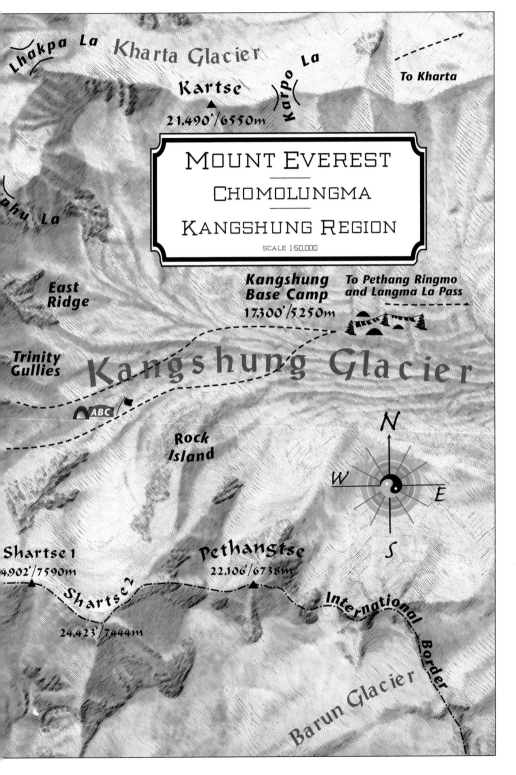

Lhakpa La   Kharta Glacier   Karpo La   To Kharta

Kartse
▲
21,490'/6550m

...ahu La

MOUNT EVEREST
CHOMOLUNGMA
KANGSHUNG REGION
SCALE 1:50,000

East
Ridge

Kangshung
Base Camp
17,300'/5250m

To Pethang Ringmo
and Langma La Pass

Trinity
Gullies

Kangshung Glacier

ABC

Rock
Island

N
W   E
S

Shartse 1
24,902'/7590m

Pethangtse
22,106'/6738m

Shartse 2
24,423'/7444m

International Border

Barun Glacier

Scouting the site for Advanced Base Camp, we approached Lhotse (left) *and Everest.*

"Does it feel great to get out and accomplish something!" Robert sang out with extra gusto.

We didn't cairn the trail on the way up. We preferred to figure out the best route first, then mark it on our return. We walked, slipped, and stumbled over the loose debris toward the large rocky island protruding from the center of the upper Kangshung basin. An ice slab coated with a frosting of snow required several minutes of extra care before we reached the island. To our delight, a convenient path of hard snow girdled the base of the rocky atoll. We trod quickly along crunchy snow, circling toward what Paul had named the Witches' Cauldron, the eerie avalanche catch basin beneath the two-mile-high North Face of Lhotse. Spoiling the Tibetans with frequent stops and cigarettes, we enjoyed getting to know them as individuals, away from the other porters.

All morning long, our eyes were riveted to the two major buttresses protruding from the lower portion of Everest's East Face. The *Lowe,* or *American Buttress* rose in the center, while our hoped-for climb—the smaller of the two prows—jutted out on the left, closer to Lhotse. Our candid opinion of the 1983 American route was unanimous. Although it was certainly the face's most obvious feature, it was a black hulk of fragmented rock topped by a dangerous crown of snow flutings and leering ice gargoyles. By comparison, our buttress was smaller, but more importantly it appeared to Robert and me to be a considerably more aesthetic climbing route. And while the danger level certainly looked as bad or worse than the *American Buttress,* after a binocular-aided inspection of our dream climb, we thought we might have spied a feasible way.

Our proposed new route's approach was guarded by a blocky and menacing icefall. Fortunately, a snow gully appeared to skirt the icefall's left side to gain the toe of our buttress. Easy climbing then led to a rightward traverse across two, low-angled snow terraces, before a rock headwall gained a narrow, vertical, snow-filled depression or groove—the Scottish Gully, Robert named it, after the birthplace of modern ice climbing. The gully ended beneath some protective rock overhangs jutting out from below the four cauliflower-shaped ice towers. Next, a long and potentially very dangerous diagonal, rightwards traverse led to an ice ramp that appeared to give access through several vertical rock cliffs. Topping the buttress was the cockscomb of huge, crazily perched, partially detached ice blocks (called seracs), then the immense snow and ice slopes above.

If we could navigate a safe route up the lower portion of the buttress and emerge safely onto its crest, we hoped that the Cauliflower Towers themselves would be less arduous to climb. Above them, only four thousand more vertical feet of high-altitude wallowing up the mountain's middle snow slopes would separate us from the world famous terrace of the South Col and our highest camp. The snow conditions of these middle slopes—which could be anything from deep, laborious powder to easy-to-climb, hard, compacted snow called *névé*—would determine the ease, or struggle, of our eventual ascent to the Col.

Late that afternoon, Robert signaled that he'd found a good location for Advanced Base Camp, a flat hollow on top of a stony rib of moraine. The altitude was 17,800 feet. There were several good tent sites, plus a small ice-covered pond for drinking water, and we estimated that we were far enough away from the nearest avalanche threat. Furthermore, this particular moraine continued on toward the left side of the icefall below our buttress. We marked the spot with a blue barrel and a cluster of bamboo wands, then headed back.

The others had finished sorting our food and gear. A tarpaulin extending out over the front of the cook tent now housed the food barrels stacked up in neat rows, each barrel containing a different foodstuff. In the kitchen, Pasang and the

Tibetans had built a large rock table for our double-burner Coleman stove—and to store our pots, pans, utensils, and large array of condiments. In all, Base Camp had a semblance of home and looked wonderfully cheery.

The next morning the pitter-patter on my tent fly told me that yesterday's "afternoon mist" had turned to snow overnight. The temperature was also bitingly cold, and visibility was less than one hundred yards. I didn't think the Tibetans would carry up any loads on this day, but when I questioned Stephen, he replied curtly, "Oh yes they are. Pack up the duffel that you want us to take to Advanced Base. We're never going to climb the mountain if we delay for every little snow storm!"

I didn't envy them their chilled, wet, seven- or eight-hour forced march. I gave Stephen and Paul brief directions to the proposed site for our Advanced Camp, and moments later they set off cheerfully into the murk, the porters trailing behind them. I was glad my rest day had come, but was sorry we couldn't set out the sun showers. Journal and Walkman in hand, I stepped into the cook tent to intercept the tail end of a conversation. Robert glanced up.

"Oh, Ed—You don't mind what happens to your body if you get killed, do you? We'll dump you in a crevasse. That is okay, isn't it?" he asked.

I was, I must admit, shocked by his candor. As if I needed to be reminded of the possibly fatal outcome of the high-stakes game we were playing—just before starting the climb! But Robert was deadly serious. "Could you please show Joe and Mimi where your passport and money are? It just makes everything so much easier if you do get killed." Later I recalled that one of Robert's climbing partners had died on a climb they had been attempting in the Peruvian Andes; his concern was the product of experience.

For over a year, I had examined my reasons for coming to the Kangshung Face. Utterly remote, a four to five day hike from the nearest village or outside help, and raked by avalanches of truly massive proportion, Everest's East Face has one of the most fearsome reputations of any mountain wall in the world. Before we left home and during the long weeks of our approach, we'd each had plenty of time to look into our souls, to ponder, to rationalize—to try and explain to ourselves why we were here. The reasons were not easy to put into words.

By coincidence, I think that Robert, Stephen, Paul, and I had each reached personal junctures in our lives where we were willing to risk everything, even our lives, to attempt this one climb. There could honestly be no other explanation for our being here, at the base of a proposed new route up Mount Everest that our peers, without exception, thought was suicidal. Over many years, on our individual paths, we'd acquired the climbing skills and confidence-building experiences required to seriously contemplate climbing Everest's East Face. Being injured or killed was a frighteningly real possibility. We'd been repeatedly warned off by several of the world's best mountaineers. Yet here we were. Rock and ice fall, avalanches, hidden crevasses, frostbite, high-altitude illnesses, cerebral edema, pulmonary edema—the hazards were many, and undeniable.

Robert, I realized as I snapped back to the present, was simply being his usual pragmatic self. Slightly numbed, I showed Joe where I'd hidden my passport and money in my tent. Gently, he thanked me.

I had never started a climb while thinking that my chances of being killed were so great. But to dwell on the reality of death is hardly productive for a climber. Fatalism and pessimism rob you of energy; negativity and doubt destroy the self-assurance a mountaineer must cultivate in order to succeed. Climbers climb to live—not to die pointlessly. We climb to reaffirm the beauty and joy of existence, so why imbue that experience with a fatalistic or morbid attitude? I had examined the inner strength of my conviction to climb Everest's Kangshung Face, but Robert's blunt words brought all my fears to the fore.

The previous autumn, only two years after Lauren's death, I'd nearly been killed myself while climbing in the Black Canyon in Colorado. My partner was the legendary American rock climber Layton Kor. We'd nearly completed the first ascent of *The Gothic Pillar,* a two-thousand-foot granitic ship's prow. Only a seventy-foot-deep notch separated us from the top and the canyon rim. Looking for a suitable rappel anchor, I pulled down on an outcrop beside me, testing it—and it broke without warning. Falling forward, I tumbled head-over-heels, and rolled toward the canyon edge, then miraculously I stopped a scant ten feet short of the void.

"Don't *ever* do that again!" Layton yelled in horror at me.

"And you're going to Everest next year?" he added questioningly.

The need for caution and safety had been repeatedly drilled into me during twenty years of climbing. Yet in 1985, on my first Everest trip, I was criticized by some on my team for being too careful, for "not going for it." After witnessing Lauren's death and having had a few too many close calls of my own, I knew the importance of triple-checking every knot, anchor, and decision. Hopefully this year we could eliminate all preventable mistakes and lapses in judgment.

Mulling things over while sitting in my tent, I knew that I at least felt very comfortable with my companions' climbing skills. Robert, Paul, and Stephen each had solid qualifications. I had an innate trust and confidence in their capabilities; and they, I'd like to think, had equal faith in me. When any of us gave the go-ahead to climb, voted where we thought the route should go, or declared a section to be too dangerous, our judgment was mutually accepted, and respected. I was convinced there'd be no avoidable errors on this climb.

Stephen, Paul, and the Tibetan porters ferried all twenty-three loads up to ABC in the storm. At dinner, we discussed our proposed route.

"I take it we are doing *our buttress?*" I asked.

"I didn't see any other ways up the face, did you?" Stephen asked. Our only alternative was to repeat the original route up the Kangshung Face, the 1983 *American Buttress*—which none of us really wanted to do.

"You can see why it took them two years and rocket launchers. It looks like a nightmare!" Paul exclaimed. "Our climb," in Stephen's words, would be "rather more subtle." With only four of us, it would have to be.

We held our blessing ceremony, appropriately enough, on April 1, April Fool's day. Pasang and I collected rocks, and we all pitched in and built two ceremonial *chortens* on the hill behind the cook tent. Masonry was good training at seventeen thousand feet! We also made a small altar where Pasang would burn juniper boughs to bring us additional luck, then strung prayer flags. Before the ceremony, Robert set up his binoculars, and we took turns inspecting the route.

"Horrendous!" Paul shouted.

"No easy way at all," Robert declared.

"It looks like one of those Andean climbs where you always have big nasty lumps hanging over your head," Stephen commented.

After Pasang conducted our *puja* ceremony and read prayers, Mimi subjected us each to a series of physical and mental tests as part of her medical school research project. She'd been given a special leave of absence to come on the expedition. "I want to test you *before* the climb so I can tell how strange you guys are *after* you get down," she half-joked, sitting in my tent. I felt dazed by the surprising strenuousness of the mental aptitude tests—plus her cold medical instruments touching against my skin made me shriek.

"You all right, Ed?" Paul shouted from his tent next door, laughing.

At dinner, Mimi led us through the ceremony of Passover. She was the only Jewish member of the team. Her explanations of the symbolism of each item and of her ritual gestures were heartfelt and touching; she was obviously missing home. And, although her voice wavered as she began to paint a word picture of what her family back home would be doing tonight, she did manage to also keep her sense of humor:

Mimi Zieman at our puja blessing ceremony at Kangshung Base Camp.

"A traditional Jewish family has four sons. The smart son, the silent son, the stupid son—and the bad son," Mimi explained, glancing lastly over at Paul. Everyone laughed, Paul too. We'd been blessed today not just by Pasang's prayers, but by each other's company. Now the climb could begin.

* * * * * * * * * * * * * *

Kasang's unfailing greeting of *"Goo mournu!"* announced bed tea at 6:30 A.M. "New horizons to conquer, new moraines to stumble over, and new crevasses to fall into!" Robert shouted. And it was perfect weather for the job, too, as George Mallory would say. All hands except Pasang (who would stay behind to watch camp) soon set off to Advanced Base.

My backpack was much too heavy. Joe, also, I noted, was doing his Mr. Atlas imitation, and carting up everything but the proverbial kitchen sink. Joe was the sort of person who couldn't leave anything behind if he thought that eventually he might need it. As a boy, he'd been an exemplary Boy Scout. It showed. His Swiss army knife could have repaired a tank! Joe and I, the two turtles, ambled up and down the stony moraines as the hares accelerated rapidly out of sight. Our leisurely pace gave us ample time to ponder the many features, and multitude of dangers, of Chomolungma's East Face.

Advanced Base Camp was situated roughly two miles away from Lhotse's imposing North Face, and one and a half miles out from the base of Everest's Kangshung Face. Unlike the other two sides of pyramidally-shaped Everest—the mountain's Southwest Face, and its North Face—the upper half of the entire East Face of Mount Everest is dominated (and threatened) by a singularly immense hanging glacier. The bottom three to four thousand feet of the face, however, is vertical to overhanging, and as a result it does not collect snow. The Face's two major buttresses are flanked on all sides by active avalanche gullies that funnel broken chunks of the hanging glacier earthwards with alarming frequency and resultant devastation. This glacier's bottom edge runs horizontally across the face's entire midriff, and is composed of splintered ice walls and semidetached seracs, or ice blocks. On Everest's Kangshung Face, in other words, there were very, very few safe places to hide.

Quite early in the expedition, Paul, our resident humorist, had named the avalanche gully separating our buttress from the *American Buttress* with the colorful name "Big Al." Mount McKinley (also called Denali) in Alaska is home to another famous death trap and hanging glacier named Big Bertha, and Paul evidently thought we should have sexual equality in our mountain nomenclature.

Our first night in Advanced Base, I was so keyed up that I couldn't sleep. When I stood watching the full moon's slow rise from behind Chomolönzo, I also perceived that the quietness surrounding us was deafening. My ears rung.

*Pasang Norbu
cooks up an
omelette in Kharta.
Joe Blackburn*

Clockwise from Top Left:

*Ed Webster bathes in the Kharta Chu,
to the delight of local children.*
Stephen Venables

*Ed's thirty-second birthday: Teare,
Venables, Webster, Anderson, Zieman.*
Joe Blackburn

Your friendly yak driver from Kharta.

*Villagers from Kharta watch disco
in a blizzard at Pre-Base Camp,
with music by the Rolling Stones.*

Norbu Tenzing Norgay with Everest good luck pieces.
Joe Blackburn

Tashi (center) points to the boyhood home of
Tenzing Norgay, as Norbu Tenzing Norgay (left) meets
his long lost relatives in Moyun village near Kharta.

Edmund Hillary on 1953 British Mount Everest Expedition. Royal Geographical Society

Tenzing and Hillary several days after their triumph. Peter Jackson / AAC Library

Stephen Venables admires the view of Makalu, Chomolönzo, Lhotse, and Everest.

Sunrise on Makalu and Chomolönzo from the Gangla.

Beautiful weather at Boulder Camp in the Kama Valley.

Paul Teare having fun at Pethang Ringmo.

Sunset on
Chomolönzo at
Pethang Ringmo
Inset: Ed Webster

Prayer flags
and our puja,
at Kangshung
Base Camp.

The Kangshung Face of Chomolungma, Tibet.

Above: *Sunrise on the* Neverest Buttress *and* American Buttress.

Below: *The Gang of Four, Venables, Anderson, Webster, and Teare.*
Joe Blackburn

Above: *Venables, Teare, and Anderson at ABC, below the face.*

Below: *Another monster avalanche roars down Big Al.*

Moonrise over Chomolönzo.

Time exposure of Everest's Kangshung Face from Advanced Base Camp.

Stephen Venables hanging out
on the fixed ropes next to Big Al.

Paul Teare leads the harrowing no-man's-land of the Traverse alongside Big Al.

Ed Webster leads brittle water ice below the Greyhound Bus. Stephen Venables

Serious Ice-capades: the view down Big Al, with Paul below. Stephen Venables

The
Cauliflower Ridge

Spot the
climber!

Robert Anderson
"on belay."

Stephen Venables jumars Paul's Ice Pitch, with Big Al dropping below.
(Each climber in these photos is in the exact same location on the climb.)

Robert Anderson at Camp One at 22,500 feet.

Stephen Venables on the Headwall.

Robert and Stephen proving that Everest can be climbed without oxygen.
Joe Blackburn

And above our small camp, the bright glow of moonlight fell like a celestial cascade of molten silver down the Kangshung Face. Eventually I dozed off—then, at dawn, I was rudely awakened by the sudden explosion of real sound into our quiet world. A mile above our heads, a large ice block had detached.

"Here comes the big one down the Lhotse Wall!" Robert screamed. Hands tore madly at zippers and nylon tent doors as we scrambled outside to watch the wave of snow and ice roar down the two-mile-high, vertical precipice. Seconds later, when the avalanche exploded at the back of the Witches' Cauldron (the no-man's-land where the faces of Everest and Lhotse merged), the avalanche hit ground zero with resounding violence. From the back of the cauldron, huge foaming clouds of snow and ice crystals billowed straight toward us like an out-of-control freight train. Luckily, just before blasting our camp, they dissipated, floating upward, harmlessly, into thin air.

"Good. It didn't clobber our route," Stephen commented with seeming nonchalance, while finishing buckling his harness and departing for the climb. What a way to start the first day on the hill, I thought. April 3, 1988, began like every other day would for the next six weeks. Mornings appeared to be the most active time for avalanches, and we soon grew accustomed to these daily symphonies of destruction pouring off the surrounding mountain walls.

But on this initial morning on our route, we were still warming up to routine—both to the mountain's many moods, and to our own individual and idiosyncratic climbing habits. "Now don't go falling into any crevasses," Robert told Stephen as they left camp. "I haven't practiced my rope work in months."

"My boot-ax belay is a bit rusty, too," Stephen admitted.

Paul and I didn't leave until ten. The first day out on a big climb is always a dry run. Gear must be sorted, knots and straps checked, and I always seem to misplace something essential. Robert and Stephen's trail followed our small moraine rib for a short ways, then headed slightly left onto the immense flat snowfield leading toward Lhotse—and the Witches' Cauldron. After about twenty minutes, Paul and I gained the crest of an ice shelf and contoured left around the foot of the heavily-crevassed icefall directly below Big Al.

The closer we got to the base of Lhotse's colossal, ten-thousand-foot shooting gallery of avalanche-swept black rock, the more buckets of adrenaline dumped into my veins. Shattered cliffs of ice threatened death from two miles above us; did one of those ice blocks have my name on it? Raw fear welled up inside me. It was the overpowering silence of the Witches' Cauldron that I hated most, because it was a false yet irresistibly welcoming quiet. But we well

SHARTSE II   Rock Island   SHARTSE I

OTSE 1988 Route South Col Lowe Buttress MOUNT EVEREST Everest's East Ridge

Panoramic view of the Kangshung Glacier cirque, looking west from Base Camp.

knew that at virtually any second, hundreds of thousands of tons of ice could come thundering down onto our heads. Not to be deceived, we listened expectantly, waiting for the inevitable *CRACK!* that signaled the next avalanche.

In fact, we nearly sprinted across the glacier to get out of firing range, then crouched, panting for breath, under a protective rock overhang. A fifty degree snow gully bordered the ice fall's left side. We zigzagged up it, cursing under our loads. I felt unusually apprehensive that one of the big ice blocks on the Cauliflower Ridge might collapse, while Paul appeared completely relaxed. I told myself to just get on with the job. Above, Stephen and Robert were crossing a snowfield on the toe of the buttress, fixing rope as they went. They looked to be moving well and were about to dispatch the rock headwall beneath the Scottish Gully, the section of our route that I had long coveted.

I felt better once I clipped my jumar ascender into the initial fixed line and started up. The terrain was snow and rock, not very steep or terribly hard, but fun! However, the moment I reached the first anchor that Robert or Stephen had placed, I knew I had a job. Testing the two rock pitons with a sharp tug, I pulled one piton straight out. Coincidentally, just then Stephen came sliding down the rope from above. Holding up the piton, I asked him who'd placed it.

"But—I put that pin in!" he protested.

"Yes—and I just took it out with my fingers." Stephen was very dismayed. I tapped a nut into the same crack using my hammer, then equalized the force exerted on each anchor using a short nylon sling. Robert arrived; they had indeed climbed the Headwall. Stephen led it brilliantly, and it was about 5.8 in difficulty. Stephen apologized because he knew I'd wanted to lead that part, but I really didn't mind. Daily progress was more crucial than who got to lead which parts of the climb. Ultimately, there would be plenty of leading for all.

Robert and Stephen descended, leaving Paul and me to carry extra rope and hardware to their high point. Paul continued up the newly fixed ropes, climbing an easy snowslope and a steeper forty-foot cliff. "I'm twittering!" he yelled upon reaching the next anchor, using one of his pet expressions, before unleashing a defaming string of expletives. "This piton was placed into mud!" he raved. "It wasn't even in a crack. It was just lying there on the ledge—I'm twittering!"

He hammered the piton into a better crack, and I came up. Stephen and Robert's anchors obviously left a lot to be desired. They had soloed across the next snowfield to save their remaining rope to fix up the Headwall, so Paul strung out a one-hundred-meter roll of eight-millimeter cord across the gap. The afternoon fog rolling up the Kama Valley had engulfed us, so I couldn't

Day One: Paul Teare approaching the base of the Kangshung Face. Lhotse on left.

Paul and Robert (circled) at the start of the fixed ropes.

see or hear a thing. I soloed up a fifteen-foot rock band, lightly holding Paul's orange rope in my right hand—which he was still trailing behind him—then I happened to glance down at the four-hundred-foot drop to the glacier. What was I doing up here, climbing unroped and without a belay? Unable to see any of the lurking, fog-shrouded dangers around me, I got very nervous.

"Paul—I'm going down!" I shouted repeatedly. Finally, he reappeared.

We slid back down the ropes to the deceptively silent glacier. The snow crust froze over instantly once the sun dipped behind our giant sun marker, the South Col. We roped together on our seventy-five-foot half rope to guard against falling into any hidden crevasses. Arriving at camp dead-tired, we ate dinner just before dark. Mimi and Joe served, plying us with endless cups of tea.

"Joe, you're a married man," I said. "I hate to tell you, but this is definitely an unmarried man's route." He looked crestfallen.

"You mean I couldn't climb up the first couple of rope lengths?"

"The route is way too dangerous. Take my word for it," I answered, putting an immediate end to idle speculation that Joe and Mimi might climb with us. They'd have to find other diversions for the next two months. Then I told Robert I might need a rest day.

"Don't burn yourself out doing too much, too early," he answered, letting me make my own decision to go back up, or not. Robert's leadership style was completely casual and democratic, which we all liked. There were no mind games within this team; open communication was our password from day one.

"Anyway, Stephen and I are going up," Robert continued. "I'm pretty psyched to lead the Scottish Gully. You and Paul can rest if you want to."

"Not me," Paul spoke up. "I want to lead tomorrow, too."

I decided to see how I felt in the morning. We were finally established on the mountain, and I'd broken through some of my fears, but not all of them.

The planned 3 A.M. alpine start became a 7 A.M. start when the alarms failed to go off. I lay in my tent feeling perfectly fine, listening to the others preparing to go, knowing that if I didn't go, I'd feel guilt ridden later. My good luck charms—Fritz Wiessner's piton and carabiner—hung suspended, not so silently, from my tent roof. Fritz would never have wasted a day of good weather.

"I'm coming!" I shouted to everyone's immediate approval. Quickly donning my boots, harness, crampons, and helmet, I grabbed my ski pole and ice ax, we roped up, and left. The snow was firmly frozen. We reached the base of the buttress in an hour and a half. Stephen quickly caught up to Paul and Robert, while I rearranged the various anchors and knots to increase our safety

Robert Anderson—with the Himalayan grandeur of the Kangshung Glacier.

Ed ascends the Scottish Gully. Chomolönzo is in the distance. Stephen Venables

margin, plus speed our ascents and descents. "Ed, the Anchorman," Paul called me. Well, the name definitely had a better ring than "the Turtle!"

The seventy-degree, two-hundred-foot-high Headwall was broken by one weakness: a shallow, right-facing corner. The rock itself was a metamorphic banded schist-gneiss, similar to that found in Colorado's Black Canyon. I felt right at home. The edges and holds were positive, comfortably in-cut and easy to grab hold of, not downsloping and insecure like the rock on Everest's north and west sides. At the top of the corner, a delicate traverse on crampon points led rightward across a steep slab to a near-vertical, thirty-foot rock wall.

I worked up the fixed line, sliding my ascender, attached with a sling to my sit harness, up the rope. I could lean back for a rest every fifteen feet. We might reach the magic, numeric altitude of twenty thousand feet today, but I also knew that I was not quite acclimatized, so I consciously paced myself. Left foot, right foot, slide the ascender, take two deep breaths, then repeat.

I pulled over the top of the Headwall and stood at the base of the Scottish Gully. It was very well-named, a beautiful forty- to fifty-degree snow ribbon bordered by vertical rock walls on each side. Fortuitously, the gully's right-hand retaining wall formed a semiprotective divider, which in theory would keep rocks, ice blocks, and avalanches within Big Al gully, 150 yards further to my right. There was, in fact, probably more danger from one of the Cauliflower Towers collapsing into the Scottish Gully than there was from being clobbered by an avalanche roaring down Big Al.

"It's wet up here; you might want to stay below," Paul cautioned. He and Stephen stood on a stance belaying Robert, who was leading over a tricky ice bulge fifty feet higher. With our longer-than-normal three-hundred-foot ropes, belaying the leader could be a lengthy affair. But soon Robert had anchored his rope, which Paul and Stephen climbed with their ascenders to join him.

We intended to climb the steep, bottom buttress in traditional siege style, anchoring a continuous safety line of fixed rope up the mountainside. Once the rope was installed, it would be relatively easy and quick to either ascend or descend the mountain as needed—even at night, or in a storm. Each three-hundred-foot rope was tied securely into the ropes above and below it, and since we used both nine- and eleven-millimeter diameter static ropes, it was an extremely safe system. The end of each rope length, however, didn't always coincide with a natural ledge or rest spot, so as I followed the others I placed new anchors where needed. After hammering in two securely-driven, side-by-side pitons, I readjusted, reknotted, and reclipped the ropes.

Stephen and Robert take cover at the start of the Traverse. Big Al is on the right.

Standing at the top of the Scottish Gully, Robert was hunkered under a protective rock overhang amongst a tangle of ropes and pitons. Stephen was about to rappel back down, and Paul was leading the wild traverse across the snow-and-rock "no-man's-land" on the left-hand wall of Big Al gully. At last, the Real Climbing had begun! Awestruck, I stared up at the colossal, U-shaped avalanche funnel of Big Al. The amphitheater was ringed with black rock cliffs, serac blocks, ice flutings, and ice walls. Some of the ice cliffs were up to a vertical mile above us, and the back of the gully showed the relentless scouring and pounding of hundreds of thousands of avalanches—since Chomolungma was created.

"It's the grandest climbing situation I've ever seen," Stephen raved.

Robert was equally enthused. "It's a route now, following but not forcing the natural line of weakness up the mountain. That's what I like."

It was indeed a phenomenally aesthetic line, the kind of route mountaineers dream of finding. Paul had embarked on a traverse out right; above him, moderate snow led to more rock outcrops sheltering the next resting ledge. Beyond, we hoped, was an exit ramp. Higher, it was too early to say. For the moment, we were thrilled to have discovered such a logical and "reasonably safe" route.

Down at Advanced Base, Joe and Mimi had thoroughly enjoyed watching our progress through the telescope. "We can see your every move, so you'd better watch it!" Mimi laughed. I was glad that they had discovered such handy entertainment. For the next six weeks while we climbed, they'd need it.

The view straight up our route as the Kangshung Face greets a new dawn.

Stephen and I had decided to get an early start the following morning. My initial fears had mostly vanished, and I couldn't wait to come to grips with the next section. I heard Stephen light the stove at 2:30 A.M., putting on water for tea and oatmeal. A deep sleep made my extrication from the blissful warmth of my sleeping bag all the more painful. We left camp at four, crunching across the frozen glacier in the pitch dark, our sole illumination the tiny orbs of light from our headlamps. Later, we stopped, halted by the call of nature and admiration of the clear Himalayan sky with its multitude of stars. The Kangshung Face brooded silently above us, waiting to catch the sun.

Stephen ascended the ropes while I photographed the spectacular sunrise over the Gyankar Range to the east of us, beyond the Arun River. You could capture the most sublime colors photographing Himalayan sunrises and sunsets, but it was such a labor of love. Could I get frostbitten? The cold was bitter. Holding my camera, my fingers ached with each picture. But Everest's East Face embraced the sun's first rays at dawn, and boasted the loveliest of alpenglow colors. The suffering of cold fingers and hands seemed worth it.

I was hurrying to catch up to Stephen—a now familiar pastime—when I noticed that the sharpened metal front points on my right crampon had fallen off! They'd been attached by a single screw, and even though I'd tightened it the day before, it had loosened. I continued up the ropes and told Stephen the bad news. He was only too happy to keep the lead, so I belayed him as he continued above Paul's high point. Steepening mixed ground led toward the Terrace, a narrow platform beneath several more jutting rock overhangs.

Feeding out the climbing rope to match Stephen's upward progress, I quickly noticed that we were perched on a north-facing wall in permanent shade. Luckily I'd taken Stephen's advice to bring my expedition parka. I put it on and settled in for the Big Chill. Stephen led up and right through steep sugary snow, placed two pitons in a rock outcrop, and continued pigeon-holing upward by thrusting his ice ax shafts into the unconsolidated snow headwall just beneath the Terrace. Conquering an eighty-degree snow wall at twenty thousand feet, a full fifty feet above his last protection (risking a hundred-foot fall) was quite a feat. I yelled congratulations, but still felt uneasy trusting his piton placements.

"Do—You—Have—Good—Anchors?" I shouted evenly.

Stephen replied that he did.

"How—Many?" I yelled back, still unconvinced.

"Four!"

I figured that was enough. I ascended his rope and collapsed onto the Terrace—tired, but warmed from my exertions. A large rock overhang gave us complete protection from the perils lurking above, but it also blocked our path upward. After I pounded in another piton for good luck, Stephen set off once again, this time to peek around the corner to the right.

As Stephen climbed farther away from me, the wind began to rise, and communication became increasingly difficult. When I finally yelled "Thirty feet!" to tell Stephen just how much rope he had left, he thought I was shouting that he was completely out of rope. Not seeing another belay ledge near by, he constructed an exposed, semihanging belay in the center of an exposed ice slope. After more incomprehensible shouting and escalating tensions, I eventually understood that he was off belay and ready for me to ascend the rope. Then I followed him—to what we instantly decided would be our high point.

It was 4 P.M. before we straggled back into Advanced Base, exhausted and dehydrated. After only three days on the mountain, I was already beginning to despise two parts of the climb: the approach gully up to the bottom of the fixed ropes, and the long walk home across the glacier at day's end. We found Paul and Robert in camp, and rested. They were supposed to have spent the day ferrying loads, but as Paul explained: "I couldn't move this morning." We didn't begrudge them the time off, which tomorrow we would also savor.

Evening brought a rustling wind, however, and the appearance of warning clouds—high cirrus, herringbone clouds, and mare's tails—storm indicators in

Stephen leading steep mixed ground to the Terrace—hidden under the next overhang.

the sky. We went to bed nervous about a change in the weather, but awoke to another perfectly still and cloudless day. Robert and Paul got an early start, while Stephen and I lounged in bed until nine, sinfully late! After rousing ourselves, we hung out our sleeping bags and clothes to dry. It was a luxurious day spent spinning tales of our own past climbing epics, and how we had each managed to become involved in this ridiculous project.

Before Joe and Mimi left to hike back to Base for a rest, we also experimented with Joe's astonishing array of Nikon lenses, including a 300mm lens with a doubler—the perfect tool for keeping tabs on the lads' upward progress. Initially, Paul led an exit ramp, then for five long hours Robert stood motionless while belaying Paul on the next ice pitch. Silhouetted against the dramatic sweep of the snow and ice slopes of Big Al gully, Robert stood on a sharp snow arête and was barely visible as a tiny black dot. The climbing, we surmised, must be extremely difficult for Paul to take so long. This was confirmed when they returned to camp at 6 P.M., dog tired. Paul's Ice Pitch, as it came to be known, featured sustained seventy-degree ice with two vertical sections—and an overhang. Yet Paul, somewhat inexplicably, was disappointed with his performance.

"Back home I could have cruised it," he related after he and Robert returned to camp. "But at twenty-one thousand feet, my arms were dying! It was all I could do to hang on. I think it's the hardest ice pitch I've ever done."

Then came the real explanation: Paul was chagrined because he'd had to rest on aid from an ice screw! As if anyone would scold him for such a serious ethical infraction while leading a new ice pitch on Everest. And Robert, standing immobilized at the belay stance for five hours, had nearly frozen to death.

"Remember the gully farther right," Paul added, "you know, the one that we were thinking of climbing? A couple of big frisbees—rocks—came flying down it while I was leading today. We definitely don't want to go over there."

Earlier, we had considered continuing up and right, moving closer to the back of Big Al. Now it appeared we had no choice but to meet the Cauliflower Ridge head on, climbing up and over each of the individual ice towers.

"There's a continuous weakness above our high point," Robert continued, "up a shallow but steep ice gully to a notch in the ridge. You two should be able to reach the crest tomorrow. This climb is probably one of the wildest things attempted in the Himalaya in the last few years, especially by a team of four!"

"Four against the Kangshung Face? YOU'RE MAD!" Stephen bellowed, repeating Charlie Houston's candid opinion of our sanity. While some might consider us "mad," we were increasingly positive that our climb "would go."

We hoped "the Greyhound Bus" (top left) *would stay "in park." Spot the climber!*

April 7 was Day Five on the buttress. I'd never met a climber with such a zeal for alpine starts as Stephen, our Himalayan veteran of a dozen previous expeditions. Unfortunately, his zest for predawn movement was beginning to run counter to this Yank's favorite habit of dozing an extra hour or two.

"It's all those five-hundred-mile drives from London to Scotland to go ice climbing, and getting up at 5 A.M. to hike up to Ben Nevis," Stephen explained. Maybe, but I was beginning to think that it was also something much deeper, that Stephen possessed a hunger to succeed on Everest *no matter what.* My own preference at altitude was to hold back a fraction, pace myself, and preserve an emergency reserve of strength—to maintain an extra margin of safety.

Although I was excited to be coming to grips with the route's difficulties, as we grimly ate our oatmeal in the dark, I was nonetheless haunted by any one of several visions of a violent death—perhaps my own—tumbling into the void when a rope broke, or getting my head smashed in by a falling rock or an ice block. Could I overcome my fears? I wasn't totally sure.

Stephen, conversely, was completely let's-get-down-to-business. I was more asleep than awake as we crossed the glacier in the subzero night. Stephen must have been temporarily groggy too, because he missed the trail where it forked to the right—and we walked too far left, directly toward the Witches' Cauldron. Nearing Lhotse, we encountered an evil maze of crevasses. All around us the glacier was a silver ocean of ice: alive, creaking, and crackling. I couldn't shake off my earlier sense of foreboding. I kept imagining a colossal avalanche appearing out of the darkness—too late for us to run or hide. When an icicle spontaneously exploded because of the intense cold, I nearly jumped out of my skin.

Stephen stopped briefly, so I went ahead up the approach gully. I thought maybe just once I'd beat him to the fixed ropes, but he soon overtook me, churning stubbornly uphill while I gasped for air, pulling it down my parched throat. How could Stephen maintain such a hard pace—and smoke cigarettes?

"Sorry I'm so bloody slow," I croaked as he passed me. "I keep trying to go faster, but I can't."

"Oh, don't worry," Stephen replied. "Chris Bonington is slow, too—and he always reaches the summit."

Twenty minutes later, as I started to ascend the Headwall, sliding my jumar clamps up the rope, to my surprise Stephen leaned back from the base of the Scottish Gully and shouted, "What's taking you so long? It's getting late! The snow will be all softened up by the time we get up there."

After opening up to him about my sensitivity to being slow, I got angry.

The Cauliflower Ridge was an eerie spectacle in the moonlight.

"What's the problem?" I yelled back, "I'm a good hour in front of my time the other day." I pushed on, determined to catch him. Ironically, when we met at the top of the Scottish Gully, Stephen asked if I'd climb on ahead and go first—so that he could take pictures of me! We continued up the ropes, having, as Stephen later phrased it, "an orgy of photography."

When I reached the anchors at the start of Paul's Ice Pitch, I gasped in awe and disbelief. A vast boilerplate slab of seventy-five-degree black ice led straight up for 150 feet to a thirty-foot, vertical ice wall. Just above, a body-length-wide ice overhang bulged at the horizon. Higher still, the First and Second Cauliflower Towers reared out into the blue sky, hundreds of tons of sparkling white ice temporarily defying gravity—for a little bit longer, I prayed. Then I heard Stephen's voice: "Keep jumaring, or we won't get anything done!"

He needn't have worried.

Paul and Robert had anchored the high point of our fixed ropes at a narrow shelf beneath an imposing ice wall. It was my turn to "push out the route." My crampon front points hadn't fallen off yet (always a good sign), and now I was handed one of the hardest ice pitches of the climb—and my first lead ever on Everest—at twenty-two-thousand feet. Diagonally to our left loomed the ominously unstable and leaning First Cauliflower Tower (or as Paul nicknamed it, the "Greyhound Bus"); on the right rose the Second Cauliflower. Although these ice skyscrapers looked *relatively stable,* the Second Tower was fractured along its entire base. Between the towers dipped a col or saddle, the obvious chink in the mountain's armor.

Stephen put me on belay and held my rope as I began front-pointing up the iron-hard, seventy-five-degree ice. After placing two ice screws for protection, I was still trying to placate Stephen; I apologized to him for my caution and even for stopping to place the screws. The ice, however, was brittle and cold. It broke apart in shards with every blow of my axes, whose sharpened picks barely penetrated the ice's metallic hardness. Teetering and insecure, I impulsively tackled a short vertical bulge (sending my heart rate and breathing racing), then gingerly stepped right into the base of a V-groove leading toward the Second Cauliflower Tower. Hyperventilating from my exertions, unable to suck enough oxygen into my lungs, for a moment I believed I was suffocating. Breathing as fully and as deeply as I possibly could, I tried to stay calm—and avoided looking at the hundreds of tons of fractured ice thirty feet overhead.

After placing another ice screw as high as possible, I gulped several draughts of air, then hesitantly traversed left onto a vertical wall of unconsolidated sugar snow. A wobbly ice screw gave fleeting security to more awkward moves as I thrust my arms into holes I punched into the snow, pigeon-holing upwards, while my boots stamped out equally insecure footing. Pulling round the corner to my left, I adrenaline-surged past the crux—and was rewarded with an unobstructed two-thousand-foot view straight down Big Al. Continuing up a moderately-angled snow slope, I finally collapsed onto a level platform, still heaving for breath. This snow terrace was the first place on the climb where we could sit comfortably and not be constantly worried about getting obliterated by multiple tons of falling ice and snow.

I anchored the rope and signaled to Stephen. "Nice lead!" he congratulated as he came into view. We sat down for lunch in the midday sun, enjoying each other's company and the view east to our neighbors, Makalu and Chomolönzo. It was not, however, readily apparent where to go next. An eighty-foot-high ice wall (the smooth, ninety-five-degree overhanging face of the Third Cauliflower Tower) appeared to obstruct all hope of progress. At this elevation, overhanging ice climbing was indeed a formidable challenge. It was Stephen's turn to lead, but I couldn't tell if he wanted to go first—or not.

"You could try circling round it to the left," he said, handing me the gear.

I plowed ahead through sun-softened snow into the cold shadow of the ice cliff. Front-pointing up a seventy-degree slab of brittle ice, I reached a small ledge at the base of the overhanging wall. After searching left and right for potential alternatives, and finding none, I decided to try climbing directly up the wall's center. To shed extra weight, I left my pack hanging on an ice piton, and started.

Ed on the Webster Wall. Stephen Venables

Something came over me. This was exactly the technical challenge I needed to restore my self-confidence, provided that I could actually climb it. I moved up a short ramp inset into the wall, reached as high as possible, and hammered in two ice pitons before launching left across the overhanging ice face. The wall was formed of dense snow, a porous white Styrofoam into which the dagger-like picks of my two Stubai ice hammers penetrated right up to the hilt.

Feeling lighter than air, I danced left, hanging one-armed from my right ice hammer every eight feet while I pounded in another ice piton for protection with my left. I free-climbed all of the moves, even while placing protection and pulling up the rope to clip it into each anchor. The situation—suspended on an overhanging ice serac at 22,500 feet—made me dizzy.

Resting on aid, hanging from an ice piton just below the overhang's lip, I hacked away at the soft edge with my hammer, dug a trough, and finally found hard snow. And, at one memorably hazardous moment, I hung off a single ice hammer, then frantically removed my last ice screw so I could use it again higher.

But how to surmount the top of the overhang? Aiding off of two snow pickets—three-foot-long aluminum stakes—I swung awkwardly in slings and groveled over the edge onto another snow terrace. I knew I'd been in full view of the Advanced Base binoculars; little did I know how appreciative my audience was!

Stephen came up and began to remove the ice pitons. Since the pitch both overhung and diagonalled, ascending it on jumars was tricky work. Each time he removed a piton, he swung out sideways into space, well away from any contact with the ice. I scampered back down to the edge, and enjoyed watching him get scared. When Stephen finally arrived at my belay, he said in greeting, and in earnest, "Really, that was the best ice lead I've ever seen."

It was 3:30 P.M. The sun had set behind the South Col, and the temperature was plummeting by the second. Congratulating ourselves, we hurriedly began our descent. Rappelling three thousand feet took an hour. Buoyed by my day-long adrenaline rush, I felt strong until we began crossing the glacier, whereupon I felt more like a limp marionette swinging on a string. Stephen kept pulling at the rope, trying to move faster than me, but every fifty feet I slowed him down by falling up to my waist into another hole in the sun-softened snow.

The next afternoon, Paul was to share an identical experience. He and Stephen were heading home across the glacier, with Stephen, once again, in the lead, rushing, tugging on the rope, pulling at Paul. At last, in exasperation, Paul shouted: "Finesse, Stephen, finesse! Let's slow down some."

To which Stephen replied succinctly and memorably:

"F___ finesse; I want my bloody cup of tea!"

Today, whoops and hollers greeted our return. We embraced Robert and Paul, who then thrust steaming cups of sugared milk tea into our hands. It was 6 P.M. We'd been on the go for fifteen and a half hours, since 2:30 A.M. We really felt we'd cracked the nut, and that the route to the upper slopes was assured.

Paul and Robert had watched our progress all day long through the high-powered binoculars. "When I saw you clip your pack into the ice screw," Robert exclaimed, "I thought, *'OH, NO! Ed's going straight up the wall,'* and you did."

"I bet no one's done an ice lead like that, at that altitude, on Everest before!" Paul added. They were already calling the cliff the Webster Wall. Tomorrow, Robert and Paul—and Stephen, that glutton for punishment—would try to reach the mountain's upper slopes. For the first time, we began to feel like the route could be ascended by our four-man team. We also agreed that our climb, in a fitting play on words, should be called the *Neverest Buttress*. (And, with great irony, years later we discovered that "Neverrest" was Sir George Everest's nickname.)

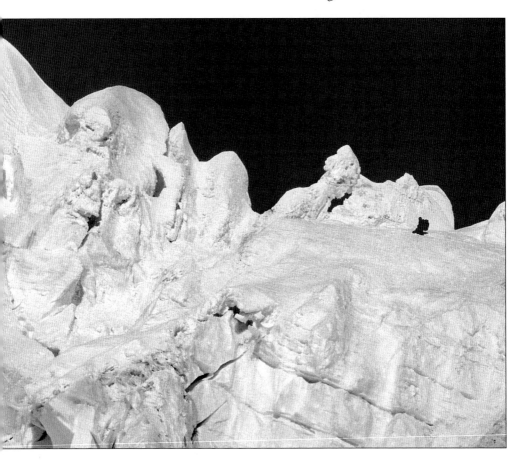

Stephen on top of the Fourth Cauliflower Tower—about to get a "little surprise."

It was a rare treat to be alone in camp and sleep for as long as I wanted. On that day, I lounged in my sleeping bag, began to read *The Razor's Edge* by Somerset Maugham, then watched through the binoculars as the Gang of Three reached a new high point. A day of domesticity was a welcome diversion from the life-and-limb struggle on the buttress.

It was nearly dark when they returned. Stephen had sacked his cherished ice runnel up the front of the Fourth Cauliflower Tower (directly above the Webster Wall), climbing a shallow vertical groove inclined from sixty-five to ninety degrees for almost two hundred feet up the tower's prow. How he had mustered the necessary energy to lead it after ascending six thousand feet of fixed rope in two days, I didn't know. But just when Stephen thought the mountain would drop its defenses, he met an unexpected foe.

LHOTSE

MOUNT EVEREST

South
Col

Cow's
Mouth

Jaws
of Doom
Crevasse

Fourth
Cauliflower
Tower

Webster
Wall

Camp One
(22,500 feet)

Cauliflower Ridge

The
Greyhound
Bus

Paul's
Ice
Pitch

Big
Al

Gully

American
Buttress

The
Terrace

Neverest
Buttress

The
Traverse

Scottish Gully →

"I traversed left from the belay at the top of the fourth tower," he later recounted, "climbed up another narrow ice groove, placed an ice screw, then reached up—and grabbed a sharp edge of ice."

"'I have an unfortunate little surprise for you,' is how you put it, I think," Robert broke in.

"It was a huge crevasse, completely hidden from below. It's a hundred feet deep, and a full forty or fifty feet across," Stephen continued. "And what's so damnably frustrating, is that the easy upper slopes are right on the other side! It looks like we'll have to bypass it on the right or the left, which would mean a huge detour. Or we could establish a rope bridge, and do a Tyrolean traverse across it."

There was only one problem with actually doing a rope bridge or a Tyrolean traverse: they are incredibly scary, those few minutes of tenuous spider-like suspension while you dangle, upside down, suspended in your harness from the climbing rope, completely at the mercy of your equipment and the anchors— and whether they hold or not—as you bounce and bob unnervingly above the gaping chasm.

"I slid across one once in Outward Bound," Robert said turning serious, "and I vowed I'd never do it again!"

Chapter 9

Bridging the Jaws of Doom

Take risks. It is better to live and die than to never live.

—Chinese fortune

W e stayed at Advanced Base Camp on April 9 to savor our first communal rest day. The weather had worsened considerably. Low clouds wreathed the mountain's base, and by afternoon stray flakes fluttered from a somber sky.

"This weather's all the more reason to get to the summit by the end of April and go home," Robert advocated. "Well, it looks like a good day to replenish a few lost calories."

"Eating is one of the troubles with alpine starts," Stephen admitted. "You can never stomach a full meal at 3 A.M."

For the first time I noticed we were all looking quite skinny.

Left: *Robert Anderson deep in the depths of the Jaws of Doom crevasse.*

"Bantam weight," Paul crowed. "We've just begun to fight!"

Or be blown away by Everest's winds, I thought.

In his quest for a fattening breakfast, Robert concocted a pancake mix of precooked Ralston breakfast cereal, wheat germ, and dried egg mix. In fact, his "pancakes" were so tasty that we all ate seconds.

By midafternoon, another blizzard was upon us. Robert and I would not be establishing Camp One the next day, as we had planned. Then the Lhotse Face came alive. Although we couldn't see them through the snowstorm, we certainly *heard* the avalanches. Many of them were absolute monsters. When Big Al also rumbled, it was time to heed Pasang's wise words: "Come to Base if weather bad. Eat and rest."

"This route sure is psychologically draining," Robert said.

"It's no vacation," Paul agreed. "Listen to that symphony!"

The avalanches, which continued all night, sounded like a continuous cascade of runaway trains—barreling full steam to resounding explosions on the Kangshung Glacier. Many of them were a little too loud for my comfort level. We prayed we were camped far enough away from their danger.

I awoke to the loud cracking of a crevasse widening directly underneath my tent. I envisioned a bottomless, icy pit yawning open, and.... More paranoid delusions of glacial living. The storm persisted; no one appeared in any hurry to get up and start the day. I finished reading the climax of *The Razor's Edge*, where Larry unfolds the depth of his experiences in India to Maugham in a Paris cafe. Reading this passage made me think back to my adventurous old school friend, Lisa Stamas, and how years ago she'd shared with me her vivid experiences of studying and trekking in Asia when India, Nepal, and Tibet were far-off lands, places that I doubted I would ever visit. Her words had inspired me.

I fell back into a sleep as deep as death. I did not dream. When I came to, I was tied to the ground by an unimaginable lethargy. I could hardly move. Stephen claimed our immobility was due to the storm and the drop in barometric pressure. With little discussion, we decided to return to Base Camp. After making four trips in a week to twenty thousand feet and higher, working eight to sixteen hours a day, leading tough pitches, and carrying heavy loads, our bodies and minds craved rest.

Paul had an unfortunate accident on the hike back to Base. Sliding down a short ice slab, he put his right hand out to steady himself, and cut open his palm on a sharp edge of ice. Mimi sterilized the painful wound, then carefully bandaged it.

Base Camp. Beyond the Kangshung Glacier rise Chomolönzo (left) *and Makalu.*

Pasang Norbu Sherpa—Sirdar, cook, confidant, and friend.

Joe, Mimi, Pasang, and Kasang were relieved and happy to see us, and we them. We swapped stories in the cozy warmth of the cook tent, ate snacks, and drank endless cups of tea. The storm broke late in the day, and the clouds parted to reveal the panorama we'd grown to know so well. At dusk an angelic white light fell upon the high peaks. The mountains of the Kama Valley and the Kangshung cirque were now our friends.

I began reading a biography of Vincent Van Gogh. His bright bold colors were a great comfort amongst the rocks, stones, snow, and ice of Base Camp. Reading was also a solace because now my stomach felt bad. I knew I should be eating foods high in calories and carbohydrates, to counteract the muscle-wasting effects of high altitude. I needed to rebuild my reserves for pushing the route higher, but instead I felt weak and listless. Unbeknownst to us, after our lovely trickling stream of clean drinking water dried up a week before, Kasang began fetching water from the yak-dung-contaminated trough in front of our Base Camp. No wonder the tea had begun to have a distinctly earthy aftertaste!

Nonetheless, yak dung was handy stuff. Pasang and I talked outside my tent while waiting for a fire of smoldering dung to heat up some bathing water. (To conserve propane for cooking, we heated all our washing water with sun-dried yak patties.) Pasang very much wanted me to come to his home in Namche Bazaar, and to go on a trek "with the future Mrs. Ed," he said, grinning. We spoke of trekking to the idyllic Gokyo Lakes and of attending the Mani Rimdu festival at Thame Monastery in the month of June. I was so glad that my friendship with Pasang had extended beyond Roger's Everest expedition. Two years before, I had first cast Pasang in the role of father figure; this year, the rest of the team had also adopted him. Although short in stature, Pasang—with his big heart, concern for others, and genuine friendliness—was an integral part of the strong glue that bound our expedition together.

Reading about Van Gogh also had made me realize the importance of art in everyday life. Since childhood, I had identified with the renegade lives of artists, feeling kinship with the independence that being an artist brings. As Somerset Maugham himself once wrote, "It's a perfect life because you can freely tell anyone you disagree with to go to hell." Being master of my own fate, shaky as my material foundation might be, I found very satisfying. For me, at present there was no better life than to be a full-time climber, combining rock climbing and mountaineering with the arts of photography and writing.

Later, when I couldn't shake my upset stomach, Mimi checked me over. I was breathing irregularly, hyperventilating slightly, and my head felt light and cottony. Quite honestly, I thought I was having an onset of cerebral edema. I lay in a daze till noon, then forced myself to get up and go for a walk. At altitude, movement is often the simplest and most effective cure for lethargy.

I hiked to the west to the site of the 1983 American Base Camp. Although five years had passed, a considerable amount of trash still littered the meadow. A heap of rusty tin cans filled a prominent ditch; nearby, two unnecessary expansion bolts disfigured a beautiful granite boulder.

Captive to my strange mood, I continued hiking along the green grassy bench beside the glacier. My thoughts returned to Van Gogh, a man who yearned for what he called "the fruitful life," a life shared with a wife and children, yet he died penniless, childless, and alone. I stared hard into a pool of meltwater and vowed, bringing tears to my eyes, that I would not suffer the same fate. In camp, Robert gave me a look filled with extra concern.

"How you feeling?" he asked.

"Lousy," I answered. "It's the worst day of the trip."

"I noticed you weren't your old self."

I was convinced that the cause of my illness was the yak-dung-flavored water we'd been drinking. Pasang and I hiked uphill to find a new water source. A rivulet bubbling beneath a field of clean granite boulders looked good. Pasang yanked a frozen rock out of place. "No yak shit here; good water," he said.

The sun peeped out. It was a peaceful moment. I asked Pasang a question that had long been on my mind.

"On last year's Everest expedition with Ruth and Roger, was Roger happy?"

Pasang thought a moment. "Yes, he mostly happy."

"Did you have premonitions something bad would happen?"

"I worry about Roger because he have bad cough from early in expedition," Pasang explained. "He sick and run down. And often he and Ruth fight, argue. She have tears. Roger not so happy when he went on climb."

Pasang continued: "I stay at Tilman's Lake Camp, our Base Camp, while Ruth she stay higher, at Advanced Camp below Changtse. Roger climb well on first day, May 19. He camp in rocks below 1986 Swiss bivouac. Next day he climb up to Swiss bivouac, to 25,500 feet, but he go very slow. He go for ten minutes, rest, then again. Over and over and over.

"Third day, I pray Roger he go to summit! I look and look, and no. He going down! I very sad. I come to Advanced Camp on May 21, and Ruth tell me Roger slip on blue ice near bottom. No one see him fall. Ruth crying and Roger dead. What more to do?"

The pained expression on Pasang's face I had never seen the likes of. It obviously pained him to talk about Roger's death. They'd been good friends. The afternoon sun warmed us as he spoke, and for a few moments we were transported back to 1986 when Roger was alive. Although that expedition, too, had at times been stressful, in our memories, our shared experiences of that trip now seemed festive.

"But solo expedition is very, very difficult," Pasang exclaimed, continuing. "Roger, he have so many plan: Everest, Lhotse, Makalu, K2. He always thinking, thinking: 'what I can climb next?' So now what? All gone, dead, finish. Your expedition much better, happy, laughing."

But how did Roger Marshall fall? Ruth De Cew believes he slipped on his descent while making the transition from the snowfield below the *Hornbein Couloir* onto the hard, unforgiving ice of the *Japanese Couloir*. Whatever happened, death on Everest was a tragically appropriate way for such a brazenly outspoken individualist as Roger to die. That summer, friends gathered in Colorado to memorialize him, built a *chorten,* and strung it with prayer flags.

"Roger created so much pressure around himself and his Everest solo," Ruth told me at Roger's memorial, "that in 1987 he had to do it. Everest was his destiny. In 1986, we had fun. In 1987, life was tense. Death was such a real possibility that we never discussed it."

Bravely, Ruth had crossed the glacier alone to where Roger's body lay at the foot of the mountain. The six-millimeter rope he had carried with him was coiled over one shoulder. Roger wore no harness, but the leashes from his two ice axes were still looped around each of his wrists. Roger's neck was broken. The following day, Pasang and two other Sherpas buried Roger Marshall in the bergschrund crevasse at the foot of Mount Everest's North Face.

* * * * * * * * * * * * * *

Sun and spring-like weather returned, good omens for returning to the route. Establishing Camp One and bridging Stephen's hidden crevasse were our primary goals. With my aid-climbing skills, I advocated battling the crevasse's far wall, if we couldn't find an easier way to circumnavigate the impasse. Our latest plan called for a four-man load carry to establish Camp One just below the Webster Wall. The site was safely situated, away from avalanche danger and falling ice (so we thought), plus it was logistically well placed, a seven-hour carry from Advanced Base. Robert and I would climb to

Camp One for a two- to three-day effort to cross the crevasse, while Stephen and Paul did "yak duty" hauling supplies to stock the camp. When we tired, we'd switch, and they'd investigate the upper slopes toward Camp Two.

Early in the morning, waking at Base Camp, I'd had one of my most memorable experiences of expedition life. Most Himalayan climbers use a pee bottle to avoid the nighttime discomfort of having to brave the elements outside the tent. (Even women—so I've been told—with practice can become highly skilled using wide mouth plastic bottles.) This morning, my pee bottle was almost full, but I hoped to get one more use out of it. Unfortunately, no! As it brimmed, I clamped down hard as both bladder and pee bottle threatened to overflow simultaneously. Then, with impeccably bad timing, from just outside my tent door I heard an abrupt and cheery greeting: *"Goo mournu!"*

Bed tea had arrived at just the wrong moment.

Trying not to panic, I kept a firm grip, maintaining the necessary pressure to keep my sleeping bag from being flooded, carefully set down the sloshing bottle, screwed on the lid, then unzipped the tent door with my one free hand.

"Oh, good morning, Kasang," I said pleasantly. Not having a clue of the agony I was in, he handed me a hot mug of milk tea, smiled, and departed. Just before I burst, I emptied the bottle's contents out the tent door—and hastily completed my urgent chore.

Although Mimi accompanied us back to Advanced Base, Joe had decided to remain temporarily at Base Camp. Part of his job as expedition photographer was to do high-altitude film testing for Kodak. He wanted to develop the 4 x 5 inch black-and-white T-Max negatives he'd taken of our route up Everest. In the variable (and usually chilly) weather at 16,500 feet, obtaining a precise temperature for the development chemicals—and keeping it steady—was quite a feat. I doubted that a full darkroom had been brought to Everest Base Camp in decades, perhaps since the British Everest expeditions of the 1930s.

The return to ABC was uneventful, another good portent, and we retired promptly, determined to get back to work on our route early the next morning.

The early birds got the hard-frozen snow on this climb. Robert's word-play name for our route, the *Neverest Buttress,* was sounding increasingly appropriate with each of our middle-of-the-night 2:30 A.M. starts. On this night the weather held, and Robert and I left thirty minutes after Stephen and Paul. In the distance, we could see the lights from their headlamps bobbing across the glacier—then a loud crack echoed through the darkness, followed by a thunderous roar. A serac avalanche cascaded tons of ice into the bottom of the Witches'

Robert on the Kangshung Glacier at first light.

Cauldron before the blast careened directly toward Stephen and Paul. Their headlamps darted back and forth like agitated fireflies about to be swatted, but the avalanche was too big to run from. When the ice crystal cloud from the blast enveloped them seconds later, the two tiny dots of light disappeared.

"Looks like it's going to snow on us, too," Robert declared fatalistically. We turned our backs toward the approaching maelstrom and pulled the drawstrings tight on our hoods. The fallout swept over us with a single dramatic gust and a chaotic swirling of snow. Afterward, Robert's pack resembled a cake sprinkled with powdered sugar. Up ahead, Paul and Stephen's lights reappeared, and we continued on our nocturnal trudge.

Robert's and my pace were almost identical. "Not as fast as speedy Venables, the stomach churner," Robert quipped. Neither of us could match Stephen's quick gait, Paul couldn't either—nor did any of us really want to. All that hurrying just dried my parched throat and tired me out. "It's not efficient to push yourself *that* hard," Robert reflected, before adding prophetically, "but in most athletic endeavors, it's usually that extra 10 percent of effort that makes the difference between winning and losing."

The sky lightened behind Chomolönzo as the luminous white glow of the preborn sun swelled behind the mountain's castle-dark granite ramparts. For a few moments, high wisps of cloud caught and displayed the rainbow-banded wet seashell colors of the sunrise's first subtle hues, before the sun's fiery red-orange orb broke over the jagged edge of the Gyankar Range to our east. We stopped to watch the soft light flood the glacial stillness surrounding us.

I was glad to be here with Robert. It was our friendship and strength as climbing partners that had brought me here to Tibet, to Everest's East Face. Colorado-born, Robert always shot straight from the hip. His western genuineness and directness made me feel calmly confident. We had that unspoken, implicit trust in each other's capabilities—which we also had with Stephen and Paul—that is so essential to the success of any team endeavor. No matter how dangerous this climb might become, I reflected as I trudged across the glacier, I felt firmly and warmly embraced by the comradeship of my teammates.

The recent storm had deposited several feet of wet monsoon snow. We watched Stephen and Paul rip out the fixed ropes from beneath their heavy blanket. Our line of ropes was now a well-known highway, and we traveled most sections up the buttress by memory, paring our time to Camp One to just under seven hours. After the four of us regathered on the snow terrace below the Webster Wall, we dug two platforms for our lightweight Bibler tents.

Robert makes tea at Camp One at 22,500 feet. Lowe Buttress *in profile on right.*

It was a beautiful camp, situated on an open terrace that welcomed the morning sun and featured a panoramic view of Lhotse Shar, Peak 38 (also called Shartse I), Shartse II (known also as Junction Peak), Pethangtse, Makalu, Kangchungtse (also referred to as Makalu II), Chomolönzo, the Gyankar Range in the far distance to the east, and, behind our Base Camp, the two lovely snow peaks of Kartse and Kama Changri—both first ascended by George Mallory in 1921. We also had a close-up view of the Kangshung Face's massive central rib, the *American,* or *Lowe, Buttress.* Its spectacular bulwark of somber black rock was laced with white pegmatite veins and draped with fragile snow icing.

Stephen and Paul zipped back to Advanced Base while Robert and I ascended gingerly up the free-hanging, eight-millimeter rope on the Webster Wall. After retrieving a cache of food, stoves, and fuel canisters, we retreated quickly to the tent, and buried ourselves in the warmth of our Gore-tex down sleeping bags, rated to minus thirty degrees and cut extra long with plenty of toe-wiggling room. Inside of our bags, additionally, we each wore very comfortable, capilene fiber Patagonia long underwear. Our two French-made Bluet propane-burning stoves hung from the tent poles, hissing away as they melted snow for water. The stoves, in turn, were screwed into Markill pot sets, an ingenious German invention featuring a pot and lid stacked vertically above a windscreen protecting the stove's flame from unwanted drafts. Cold fingers soon curled lovingly around mugs of Earl Grey tea generously laced with sugar and powdered milk.

"Here we are at 22,500 feet, suffering through another day in Tibet," Robert beamed. It was the highest we had camped since 1985, when Robert spent two nights at twenty-seven thousand feet on Everest and I several nights at 23,500. After dinner, we took our Hypnovel sleeping pills, then I listened to Sting's *Nothing Like The Sun* on my Walkman, waited for sleep—but sleep never came.

The next morning, April 15, we saw and felt the heat of the sun, but we could not move. We could not sit up, nor could we speak more than two consecutive sentences. By 11 A.M., we had melted snow for tea. My pounding headache was the worst that I could remember; our lethargy was crippling. The rude clinking of gear as Venables and Teare arrived in camp completed our dishonor. We weren't even out of bed—and they had already ferried loads! Rarely had Robert or I been so chagrined. Fortunately, Paul and Stephen didn't ridicule us too much. We placated them with tea, and they sped back down.

Ed and Robert at Camp One. The worst headache—ever. Stephen Venables

Roused by their ribald joviality, we finally managed to force ourselves to reascend the fixed rope up the Webster Wall. Higher still, when we reached the top of the Fourth Cauliflower Tower, swirling clouds obscured all visibility. Robert was feeling a bit ill, so I led. Eighty feet higher, I reached a platform just beneath the crevasse. Under a giant fractured blade of ice—soon nicknamed the Cleaver—a window or gap opened through the crevasse wall, revealing the ice-blue tomb below. If there wasn't a lucky way around this behemoth of a crevasse, we'd have to rappel into its interior and search for an escape up the far wall. I hammered in two ice pitons—threaded aluminum tubes—for my anchor, fixed the rope, and a very cold and lethargic Robert joined me. Then I decided to try and circumnavigate the crevasse on the right.

"Ed disappearing into oblivion!" Robert exclaimed optimistically as I rappelled down a one-hundred-meter length of skinny, eight-millimeter rope toward Big Al gully. Unfortunately, it soon became evident there was no "easy way" to bypass the crevasse. Vertical ice walls and detached ice blocks presented me with a chilling spectacle. On my left, however, a sentrybox-wide entrance beckoned me into the crevasse's snow-smothered interior. I waded through several drifts and entered into the ice gallery.

Cautiously, I fed out my safety rope and anchored it every fifteen or twenty feet into ice pitons that I drove into the crevasse's polished, well-frozen walls. The silence inside the great fissure's interior was unearthly, and yet there was something equally magical about standing between these two vertical faces of sheer ice—a realization of and a feeling for the earth's primordial, ageless nature that was simultaneously terrifying and captivating. Horizontally banded dust layers (the wind-borne glacial dating equivalent of tree rings) striated the white-blue walls. Above, the ice ramparts arced inward over my head and suffocated my view of the sky. My breath came in short rapid gulps; I felt like a soon-to-be victim exploring a haunted house. The crevasse did indeed hold a secret passageway which, with luck, might lead to the upper snow slopes. Then, blocking my way ahead, I saw two giant detached ice blades resembling shark fins.

"Ed! What—are—you—doing?" reverberated a calling from the heavens.

It was reassuring to know that another human being was alive nearby.

"I'm—exploring—a—passageway!"

It was impossible to tell if the crevasse's snow floor was firm, or only a deceptively thin layer masking a bottomless black hole. I took a step forward—and promptly fell into a pit, frantically grabbed at my belay rope, caught it, and hauled myself out. I tried to catch my breath, couldn't, then scurried under the

Shark Fins and into a claustrophobic body-width passage. Chimneying through the slot, I stabbed the pick of my hammer into the ice for security, then entered a new and larger chamber. In the distance loomed another grim prospect, a forty-foot-in-diameter ice block wedged between the crevasse walls like a giant cork. Unfortunately, from where I stood, I couldn't see if an escape was feasible beyond the ice chockstone—that is, if anyone might dare walk beneath it.

Suddenly shivering, I realized I'd come far enough. I retraced my steps, fought back my now-unbottled panic, and hurriedly rejoined Robert.

"I'm freezing. I'll put the tea on!" he volunteered, descending instantly for the warmth and security of our nylon sanctuary at Camp One.

After my tour through the crypt, our tiny tent felt absolutely spacious.

"You really think that's the right way to go?" Robert asked as he dropped two tea bags into a pot of boiling water. "It looked fearsome to me."

"Well, going to the right around the crevasse is definitely out. First, there's danger from falling ice, plus it would require miles of fixed rope. I think that the secret passageway is the best way, actually. It's the jammed ice chockstone that worries me," I said. But how stable was the cork? We'd have to find out.

More Hypnovel pills worked marvels that night. We were reclimbing the fixed ropes by 7:15 A.M. the next morning, astonishingly early for two Yanks! We both felt fit, and I rigged our blue, eleven-millimeter lead rope through the crevasse window, giving us a direct descent into the secret passageway one hundred feet lower. Rappelling into the crevasse, however, was frighteningly reminiscent of entering a cave. I hated caves. I went first, then came Robert.

Ed prepares to enter the crevasse. Robert Anderson

352

Robert happy to be inside of Mount Everest.

"This is the freakiest place I've ever been!" he gasped. "We're *inside* Everest."

Robert belayed me while I retraced my steps below the Shark Fins, through the tight squeeze, and into the far chamber, where I placed an ice screw and belayed. I gathered by Robert's expression as he emerged from the crawlway that he thought I was completely out of my mind. Maybe I was—but what other choices did we have? I advocated aid climbing up the crevasse's far side, up a ninety five-degree ice wall, but Robert disagreed. He felt we should check out the easier alternative—walking under the wedged ice block to see what was on the other side—first.

"Why don't you go check it out?" he said.

Blind to the danger, I agreed. Thirty feet from Robert's belay stance, I halted. In front of me, the crevasse floor dipped, forming a snowy hollow below the cork. It seemed a wise place for a piece of protection. I took a drive-in ice piton off my harness and began pounding it into the crevasse wall. The ice was rubbery and unyielding. I hit the piton hard, then harder still. The piton wasn't going in. I knew that the ice chockstone, the cork, was unstable, but high altitude had dulled my ability to detect danger. Now the ice piton was nearly in....

The sound of an atomic blast detonated beside my right ear. I recognized what was happening—that the ice chockstone had exploded—and I ran back toward Robert, my arms, legs, feet, and hands whirling, reacting, propelling me away, away, as fast as was possible at twenty-three thousand feet from the terrifying din, as millions of ice crystals blasted us in a continuous falling wave.

When I opened my eyes again, we were huddled right next to each other, cowering, and engulfed by the explosion's fallout of swirling snow and ice.

"Where's Ed?" Robert continued to shout frantically.

"I'm okay! I'm okay! I'm right here," I yelled back, energized by the several gallons of adrenaline that had just dumped into my veins. Robert stared at me in blank astonishment; his bearded face was completely sugar-coated with snow.

"How'd you get here—fly?" he wondered aloud. Realizing in the very next moment that we were still alive, we both instinctively looked up, expecting even more debris to fall. Then, turning my gaze to my right, I gasped when I saw the unbelievable destruction. The chockstone had collapsed into a chaotic pile of multi-ton ice blocks a good thirty feet thick. They could easily have been my tomb. One huge shard had landed only a few feet from the infamous ice piton.

"I was watching you hammering when I heard a crackling noise. I looked up, and in an instant, the chockstone exploded. It didn't just fall. It blew up," Robert explained.

"Yeah, close one, huh?" I said dryly.

"Well, it's safe now," Robert quipped. "Go stand over there and I'll take your picture. You might as well see what it's like around the corner."

I clipped into the ice piton, then posed for the camera like Teddy Roosevelt on top of the ice blocks. Beyond, the secret passageway was literally a dead end, terminating with a dizzying drop-off to the Kangshung Glacier three thousand feet below. With no easy escape, we now had no alternative but to aid climb up the crevasse's far wall. I collected our ice pitons and ice screws, my four-step nylon webbing stirrups, and began front-pointing up the seventy-five-degree ice face above Robert's belay. The two crevasse walls tilted close enough together so that when I tensioned off an ice screw and leaned to my left, I could just stem across and touch the far wall with my left leg and crampon front points. One piton higher, I launched up the far wall.

It was exhilarating climbing. The crevasse wall was formed of compacted snow—luckily it was not hard ice—and I hammered in pitons and screws like I was driving them into Styrofoam. The danger was that if I fell, all the ice pitons and screws might pull out. After forty-five minutes of high-altitude construction work, I neared the top of the overhanging wall. "How'm I doing?" I asked.

"Great!" Robert answered. "Keep going! This is why I invited you to come on this expedition."

Right: *Ed climbing out of the Jaws of Doom crevasse.* Photos by Robert Anderson

We witnessed immense avalanches. This blast explodes out of the Witches' Cauldron.

The wall's final twenty feet deteriorated into soft granular snow. This top section I aid climbed on snow pickets, driving the aluminum stakes into the wall at a steeply inclined angle, so that even if the picket sheared through the snow for an inch or two, it hopefully wouldn't come out. When I swung my right leg up onto a powdery shoulder—we were on Everest's middle slopes.

After eight days, we'd climbed the buttress. Robert and I shook hands. It'd taken a team effort from the four of us to get here. Now we had to establish a Tyrolean traverse—a rope bridge—across the Jaws of Doom, my new name for the crevasse. Robert's "modified-bullet-coil-overhand-fastball" finally sent our spare rope sailing through Stephen's notch in the crevasse's opposite side.

Reluctantly, we rappelled carefully back into the crevasse, then retraced our steps to our original rappel rope. We were each terrified of being killed by the Cleaver, the detached ice flake suspended directly above the rappel anchor. I jumared the rope first. Nothing happened. Nervously, I waited for Robert.

"I didn't think I could climb so quickly up a hundred feet of fixed rope at twenty-three thousand feet," he gasped, totally out of breath. "You know, going through that crevasse was a bit like walking through your own coffin."

Over dinner we recounted the day's harrowing events. It had been a very close call for me when the ice chockstone exploded. It wasn't the first time I'd almost died climbing, and I doubted that it would be the last. Death was part of climbing; I knew that all too well. Himalayan climbing, with its one in ten fatality rate, was obviously not safe. But experiencing the tragic death of another could also make you strong, Robert and I agreed. Death was so undeniably final that it had forced each of us to realistically appraise why we were on Everest.

"To be honest, it's one thing I've always admired about your dedication to climbing," Robert declared. "You've seen death, and you've become a stronger person because of it." And so had Robert become toughened in character after he watched his climbing partner fall two thousand feet to his death in Peru.

"I learned it doesn't take much of a mistake to die climbing," Robert told me with a slight shrug. "I wonder if Stephen or Paul have seen someone die on a climb? Somehow I don't think so."

It was Robert's lead the following morning. After a breakfast of Pop Tarts and ramen noodle soup (high altitude does funny things to your appetite), perhaps not surprisingly my stomach took a turn for the worse. Meanwhile, Robert finished engineering the Tyrolean traverse across the Jaws of Doom. At Stephen's notch, he anchored the rope he'd thrown across yesterday. Five ice screws (equalized for both upward and downward "pulls," or forces) made for a completely "bombproof" anchor, but Robert still screamed as he bobbed uncontrollably up and down—hanging in his harness above the hundred-foot void—from halfway across the sagging, eight-millimeter-diameter rope bridge.

Blinded by another dense whiteout that had settled upon us, in the near-zero visibility I could barely discern Robert's progress. Having attained the mountain's upper slopes, he plowed methodically uphill through thigh-deep snow toward the Hump, a snow dome several hundred feet above the crevasse. Gray on gray, white on white, the cloud was so thick that I could hardly see him. Beside my belay stance at Stephen's notch, snow and ice mushrooms leered like frozen gargoyles jutting from the eaves of a fantastic haunted house. I had to keep reminding myself that I was a third of the way up a new route on Mount Everest—and there were only two of us here. It took a strong conscious effort to keep my wits about me; there was absolutely no room for error.

"Here I come!" came a shout. Robert reappeared.

"Good to have some company," he mut-  tered as he joined me. I felt the same. Snow was falling thicker and faster by the minute, so we flew down the fixed ropes to Camp One. The Tyrolean traverse was installed; the Jaws of Doom had been bridged.

"This weather's awful. Let's go back to Advanced Base," I suggested. With hearts in mouths, we rappelled down Big Al in the worsening storm. The mountain was smothered under a foot of new powder; the threat of a tremendous avalanche was very real. And because of the clouds we couldn't really see the danger, but we certainly sensed it as we hurried to escape. It was rope work by instinct: rappel down the fixed rope at a breathless run, unclip the figure-of-eight rappel brake, rewrap it using the next lower length of fixed rope, unclip the safety sling from above the anchor point, reclip it into the lower rope—and immediately start running downhill again. I didn't dare look up once.

Retreating down Big Al.

We barely recognized the glacier. In our four-day absence many familiar landmarks had apparently melted. Advanced Base was silent as a church, before one by one, people began to emerge from their tents, as dusk turned to darkness. Whenever I came down off the mountain, Paul and I always clasped with a firm handshake, then stared fixedly at each other for several seconds, eyeball to eyeball, to see if everything was okay. This evening was no exception.

"There's no dinner. Sorry. We didn't know you'd be down," Paul said, so while eating our hurriedly made soup, we regaled them with horror stories of "conquering" the Jaws of Doom.

It was a relief to have overcome the crevasse, but several more hundred feet of climbing around the Hump still separated us from the easy-angled snow slopes of the upper buttress. Stephen and Paul left early on April 19 to climb past the Hump. At 4 A.M., snuggled in my warm sleeping bag, I was immensely pleased to hear Stephen moan, "I could have slept in all day today!"—proof that he was indeed part human.

Pasang and Kasang arrived in midmorning with two loads of supplies. The day was sunny and hot, having fooled us again. We relaxed, ate well, and prepared for a load carry to Camp One the following day. That evening, the weather began to act very strange. Lightning flickered from ominous dark clouds behind Chomolönzo, while hail fell at Advanced Base. But by bedtime, the sky had again cleared.

Our 4 A.M. start verged on pure hell. Saint Mimi got up to light the stove and brew tea. "Morning," Robert said in his most deadpanned voice. "Please notice that I left out the good. There will be no more of this 2:30 A.M. stuff for me. Your most important sleep occurs between three and five in the morning. All this getting up at two or three is awful!"

Robert savors a bowl of 3 a.m. oatmeal.

After a beautiful sunrise, the weather changed in a blink. A threatening gray cloud swept across the sky and deposited an ugly black lenticular over Chomolönzo's rocky summit. The clouds certainly weren't auspicious, but at least they made the temperature much more comfortable for load carrying. Ascending the fixed ropes went easily, but a foreboding silence gripped the air. Normally a handful of sparrows and chuffs twittered and darted across the base of the buttress. Today the birds were noticeably absent.

Burdened by the silence and our loads, we plodded mechanically up the Scottish Gully. Spindrift had filled in our previous footsteps; each step had to be excavated anew. The traverse across Big Al's exposed left-hand side was equally slow and laborious. Snow then began to flutter out of the quiet sky, falling softly but steadily—"just like a Christmas morning," I yelled down to Robert.

A few minutes later, he screamed: *"Ed—Avalanche!"*

It was Big Al. The dull roar of thousands of tons of crashing ice and snow reverberated with increasing destruction through the clouds that cloaked the mountain. With each passing second, Everest became more of a living, breathing, *and moving* entity as the cataclysmic avalanche gathered speed and mass down Big Al's well-scoured chute. Shooting my eyes upward, I saw wave upon wave of snow emerge and explode out of the storm clouds. Since I was clipped into the fixed rope, I had nowhere to run and nowhere to hide. The avalanche would engulf us in two or three seconds. My mind and limbs scrambled. My crampons scratched uselessly against some rock, then I slipped and fell onto the fixed rope. Poor Robert, I thought to myself: he was several hundred feet below me, stranded at the lowest and most exposed part of the traverse.

A second later, the powerful cascade of snow and ice crystals hit me like a sharp right to the jaw. The force knocked my face sideways. I bent down, inhaled a deep breath, but not quite big enough, covered my face with a glove to keep from breathing in any more snow crystals, then instinctively shielded the back of my neck with my other hand, praying that I wouldn't be hit by a falling ice block or a rock. Soon running out of oxygen, I was forced to gasp for air but, drowning in the avalanche, I swallowed a big mouthful of snow instead. Coughing and sputtering was accompanied by spitting out snow; I finally could breathe again twenty or thirty seconds after the avalanche blasts had subsided. Hanging limply on the rope, hyperventilating and heaving for breathe, I listened to the cacophony of the snow torrent colliding with the glacier far beneath us.

Then Robert and I shouted profanities back and forth, releasing adrenaline, each amazed that we were still alive, before we inquired in greater detail about the other's condition. Neither he nor I had been injured, so we brushed the snow off ourselves as though nothing had happened—but in reality something had. We'd cheated death again. How much longer would our luck hold out?

When we finally reached Camp One, we discovered that Paul and Stephen were up above, pushing the route ever higher. They'd left us a note:

"19-4-88 Neverest Villas. Terrible mess in the neighbourhood.... Please tell Mimi we both have sore backs and need a massage. We also need / may need: 1. An extra shovel head. 2. the snow saw. 3. a Bluet burner top—one of the ones here is broken. It has a blocked nipple and we have no needles to clean it. We will see how far we can get tomorrow. If we get a good distance, we will try to go up and camp on the 21st (headaches permitting.) Happy jumaring!"
Stephen and Paul

We dropped off our loads and descended to ABC, where Joe had been hard at work. He'd built a new cook shelter by stretching a blue tarp over a rock retaining wall—so at last we could prepare meals and sit and eat, out of any snowstorms. We spent the afternoon leisurely catching up with Mimi and Joe, both of whom, I noticed, now talked only about what their first meal would be upon getting home, a predictable shift in conversation at this stage of the trip.

Clouds obscured every inch of Everest. When the weather cleared at dusk, there was no sign at all of Stephen and Paul. We surmised they must be in their tent at Camp One. Then Robert screamed, *"Avalanche! Big Al!"* and another colossal boomer roared down the gully. The snow wave multiplied upon itself, feeding in a frenzy on the recent snowfall, and finally engulfed not only Big Al gully, but the entire lower portion of our buttress, from the Scottish Gully on down. Thinking of Paul and Stephen caught at Camp One made me shudder. The churning snow resounded upon impact with the glacier, then billowed skyward and slowly dissipated.

"That one could have killed you," Robert said simply.

For the next thirty minutes, an eerie spectacle mesmerized us. Avalanche after avalanche poured down the cirque's enclosing walls, falling first from Lhotse Shar, then from the Trinity Gullies—as Stephen named the prominent gullies to the right, or north of, the *Lowe Buttress*—then down Lhotse again, before Big Al disgorged a second massive flow. It seemed that the Earth's gravitational field had suddenly been switched to "high," with the result that every avalanche trough and loose serac spewed its waste in one prolonged destructive riot. We decided not to return to the mountain the next day as planned.

Later that evening, after Joe and I had retired to the tent we were sharing, he asked if I thought he might climb up onto the bottom part of the route. We'd often had talks long into the night during the past week, and Joe and I felt comfortable speaking candidly. I answered that having him along would scare the hell out of me—and Joe admitted that he too would be worried, for his family's sake, that something might happen to him. Our concern for Paul and Stephen's safety at the moment only strengthened the importance of Joe's remark about his family, and although I knew he craved the opportunity to get up on the mountain and photograph us, the issue was closed.

The morning quiet was interrupted by Robert's shout: "I can see them! They're coming down. Paul's on the middle snowfield at the bottom of the fixed ropes, and Stephen's just below him." Whew—they were safe.

"But this weather is the pits!" Robert added. "Time for resting and eating at Base Camp, I should think."

The A Team arrived, tired, sore, and relieved to be down. Stephen proffered the obviously acceptable excuse that the upper slopes were loaded with fresh snow, unstable, and avalanche-prone—"so we thought we'd better come down."

Paul glanced at him in mock shock. "Actually, we had quite a confab over the pros and cons of going down, or waiting out the bad weather, and I was rather surprised when Stephen agreed we should descend," Paul claimed.

They had loved the Tyrolean—the world's highest rope bridge—and were equally glad that they hadn't needed to descend into the Jaws of Doom. Another crevasse lay just above the Hump, but it hadn't been nearly as threatening.

"It cut across most of the buttress, but we passed it on the left," Stephen said.

Then Paul cut in: "I was belaying Stephen toward the Hump on the far side of the Tyrol, when I felt three tugs on the belay rope—you know, the signal for off belay. So I undid the belay rope, clipped my ascenders onto the rope, pulled down any slack, and right when I'm ready to climb up after him, *WHAM*, I get hit in the chest by a two-foot-thick slab avalanche. *BANG!* It knocked me right over. Then I stood back up, slid the ascenders up the rope—and suddenly, *I'M FALLING!* Took a thirty-footer! Turns out the rope had straightened out, and sliced through the snow where Stephen had done a big traverse."

"Eventually," Stephen continued, jumping back into the verbal fray, "we got to another crevasse filled with huge jumbled blocks making a sort of snow bridge, and we anchored a fixed rope across them."

"So, only twice as much climbing as we've already done," Paul summarized, "and we'll be at the South Col in no time!"

The climbing on the lower buttress had been nervy, strenuous, and utterly committing. Every day on the Kangshung Face we had put our lives on the line. We had alternated the duties of leading, switching that fatiguing role back and forth between whichever pair was feeling fittest at the time. During the past week, the lead pair of climbers, due to various circumstances, had always been alone on the mountain. They had been required to be entirely self-reliant, completely self-sufficient, and fully responsible for their own decisions and actions, and whatever else might befall them. The thrill of figuring out a new route up Everest's unknown East Face was extraordinarily exhilarating—and at the same time, scary as all hell. This climb, we had each now come to realize, was the adventure of our lifetimes, the one climb whose memory was likely to linger on, in one form or another, for the rest of our days.

Chapter 10

Snow in the Kingdom

If a man will begin with certainties,
he shall end in doubts;
but if he will be content to begin with doubts,
he shall end in certainties.

—Sir Francis Bacon

Pasang's Lodge was a welcome sight at the end of the long trek back across the Kangshung Glacier. At 16,500 feet, the Base Camp air was so rich with oxygen that we felt like we were at the beach. Our hosts wasted no time in spoiling us, either. We dined on spaghetti and tomato sauce spiced by black olives, mushrooms, peas, ginger, and garlic. And, at exactly 8 P.M., Pasang tuned our yellow ghetto blaster to Radio Nepal, broadcasting from Kathmandu. The nightly weather forecast did little to factually foretell the Kangshung microclimate's fickle whims, but it did provide, most importantly, our sole link with civilization.

Left: *Big Al erupts with a killer avalanche.*

"Good eeevening. This is the weather forecast from Radio Nepal. In the eastern sector there will be thunderstorms tonight and tomorrow. In the central sector there will be the same."

The reports weren't known for their in-depth coverage. First came the temperature listings, for Kathmandu, then Pokhara (near Annapurna), and finally for a number of more obscure locales. Next, a blaring round of Hindi music announced the program's highlight: the "special weather bulletin for the mountaineering expeditions in the Kingdom of Nepal," a phrase that Paul took great pleasure at parroting, either back at the announcer—or at any opportune moment in the middle of a raging blizzard. What followed was the dutiful recitation of a list of wind speeds and direction, plus centigrade temperatures for elevations of five-, seven-, and nine-thousand-meters. Tonight's forecast was bad.

"We hit it spot on, deciding to come down," Stephen exclaimed gleefully, relieved to hear Radio Nepal's validation of his and Paul's decision to descend.

The weather bulletin's forecast prompted us to make a cursory inspection of our food supplies, which appeared adequate for another month. "Good thing," said Robert, "because it looks like we might be here a while yet."

"Americans come down, weather good. Americans go back up, weather bad," was Pasang's comment. And true to form, the next day in the Kingdom dawned resplendent. Pethangtse gleamed like a shining obelisk opposite camp.

"Yes, we should be up there right now," Paul said pointedly in a somewhat antsy voice, still believing we should be climbing regardless of the weather.

I didn't agree with him. The snow needed to settle, and I was hopeful yet that there'd be plenty of clear skies and sun during May. I saw no need to rush—at least not yet. I advocated that we should prepare the route to the South Col, descend one more time, rest fully at Base Camp, then make a lightning attempt on the summit during the first settled weather in early May. We had just had a thrilling week of climbing, maybe the best of our lives. We'd attained twenty-three thousand feet, "knocked off" the buttress, as Ed Hillary would say, and boosted our acclimatization. With Everest's upper, avalanche-prone slopes laden with fresh snow, now was the ideal time to recuperate.

A world of white—yet another storm—arrived that night. We lay in the "como-sutra" position (another Paulism) until the next morning's pan-banging signaled the start of a hearty pancake breakfast. It was time to store energy for the final push. After gorging on "lead cakes," the blood sunk to our stomachs, and one by one, we crept, well-fed, back to our tents to digest and hibernate. Cassettes were duly exchanged, paperbacks finished, and diaries updated.

Kasang serves up a gourmet meal at Base Camp.

At lunch we had a tasty treat. Kasang had been hauling water the previous afternoon when he saw an eagle dive-bomb a snow grouse, kill it, but fail to carry it away. Before the eagle could return, Kasang grabbed it. "Charlie"—as Paul christened the unfortunate fowl—now hung fully plucked from the cook tent rafters, ready for our midday meal.

Our mostly vegetarian diet had left several of us craving meat, an urge only semisatisfied by tuna fish and Stephen's limited gourmet supplies of provolone ham and Negroni salami. Toward the end of my 1986 Everest trip, I'd experienced an intense hunger for meat and protein—and dug right in when the departing Chilean team left behind cans of meatballs in tomato sauce. Then, on my return journey home, in Hawaii I'd feasted daily on hamburgers and hot dogs, foods not normally a regular part of my diet. So, while I can't completely explain my meat craving, our special lunch of spicy "stewed Charlie" was a welcome addition to the menu—although our stomachs were a bit queasy afterward. Only Mimi, whose dedication to the principles of vegetarianism could not be swayed, turned up her nose in disgust.

With the climbing up the lower buttress completed, our expedition now appeared to have entered into a period of indecision, which I found striking in its contrast to our previous strong focus. We found ourselves engaged in endless speculation: about the weather, our health, and whether we had the requisite stamina for a serious summit attempt without bottled oxygen. The logistics of load-carrying and climbing timetables for the ascent rounded out these discussions. All ideas were taken into consideration, tossed around, accepted, rejected, or reformulated. We were such a small team by traditional Himalayan standards that each of us recognized that our hopes of reaching Everest's summit now demanded the free and open expression of our fears, concerns, and opinions about the climb's next stage.

There were countless unknowns. Should we fix ropes up the steep ice slopes leading to the South Col? Should we carry loads up to the Col, then retreat to Base Camp, rest, and return for a concerted effort—or should we push straight through, climb to the South Col with one big load carry, then aim for the summit early the following day? Each scenario had its pluses and minuses.

The best plan for now, we decided, was to read up on past lightweight expeditions to Everest so that we could (hopefully) emulate their success. Back in Kathmandu, I'd bought a copy of H.W. Tilman's *Mount Everest 1938,* which I now started. Stephen, meanwhile, was reading Lincoln Hall's *White Limbo,* about the successful 1984 Australian Everest expedition. These trips were the finest examples of what small-sized teams had done on Everest. With the right blend of self-confidence, group spirit, and willpower—anything was possible.

The Australian ascent of Everest's North Face by a new route lay closest to our hearts. They were, prior to their Everest climb, a group of relatively unknown mountaineers, yet the tremendous success of Tim Macartney-Snape, Greg Mortimer, and Andy Henderson gave us constant hope that we too might pull off the impossible. The Aussies weren't such highly trained professional mountaineers like the European élites Reinhold Messner, Jean Troillet, and Pierre Béghin; rather, they were close friends and highly motivated individuals who shared a common dream. It was their belief in themselves, and the obvious and admirable harmony within their small group, that allowed them to climb a very audacious new route, without bottled oxygen, up Everest's Great Couloir.

With just five climbers, two climbing Sherpas, and two film cameramen, the unheralded Australians had become the smallest team to ascend a major new route up Mount Everest. They'd gone against the accepted notion that a new route on the world's highest mountain could not be made by such a small team.

As we read their story, we honestly felt we could disprove the skeptics, too.

But the success or failure of every high-altitude mountaineer is ultimately dependent not simply on climbing prowess, but also upon his or her body's ability to acclimatize, and the individual's own mental willingness to accept danger. The latter we'd obviously dealt with successfully, and fortunately we also appeared to be acclimatizing well. So far no one had developed any serious symptoms of high-altitude illness. The physical and aerobic rigor of the dozen load carries up and down the initial buttress, of establishing and stocking supplies at Camp One, had greatly facilitated our acclimatization. Even more strengthening than load carrying—but in the long run, it was obviously wearing—was the mental strain of putting our lives in peril on a daily basis. Call it arrogance, but so far, like the Australian team before us, we'd managed to maintain that essential fanaticism that *we could do it*.

Why did we have such confidence? I looked for an answer. A common thread was woven through each of our climbing careers. Robert, Paul, Stephen and I had all habitually climbed very dangerous routes alone. Robert had soloed a new route up the Matterhorn in winter, then climbed Peru's tallest peak, Huascaren (22,206 feet), by himself. Paul soloed *The Silver Strand* ice climb in Yosemite and additional ice routes in California's Sierra Nevada. Stephen soloed the Aiguille du Plan North Face in the Alps, a new route on Ancohuma (21,086 feet) in Peru, and an unclimbed granite monolith, Solu Tower at 19,616 feet, in the Karakoram in Pakistan. I'd soloed numerous big wall rock climbs in the United States, including a new route up the Diamond on Longs Peak in Colorado, first ascents on Moses and Cottontail Towers in Canyonlands, Utah, plus the East Face of Changtse (24,879 feet) in Tibet.

Climbing alone, as opposed to climbing with one or more partners, is an infinitely more serious game. Even seemingly minor injuries or miscalculations can become deadly. Soloing exacts the ultimate test of a climber's wits, nerves, stamina, and raw ability. It also breeds other harder-to-define qualities, primarily the ability to endure high risk situations and hardships that would make most other climbers look for the quickest retreat, or the nearest bar, or both. By surviving such extreme situations, the soloist discovers hidden strengths; unknown capabilities are revealed, explored, and built upon. If an accident occurs when climbing alone, usually there will be no rescue except self-rescue. Self-reliance and, more crucially, self-knowledge of one's abilities, plus adequate preparation, and skillful timing (with weather and snow and ice conditions) are of paramount importance to the success and safety of the soloist climber and mountaineer.

The daunting precipices of Mount Everest's Kangshung Face. South Col at upper left.

As individuals, we brought this vital background of climbing alone and on the edge to enrich the strength of our four-man team. In the past month, we had merged the soloist's heady egotistical self-confidence into a collective, previously unfathomable "team-will," which allowed us to extend ourselves well beyond any prior boundaries or limitations. But ultimately, our inner faith propelled us to the very precipice separating life and death because it made us believe—at least at this point in our Everest climb—that we were immortal.

The deadly seriousness of climbing the Kangshung Face was self-evident, yet rarely did we voice the unspoken code that we each were responsible for our own safety on the mountain. We were all in tacit agreement that once above the South Col, where we'd be climbing above the twenty-six-thousand-foot / eight-thousand-meter level without oxygen, that realistically, it would be every man for himself. Once we entered the so-called Death Zone, the realm above that altitude, the lack of atmospheric oxygen to breathe limits human survival to a mere handful of days. So profoundly muscle-wasting and brain-debilitating is the dearth of oxygen at these extreme high altitudes that to remain there unnecessarily is to invite death. If one of us had an accident or were injured in the Death Zone, there is virtually no possibility of a rescue. Of course we would certainly do our very best to assist a stricken partner, or partners, back down the mountain to safety, but in reality, we knew the truth full well.

High-altitude mountaineering was really *high stakes* mountaineering.

* * * * * * * * * * * * * *

The day after we ate Charlie, it snowed. A thick cold cloud clung to the ground. I lay in my tent enjoying a good read: Tilman's 1938 Everest account. Fifty years earlier, they'd also experienced horrible spring weather.

"I can't take it! I'm cracking up," Paul screamed from his tent.

"Ahhh! Help!" came a second yell.

In the far distance, the rumblings of avalanches signaled that Everest would be out of condition for several more days. One avalanche down Lhotse's sheer North Face, noticeably louder than the rest, Paul called "the triple-sonic-boomer."

The morning of April 24 dawned clear, but revealed a new load of snow on Everest. "Looks like the South Col is several feet higher," Robert quipped. But all too soon, clouds billowing up from the Arun Gorge recaptured Everest's summit, and a menacing cloudcap also gripped Makalu. There was no rush to go back up yet; and another thing, Stephen and I hadn't taken our baths yet!

R&R at Base Camp: Stephen, Paul, Robert, Joe, Mimi.

Outside my tent, the mist clumped as thick as overcooked oatmeal. One day I knew that this particular adventure would eventually end, and that my life would continue, after Everest. But what did my future hold?

"When all of our books have been read, the expedition will be over," Robert explained.

"Tonight there will be snow in the Kingdom," Radio Nepal prophesied.

At the new dawn, I peeked expectantly out of my tent door. Everest and Lhotse glowed pink. Dressing in an instant, I grabbed my Roliflex and Nikon FM2, and leapt into the quiet, bitterly frozen air. I sprinted up the hill behind camp, hoping to catch a better angle. Holding the cameras was sure tough on the fingertips! I blew on them for warmth, and told myself that photography was better training for the cold than holding snowballs in your bare hands.

Later, Stephen, Joe, and I went on an extended hike toward Kartse, the mountain immediately north of Base Camp. Joe and I surprised ourselves by being able to keep up with Stephen; obviously, something was wrong with him. His stomach was off. When we stumbled onto the crest of the moraine north of camp, we were astonished to discover a large frozen lake directly below the Karpo La pass, which George Mallory and Guy Bullock crossed way back in August, 1921—when Mallory also made the first ascent of Kartse.

Getting a second wind, we decided to attempt a circle, looping west over a suspected col below Kartse's South Face, and returning to Base Camp along the Kangshung Glacier's grassy northern bench. The Kartse Glacier ended abruptly in a forty-foot-high ice escarpment. Dedicated photographers all, we studiously framed Chomolönzo and Makalu between the cliff's dripping icicles.

Reaching a rocky col, we built a cairn and christened the pass the "Blackburn La" for Joe, and his new altitude record. Sitting on some boulders, we looked south across the Kangshung Glacier's large expanse of moraine and rubble to our route. I asked Stephen how soon he thought we should go back up.

"This unstable weather could go on for weeks," he answered. "My intuition is that we could be doing some useful work getting up to Camp Two."

Just then, Big Al thundered to life. The avalanche was by far the largest we had witnessed. Within seconds, huge cannon-like blasts of snow and debris shot out over the Scottish Gully and completely obscured the bottom of our climb. A mushrooming snow cloud boiled across the lower icefall then raced toward our Advanced Base Camp. We stared at the spectacle in numb shock.

"That one sure was a killer," Stephen said, a bit chagrined.

Radio Nepal's anticipated evening weather forecast was equally unpromising. Afterwards, standing outside of the cook tent, I watched lightning flash in regular bursts near Kanchenjunga to the southeast.

For the past several days, at least in general, Everest had been pleasantly absent from my thoughts. After the psychological pressures of the past weeks, this week had felt like a seaside vacation, far from Chomolungma's menacing stare. In fact, I had been quite content *not* climbing. Advanced Base Camp wasn't more than five miles away, but seeing sprouts of grass greening underfoot here at Base Camp made me feel like I was on another planet.

"So when do you think you'll be going back up?" Joe asked at dinner.

After a noticeable silence, Robert answered, "I should think in a few days, when we're healthy." Several stomachs were currently out of commission, and Stephen and Robert were taking Flagyl to treat suspected giardia.

We were also keenly aware of the large volume of snow that the stormy, unsettled weather was currently depositing on the mountain's upper slopes.

"Did you notice?" Paul asked. "The ice slopes below the South Col are completely buried. Ten feet of new snow must have fallen up there."

"The snow could certainly use a few sunny days to consolidate," was my answer. "No point returning to ABC when the weather's so unsettled."

"But this weather could be like this for the next three weeks," Stephen threw in, "and when it does clear, we'll still be messing around getting Camp Two established. It's important we have Camp Two stocked and ready, so that when the weather improves, we'll be poised to go for the top."

Eventually, we all agreed with Stephen. We'd head back up tomorrow or the next day. It was becoming increasingly frustrating trying to predict the weather in the Kama Valley. Except for the relatively clear spell during the first two weeks of April when we'd climbed the buttress, we'd been swamped by a depressing amount of cloud ever since. Now nearly every day, moist air blew up the Kama Valley from the Arun River drainage to the east of Makalu. The Arun Gorge formed a natural conduit for wet monsoon weather heading north from the Bay of Bengal. Even mornings that began moderately clear were usually whitewashed by the Arun's insidious clouds by as early as 8 or 9 A.M.

I took a delicious shower, my first in two weeks.

* * * * * * * * * * * * * *

April 27 started like a day in heaven. A strong west wind from Nepal pushed the constant clouds back down into the lower Kama Valley, and the sky was even completely clear of any high cirrus. Robert and Paul decided to return to Advanced Base, and Joe and Mimi were overjoyed; for the sooner we reached the summit, the sooner we could go home.

"But it's fine if you and Stephen want to wait another day," Robert said.
We did.

Stephen, as usual, was the first to leave the next morning, eager to return to the fray. I packed up leisurely with Joe, then drank several sociable cups of tea with Pasang, Kasang, and Mimi, who'd decided to remain at Base for the next five days. "I'm beginning to feel caged at Advanced Base," she explained. I didn't blame her for wanting to stay low, and to hang out in the green at Base. Pasang walked me to the edge of camp, hugged me, and said, "Be safe."

Back at Advanced Base Camp, it was winter again. Not liking the appearances of the weather, Robert and Paul had decided to remain in camp. Once more, snow began to fall steadily, and the wet and cold was miserable. It was useless pitting ourselves against such fickle weather; we had to bend so we wouldn't break. Remaining optimistic, we made plans for another alpine start.

Stephen Venables ascends the fixed ropes up the Scottish Gully.

At 2 A.M., Stephen yelled out, "It doesn't look too bad. Let's go!" I lay in my bag for half an hour of beauty rest—but with my headlamp switched on, feigning that I was getting up. Dressing was a lengthy and complex ritual. Putting on polypropylene tube socks, ragg wool socks, expedition weight capilene long underwear, wind pants, a pile jacket, down bibs, an expedition down jacket, inner boots, plastic mountaineering boots, gaiters, a hat, and gloves took nearly twenty minutes. Getting up at 2:30 A.M. in subzero temperatures was what climbing Mount Everest, bottom line, was really all about: SUFFERING.

Dark swathes of cloud dominated the eastern sky as we walked toward the base of the buttress. Were Robert and Paul coming? They hadn't made a sound as we left. I was now beginning to think that the real reason that I was paired with Stephen was thoroughly by default, because I was the only one of the three of us willing to get up so damn early and go with him!

Today (at least for the first several hours), I was proud of myself for keeping pace with him. Above, Stephen had just disappeared over the top of the Scottish Gully when I heard the mountain let loose a loud rumble overhead. Fearing the worst—that the Greyhound Bus was going for a joy ride—I ran to my right and slammed myself against the Scottish Gully's right-hand rock wall. The sound intensified; my heart raced. At any moment, I expected an avalanche of debris to roar over the top of the gully. I waited. It never came.

I continued up the fixed ropes. Thirty feet higher, another roar sounded. Again, I "postage-stamped" myself flat against the rock wall. And again, nothing happened! Where had the avalanche fallen? I was nervously perplexed.

"Oh, I'm sorry you were in such a panic," Stephen said when I caught up to him. "The avalanches went straight down Big Al. You were quite safe."

Making incredibly good time, we reached Camp One at 9:45 A.M., in only five and a half hours from ABC, our best time yet. Even though there was an immense halo round the sun—usually a portent of bad weather—it turned out to be a glorious day. There was still no sign of the others. We dropped our loads and zipped back down the fixed ropes, astonished at how fast we could descend from Camp One. Each length of rope was so well engraved in our memory that seemingly we could climb or rappel virtually any section with our eyes closed. I didn't realize then just what an asset this would later prove to be.

Stopping on the Headwall to duct tape several worn sections of rope, I saw two small figures down below. Paul and Robert. They'd gotten what became known as "a Robert start," at 6 or 7 A.M. They were going up for five days, weather permitting, to push the route to Camp Two.

Stephen pauses at the safe haven of the Terrace, protected by rock overhangs above.

"No reason to get up at the crack of dawn and kill yourself!" Paul shouted as I rappelled down to him. Except that now, instead of frozen crust, there was a foot of soft slush to wade through. Elevation, and full or partial exposure to the sun, determined the snow's consistency. The higher the altitude, the less the sun's rays melted the snow, metamorphosing and compacting it. I'd been astonished to find over a foot of fluffy powder blanketing Camp One this morning.

Walking back to camp, Stephen and I paused momentarily to gaze up at the enormous expanse of the Kangshung Face. The midday light was unusually clear and strong. An unbroken white band of sparkling ice cliffs spanned the mountain's entire waist, from the brooding North Face of Lhotse on the left to the *American Buttress* on the right. We shook our heads in astonishment.

"Amazing to think there's a route there at all!" Stephen proclaimed.

Eight hours after leaving, we were back in Advanced Base drinking tea with Kasang, Ang Chu's younger brother Sonam, and Joe. Kasang delivered a letter from Mr. Yang and Mr. Shi. They'd reserved our return flight from Lhasa for May 22, according to Robert's departure schedule. They also sent us some sugar, rice, and Chinese crackers, which was nice. When did we want the yaks to come and fetch us? That we could not possibly predict. I wrote them back and suggested several possible dates.

At 2:30 A.M. I heard Stephen yell: "Webster, what the hell are you doing in there that's taking so long?" I was so tired that I couldn't get out of my sleeping bag for the life of me. Joe, my tentmate, looked at me in sympathy.

"He really isn't very patient, is he?"

"I'm coming," I answered. "We'll still get out of here by four." And we did. I went first across the glacier. My legs didn't have nearly the pep they'd had yesterday, I told Stephen. I felt like a robot in need of a grease job.

"They never do, the second day in a row," he replied. I looked up and saw several strange, fan-shaped clouds blowing into Tibet from the Nepalese side of the South Col. Then, just short of the approach gully at the foot of the buttress, I was rudely startled out of my stupor.

"ED!" Stephen screamed. He didn't have time to say more. A huge avalanche exploded from Big Al and boiled violently upwards into the awakening twilight—directly over our heads. I immediately sat down on the snow and had covered my mouth with my mittens before the force of the blast hit us. My rucksack protected my back; my helmet shielded my head. After several elongated minutes, the riptide of snow subsided, and the dawn air returned to its stillness. We'd been really lucky that nothing big had hit us.

Stephen had a real zeal for alpine starts.

Stephen, however, had been "hit" once—rather comically, I thought—by a single, softball-sized ice chunk that I happened to watch bounce down the snow slope above us—and unerringly clunk him in the helmet. "Oh well, hit by an avalanche," Stephen lamented. "Just another average day at the office."

At Camp One, we rested in the sun, dried clothes and sleeping bags, drank tea, snacked, and lounged about. We also made plans to visit each other's homes after the expedition was over. Stephen wanted to climb in Eldorado Canyon and the Black Canyon in Colorado, plus the Canyonlands of Utah, while I would meet him in the Lake District in England. I'd climbed there once already, but Stephen insisted that I must return to visit his favorite pub!

Under fair skies, Robert and Paul slipped back down the Webster Wall at 4 P.M., after their exploration of the buttress's middle slopes. Their happy smiles spoke of success. They had made eight hundred feet of progress above the Jumble, Stephen's high point at the top of the fixed ropes, pushing out the route into a maze of snow slopes. They saw no obstacles to stop us.

"It's like a ski run! You won't believe it," Paul exclaimed.

"And it's not avalanche prone either," Robert added. "I like that."

Just before dusk, the full moon floated majestically over Chomolönzo, whose granite pillars caught the fading sunlight that fled upward before turning the peak's summit slopes to crimson. Tomorrow, May 1, we'd make our long-awaited sortie to establish Camp Two.

Stephen's predawn efficiency was something the rest of us could only watch with incredulity. When I mentioned to him that I'd only routinely begun making alpine starts several years ago, Stephen blasted back: "No wonder. It's because you weren't weaned on them! No one except bloody Americans climb Himalayan peaks in the heat of the day."

Camp One: Paul, Robert, and Stephen. The Webster Wall is directly behind the tents.

Ed at 4 A.M., ready to start for Camp Two. Stephen Venables

Stephen ascended the ropes up the Webster Wall in the dark. At first light, I followed him. Then we photographed each other suspended on the "world's most spectacular rope bridge." It was Stephen's second crossing, and my very first Tyrolean traverse ever. After each of us got scared witless dangling above the Jaws of Doom, we continued up the fixed lines to the Hump and the Jumble.

Today's mission was to ferry basic supplies to the site of Camp Two, which we hoped to situate at a prominent bergschrund or ice cliff about fifteen hundred feet below the South Col. Stephen's and my loads were identical: a two-man Bibler tent, six Bluet fuel cartridges, a Bluet stove, and a Markill hanging pot set. On our following trip up to Camp Two—heading to the summit, we hoped—we would *only* have to carry sleeping bags, foam pads, our super warm, extra-insulated down jacket and bib overalls, supergaiters, and food.

Stephen led us, plowing his way relentlessly uphill. It was hard to comprehend that we four humans had made ourselves a part of this towering world of ice and rock whose scale and beauty was so utterly vast and unearthly. All day long, vistas of sparkling snow and ice and seracs, plunging rock walls, and a sky so immense that it seemed to swallow us, made me think we were no longer on Earth at all. We really had been thrust up to the doors of Heaven, carried into a realm of pureness and tranquility beyond human consciousness or thought.

Crossing "the world's highest rope bridge" over the Jaws of Doom at 23,000 feet.

Stephen pauses at 23,500 feet during the climb to Camp Two.

Chain upon chain of distant snow peaks, each cast in a golden blue light, extended to the horizon in jagged, white waves that broke the dusty brown monotony of the Tibetan plateau. Our hard breathing and sweat was not for naught.

Leaving the fixed ropes behind us, Stephen and I roped together on a seventy-five-foot length of seven-millimeter rope, and set off through knee-deep snow, balancing with a ski pole in one hand, and an ice ax in the other. Paul and Robert's tracks were still fresh. The terrain, though not steep, was convoluted. We wound our way between snow blocks and thirty-foot ice cliffs, always seeking the lowest-angled slope. I'd just snapped a photo of Stephen solving this maze when he yelled, "We're not getting anywhere, Ed. Let's get on with it."

I should have realized he wouldn't be easily amused today. But when I saw another good picture form of him approaching a spectacular ice cliff, I asked if we could stop for a photo—and that did it. The charge had been primed; next came the detonation. Stephen immediately turned around and began shouting at the top of his lungs at me.

"All I've done for the last month is wait for you! I wait for you to get up, I wait for you to get dressed, I wait for you to put on your boots! This isn't the bloody Black Canyon, you know. I want to climb this mountain! And now it's the middle of the day, hotter than blazes, and we still have a long way to go...."

Finally his voice trailed off. He'd run out of oxygen to breathe. Part of me knew that Stephen was right. I was slow, but I was also thinking that this was quite a place for a scene like this—for two people, alone amidst the great white vastness of Mount Everest's Kangshung Face—to have a yelling match.

"Stephen, it's only 8:30 in the morning," I replied. "I'm not fast. I've told you that countless times. If you're so incredibly unhappy with me, then why don't you go back to climbing with Paul, and I'll climb with Robert?"

"I'm sorry," Stephen answered. "It was stupid of me to blow up. I just get frustrated by the slow going."

I took my picture and we continued on in silence. At Paul and Robert's high point—a snow shoulder festooned with a bright bouquet of orange-flagged bamboo wands—we halted for a candy bar. But the tension lingered. Stephen tried to be upbeat; I was too tired to drag out our squabble.

"I guess I've really lived up to my nickname today," I said in monotone.

"What's that?" Stephen asked, trying to inject some pep into his voice.

"The Turtle." We both laughed. I apologized to him for my repetitive lateness, as did Stephen for his outburst.

"Do you want me to break trail?" I queried.

"No, I'm happy to do it," Stephen said. "It gives me a purpose in life."

"And a chance to get your aggressions out," I threw in. Luckily, we laughed again, although not quite as heartily as before.

The trail now wound along the tops of several snow mounds. In general, the slopes were small isolated snow facets, with no avalanche danger. For once I felt completely safe, and the clear weather showed us the best line to take. Still, knee-deep powder made tiring work as each uphill step had to be excavated or the snow compressed. Luckily, the underlying snow was reasonably firm. Stephen's twenty continuous steps between breathers ebbed to ten, and then five.

We heard a yell. It was Robert and Paul, following in our tracks. As the South Col grew perceptibly closer, we felt a surge of excitement.

"Where no human foot has ever trod!" Stephen exclaimed like a true British explorer—then he added, "With so much history on the Col, it's a thrill to finally be getting so close."

Coming around the right side of two snow domes, I saw that a twenty-foot-wide crevasse sliced horizontally across the entire width of the buttress. A snow bridge fortuitously allowed us to cross this obstacle. Then, as the weather worsened, Stephen front-pointed up a fifty-degree snow and ice slope above the far side of the crevasse. He led it masterfully, with no protection, using only his eighty-centimeter ice ax. When the rope came tight, I followed him. We were now at the base of an unbroken slope buried under several feet of fresh snow, thirty to forty degrees in inclination. Perfect avalanche terrain. The snow base felt solid, however, when kicked. Stephen once again took the lead. His pace slowed, I noticed, in proportion to an increase in his high-altitude cough.

As I gained ground on Stephen, I coiled up the slack climbing rope in one hand. "Want me to break trail?" I asked, catching up to him.

"Yes," he muttered before doubling over in another coughing fit.

Through the mists now rising in the midday heat, we could glimpse the Flying Wing, Paul's name for the massive bergschrund below the South Col. I headed toward it, up the easiest-looking route. The powder snow lay deep, and slowed by it, I had to rest and breath every two to four steps. To make matters worse, snow clouds were creeping over Everest's Northeast Ridge far to our right, and over Makalu and Lhotse on our left. The weather was breaking.

Ten minutes later, it was snowing steadily. Our tracks would soon be buried, and we became lost in the whiteout. We were not noticeably closer to the Flying Wing either, and Stephen was tiring. He suggested that we drop our loads at the bottom of an ice cliff on our left. I said I'd check it out. When I

At 24,000 feet, Stephen leads his eponymous ice pitch en route to Camp Two.

realized there wasn't a ledge below the cliff, I headed straight up toward the Flying Wing instead. Glancing down, I saw three black dots in the white mist.

"I don't know where he's going!" I heard Stephen yell to Robert. "And I don't think he knows either."

"Ed!" Stephen shouted up to me, "I thought we were going left?" That did it.

"Will you please shut up?" I replied. "I know exactly where I'm going!"

In the whiteout, distances became guesses. The bergschrund was certainly farther away than we thought. Circling left through a particularly bad maze of crevasses, I finally gained a snow ramp that led to the left-hand end of the Flying Wing—the only safe campsite hereabouts. Ascending a final, tiring slope, I utilized my favorite "Scottish-burrowing" technique, plowing an uphill trench through the soft and feathery snow. The work was grueling, but just this once I wanted to show Stephen what I was made of.

At 3:45 P.M., exhausted, but happy, I reached a hidden flat platform beneath the 120-degree overhanging ice cliff of the Flying Wing. One by one, the others joined me. Everyone was completely out of breath.

"You really pushed it," Stephen said, slapping me on the back. "Good job."

(From right): Stephen, Robert, and Paul arrive at Camp Two—after an eleven-hour climb.

"I had to show you," I answered, "after all the grief you gave me." We anchored our cache of gear to two ice screws hammered into the overhanging wall, snacked, gulped some water, and left. We had reached 24,500 feet, which was an altitude record for Paul, and almost tied my highest altitude.

Stephen ran off downhill and was soon towing me down our footsteps, nearly yanking me off my feet. I shouted at him to slow down. "You've pulled me up the mountain today," I yelled angrily, "and I'm not about to be hauled down it, too!" Again, Stephen cursed the incurable slowness of Americans.

Paul glissading.
Stephen Venables

"Hey—that's how accidents happen," Paul said sharply to Stephen. "We don't need that here." Stephen stopped and scowled, and I swung into the lead.

The snow was near perfect for glissading, though, and we slid down the next slopes roped together, laughing and hollering, making incredibly rapid time. What had required eleven backbreaking hours to ascend took us just over an hour to descend. It was hard to believe that we could escape off the mountain so quickly. And, as a result, we were confident that if we wanted to descend rapidly from the face's upper slopes to the safety of Advanced Base Camp, we could do it in just a single day.

Back at Camp One, Stephen cooked as I coughed away, lying in my sleeping bag. While I still felt proud of my afternoon performance, I now had to admit to myself that the last grueling push to Camp Two had just about finished me. My throat was painfully raw, and my body exhausted. I also felt badly about our quarreling, and I apologized to Stephen again.

"They say you're supposed to bicker at high altitude, don't they?" was his nonchalant reply. "It must be true," he added. We shook hands.

While Stephen and I had achieved some measure of reconciliation, our team as a whole soon found itself in conflict over what to do next. We'd long speculated that we might see clear, stable weather only once in May—and what if this was it? Even though everyone was clearly very tired, the evening's decision was to seize the moment, *reascend to Camp Two tomorrow*, and *then push on with our summit attempt*. "Right—somehow," I thought to myself with fatigued resignation. I argued that to return to Camp Two without adequate rest would be a substantial handicap, and that several days of recuperation, preferably at Base Camp, would be crucial to success, all the more so since we were attempting the summit without oxygen. However, the fear of missing our only opportunity for good weather continued to sway my teammates, and to my dismay, our summit plans remained "on" the next morning. I knew that I needed to be fully rested to stand any chance of summiting, and I felt that pushing ahead to the South Col now was a completely idiotic idea.

I had a terrible night fighting insomnia, and was roused to an exhausted consciousness at 4:30 A.M., when Stephen lit the stove and filled the pot with snow chunks. The weather, he claimed, "looked reasonable." Below us we could see heavily layered clouds; the day could be either good or bad. Having had such a poor night's sleep, I felt that my resolve had completely crumbled. More debate ensued.

Paul asked how we'd feel if we got to the South Col and found that we'd missed the good weather by a day. "I'd never be able to live with myself," he said.

Stephen then related how that very circumstance had happened to him on Kunyang Kish in Pakistan. "We were hit by a storm on the summit ridge. A day earlier it had been clear. Timing is everything in the Himalaya."

Timing is indeed everything, but how could we foretell when the time to strike would be exactly right? The desire to be high on the mountain when the weather was at its best drove my friends to argue for continuing, but in their hearts I think they also knew how bone-tired we were. Somewhat later, Paul announced, less than cheerfully, that he'd thrown up his dinner last night.

"What's the feeling guys?" Robert then asked, acknowledging the team's underlying indecision.

"Most people making an Everest summit bid haven't done a three-thousand-foot load carry the day before," I answered, trying to sway them to descend.

"I am tired," Stephen then admitted, momentarily appraising his physical condition with uncharacteristic honesty, "but I could still climb today. By all standards, though, I suppose we do deserve a rest."

"The weather looks fairly settled," Paul chipped in. "One day of rest here at camp will set us up mentally and physically for the top."

"Okay," Robert said, confirming our lack of momentum. "We're resting."

Our rest day, May 2, was also Stephen's thirty-fourth birthday. We presented him with a "cake"—a Mars bar with a Bic lighter stuck in the middle—and he dutifully made a wish, blew out the flame, and we shared the cake after singing Happy Birthday. "And many more," Robert sang in the refrain.

We improvised a cake for Stephen's birthday.

"Yes, I like that last part," Stephen told me. "Imagine; half a lifetime already used up! Sometimes, when I look at the state of my own life, I get envious of my friends who already have children and families, or jobs with pensions."

"But then again," he reflected, "I do have my freedom."

I collapsed into a much-needed sleep. When I awoke at mid-morning, it was snowing steadily, and it snowed the rest of the day, burying our hard-won footsteps to the Flying Wing. That afternoon, I peeked in on Paul and Robert.

"Well, do we look absolutely primitive?" Robert asked. Their hollow eyes, sunken cheeks, and sunburned faces revealed the new depths of high-altitude depravity to which they had sunk, and I had to answer: "Yes."

"I can't sit here at twenty-two thousand for another day," Robert declared. "It's either up or down tomorrow."

The following morning's verdict was unanimous: retreat. Overnight, the Kangshung microclimate had moved in to stay. I descended last, zipping up the tents (assuming we'd be back soon, we didn't collapse them), and rappelled off into the whiteout. A foot of powder snow had buried everything. We'd always absolutely dreaded being forced to rappel down Big Al in such high avalanche conditions, so I virtually sprinted across the traverse, wincing with the expectation that an avalanche would overwhelm us. But one never came. I caught up to the others and we methodically rappelled down the Headwall. For one of the few times on the entire expedition, the four of us walked together across the glacier back to Advanced Base. At 10 A.M., it was clear what was on our minds:

"Fried eggs and bacon!" Stephen yelled.

"Pancakes and sausage!" Paul shouted.

"Denny's Grand Slam!" Robert bellowed. Joe and Mimi came out to greet us, but they seemed genuinely sorry to see us back.

"You were supposed to be summiting tomorrow!" Joe exclaimed.

"Sorry to disappoint, but we weren't going anywhere in this stuff," Paul said.

The following morn, a foot of heavy wet snow plastered the ground. Not a soul stirred. The weather tried gamely to clear, some blue patches opened, but the mountain remained dark and welcomed a continuous delivery of new snow. Paul, Stephen, and I had decided to descend to Base when Stephen opted to stay behind after all, just in case it cleared up. If the weather did turn good tomorrow, Paul and I would return to ABC right away. Joe thought it was absolutely ludicrous to hike five miles to Base Camp for a single night's rest, but Paul and I were longing for low altitude and a home-cooked meal.

We reached Base Camp, much to the delight of Pasang and Kasang, Ang Chu, and his musically talented brother, Sonam. Pasang had attentively watched our progress to Camp Two through our high-powered binoculars. "South Col, now very close!" he said excitedly. He appreciated that Paul and I had hiked down mostly to eat a good meal before going back up the mountain, and Pasang cooked us a banquet. Afterwards, he and the Tibetans danced to several traditional Tibetan and Sherpa songs, arm in arm, stamping out the complex rhythm with their feet. One tune was even about Chomolungma, but Pasang said that it

Mimi and Joe dancing at Base Camp.

was too hard to translate. However, all of the songs were for good luck. It was a particularly heartfelt evening. The sky cleared after sunset, the stars shone brightly, and Everest's great white bulk stood illuminated against the night sky.

"You've just got to want it," Paul said. "And I know we want it."

At dawn, Everest was aglow, colored pink and gold. A few puffy clouds hugged its base, and a high thin lenticular shadowed the summit. Otherwise, the weather looked superb.

"I watch juniper smoke this morning," Pasang said. "Wind blowing down-valley, good sign!" As usual, Pasang had risen early to musically chant his prayers, then to burn green, thick-scented juniper boughs to bring us luck.

This morning and the previous evening, we had listened to reports on Radio Nepal about the Asian Friendship Expedition. Their well-provisioned team had weathered the storm at the high camps while we'd been blown down from Camp One. Two groups of six climbers each were bound for the summit today, May 5. I was taken aback to hear the names of the individual climbers announced over the air. Obviously, this was big news in the Kingdom!

On the return to Advanced Base, Kasang and Ang Chu volunteered to carry our packs. Paul and I started on our way, but we'd only reached the moraine ridge five minutes from Base Camp when I heard Pasang yelling frantically. Had we had forgotten something? Then I saw the binoculars in his hand. He had seen climbers nearing Everest's summit! Three infinitely small black specks of humanity were silhouetted against the white snows of Everest's Southeast Ridge. They were approaching the South Summit. Looking up at them through the binoculars, I tried to fathom that in a few days we might be up there, too.

When Paul and I told Stephen and Robert we'd seen the TV team near the top, the push was on for us to make our own summit bid as soon as possible.

"Mimi suggested that we leave this afternoon, and I think we will," Robert said. We sorted through our summit food supply, and each picked our fancy. I wondered, very seriously, about the lateness of the day. It was already 3 P.M. Darkness fell at six. Our best time to Camp One was five hours. Nervously, I eyed some high clouds that were pouring over Lhotse. What was the rush?

My worries were temporarily displaced by the other woman who had joined our expedition. She was Joe's female ice fantasy, the Lady of the Lake. Keenly missing his wife, Ellen, Joe had put his creative energies to work and sculpted a life-sized nude woman reclining on the small frozen lake in the middle of Advanced Base Camp! He now photographed the four of us beside her— our presummit photograph—as we departed.

The glacier was in horrible condition. Beneath a thin snow crust was a mire of bottomless depth hoar (lumpy, oatmeal-like snow) into which we occasionally sank up to our waist. Then the weather deteriorated, and by the time we reached the base of the fixed ropes it was snowing heavily. A foot of dense monsoon snow, thick as wet concrete, had smothered the bottom terraces. Stephen plunged aggressively up the slope, ripping and pulling the buried ropes out of the snow with both hands, foot by foot.

Suddenly I had a very strong negative feeling. It was almost dark, and the snowfall was worsening.

"You know, I'm not so sure leaving this late in the day was such a great idea," I said.

I didn't expect Paul to join in, but he quickly added: "I think this is really pretty stupid, with it snowing like this."

"But it always snows in the afternoon in the Himalaya!" Stephen retorted.

I calculated mentally that if we continued to Camp One it would be after midnight before we ate dinner. I then said, "Well, I'd like to go down."

"We're very democratic here," Robert replied. "We don't all have to do the same thing. We have two independent groups of two climbers each. Stephen and I will break trail tonight to Camp One, and you and Paul can descend."

With no hard feelings, Paul and I turned around. Soon it was pitch dark.

"You've got to trust your instincts on a big climb like this," Paul said, as we returned across the glacier. "It's being cautious and making conservative decisions that's kept me alive," he added. The light from our headlamps shafted into the blackness and illuminated the storm's eerie phantasm of swirling snow.

"Have you ever lost any friends to climbing?" I asked Paul.

"Yes, two," he said.

"Were you with either of them when it happened?"

"No. Why? Have you been with someone who was killed climbing?"

"Yes—once," I said. We stopped walking.

"Who was it?" Paul asked. I took a deep breath.

"I was with my girlfriend in the Black Canyon, in Colorado, about four years ago. Her name was Lauren. I guess you never heard the story."

Paul looked at me in stunned silence. Then he shook his head sideways. I recounted for him how Lauren had died. He listened quietly until I was finished. Then, in the darkness and the falling snow, Paul turned away from me, started to walk, bent forward, and began to cry. Soon he was wracked by sobs. I walked over to him, and we stood together on the glacier, hugging each other, crying.

"I've never heard of anything so sad and tragic, so terrible. How did you ever keep climbing?" he implored, looking at me in anguish.

"It took me a long time. But here I am, still climbing. I think about Lauren almost every day. I remember her positively, and over the years I've done some special things in her memory."

I hadn't meant for our conversation to have turned the way it did, but as we hiked back to Advanced Base, I was positive that Paul and I would be friends for the rest of our lives.

Joe fixed us dinner. I set my alarm for 4 A.M., for yet another alpine start. When it went off, I peered outside my tent and saw only a blanket of white.

"What's up?" Paul asked.

"Looks like new snow."

"Right, more sleep," he replied. I didn't disagree.

Last evening's romp now seemed like a bad joke. This morning, the entire Kangshung basin was fogged in, and we had a hard time deciding whether to go back up, or not. We fully expected Robert and Stephen to continue to

Camp Two today, which meant we were now a divided team. Personality-wise, I was fine with that because Paul and I shared the same relaxed attitude, and despite our attempts at reconciliation, Stephen—the Greyhound—had still been getting on my nerves. Paul and I didn't leave Advanced Base till nine. Joe encouraged us to hurry, though, and to catch up to Robert and Stephen.

"Maybe if I don't take a photo of you guys leaving today, then you'll get to the top," he quipped. Joe had already taken approximately one zillion photos of "the climbers leaving camp and heading for the summit."

"We'll expect you back for lunch," Mimi cracked.

When the sun burned through the low clouds, the heat poured down. But up above the Scottish Gully, the mountain remained solidly socked in. It was impossible for us to tell if Stephen and Robert had continued to Camp Two.

"Situation change!" Paul crowed as it began to snow in earnest as we kick-stepped up the Scottish Gully. Last night's blizzard had filled in Robert and Stephen's tracks; our pace was miserable. I didn't want to admit it, but climbing for two months above sixteen thousand feet was finally taking its toll on me.

The traverse across Big Al was absolutely buried with snow. Flakes swirled around Paul's ghostly shape as he shuffled along the rope in front of me. The entire mountain felt deathly avalanche prone. We were really pushing our luck.

"I don't like this!" I shouted out. "The avalanche conditions are very—"

"I know," Paul responded. "I was just thinking the same...."

"OOOYYY!" came a cry through the mist. It was Robert.

"Oh no, not you!" Paul yelled. "You're supposed to be going for the summit."

"Too much snow," Robert answered glumly, emerging from the gloom with Stephen. "Four feet of powder at Camp One. 'We used to have a camp here, didn't we?' I thought when I got there last night. The tents were completely buried by new snow, tent poles broken in a dozen places, fabric ripped."

Paul was steaming mad. He'd suggested that we collapse the tents when we'd descended last time, but no one had listened to him. Now both tents were apparently destroyed, and we were already short of tents.

"We thought you'd have more sense than us, coming up here on a day like this!" Stephen reprimanded. He looked like a snow-frosted ghoul. Robert and Stephen retreated while Paul and I ascended one more rope length to the Terrace, where we deposited our loads.

"We should never have left ABC," Paul moaned.

"We should have stayed in Base Camp during this unsettled weather, rested, and come back up when the weather really cleared," I declared once again.

Stephen and Robert in Big Al after the "midnight-sport-jumaring episode."

"Too late for that," Paul lamented. "I'm beginning to feel some not so subtle pressure from Joe and Mimi that we climb the route NOW. I know that they want to go home. We all want to go home, but we can't keep throwing ourselves against the mountain regardless of the weather."

Anymore false starts and our expedition would be finished. We would be too exhausted to make a concerted summit push, our muscles and minds too enfeebled from the prolonged exertion at high altitude. As we descended, once again, the monster-avalanche-in-waiting spared us. We slid down the ropes, laughing at the sheer absurdity of our meek, puny effort on the greatest mountain on earth. "Situation change," Paul announced gleefully again.

I felt more tired than on any other day of the trip, except after our carry to Camp Two. I felt spiritually and physically broken. The chill and the wet crept deep into my bones, and I crawled off to my tent. Joe fixed us a chili dinner, but I hardly had the energy to unzip the tent door and accept his gourmet delight.

At 6:30 A.M. the next morning, Paul screamed: *"Oh my god, it's Big Al!"*

Above: *Stephen, Robert, and Paul at Advanced Base Camp.*
Below: *Paul inspects the mountain through our high-powered binoculars.*

A huge avalanche had detonated in the Cow's Mouth, the icy cul-de-sac high in Big Al. In seconds, it swept up all the fresh snow in the entire gully, exploded with colossal power, and ejected massive hundred-mile-per-hour jets of snow over the lower half of our route. We watched, open-mouthed. If that avalanche had happened yesterday afternoon, it would have wiped us off the mountain.

"Gee, I'm glad I didn't suggest we get an early start today," Paul said.

I returned to the haven of my sleeping bag, unable to think or to act. Later, Paul came by. "Robert and Stephen think we should leave today at 3 P.M.," he said, suppressing a laugh. Then we reconvened, inspected Everest's upper snow slopes with Robert's telescope, and discussed our options. No one wanted to leave for the summit today; everyone was nursing their wounds. Robert even admitted that the "midnight-sport-jumaring" had been an "ill-conceived" idea.

Instead, the new plan was to start early tomorrow morning. Stephen and I agreed to an alpine start; Robert and Paul would follow. We'd also carry up Stephen's Bibler tent to replace the damaged tent at Camp One. To bolster our physical reserves and strength, we spent the day eating: cereal, pancakes with real butter and freeze-dried maple syrup for breakfast, crackers, sardines, cheese and mustard for lunch, and finally noodles, ham, and fettuccini for dinner. We also tanked up on Carboplex, a complex carbohydrate powdered drink mix.

That afternoon the sun arched high above the South Col, crossing a clear and radiant sky. I sat on my foam pad doing yoga, stretching, breathing, and invigorating myself. I felt vastly restored from the previous day's torpor. I pre-visualized our push for the summit, the jet stream-blasted snow slopes, the gray limestone outcrops, the controlled breathing. The summit loomed twelve thousand vertical feet above me—dazzlingly white against a blue-black sky. If the weather held, in three or four days we could be climbing for the top.

The ribald joking at dinner belied the fact that tomorrow morning we would rise for what we hoped was our last trip to Camp One. I lay in my sleeping bag, listening to music, unable to calm the adrenaline rushing through my body. I thought of my mentor, the eighty-eight-year-old mountaineer Fritz Wiessner, and knew that I'd be thinking of him as I plodded up Everest's summit ridge. I hoped that I had the same determination within me that Fritz had shown when he attempted the first ascent of K2—without bottled oxygen—in 1939. But I also hoped that I'd know when to stop, when to listen to my inner self if things went wrong. Brushing away my fears that one of us might die, and that it could even possibly be me who died, I concentrated instead on the prize, the dream: that for a single day I might coexist with the roof of the world.

Chapter 11

To the South Col—
from Tibet

Life itself cannot give you joy unless you really will it.
Life just gives you time and space. It's up to you to fill it.

—Unknown

There was no fanfare when we left Advanced Base Camp at 4 A.M. on May 8. We were determined not to return before we had at least attempted the summit. Our ascent to Camp One felt routine. Stephen blazed the trail in only four hours while Paul, Robert, and I paced ourselves, conserving our strength for the high-altitude marathon to come. I had long since adopted a fatalistic attitude toward climbing the lower buttress. I no longer worried about the Greyhound Bus or one of the other Cauliflower Towers collapsing on top of us, nor feared that falling rocks would slice through our fixed ropes. We had traveled up and down the buttress a dozen times now

Left: *In view of Chomolönzo, Ed and Paul ascend to Camp Two.* Stephen Venables

Stephen ascends fixed ropes up vertical ice to Camp One on the saddle above him.

without injury. Higher on Everest, I knew that increasingly perilous dangers—frostbite and the frequently quick-killing high-altitude illnesses of pulmonary and cerebral edema—would test us to our limit in the days to come.

We arrived at Camp One in sunshine. Paul and Robert quickly erected the replacement Bibler tent to substitute for the one destroyed in the storm the previous week. Stephen's and my Camp One tent had survived; we just shoveled it out. As this campsite was now well stocked with food, we indulged in a banquet that afternoon, eating as many calories and carbohydrates as possible. We knew that above this altitude our desire to eat food of almost any type would decrease dramatically. At twenty-six thousand feet on the South Col, meals would consist of instant oatmeal and Pop Tarts, ramen noodle soup, candy, tea, and drink mixes.

Although this was the biggest climb of our lives, none of my companions seemed to be the least bit nervous about our approaching endeavor. If they were fearful, they kept their feelings private. The rigors of the past five weeks had been a trial by fire—and sweat and storm and avalanche. We had been molded into a well-oiled, cohesive team, and furthermore, the climb's high technical difficulty and danger had forged the unbreakable trust that we needed in each other's capabilities. And that we had quite genuinely become the best of friends would soon be the single most important fact of all.

At midnight we began the time-consuming process of brewing hot water from snow chunks. Groans and moans emanated from both tents, but outside, for once, the weather actually looked promising. Stephen and Robert left first; Paul and I followed. Dawn broke as we slid across the ropes spanning the Jaws of Doom, and by the time we began plodding up the snow slopes toward the Hump, a sublimely beautiful sunrise was unfolding all around us. Below, at the sun's urging, a boiling sea of silver-white puffy clouds melted into spellbinding hues of pink, orange and gold. The beauty stopped us in our tracks.

"God loves those who grow young," Paul said. Although I wasn't exactly sure what he meant, it seemed an apt statement.

Try as we might, Paul and I remained well behind Robert and Stephen until we were just below the largest of the crevasses, halfway to Camp Two. When we finally did catch them, they seemed a bit annoyed that we hadn't overtaken them sooner. The new snow was thigh deep and made for laborious wallowing. I volunteered to lead, mostly because I wanted to get my stint over. I didn't want to have to break trail again up that wretched, last steep slope to Camp Two.

Predictably, the weather deteriorated into a whiteout as I took over and began excavating a trench through the deep powder. Suddenly, a loud, ominous

Dawn breaks over Tibet, our Camp One, and the Kangshung Glacier.

Paul waves with relief. This time the snow slopes held.

crack split the air. I glanced up nervously—and watched in horror as an eighty-foot-tall ice wall two hundred feet above us spontaneously splintered apart and collapsed. Fortunately, most of the debris fell into a crevasse, but the demolition didn't end there. The underlying ice, yielding to the outward release of pressure, began to complain and groan like an old house rocking on unstable foundations.

A moment later, the ice wall shattered a second time. This time, more multi-ton blocks of glass-sharp ice detached and fell from the disintegrating serac. I stood my ground, braced but motionless, my eyes riveted to the destruction, debating whether to stand, or run for my life. The largest ice block was the size of a taxi cab. Falling, it smashed into the debris jamming the crevasse, bounced forward, then careened down the snow slope only one hundred feet to my right. Ready to flee if the impact of the block ramming the slope triggered an avalanche, I watched the taxi swoosh effortlessly downhill—then leap over the edge, crashing into the upper reaches of Big Al. This time, the slope held.

Nevertheless, I was traumatized. "Why does this always have to happen to me?" I shouted angrily, vividly recalling my previous near-fatal accident when the ice chockstone exploded inside the Jaws of Doom.

Down below, I heard Paul laughing. "Just your luck, I guess!" he shouted up.

The danger passed. In its place, we confronted a new but well known enemy: the enervating heat. The whiteout had lifted, and the new culprit was a thin, gauze-like cloud that had crept over the sun. After the sun's rays passed through the cloud, they reflected off the vast Himalayan snow slopes, then became sandwiched between the two surfaces. As the rays bounced back and forth, the net effect was a doubling and tripling of their intensity—and the heat. The fluctuating temperatures we experienced during our ascent to the South Col could not have been more extreme. Plodding uphill an hour later, I felt my eyelids sag in the suffocating heat. I was barely maintaining consciousness. Overheating is not an adversity most people readily associate with Himalayan mountaineering, but that afternoon the heat was nothing short of staggering.

My eyes shut involuntarily. Then, with a start, they blinked open. The heat was worsening. Everyone was affected; even Stephen was heard to shout woefully, "This is the longest day of purgatory!" To add to our problems, the snow was much deeper and softer than it had been during our first ascent to the Flying Wing on May 1.

We tiptoed across a snow bridge, repeated Stephen's Ice Pitch (buried under two feet of new powder), then wallowed up an interminable featureless slope to a small flat crest marked by another of our orange-flagged bamboo wands.

We'd already passed several other wands; some leaned to one side, and a few had fallen over into the snow. We rested, snacked, then continued our uphill marathon one last stretch to the bergschrund at the Flying Wing, Camp Two.

Paul was upset by the dangerous condition of the snow. "Hey, these slopes are incredibly loaded. They're ready to avalanche; just look at them!" he warned.

The feathery powder appeared bottomless. It felt only loosely attached to the rest of the mountain. And, at an angle of twenty-five to thirty-five degrees, the slope had the perfect tilt for an avalanche. I was genuinely frightened, and as if we needed something to make matters worse, another snow storm had moved in, prompting additional flakes to fall from the congealed-porridge sky.

I burrowed out a trough up the slope, clearing off the top foot of snow using swinging motions with my mittened hands, then excavated another two feet using a backward kick from my left foot. It was slow going, digging down to the more stable bottom layers, but this was the safest technique. I headed directly uphill in a straight line. Theoretically, if the slope did avalanche, it would do so on only one side of the trench—and we could leap to safety on the other side, if we were lucky.

Unsatisfied with my rate of progress, Stephen suddenly sped up and passed me. I was grateful for his help, but I immediately worried about him triggering the slope. However, when we were unsure of the snow conditions, as we were now, we usually asked Stephen, "our expedition man," for his sage advice.

"What do you think about the snow here?" I asked him as he kick-stepped up the slope above me. "Have you ever been caught in a big avalanche?"

"No, luckily not," he replied. Stephen seemed unfazed and unperturbed. "You know, I really don't think the snow here is all that unstable," he added.

Again, fortunately, the slope did not avalanche. We arrived intact at Camp Two at 4 P.M., after Stephen vanquished the much-reviled final incline. Breathing a collective—if extremely out of breath—sigh of relief, we flattened out two tent platforms under the Flying Wing's radically overhanging ice roof. The snow stopped falling, the clouds lifted, and I alternated between taking photos and helping Stephen prepare our quarters. After he swore at me for taking pictures and not concentrating on setting up the tent, I helped more, albeit a bit too late. But when we crawled inside the tent, I vented my spleen.

"There's one thing that really gets to me, Venables, and that's you complaining about my photography!" I bellowed at him. "And invariably, when I turn around a moment later—you're taking pictures too! You know, there's no need to be in such a bloody hurry all the time."

Paul, Stephen, and Robert arrive at the Flying Wing—Camp Two (24,500 feet).

It was the angriest I'd been at Stephen. Taking pictures was such a big part of my climbing. For someone to criticize my photography verged on sacrilege. It was the one thing I couldn't tolerate. Stephen realized this, apologized, and the quarrel ended as quickly as it began.

Even though we squabbled occasionally, Stephen and I really did enjoy each other's company. The natural pairing of Robert and Paul, and Stephen and I— which we'd adopted while tenting at Camp One—was successful enough that we didn't tamper with the arrangement as we climbed higher on the mountain. My harmony with Stephen I attributed to my provident half-English ancestry, a respectably cultured and energetic addition to my otherwise lazy Yankee blood!

With steaming mugs of tea cradled in numb hands, we began the vital task of rehydrating and eating after another long fatiguing day. As we ate, I was pleased that I still had a healthy appetite. We'd pushed ourselves for a dozen hours straight today—so to better our chances of arriving on the South Col the next day feeling relatively fit, we brewed endless rounds of herb tea long into the night. I was astonished by how much I could drink without having to relieve

Stephen in the lead, heading toward the South Col (at upper right). *Lhotse on left.*

myself. On a cellular level, my body felt bone dry. Drinking cup after cup of hydrating tea, we savored our high solitude together in the tiny tent, talked amiably, finally lost the energy to refill the pot with snow chunks, and slept.

May 10 began as a perfect morning with a half moon hanging in a radiant blue sky. Stephen (of course) had hoped for an alpine start, but after yesterday's marathon, we needed the sleep, plus time to dry boots, clothes, and sleeping bags. Sitting drinking tea outside the tents, I relaxed on my haunches and relished the extraordinary "front porch" view of the colossal Lhotse Wall, composed of Lhotse's North Face, Lhotse Shar, Peak 38, and Shartse II. Pethangtse was now well beneath us; Makalu, the black pyramid, and Chomolönzo's golden granite walls framed the remainder of the jagged skyline. Camp Two was a hauntingly beautiful site, a flat platform tucked under a dramatically overhanging serac wall. Although it was sheltered from wind and avalanche, it did feel somewhat dangerous camping beneath the leaning tombstone slab of sparkling white ice.

The next morning, I led off through waist-deep snow around the right end of the bergschrund by 7:30 A.M. Rounding the corner, I discovered that the

Robert enjoying "the Great Day" of hard snow, sunshine—and endless mountains.

Flying Wing was, in fact, a completely detached ice block tilted downhill at a precariously steep angle. I yelled for Stephen to tighten up and watch the rope, stepped quickly across a narrow snow bridge spanning the bergschrund, and planted our last bamboo wand to mark this key location for the descent.

We'd long speculated how best to reach the South Col from here. Back in April, the bowl immediately below the Col had shown plenty of bare ice, and Stephen and I had voted to climb a vertical snow gully through low-angled rock slabs on the far right, arguing that climbing up snow was preferable to iron-hard ice. Six weeks later, conditions had completely changed. So much snow had fallen that now barely a speck of ice was visible. Even though we'd have to forge a long leftward diagonal across a single immense snow slope, we decided that the snow bowl gave us the easiest and most direct line to the Col. Stephen took the lead, treading happily up the unbroken new ground.

It was evident, however, that the slope had recently avalanched. Runnels and grooves carved in the snow showed where avalanches had scoured the soft surface to expose the harder foundation. Although we never openly discussed the danger, it was obvious that after only a moderate snowstorm, these wide-open slopes beneath the South Col would become an avalanche deathtrap.

Fortunately, at the moment this snow was the best we'd seen. We merrily crunched across the hard-packed, thirty- to forty-degree incline. Smiles broke across our faces as, for the first time, I think, we started to sense we would actually complete this new route up Everest's Kangshung Face. The combination of easier terrain, beautiful weather, and good camaraderie made us giddy. It was one of the most memorable and wonderful days of my life: climbing at twenty-five thousand feet with Stephen, Paul, and Robert, striding upward across those perfect snow slopes under sunny blue skies, glancing idly up at the legendary South Col growing ever nearer, and daring to think, "We're going to make it!"

I shot two rolls of film as we climbed the long leftward traverse into the center of the snow bowl. The icy views of Makalu and Chomolönzo were absolutely breathtaking; farther east we could see to the distant reaches of Tibet's crystalline horizon dotted with a multitude of snowy peaks, especially rock-toothed Jannu, and its dominant, towering neighbor, Kanchenjunga.

Then the ecstasy faded and the grind resumed. Paul led across a small bergschrund and began wading up a laborious snow slope, aiming for the safe haven of a large rock outcrop five hundred feet higher. Because the four of us were muscling all of our equipment to the South Col in only one load carry, our packs weighed fifty pounds or more. Accordingly, there was no need to exhaust one person unnecessarily, so we alternated trail-breaking every half hour to an hour. We had no

Paul and Robert at 25,000 feet.

The South Col presented us with the most inhospitable scene imaginable. Its subzero wasteland of snow, ice, and rock was being raked by hurricane-strength jet stream winds. Terrific snow plumes streamed from the summits of Everest and Lhotse, while pummeling gusts tore at my clothing and face. At first I attempted to comprehend the hauntingly bleak desolation, remote as outer space; then, after taking two faltering steps, I doubled over. My lungs heaved and fought for the even the smallest volume of life-giving oxygen. I was suffocating for several seconds, and thinking I was dying, mortal panic speared into my brain. I pulled and rasped as much air down my throat as each convulsion allowed. Gradually regaining my equilibrium, I stumbled doggedly to my right and looked for a campsite. When I glanced back at my companions, I noticed them falter, too, bending over their ice axes, panting and struggling for breath.

Like blind drunks, we fumbled across the Col's lunar-like frozen landscape, repeatedly snagging our ropes on rocks as we searched for two relatively level spots for the tents. The ferocious wind penetrated all four of my layers of clothing; it was imperative that we find shelter at once. We finally stamped down two flat platforms of snow fifteen feet apart. I finished leveling the snow while Stephen unrolled our tent and struggled to fit the poles together.

"Ed, Ed! Come here," he yelled, as the tent snapped like machine gun fire in the gusts, threatening to be blown from his grasp. "Help me!"

I held down the tent as Stephen inserted the tent poles. We anchored the tent's guy ropes to several small boulders, then stacked additional rocks inside each corner of the tent for extra stability—and in case the winds increased. Remembering stories of South Col winds *picking up tents with climbers inside them,* as a final precaution we took one of our seven-millimeter ropes and anchored both tents to a big boulder nearby. At twenty-six thousand feet, every effort was utterly exhausting. Hyperventilating for breath, gaining shelter none too soon, we sprawled inside our haven of yellow nylon fabric, grateful to be out of the wind that flapped the tent walls incessantly. Camp Three was established.

Immediately we began the tiresome task of melting ice chunks and boiling water for tea and soup in our hanging propane cartridge stove. My stomach felt weak and queasy, and every few minutes, Stephen doubled over, clutching at his chest, in a high-altitude coughing fit. We made a healthy pair. At any given moment, only one of us, seemingly, could muster the necessary energy to tend the stove; the other lay comatose in his sleeping bag. Then we'd switch roles; the other would gain momentum with a significant mustering of sheer will, haul himself up on one elbow with a titanic effort—and see if the pot needed another snow lump, or was near to a boil. This high drama pretty well sums up life in the Death Zone, at or above eight thousand meters (roughly twenty-six thousand feet) in altitude. We knew we could survive here at most for three days; any longer and the oxygenless atmosphere would slowly but surely kill us—as it had depleted and killed many other Himalayan mountaineers.

Headaches of previously unknown severity walloped us next. Extra-strength Tylenol was our most trusted friend. We each gulped three as soon as we were in the tent. And always there was the screaming wind, the unnerving, wolf-howl gale. The blasts were so loud that even though Paul and Robert weren't more than fifteen feet away from Stephen and I, we couldn't communicate with them. Instead, we lay inert and silent, trapped in our own hallucinatory dreams. By 10:30 P.M., we'd produced three cups of herb tea apiece, and forced down a bowl of ramen noodle soup. My stomach churned with nausea; I was convinced I'd vomit, but through a great force of will I held down the precious liquids. After our ten-hour climb to the South Col with fifty-pound packs, plus the twelve-hour forced march the previous day, it was no small wonder talk was at a minimum.

Our original plan was to gain the South Col early enough in the day so that we could recuperate and still try for the summit the next morning—the game plan most mountaineers use. But we hadn't reached the Col until 4 P.M., and we were utterly shattered and dehydrated from our load carry. The plan needed changing. We decided to postpone the summit attempt for one day, until May 12, to let us recover—if we could. Listening to the wind's sustained roar, it was fairly obvious that we weren't going anywhere soon.

Beset by a constantly throbbing headache, I slept badly. The wind's din was near deafening, and the constant flapping of the tent fabric only reinforced the nightmare. I awoke with a migraine-level high-altitude headache. My throat was severely raspy, and my brain was fogged from lack of sleep. At about 6 A.M., the sun shone gold through the tent walls, and I noticed that the wind appeared to have diminished slightly.

"Any life over here?" a voice asked from the outside world. Robert unzipped our tent door and peered in. He didn't mince words. "Paul's sick. He needs to go down right now. He threw up last night. One of you needs to go with him."

The news of Paul's illness and his need to descend hit us like a hammer blow. My enfeebled brain mulled over the ramifications. Stephen and I were each reasonably healthy and relatively strong. But for one of us, the time-honored mountaineering obligation to help your fellow climber, no matter what the circumstances, meant that our chance of reaching Everest's summit had just ended.

I asked if Paul was well enough to stay on the South Col for one more day.

"No. He might be having an onset of cerebral edema," Robert answered. "He's got to descend immediately. Listen, I'm getting cold. Let me know, okay?"

As leader, it was Robert's prerogative to stay for the summit bid. I accepted that. But instantaneously, a noticeable tension arose between Stephen and me. Neither of us wanted to give up the summit. After at first becoming as silent as a church mouse, Stephen finally said that he "definitely wanted a go at the top."

An awkward silence filled our tent. I hadn't slept well last night. Stephen, furthermore, had consistently been our team's strongest member. Several factors made me Paul's logical partner, but my life's great ambition—the top of the world—was tangibly close, only three thousand vertical feet above our campsite. I felt hard pressed to deny myself the chance to reach Everest's summit, but mountaineering safety and common sense each dictated that Paul needed a companion to accompany him back down. Or did he? Outside, I heard more talking.

"Shall I ask Ed to get ready to accompany you?" Robert asked.

"No, I have another idea," Paul said. I looked out the tent door. Clad in their expedition suits, Robert and Paul sat next to each other on a boulder beside their tent. Then Paul got up, walked over, and knelt at our doorway.

"I'm out of here," he said unemotionally, adding, "I'm going down alone."

"You're descending by yourself?" I asked, shocked. The possibility that Paul would volunteer to descend the entire eight-thousand-foot face from the South Col to Advanced Base Camp, alone, had never occurred to any of us.

"I'll be fine. There's no worry, really," he said without a trace of regret or ego. "The important thing is that you guys be strong and go for the top without worrying about me. The last thing I want is for one of you to give up your chances just to help me get down."

Pausing a moment, Paul added, "Make me proud? Just get to the top, okay?"

Tears welled in my eyes. I'd been a few seconds away from telling Paul that we should descend together. I knew what a sacrifice he was making so that the three of us could try for the summit.

"I guess we knew this might happen, that if one of us got sick, he'd have to descend immediately, and maybe by himself," I mumbled awkwardly.

"In a way, we've been alone on this climb all along," Paul answered. "Up here, you've got to take care of yourself first. And I honestly don't feel that bad. If I leave now, I might still be able to reach Advanced Base today."

He sounded nonchalant, but I knew that inside Paul must be agonizing over this unexpected turn of events. We'd all worked so hard to complete our climb.

"I love you, Paul. Take care," I said emotionally. We shook hands firmly all around, Stephen and Robert wished him luck, and a minute later, after crossing the frozen plateau of the South Col, Paul disappeared over the edge of the Kangshung Face, back down our route, alone.

Now we were three. It was on to the summit. I felt great relief that Paul, in effect, had made my decision for me, but lingering doubts made me question whether I was right to have let him descend by himself. Maybe I should have insisted that I accompany him down? Would Paul be safe; would he be all right? I then reminded myself not to second guess what had just happened. Paul had made his own decision to descend. I banished away any further misgivings, and Stephen and I settled into doing our chores, believing that nothing would now keep us from reaching Everest's summit.

We were in as good a shape as human beings can be at twenty-six thousand feet, and I reckoned we were as well-acclimatized as any of the dozen other mountaineers who, to date, had climbed Everest without using bottled oxygen. Our three-week "vacation" below the Langma La at fifteen thousand feet had given our bodies plenty of time to adjust to the thin air, and the month of hard climbing and ferrying heavy loads up the lower buttress between eighteen and twenty-three thousand feet had actually only enhanced the process.

By comparison, the other two hundred climbers who had summited on Mount Everest had all breathed supplementary bottled oxygen. Without any life-giving oxygen cylinders, our bid for the summit was clearly a race against time. The lack of atmospheric oxygen was slowly strangling the life from our bodies and minds. We'd survived in the Death Zone for one day and one night, and already I could feel the slow ebb of life and energy draining from my cells and body. If the wind didn't drop soon, if we couldn't attempt the summit tomorrow, we would have no choice but to descend. We couldn't suffer in this bleak frozen hell very much longer. Of all the mountaineers before us who had climbed Everest without using bottled oxygen, none had endured longer than seventy-two hours above 26,000 feet—and lived to tell the tale.

After several more Tylenol, my headache only slightly subsided. Up here, headaches never fully go away. Before attempting to sleep, we brewed more tea, ate lunch, then stowed all earthly belongings—socks, inner boots, outer boots, glove liners, mittens, water bottle, and pee bottle—into our sleeping bags, to prevent them from freezing solid during the night. Then I wrote the following in my diary, jotting down notes on folded scraps of paper, unfreezing my pen by holding it over the stove between thoughts:

Ed writing in his diary. Stephen Venables

Without an altimeter (the one essential piece of gear we should have brought), we are left to predict weather changes by the seat of our pants, betting on hunches, picking up clues from cloud patterns, wind direction, and changing weather—lenticular clouds or halos around the sun and moon.

Below, the Kama Valley is covered by a giant cloud. A strong fierce wind blows up over the South Col from the Khumbu Valley, making for blue skies in Nepal while immense snow plumes stream from the summits of Everest and Lhotse. There's no hope of climbing now. The tent has rattled all day in the gusts [shaking] the stove, occasionally putting it out, and splattering water over our sleeping bags. Time for Nap #2. In a couple of hours, we're going to have plenty of exercise.

I no longer feel as unnerved being on the Col as I did yesterday afternoon when we first arrived. I feel better acclimatized, more in control, but if this damn wind doesn't stop, we don't stand a chance.

The author on the South Col. Stephen Venables

When we awoke from our nap, we heard a miraculous change. Near silence! The wind had almost stopped. Chomolungma had decided to give us a chance after all. Stephen and I gave each other wide-eyed looks, then yelled the news over to Robert. "Let's go!" came his reply. We all felt a surge of excitement.

I was so focused on what I needed to do to get ready, and so caught up in the expectation of our summit day, that my thoughts did not venture far from the immediate needs of my situation: that of being prepared and dressed and ready to start on time, and of the struggle we would face in a few scant hours outside our tent door. On the Kangshung Face, I had found a comradeship with Stephen, Paul, and Robert that I knew I would never duplicate.

It had been almost two months before, on the approach to Base Camp, that I had dreamt of Lauren. Since then, I had felt a genuine sense of peace whenever I thought of her. She had told me then that she had been carried "down a long river"—which I interpreted to mean that at last she had found her destiny.

In the dream, Lauren had radiated happiness and contentment, and by following the river, she had met her future. Here on the South Col, I felt that I had now been carried upstream, to the highest and most sanctified realms upon the world's tallest mountain. Three years earlier, Lauren's memory had driven me to push higher. A year later, on Changtse, I had conquered my fear of high altitude; and now, I was climbing for no other reason than because I simply wanted to. I wanted to challenge myself as never before—and I was savoring each moment of making my childhood dream, of Chomolungma, of Everest, slowly come true.

With the top only a one-day climb away, I was about to meet my destiny.

Packing for the summit was easy, since we planned to carry almost nothing with us. In the pockets of my parka, I stowed a one pint and a one quart water bottle each filled with Rehydrate (an energy drink mix), plus two candy bars, extra mittens, a second hat, and ski goggles. I also brought a headlamp with an extra lithium battery. And I carried two cameras: my trusty Nikon FM2, with a 24mm wide-angle lens and polarizing filter, and my Yashica auto-focus pocket camera. Each contained a thirty-six-exposure roll of Kodachrome 25 slide film.

Pasang had told me that his Sherpa friends usually left the South Col for the summit at 2 A.M., but since we were climbing without bottled oxygen and would be noticeably slower, I advocated leaving even earlier, an hour or two before midnight, to give ourselves an extra margin of safety. When I'd climbed Changtse, I'd begun at 9 P.M., and had summited at eight the next morning.

I joked to Stephen that I realized it was a fairly extreme time to leave camp, even for him, but he concurred that those few extra hours might mean the difference between success and failure. We yelled the plan over to Robert; our summit departure would be at 11 P.M. sharp.

"I guess getting going this early once every year or two probably won't kill us," I said to Stephen, aware that there could also be a serious side to my comment. His response was surprisingly placid:

"You know, when we leave actually doesn't make a whole lot of difference to me, because I really have very little sense of time."

So that was how Stephen managed all of those early, middle-of-the-night alpine starts!

Chapter 12

Cold Courage: To the Summit

What you write with ink in small black letters
can be lost through the work of a single drop of water.
But what is written in your mind
is there for eternity.

—Tsangyang Gyatso, Tibetan Folk Tales

Considering the time of night, we were relatively awake and in good spirits. Inside the tent we adjusted clothing, mittens, hats, and head-lamps. Once we stood outside, the minus thirty degree Fahrenheit air felt colder than frigid. It drove punishingly through our multiple layers of protective clothing, instantly numbing any exposed skin around our eyes and nose that our hats and face masks didn't cover, and tore at our throats. I was more conscious than ever of the absolute necessity that we be ready to leave camp at exactly the same time—and begin climbing to warm up. Sitting beside

Left: *Footsteps in the snow at 27,000 feet on Everest's Southeast Ridge, with Makalu.*

our tent, Stephen cursed as he struggled to fit the toe bail of his crampons over the welt of his supergaiters. Working together, we finally succeeded. The short intense battle of gloved fingers against metal left us breathless. At precisely 11 P.M. we were ready.

During the entire expedition, we had conscientiously belayed each other at all times, and had always climbed roped. Still clinging to this cautious mindset, I asked Robert and Stephen to rope up on our seventy-five-foot length of seven-millimeter rope. They agreed. The three beams of light from our headlamps shone weakly across the South Col's lifeless plateau as we walked toward the beginning slopes of

Stephen ready to depart for the summit.

Everest's Southeast Ridge, concentrating on each of our advancing footsteps across the small dark stones and hard-frozen snow.

It was a decisive moment. The passage of events had clearly differed, but Robert, Stephen, and I had waited our entire lives to be poised within reach of earth's highest summit. And incredibly, the weather was cooperating. We'd been given our one-in-a-million gift, a clear calm night preceding a promising summit day. The ferocious winds had finally blown themselves out. Only a slight breeze was blowing across the col from Nepal, while higher on the mountain some occasional strong gusts could still be heard. May 12, 1988, was summit day. If we could reach the top and return alive, our small expedition would be a remarkable success.

I might have guessed we'd rope up backwards. Robert led, I came second, and Stephen followed. Robert's pace was slow and deliberate; Stephen and I seemed slightly faster. Stephen didn't hide his distaste for our unhurried gait.

"Robert," he asked politely, "if we can't move any faster, I really think we should unrope and travel at our own pace."

Robert and Ed at 11 P.M. at Camp Three on the South Col. Stephen Venables

We continued together in the name of safety for several more minutes, then untied from the climbing rope. Quickly assuming our natural gaits and speeds, Stephen immediately took the lead and trailed the rope behind him in case we needed it higher. Robert and I followed more or less together.

While the Southeast Ridge is indeed the easiest path to Everest's summit from the South Col, the route is not nearly as straightforward as its plodding reputation might suggest. From its start on the col, two parallel but separate vertical gullies gain the ridge proper. The right-hand gully (which attains the main ridge fairly low) is the original 1952 route pioneered by the Swiss climber Raymond Lambert and Tenzing Norgay. Succeeding expeditions, including Edmund Hillary and Tenzing's successful first ascent of Everest a year later, plus the first American ascent of Everest in 1963, also ascended the right-hand line. Today, most climbers opt for its slightly steeper companion, the left-hand gully, that ascends the center of the so-called Triangular Face. Although harder than the original *Lambert-Tenzing Gully*, this route is considerably more direct and hence a faster climb by which to attain the upper Southeast Ridge.

Edmund Hillary and Tenzing Norgay at 27,200 feet.
Alfred Gregory

We had memorized route descriptions in countless Everest expedition books, but I now realized—albeit a little too late—that these descriptions were of the original right-hand gully. Fortunately, Pasang had described for us the route of the now-standard left-hand gully. From the Col's north side, a snow fan gained a narrow snow gully near the center of a broad, relatively low-angled, triangular-shaped face. Head up that gully, Pasang had said, move slightly left, then continue up and right into a broader snow gully that narrows before it joins the upper Southeast Ridge (at a platform now commonly known as the Balcony), five hundred feet below the South Summit. The famous forty-foot rock outcrop of the Hillary Step is the mountain's final obstacle, and a gentler, but a still dangerous and heavily corniced ridge leads to the actual summit.

The previous afternoon, I had visually traced our intended route up to Everest's South Summit. (You can't actually see the main summit of Everest from the South Col; it hides coyly behind the three-hundred-foot-lower South Summit.) In broad daylight, the terrain looked straightforward enough, certainly nothing we couldn't handle. But cloaked in the black of night, the initial climbing above the South Col was dumbfounding. Several snow fans slanted uphill to form the base of the upper slopes. The next feature, the shallow

Sunrise on Lhotse (left) *and the Khumbu peaks of Nepal* (right), *from 27,000 feet.*

Robert standing at the Japanese tent at 27,000 feet, with the Black Tower on left.

the tent, Stephen ruthlessly forged ahead, switch-backing up the broad snow gully just to the right of a prominent rock outcrop called the Black Tower. The tent was pitched on a narrow, sloping snow shelf. Robert peeked inside it.

"Just food scattered on the floor and a few oxygen bottles," he said hoarsely, then crawled into the entrance for a better look. "Come on in," he added.

I knelt down and tried to enter. I had no reason to crawl into the tent. It was simple curiosity. Unexpectedly, my crampons caught in the nylon fabric. Then, in a flash, claustrophobia lunged at my throat. Precious breath escaped from my lungs—I was suffocating! My hands and arms tore wildly at the tent, I propelled myself backwards, and escaped.

Sitting in the snow, I continued to gasp for air. I was completely stunned.

"What happened?" Robert asked, perplexed, looking out of the tent.

"I . . . I . . . I don't know. I couldn't handle it in there," I panted.

While this was happening, Stephen had increased his lead over us. Already a small dot, he steadily zigzagged up the gentle snow gully overhead, breaking a trail through the snow as he went. He wasn't stopping for anything. Although it wasn't so urgently obvious to either Robert or I at the time (as it was to Stephen), precious minutes and hours of daylight were slipping by. At least the ambient air temperature had finally begun to warm up as the sun rose higher, and its rays shone on us. I set off to try to catch up to Stephen, though I wondered if I could.

Although I was following in his footsteps, I still made little headway in decreasing Stephen's lead—which was frustrating, because I was the fittest and best acclimatized I'd ever been. If I was going to climb Everest without bottled oxygen, it was now or never. This was it. Now. We had to make it. These thoughts became a mantra as I repeated, "This is it, this is it," over and over and over and over, just beneath my breath.

I did manage to slightly shorten Stephen's headway, but he'd been trail-breaking single-handedly for eight hours. Then he stopped and sat down in the snow a hundred yards above me, where the gully steepened at its crest. He said nothing. Talk was a waste of effort. What was there to say? We knew what was expected of us. My exertions had quelled my anger at Stephen. What good was anger, I thought to myself, especially here on the roof of the world? Our reality, our world on Everest, was quiet and white and primordial. And now, barely noticed mists and clouds began stealthily swirling around us, sweeping against our boots and quietly, inevitably rising to envelop us.

The upper snow gully was so steep—inclined to sixty degrees—that we had to front-point up it, balancing on the kicked-in, marginally secure, two-inch-long front metal spikes of our crampons. Stephen began edging up the hard snow, managing twenty feet in a sprint, then ten, and then five as the wind-compacted snow rose in a still steeper wall. Finally he made one last determined effort, climbed quickly up the final snow slab, stepped over the top, and immediately crumpled onto a ledge (the Balcony) located at the top of the gully, panting for breath. He had gained the upper Southeast Ridge leading to Everest's South Summit.

As soon as I started front-pointing up the same section, my breathing instantly became hyperventilated and tremendously labored. My body tensed; a slip meant a hurtling, tumbling, guaranteed-to-be-fatal fall of over five thousand feet. I slammed my ax pick into the snow as securely as I could, rested, tried to remain calm, and turned one foot sideways to placate my aching calf muscles. On the last twenty-foot dash to the ridge crest, I puffed like a steam engine, sucking in the pitifully unnourishing air, vaulted (on adrenaline) over the gully's top—and mindful of the deadly drop below—carefully collapsed onto Stephen's snow ledge.

Robert labored up the gully toward me. Another photograph formed in my mind. I took off my overmitts (again) and recorded his progress. Oblivious to my artistic efforts, Robert glanced up briefly, plodded on after a short rest, then mustered another sprint. I was completely unmindful of the metal camera that

I cradled in my fingertips. Half a dozen pictures later, Robert front-pointed up the final wall and immediately sunk down into a heap beside me. Our conversation had diminished to the bare minimum.

"You tired?"

"Just resting," he gasped.

"Okay. See you up there."

I continued in pursuit of Stephen, who was already climbing toward our next lodestone, the South Summit. Few thoughts came into my mind besides moving each boot upward one step at a time. I also tried to focus mentally on my center of balance, to keep it strong, to not falter and slip. The next long slope was covered in soft, knee-deep snow. It wasn't the best of conditions. Don't trip and fall, I thought to myself; don't do something dumb. Above, Stephen stood in the snow below the first of several rock outcrops that formed a jagged edge along the ridge's left skyline. Slowly he angled up and right, skirted along the base of the rocks, and stayed in the snow where the going was easier. I made yet another futile effort to increase my pace, to catch up to him, but I quickly collapsed, kneeling down in the snow, gasping—not a fish out of water, but a human out of air.

Robert climbing with no O² at 28,000 feet.

Without the significant benefit of breathing life-giving bottled oxygen, when we reached twenty-eight thousand feet our bodies began to function on autopilot. Although we were a team of three, Robert, Stephen, and I were each locked into our own very private and silent realms of intense—and yet decidedly fuzzy—concentration. Taken prisoner by hypoxia, the lack of oxygen, our "reality" began to more closely resemble a surreal fantasy. We had reached the limits of human existence, and our minds and limbs felt restrained, like those of an Apollo astronaut walking on the moon, caged by his space suit into a slow-motion world. I had entered into a dream-like trance, and I was unable to think of anything besides breathing, and lifting one boot at a time marginally uphill. No matter what I tried to will myself to do or to think, my brain and muscles were slowing down, and I couldn't rouse myself. Snow was streaming in plumes off the upper rock ridge, while spindrift slithered around my boots like cascading confetti. My sense of physical and mental control, and the passing of time, began to slip away like the spindrift—so many flakes of snow swirling in so many random directions that I couldn't keep track of them all.

I looked up, searching for Stephen. Instead, I saw swatches of color and fluttering objects. Several Buddhist monks had gathered on the ridge above me. They were holding a *puja,* a blessing ceremony. I didn't think that there was anything noticeably unusual about the scene. The rock outcrops along the ridge were artistically carved and brightly painted, like any prayer wall or *mani* stone that you might see while trekking in the Himalaya. Equally colorful Buddhist prayer flags were strung on cords tied between the rocks, and they flapped in the wind. The purple-robed monks paced back and forth in single file, hands folded reverently together in prayer, while they rhythmically chanted *"Om Mani Padme Hum,"*—Hail the Jewel in the Lotus.

I did not attach any great significance to the presence of the monks. Their being here near the summit of Everest was neither positive, nor negative; they simply were. Nor did I immediately think: "I must be hallucinating," because not only could I see the monks, I also clearly heard their voices and their prayers. I saw them walking, saw the folds of their dark purple robes, and admired the brightly colored *mani* stones and prayer flags just above them. Thirty feet to the right, I finally noticed Stephen sitting in the snow, next to his pack, resting.

Then an unstoppable wave of exhaustion overwhelmed me. My eyes closed, and my head slumped forward. My mind went blank; I passed out. Time elapsed. When I awoke with a start, the Buddhist monks had vanished, and I wondered where I was.

"Everest; I'm on Everest!" I thought. "I'd better try to get a grip on things."

Stephen was watching me intently. He was still sitting in the snow.

"Are you coming or not?" he yelled. "Are you going to help me break trail?"

His tone of voice was somewhat short-tempered, but who could really blame him? He'd been breaking trail single-handedly for almost fifteen hours.

"I can't stay awake! I keep falling asleep; I can't catch up to you!" I shouted back. At this, Stephen got angry.

"You mean I've wasted an hour waiting for you?" he blurted. Then, grabbing his ice ax, he stood up, picked up his pack, slung one arm and then the other through the shoulder straps, and began climbing. As Stephen stomped up the next snow slope, I was just alert enough to snap one more picture, capturing his blur of movement as he crested the South Summit's round snowy dome.

Only weeks later would I remember that none of us had carried a pack above the South Col.

Bowing my head in determined concentration, I followed Stephen's steps up the steepening slope. A strand of rope jutted out of the snow. I angled left toward it. It was some sun-bleached parachute cord, of dubious strength. Twenty feet higher it disappeared back into the slope. I moved up using several of Stephen's footsteps, held the cord in one hand and used it for balance to overcome a short steep step. The snow became shallow again. My crampons scraped against the rock. I saw other scratches on the rock, too.

Then I found a length of white, nine-millimeter fixed rope. It was tied to a snow stake thirty feet higher. Holding on to the rope, I climbed up to the stake. A slightly steeper snow slope led another fifty feet to the South Summit. The angle was probably fifty degrees, but there was no more fixed rope to safeguard this next exposed section of the climb.

Until that very moment, I had been convinced I would reach the summit of Everest. But in the next second, my resolve disintegrated. I stood immobilized and unsure of myself. Should I continue? Could I continue? I no longer knew. Maybe I just needed another rest. My head dropped forward until my forehead rested on my ice ax, its shaft plunged deeply into the soft snow.

I passed out for a second time.

When I came to, I knew I was really losing control. Of myself, of the climb, of reality. I could no longer trust my actions or my abilities; I could barely trust what little remained of my sense of judgment. I glanced at my watch: 3:30 P.M. From out of my mental haze came the inescapable conviction that if I continued I would probably be killed. I would be caught out in the dark near the summit without shelter of any kind. Or I would fall asleep and slip to my death, falling off the final corniced ridge—into eternity. I had reached 28,700 feet.

As if to seal my decision, I remembered Mick Burke, the British mountaineer who disappeared on this same section of ridge during a solo bid for the summit during the 1975 first ascent of Everest's *Southwest Face*. Mick never returned, his fate a mystery, although he probably did reach the summit. And Mick Burke had been breathing bottled oxygen. I did not want my name to be added to the

Stephen, the small blur at top center, gains the South Summit.

ever-lengthening list of Everest fatalities. I did not want to become just another statistic, and interestingly, I also briefly recognized that there were other things in my life that I wanted to accomplish besides reaching the summit of Everest.

If I descended now, I thought I might reach the South Col tents before dark. If I continued, only God knew the outcome. Then, in a strange twist of high-altitude-induced logic, I rationalized that I could rest tonight at the South Col—and then try again for the summit tomorrow! With very little emotion, I turned around. I knew that I had tried my best to reach the summit, and also that I was making the right decision to descend.

Two hundred feet below me, Robert continued to grind up the snow slope like a machine jammed in low gear. We approached one another in silence. He wanted to continue, he said. He thought he could still make it. I'd had enough, I told him. I'd descend the ridge to the top of the lower descent gully and wait there for him and Stephen. Words were at a premium. After nodding in the affirmative, Robert took one more superhuman uphill step.

"Good luck," I said.

I was astonished at how fast I could lose height, compared with the effort needed to gain it! In no time at all, I reached the top of the Triangular Face, the Balcony, and the lower descent gully—or was there more than one gully? I searched with increasing urgency for familiar landmarks, but I didn't see any, and I couldn't be absolutely sure that I was in the right place. Our footsteps from that morning had been completely covered by blowing snow.

I stamped out a small ledge in the snow and waited. Time passed, yet there was no sensation of time passing. A gauze-like mist shrouded the upper ridge. It began to flurry. Where were Stephen and Robert? They should be coming soon. But then, when I finally did see them, they were below me.

I yelled out their names. They did not respond or even turn around to see who it was, but continued heading downhill, away from me. I ran down a step or two toward them, and called out a second time, louder, as the mists and snow blew thicker and obscured them. Some moments later, after the clouds parted, I looked again, and they had disappeared! I strained my eyes, searched downhill, and then up, but they'd vanished without a trace. I returned to my snow ledge.

I now considered that I might have descended *too far* down the Southeast Ridge, *past* the top of the descent gully. What if Stephen and Robert had reached the crest of the correct descent gully—a point which was now, if I really had blundered, several hundred feet above me—and they hadn't seen me because I was below them and hidden in the clouds? My mind seized on this fatal possibility, which in fact might already have happened. Robert and Stephen could have abandoned me without even knowing it! Panicking, I climbed back up for thirty feet, looked over the windswept edge of the snow ridge to my left, and searched with increasing desperation for any familiar rock outcrops or shapes of snow that would mark the top of the descent gully back down the Triangular Face. I recognized nothing. I was lost.

I glanced back up.

Oh—thank god. There they were! Robert and Stephen were descending the ridge toward me. I was tremendously relieved to see them; it would be dark in less than an hour. I shouted up a hello and waved both my arms.

Once again they ignored me. They continued walking with an unearthly silence, moving very, very, very slowly, wearily plodding down the snow slope through the freshly fallen powder. Why wouldn't they answer me? Perhaps they were still too far away. Maybe they couldn't hear me. I stomped my feet in the snow, improved my little platform, then looked up to check on their progress.

They had vanished a second time.

I now began to contemplate spending a solitary night, bivouacking alone on Everest's upper Southeast Ridge. I hadn't the energy to climb back up to search for Robert and Stephen. I decided that I'd wait here for as long as it took them to descend from the summit to rejoin me. And, at the worst, if they had descended by another route without me, I'd just have to catch up to them tomorrow. I checked my watch. It was just before six. It would be dark in thirty minutes.

I began enlarging my ledge into a snow hole to sleep in, methodically chopping away at the unfeeling snow with my ice ax.

Then a single figure appeared. Stumbling almost blindly, lead-limbed, and utterly spent of energy, a person emerged out of the gathering dusk one hundred feet above me. It was Robert. This time he was not a mirage. His face was haggard, and encrusted with ice and snow.

"I reached the South Summit," he muttered unemotionally.

"Did you see Stephen?" I asked.

Robert shook his head. "No."

Stephen had taken his life into his own hands. He was spending the night on heaven's doorstep, alone, somewhere near Everest's summit. Or else … no. No. *Of course we wouldn't think of that, no, not yet.*

"What about the Japanese tent? We should bivouac there," Robert said. Could we reach it before nightfall? If we hurried, maybe. There was nothing that I hated more than getting stuck on a mountain in the dark—and here we were on Everest, above twenty-seven thousand feet, about to get benighted.

Looking over the side of the ridge again, this time I recognized a single identifying landmark, the shape of a particular rock outcrop. My mind registered the extreme urgency of the situation; my brain clicked on and began functioning again. Yes, this was the correct gully, the same way we'd climbed up this morning! The top of the gully was very steep. Could we safely down climb this section unroped? It seemed unlikely.

"Maybe we should just go down the ridge all the way to the Col," I said.

The firmness of Robert's answer startled me.

"No," he replied. "We've got to go down the same way we came up. Let's not make any stupid mistakes. Let's not get lost."

He was right. We had to descend the route that we knew, the way we'd climbed up. Thirty feet lower, it appeared that we could weave back and forth through several short rock steps, angle farther right, then sneak into the midsection of our correct snow gully. This we did. Astonished by our good fortune, we raced down the lower, gentler gully, and found faint signs of our morning's footprints which we followed downhill toward the Japanese tent. Five minutes before pitch darkness, we reached it and crawled inside. Luckily, I was much too exhausted and relieved to feel claustrophobic, and I immediately relaxed inside its windproof sanctuary, grateful to have shelter for the long cold night ahead.

The tent's interior was cluttered with various packets and squeeze tubes of Japanese food. The contents were written in Japanese characters. At first, we thought we might find something tasty to eat, but each time we opened up something, we discovered dried seaweed or miso soup powder. Food-wise, we were out of luck. Then we saw two yellow oxygen bottles on the tent floor.

"Let's see if they have anything in them," Robert said. He turned the on-off knob on one bottle, and I heard a slow hissing.

"This worked great on the West Ridge in 1985," Robert explained as he zipped up the tent entrance and turned on the other bottle, too. The concept was to fill up the tent with pure oxygen and breath it for as long as it lasted—which wasn't for very long, only a few minutes, but at least it made us laugh.

We lay beside each other, clad in our Bolder Designs Gore-tex down suits. In our most extreme dreams, neither of us, I'm sure, ever imagined that we'd spend a night without sleeping bags at 27,000 feet. But the suits were very well-insulated, and we tried to make the best of the situation. I was so tired that I soon fell asleep. Robert, however, was inexplicably agitated and couldn't sleep.

In the middle of the night, I awoke. Robert was still awake.

"Don't you think we should get going, maybe head down to the Col?" he asked. I looked at my watch. It was 1:30 A.M.!

"Are you crazy?" I said. "Do you know how cold it is out there? It's probably minus fifty degrees! Why would we want to go outside now?"

Robert mulled this over.

"Hmmm, you're probably right," he replied. "I guess we should stay here a while longer."

I fell back asleep.

"I really think we should go down now, Ed," Robert said at 3:30 A.M., waking me. Now I felt guilty. I was sleeping, while he was lying next to me, wide awake, shivering, slowly freezing to death.

But I said, "Robert, it's fifty below outside! Let's wait till sunrise."

"Okay, I guess you're right," he said glumly.

The next time I awoke, the yellow tent fabric was suffused with the dawn of a new day. Aching and stiff, having had nothing to eat, and with only a sip or two of Rehydrate to drink from my water bottle, Robert and I crawled from the tent at 5 A.M. At least the weather was still good, and there was no wind. We decided to keep heading down to the South Col—we certainly weren't going up—but, as yet, we hadn't had time to consider what might have happened to Stephen. Then Robert motioned behind me, and he pointed uphill. I turned around. A lone, weary figure came stumbling and staggering toward us. I thought to myself, "That is the most tired human being I have ever seen."

It was Stephen. He, too, had survived the night.

His face was ashen. His hood and climbing suit were festooned with frost feathers and ice crystals. Glacier goggles hung askew around his neck; his snowed-up headlamp was still perched on his forehead. We embraced. His voice was extremely weak.

"I made it," Stephen said, by way of an explanation. "I got to the top."

We were thrilled, and we congratulated him, shaking hands. After offering him the last few sips of slushy water from my water bottle, I then mustered the energy and concentration to click several pictures of Stephen sitting in the snow drinking it. It was a very happy moment for us all.

Later, Stephen sent me a specially written account of his summit climb.

When I separated from Ed and Robert just before midnight on May 11, I was glad to be alone. I assumed that later they would catch up to me, but for the moment I was relieved to be climbing free and unfettered, moving at my own rhythm up the couloir. I was managing ten steps at a time, with only short rests in between. I kept up this steady pace and, apart from an irritating numbness in my left foot, my body was warm. I was going to climb this mountain.

I continued alone into the darkness. At one stage, I followed some old crampon tracks too far left and realized that I was off route. My confidence wilted as I wandered back right across piles of shattered rock, wondering if this way was correct, wanting someone to show me the right way, and wishing that the faint silver glow of the waning moon would come round from behind the ridge and cheer the gloom of this lonely dark night.

Eventually my confidence was restored when the beam from my head torch picked out the Japanese tent. After four hours on the move, I had to stop and rest. I also wanted to wait and show the way to Robert and Ed whose shouts reverberated in the darkness below. I could not hear Ed's exact words, just a note of anger. Was he upset with me, with Robert, or with both of us? Soon a beam of light appeared and I switched my head torch on again to show them where I was. Then I untied from the seven-millimeter rope I'd been trailing and left it coiled beside the tent in case Robert and Ed wanted to use it. Now that they could see which direction to go, I decided to continue breaking trail and stood up to plod on into the darkness.

I had already been weakening below the tent. Now at about 27,750 feet I became even slower. The upper couloir dragged on and on, a tedious chore alleviated only briefly by the magical dawn and my first real view of the Solu

Khumbu which Paul, Robert, and Ed knew so well. Then I was back on the treadmill, zigzagging laboriously, and joylessly, up the couloir.

At its top, I rested for half an hour, sprawled in the snow, waiting for the sun's warmth to bring life back to my left foot. When I started off again I was still confident, hoping that Joe and Mimi could see me now that I was on the Tibetan side of the ridge, and hoping that I could still be on the summit by midday. But after a few more steps, my feet broke through the flaky snow crust and my doubts grew. For the next two or three hours I struggled ever more slowly up the steep flank of the ridge toward the South Summit, stumbling and slithering in a semiconscious daze of despair.

Starting to lose touch with reality, at times I imagined I was trudging the crumbling earth of some sun-drenched field; for a while I convinced myself that a nearby rock outcrop was the frozen body of Hannelore Schmatz who died near here in 1979; at other times, I was helping an imaginary old man who was to accompany me, on and off, for the rest of the day. In lucid moments, I stood back to look at myself, felt my limbs sag ever more feebly, and realized sadly that perhaps I was not good enough for this test. Just above the short length of parachute cord, I gave up in despair, cut a ledge in the snow, slumped down, and fell asleep.

It was 11 A.M. Robert and Ed were now in sight. Between dozes I stared down at Ed who was in front, climbing slowly, slowly, closer. He must have forged ahead of Robert. Typical Ed—plodding up stubbornly and patiently. We had been apart for twelve hours, but perhaps now he would take over the lead.

At noon, I swore at him. It was a curse of anger, frustration, and disappointment. As if rejecting the friendship and teamwork of the past three months, I got up and pushed on ahead alone. For thirteen hours I had been relying confidently on myself, but I was no longer strong enough. I needed their help, but Robert was too far behind, and Ed, now that he had almost caught up, was clearly even weaker than me. I had failed myself; the others had failed me; the whole thing was a disaster.

Odd, but the anger helped. It made me think, "No—you can't give in this easily. It must be possible. You've just got to try a bit harder, and move a bit faster." Knowing that Ed could not help me break trail actually made things easier, for now I knew definitely that if I was going to reach the top, it would have to be on my own. Two caffeine pills swigged down with some Rehydrate juice helped me stay awake, but it was a much stronger force, some deep reserve of willpower that I had been waiting all these years to find, that transformed me.

After a few steps, I realized that I was no longer wallowing in despair, but was once more in control of my body, directing legs and lungs in a supreme, concentrated effort to climb that final slope to the South Summit. After about an hour, I shouted down to Ed, "Nearly there!" then disappeared, treading a narrow crest to the snowy dome of Everest's South Summit, trying to absorb it all, trying to treasure this special moment up here, higher now than Lhotse, higher than any other mountain in the world. That really is the Western Cwm, I thought, far, far below, with the clouds racing toward me, and starting to swirl round the West Ridge. This really is me, here, alive, moving, breathing. I can do it after all: I can reach the summit of Everest without bottled oxygen, I told myself.

The Hillary Step. Stephen Venables

That surge of euphoria gave me the strength, after a moment's anxious fear, to continue down over to the narrow, exposed crest leading to the Hillary Step. It was 1:40 P.M. and, provided I reached the summit and turned back by four o'clock, I calculated I should be safely back down at the South Col by, or soon after, dark. Clouds were drifting around the ridge, but there was not much wind and the visibility was still quite good. A few steps along the ridge, climbing carefully, deliberately, over the rocks well to the left of the dangerous Kangshung cornices reassured me that I was still in control.

At the Hillary Step there was a choice of three fixed ropes, so I clipped my prussik loop into the newest to safeguard the fifty-foot climb up the famous steep cliff, poised right on the brink of the twelve-thousand-foot drop down the Kangshung Face.

Kicking, thrusting, and pushing up the Step left me spluttering and gasping, but I knew that there were no more difficulties before the summit. I had crossed the bridge and now it only remained to put one foot in front of the other, plodding slowly, patiently across the great white roof of Everest, over one, two, three broad humps and then up a final twenty-foot climb, stopping every few steps to gasp at the thin air and control my coughing, promising myself that surely after this climb I would give up smoking.

I would love, one day, to go back to the summit of Everest to experience it more fully. On that afternoon in 1988 I only had ten minutes. Ten short minutes of joyful disbelief, trying not very successfully to grasp what it all meant and trying to hold and remember that utterly surreal sensation of being alone on that snowy crest with its three great ridges dropping down into the clouds. I had two tasks to perform. First, to photograph a self-portrait, which sadly never came out. I also took out two envelopes containing flower petals from an ashram in southern India, talismans given to me by friends in Bombay, and scattered them on the summit. Then a final photo of the little envelopes placed in the snow beside abandoned oxygen cylinders and prayer flags.

That photograph did turn out, and shows wind-drifted snowflakes already gathering on my summit offerings. By the time I started down, the wind was growing stronger and snow was falling. I tried to hurry, but my lungs could not get enough oxygen and my legs were weak. Soon I was struggling for my life, stumbling through the whiteout, half blind and peering through frozen sunglasses at dim, blurred, half-remembered shapes, terrified of walking out onto—and falling through—one of the Kangshung Face cornices. I kept collapsing onto my knees, forcing myself each time to get up and continue, groping my way back to the top of the Hillary Step. I managed

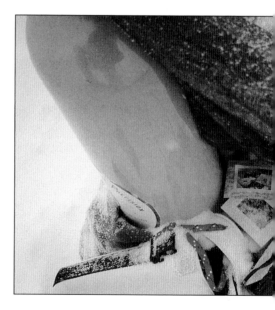

Ironically, Stephen's only summit photograph of himself shows his reflection in an empty oxygen bottle left behind by the Asian TV expedition a week earlier. Stephen Venables

to rappel back down the Step, but collapsed again at the bottom, cold, half-blind, moaning with self pity, wishing that Robert and Ed were with me. But there was no sign of them; only the old man was there and he helped rouse me to cross the bridge back to the South Summit. Together we crawled and staggered, heads down into the stinging cold, determined not to lie down and die.

I was chronically slow and by the time I reached the South Summit, it was nearly dark. Desperate to save time and energy, I sat and slid down toward the shoulder, gathering speed and racing out of control before braking with my ice ax and coming to rest in a gasping, sobbing, panic of terror. Ed and Robert must have already started down the lower couloir, I thought. Now it was dark, and after searching back and forth along the ridge and failing to find the couloir, the old man suggested that we should just wait till morning. For a while we sat on a rock, but it was sloping and precarious so I moved onto the snow and in a final desperate effort, dug a ledge just big enough to curl up on.

It was a long cold wait, but at the time it seemed less hard than other bivouacs I had endured. Perhaps my brain, so dulled by hypoxia, never really registered the cold and discomfort, or perhaps I was just too exhausted to suffer. Perhaps the old man, and Eric Shipton, the distinguished explorer and "Everester" who took over warming my hands, plus the other people crowded round my ledge that night, all helped me to endure. Luckily the wind dropped, the clouds gradually cleared, and through all the shivering, I never doubted I would live. At one stage, I think that I even became sufficiently relaxed to sleep, because there was no gradual transition from darkness to light—just the sudden realization that down there, on earth, another day was beginning.

I stood up on my numb wooden feet and started to wobble downhill. Soon I reached the couloir and slid down into the morning sunlight. Then I saw them: two strangers standing beside a tent. People. Of course—they were Ed and Robert. Thirty hours earlier, I had left them behind. For thirty hours I had been sustained by egoistic ambition, willpower, instinct, and previously untapped reserves of the subconscious; but now I really had had enough of this lonely journey. I felt a wonderful surge of joy and relief as I rejoined my friends in the bright morning sunshine and gratefully let them take me home.

Sixty-six years after the feat had first been attempted by his countrymen in 1922, at 3:30 P.M. on May 12, 1988, Stephen Venables became the first British mountaineer to successfully climb to the summit of Mount Everest without the use of supplementary bottled oxygen.

Chapter 13

The Fight

You've got to fight it. Sometimes you've just got to fight it.

—Fritz Wiessner

I t has often been said that descending a mountain is harder and more dangerous than climbing one. Perhaps nowhere is this truth more sharply evident, and statistically proven, than on Mount Everest. Now that the three of us were reunited, standing together outside of the Japanese tent at 27,000 feet, it became imperative that we descend to the South Col. We needed to reach our own tents, sleeping bags, and stoves to rewarm and rehydrate our tired, parched bodies. As of yet, I hadn't begun to consider how difficult it would be to retrace our route down the Kangshung Face. Roping-up somewhat symbolically on our seven-millimeter rope, we left the Japanese tent

Left: *Stephen Venables and Robert Anderson back on the South Col.*

Descending to the South Col on the morning of May 13. Makalu rises in the distance.

and headed back down to the col. Robert went first, guiding Stephen, who was very wobbly legged and weak, while I came last, wondering if I could belay the rope if someone slipped. Luckily the terrain quickly eased, and soon we were back on the flat, frozen, wind-swept desert of the South Col.

As we stumbled back to our two tents at Camp Three, the full realization of how extended we were began to sink in. At this extreme altitude there was absolutely no chance of rescue, or help, really, of any kind. Helicopters don't fly much above the twenty-thousand-foot level, and while several expeditions were currently climbing up the mountain's Nepalese side, none were close enough to lend assistance—nor did they even know we were here. We were three people very much alone, utterly exhausted, with virtually no possibility of any outside assistance. It was also now that we most felt the lack of the usual Sherpa companions to make hot tea and soup, care for us, carry our packs, and otherwise speed our safe return. Back down at Advanced Base Camp (a full eight thousand vertical feet lower than our present altitude), Mimi, Joe, Pasang, Kasang—and Paul, too, we hoped—would be searching for us through the binoculars.

When Stephen and Robert paused to rest, I hiked on ahead across the col toward our two tents. Then, still unaware of the extent of my frostbite injuries, I took off my gloves and pulled out my Nikon to photograph my partners walking toward me. I took two portraits of my half-frozen companions. In the first image, Stephen leans in fatigue against Robert, but in the second, Stephen stands alone, his ice ax raised in well-earned victory. It was a particularly proud moment.

I do not remember very much about the rest of that day. Oxygen deprivation, our overwhelming fatigue, and the lack of food, water, and sleep combined to make us incredibly lethargic. Our lives began to be acted out in super slow motion. I know that we lay down and rested in the tents, that we took our high-altitude climbing suits off and crawled willingly into the luscious warmth of our sleeping bags, and that we then made a brew of tea, only because somehow I took pictures of these things, too.

I dimly recall taking off my overmitts and liner gloves to inspect my fingers. Gray in color, cold, numb, and woody feeling, the fingertips of my left hand, I noted, appeared considerably worse than those of the right. Fretting over what to do, I finally decided to rewarm them in our tiny pot of hot tea water. Stephen did the same with his frozen left toes. Then of course we drank the tea. While we knew that rewarming frozen tissue should only be done when all chance of refreezing the injured tissue had passed, we were positive we'd have little trouble descending the Kangshung Face. What could possibly be worse than the nightmare that we had just survived? Our previous hour-and-a-half-long descent from Camp Two to Camp One made us assume that in two days time at the most, we'd be safely in Doctor Mimi's loving care at Advanced Base.

Finally we collapsed, dead tired and oblivious to the world, and slept. If we knew that we should have tried to descend to Camp

Stephen had pushed himself to exhaustion.

Two that day, we never discussed it. Careful, rational observations were no longer terribly important, or even possible. Subconsciously we knew that spending this third day above 26,000 feet was dangerous, perhaps even deadly, but our bodies craved only sleep and rest. The summit push had exhausted us almost beyond human limits. At last we were ready to go home; the question was: could we still get there?

Our struggle to escape from the Death Zone had begun. Stephen Venables

Time crept by. I blinked awake from the depths of sleep and peered at my watch's luminous dial. It was 2:30—but in the morning or the night? I no longer knew. My mind could not function. And what day was it? And where were we? Oh, right. We're on the South Col . . . on Mount Everest. After my long agonizing night huddled next to Robert in the Japanese tent, it felt so deliciously warm to be burrowed deeply inside my sleeping bag. Couldn't we just lie here a bit longer, I thought to myself. But wait. Who was I even asking permission of . . . ? I didn't know. I just didn't want to have to move a single inch, so I fell back asleep, never waking once, for the rest of that day and the entire night.

With no food left, the next morning we realized that our physical and mental condition had gone from bad to worse, as had our hopes for an easy, rapid descent. This was our fourth day above the 8,000-meter-level without bottled oxygen. Our bodies would not respond to signals from the brain, movement was barely possible, and every effort, no matter how large or small, became a superhuman effort. Stephen's and my last gas canister had run out the day before, but luckily Robert's stove was still going. Unable to make a single effort to prepare to descend, Stephen and I lay inert inside our bags, and waited hours for Robert to deliver us a single, half-filled pot of hot water: our breakfast. We were a pathetic sight—unmotivated, listless, and uninterested in doing anything to save ourselves from the certainty of what would happen should we not act. I began to realize the terrible truth, that slowly and inexorably, we were dying.

Standing up required an effort we could only marginally begin to grasp; to carry the weight of our two tents, or any of our additional heavier equipment back down the mountain was virtually impossible. We decided to leave the tents here on the Col, and we would risk bivouacing out in the open in our sleeping bags at Camp Two, where we had left behind a few extra gas canisters—but no food. At Camp One, we had two tents and a large food cache. Trying to cut even more weight, I also left behind my wonderfully warm down-insulated bibs. Lastly, reasoning that my wool mittens (though by now fairly worn out) would be easier to rappel down our fixed ropes with, I discarded my thick overmitts, which saved only ounces, and in retrospect was yet another costly error.

I crawled outside the tent, alternately lying and sitting in the snow until the final, most awkward task of fastening crampons to boots was accomplished. But could I stand? I glanced over at Robert, prone on his back in his tent, boots protruding out the entrance like a dead man's. Yet every so often he would come to life, sit up, fiddle with his crampons, and collapse again. Stephen was also preparing to go, and lay on the ground, corpse-like, in front of our tent. I pulled out my auto-camera to take a picture of him, and he waved at me half-heartedly to prove that he was still alive.

Ed's last photo taken on the climb was of Stephen waving. Note climbing rope in center.

Yes, I could stand up, with difficulty. Shuffling to the east side of the col, I carefully stepped down the initial steep slope and plunged into waist-deep, fresh powder snow—which was good for skiing, but not very easy to walk through! Afternoon snow storms over the past two days were the culprits. Snow had also been blown over the col onto the leeward side by the powerful winds. The avalanche danger in the upper part of the bowl was extremely high.

Earlier in the expedition we had discussed the possibility of our descending into Nepal, into the Western Cwm, if conditions or circumstances high on the mountain warranted such an extreme change of plan in our descent. And while that escape down Everest's normal *South Col Route* was probably now fully justified given that the snow conditions on the Kangshung Face were so atrociously dangerous, in my debilitated condition, I realized that several steps down Everest's East Face were several steps too many to reverse. As soon as we stepped off the South Col, we were irrevocably committed to fully descending our route. So, with no going back, I continued stumble-stepping down the slope, plunging each boot deep into the powder, my ears straining for the slightest sound of the snow cracking or settling. To make matters worse, thick moisture-laden monsoon clouds smothered my view.

I could only listen and wait for disaster.

"What's it like down there?" a voice yelled from above. It was Robert. I could see him standing in silhouette on the rim of the South Col, five hundred feet above.

"Dangerous! Whatever you do, don't glissade," I shouted back. "Don't slide down the slope. Follow in my tracks!"

Minutes later, I shook my head in disbelief. Far to my left, Robert was now almost level with me! A small and lonely figure, he stood in the very center of the vast snowfield. How did he get there so fast?

"What are you doing!?" I yelled, with not a little consternation.

"I glissaded. It looked fine," Robert replied. "I guess I got going kind of fast.... and, uh, I dropped both of my ice axes, too. Could I borrow your extra ski pole?" His voice revealed increasing alarm as he discovered the dire consequences of his slide. His two ice axes were nowhere to be seen; they were lost.

"I wanted to get down as fast as possible. So I jumped off the edge of the South Col," Robert later explained to me, using some high-altitude-riddled logic. "And everything was fine for the first few seconds. 'This is great,' I thought until I hit some rocks, tumbled forward, and the slope avalanched. Which sent me cartwheeling down the hill, but then fortunately, I stopped."

Stephen left Camp Three ten minutes after Robert, so he did not see Robert fall. When Stephen reached the col's edge, he saw only Robert's initial toboggan-slide dent in the snow. Now far below the col, Robert and I had already been swallowed by the clouds. Stephen also decided—just as unwisely—to glissade off the edge of the South Col and slide down the slope. And he also lost control and took a dangerous fall.

"It was the only time on the entire expedition that I heard Stephen's British reserve crack," Robert related. "I think he was truly frightened. He stopped above me, then he yelled down that his ice ax had been ripped off his wrist, nearly taking his Rolex with it. At least he kept his priorities straight."

Within twenty minutes of leaving our camp on the South Col, both Robert and Stephen had lost their ice axes. As a result, during the remainder of our descent of the Kangshung Face, I held in my hands our only ice ax—our *one* ice ax. I left my spare ski pole for Robert, and after his fall, Stephen now had nothing to use for safety or support, neither ice ax nor ski pole.

I continued down the snow slope. Peering through the enshrouding mists, I searched for a landmark to tell me that I was on route, hoping and praying that somehow I could still find the way to Camp Two—which, after my teammates' falls, felt increasingly distant and perhaps unreachable. I made each plunging, plowing, downhill step through the fluffy powder with the greatest of effort, lifting legs and boots and crampons, moving always forward, but finding no food to eat except for my singular desire to live, my strength flowing from a hitherto-untapped reservoir, from a life stream flowing deep within me, and of course I was thankful this new supply of energy existed, but how long would it last for?

Suddenly, I heard a dull muffled roar break loose from the mountainside high above me. I turned uphill; every muscle in my body tensed to iron. Hidden by the gray curtain of cloud, sounds of chaos and destruction multiplied wave upon wave as tons of unseen snow began to race downhill. An avalanche! Quickly I ascertained that it was not heading directly for me, but had originated above and to my left. Then, to my horror, I realized that the avalanche had started from the direction of the huge, unstable snow slope where I'd last seen Robert standing alone, and helplessly vulnerable. My stomach tightened into a fierce sick knot.

The clouds were so dense that I could not actually see the avalanche. I could only hear the crashing sound of the falling debris, emanating now well to my left, now below me, as multiple thousands of tons of snow and ice—carrying one human body—erupted over the edge of the immense Lhotse ice cliffs. A sharp, crippling wave of anguish overcame me, as I imagined Robert being swept along with the debris. I could picture the terrible sequence of events in detail: Robert standing in the center of the snowfield one moment, hopeful of survival, then his sudden panic as the billowing white tidal wave overwhelmed him, sweeping him down, down, down, before tumbling him over that horrifying edge to his final, excruciating plunge into the abyss. Robert had just died—after everything that we had been through. The finality of such a death shocked me profoundly, even through my exhaustion, even as I grappled with disbelief.

Turning back downhill, breathing hoarsely, I resumed my descent. There was nothing else to do. I imagined the two of us, Stephen and myself, walking into Advanced Base Camp, without Robert. What would we tell the others? How could we explain something so inherently unfair, that after all we had survived together, Robert had died in an avalanche on the descent? I didn't know. Robert's death was an impossibility; I wanted to cry out in anguish, to rage against Everest, to blaspheme God, to curse fate itself, but I fought back my tears and bit my lower lip to hold back my vile and desperate words. My body quivered with emotion; each breath came in a creaking, throat-tightened spasm.

My determination to reach the mountain's base became furious and indignant. Stephen and I had to survive; we could not give in and let ourselves die.

After a few minutes, I glanced back uphill. Only a single dot, a small black figure standing in the white snow, was following in my footsteps. Even as I tried to cling to the chance that Robert was not dead, I saw my worst fears confirmed. There was just one dot, not two. I was certain now that Robert had been killed. I crumpled into the snow, struggling once again to keep from breaking down. In the ultimate conviction of the truly desperate, I found myself proclaiming: "We are as alone as any humans can be. This is a fight to the end." There seemed nothing melodramatic in such a thought—in fact, I found that it clarified things wonderfully. "I am going to live," I insisted to myself. *"I AM GOING TO LIVE!"*

Adrenaline carried me downhill once again. Stopping momentarily to rest, I turned around to check on Stephen. I saw two small dots in the distance! I counted them twice, and then even a third time, just to make sure that my eyes weren't deceiving me. I had been so sure it had been otherwise! I shook my head in disbelief, then felt a surge of gratefulness and joy as I watched the dots continue down the snowfield. As quickly as disaster had seemed to descend upon our group, it had passed away again, leaving me in stunned amazement.

I still thought that we could reach the Flying Wing and the snow platform at Camp Two before nightfall. Carefully, I stepped across a partially hidden bergschrund, trying to remember at what level we had diagonalled across the

Robert Anderson rappels into the Jaws of Doom.

Ed stands on the debris of the collapsed ice chockstone. Robert Anderson

Ed climbs out of the Jaws of Doom crevasse at 23,000 feet. Robert Anderson

Stephen Venables crosses the Tyrolean traverse above the Jaws of Doom.

Ed suspended above the void, with Tibet beyond. Stephen Venables

The 1988 Everest Kangshung Face team at Advanced Base Camp:
(front): *Paul Teare, Stephen Venables, Ed Webster*
(back): *Robert Anderson, Joe Blackburn, and Mimi Zieman*

Stephen on the ropes.

Ed jotting notes.

Robert Anderson, Paul Teare, Ed Webster, and Stephen Venables
with the Lady of the Lake at Advanced Base Camp.
Photographs (Above and Below Left): Joe Blackburn

Ed and Pasang.

Stephen "in action" over Jaws.

The best cup of tea in the world. Ed soaks up the sunrise from Camp Two.
Stephen Venables

Camp Two was tucked under the Flying Wing at 24,500 feet.

We knew frostbite was a serious danger on Everest. Joe Blackburn

Ed circles around the right-hand end of the Flying Wing. Stephen Venables

The start of "the Great Day" (May 10): Stephen, Paul, Robert, and Makalu.

Stephen adjusts our tent on South Col at 26,000 feet. Everest in sunset behind.

4 P.M., May 10, 1988.
Stephen, Paul, and Robert take the first footsteps onto the South Col from Tibet.

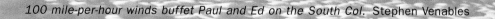
100 mile-per-hour winds buffet Paul and Ed on the South Col. Stephen Venables

The shadow of Everest projected against the horizon at sunrise, from 27,000 feet

Japanese tent, South Col, and Makalu.

Robert Anderson taking a rest at 28,000 feet, no O^2.

"*Frostbite Sunrise*" *from 27,000 feet, looking southeast, to Kancheniunga, Chomolönzo, Makalu, Shartse, Lhotse Shar, and Lhotse.*

Robert Anderson ascends Everest's SE Ridge without oxygen. Lhotse on left.

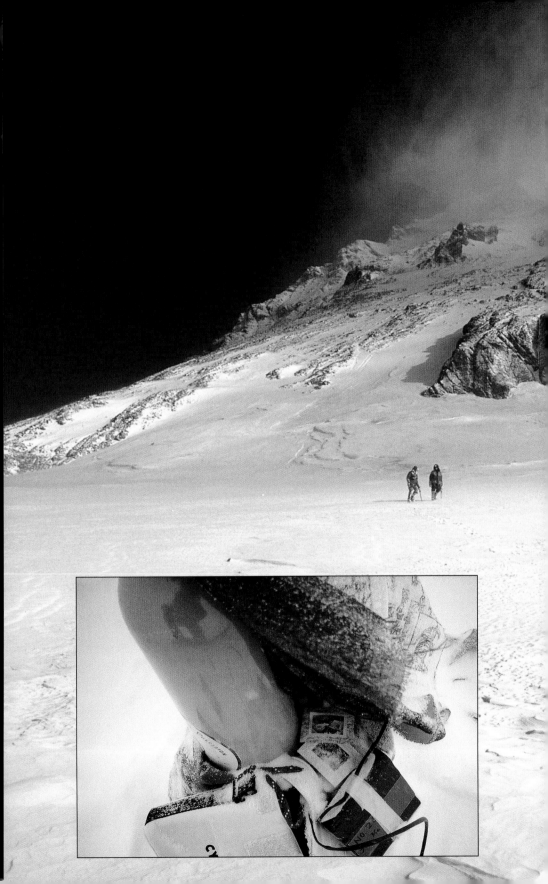

Right: *Stephen Venables raises his ice ax in victory.*

Left: *The summit photo shows Stephen's reflection in an oxygen bottle.*

Background: *Venables and Anderson stagger back across the South Col on the morning of May 13.*

Stephen after
his bivouac.

Ed's fingers.
Paul Teare

Stephen has a cup of tea back at the South Col on May 13.

Ed on oxygen at Advanced Base Camp on May 17. Paul Teare

Another bad hair day: Ed and Stephen at Advanced Base Camp, May 17.

Mimi tends Ed's fingers, and Stephen has a black nose. Photos: Paul Teare

Alive.
Paul Teare

lower portion of the treacherous snow basin below the South Col. After descending vertically several hundred more feet, I slowly began angling to my left, facing downhill. We'd made a long traverse upward to the left from the right-hand end of the Flying Wing; I now had to reverse this section. Unfortunately, the snow conditions had completely changed since our ascent. Far from the easy hardpacked snow we'd savored on our climb up, I now waded forward through thigh-deep, unconsolidated powder ripe for an avalanche of massive proportion.

As I began to traverse across the snowfield, I was cognizant that it was heavily laden with freshly fallen and windblown snow. The surface could fracture at any second, and without warning. Traversing almost horizontally to get across it, I also knew that I was breaking a cardinal rule of mountaineering—traversing straight across an avalanche slope and creating, in effect, a man-made fracture line—but here there was absolutely no alternative. Somehow, *somehow*, we had to cross to the opposite side.

We were trapped; this was sheer and utter madness! And if the snow did avalanche, as I had every belief that it would, the tumultuous deafening roar of untold tons of falling snow would send me hurtling into one of many deep and waiting crevasses, or tumbling into eternity, into the Witches' Cauldron at the base of Lhotse, seven thousand vertical feet below. There would be no escaping death if the snowfield gave way, but maybe the others would survive. Maybe the snow would fracture below them, and only I would be swept away. Perhaps they would be spared. I continued forward, making each footstep as softly and gently as possible, my heavy boots sinking nonetheless into the snow's downy cushion. We were rolling the dice to win our own lives. If I heard or felt a crack or a settling of the snow, I was prepared to run for my life—in a last futile effort.

I endured these soft sinking velvet footsteps one by one, knee-deep, waiting for death, expecting to die, experiencing the embrace of eternity known only by the condemned and the dying. Thirty minutes later, when I at last reached the slope's far side above the Flying Wing's right-hand end, I hunched over with relief. The snow should have avalanched, but miraculously, unbelievably, it had not. Slowly I recovered from this torment and prepared myself for the next one.

Days earlier, on our ascent, we had crossed the deep crevasse formed by the detached uphill side of the Flying Wing snow block. This lethal gap was somewhere just below me. We'd crossed it via a fragile snow bridge, but where?

As I stumbled downhill toward this crevasse, an alarming thought found its way into my brain. Why weren't we now roped together for safety? In fact, *where was our climbing rope?* I didn't have it. And neither, I thought, did

Robert or Stephen. Before we left the South Col, we hadn't discussed if we should rope up—tie into the rope—or not, presumably because during the summit climb we'd each become accustomed to climbing solo and unroped. No doubt we just assumed that we wouldn't need to bother roping up below the Col either. Only months later, while looking at a picture I'd taken, did I discover the missing rope lying coiled in the snow in front of Stephen's and my tent on the South Col—right where we had left it. (*See photograph on page 453.*)

Confused by the thick clouds and the almost total whiteout, I could see only about fifty feet, far enough to discern the Flying Wing's jagged and icy upper lip extending far to the right. I squinted my eyes and scanned the slope. An apparition materialized out of the clouds. Were my eyes tricking me? No: it was a tiny orange flag, the highest of our bamboo wands, which I had placed four days earlier to mark our route over the impasse. I hurried forward through the snow and grabbed the wand. It was real! Carefully I tiptoed downhill toward the snow-bridged crevasse. I couldn't tell if the snow was solid enough to support my weight, so I jumped across the span's midsection instead.

All I heard was a *"Whoompf!"* behind me when I landed on the far side— the sound of snow collapsing and falling into the mountain's unknown depths. Five feet from where I now stood, a round black hole clearly identified the part of the snow bridge that had given way. There the crevasse was much wider. I decided that the others would see the black hole and know to be careful.

Camp Two was almost in sight. I descended the next easy-angled slope, circled around the overhanging ice cliff at the right end of the Flying Wing, and waded over to our old tent platforms. At dusk, I cleared away the loose snow from where we'd tented on the way up. Then I found four or five extra fuel canisters hanging in a stuff sack suspended from ice screws pounded into the Wing.

Robert straggled in. We got into our sleeping bags and lit the stove for a brew. Stephen appeared just as darkness fell. Robert produced some tubes of Japanese instant coffee and milk he'd found two days earlier, which we drank. Unfortunately, we hadn't cached any sugar, extra tea bags, or soup here. Later the weather cleared, and Makalu and Chomolönzo thrust into view above the dissipating valley clouds, and the cold black sky, in its turn, froze around us. At Stephen's suggestion that we should try to signal Mimi, Joe, and Paul at Advanced Base Camp—to let them know that we were alive and descending— I stood up and shone my headlamp for some minutes in the direction of our friends at the mountain's base. Several more cups each of hot water quelled our thirst before we each passed out, snug inside our warm feathery wombs.

On the morning of May 15, we could not move from our sleeping bags for several hours. Merely sitting up, let alone the astoundingly difficult feat of standing completely upright, demanded impossible physical endurance. Instead, we talked sluggishly between naps, or passed out collectively. Twice Stephen tried to melt snow for drinking water, but each time the hot stove melted into the snow—and when we fell asleep, it tipped over, spilling the hard-won liquid. Well, it didn't much matter, did it? Did anything really matter? As the daytime temperature grew hotter, in our collective, numbed stupor we were lulled into a passive denial of the truth—the stark, undeniable reality that if we did not leave the Flying Wing, it would soon become our grave.

Although nearly incapacitated by lethargy and inertia, I was becoming increasingly angry at the apparent hopelessness of our situation and the near-ness of my own death. Stephen and Robert lay asleep in their sleeping bags, but for some reason I was slightly more alert. I didn't know why. As I fiddled awk-wardly with the stove canister with my frostbitten fingers, turning the on-off key and fumbling with the lighter to ignite the burner, surges of anger and rage welled up inside me. I turned and shouted at Robert and Stephen. We had to keep going, we had to move, we had to act. We couldn't just lie here and die.

I suppose at this point I recognized that maybe I'd assumed the temporary role of leader, but it was leadership by default. I did not want this duty. I was much more comfortable with a shared democratic leadership, but I also knew that personally I couldn't hold out much longer. Another day without food, two at the most, and I thought I might be finished. If it was my turn to lead us through the fray, then so be it. If through my anger and outrage at my own impending death I could rouse Stephen and Robert, then so much the better.

All three of us had been frostbitten on summit day and during our forced bivouacs during that night of May 12, but Stephen and Robert's injuries didn't appear as severe as mine. Amazingly, Stephen's hands and fingers hadn't been injured at all during his 28,600-foot bivouac. (Back on the South Col, Stephen had related to Robert and me that the miraculous preservation of his digits during his summit bivy was thanks to the warmth of a yak herder's fire, and because of some solicitous care of his health given by the spirit—or presence—of Eric Shipton, the British Everest pioneer of the 1930s.) Stephen's nose, how-ever, had been exposed to the wind that night, and the end had now turned a mottled ashen-gray. The condition of our toes we could only guess at. Because of the extra insulating layer of the supergaiters that Stephen and I each wore over our plastic mountaineering boots, neither of us had as yet inspected our toes. And the toes of his left foot, Stephen mentioned, were numb. Nine of Robert's fingertips, like mine, were covered with the sickening bulges of black frostbite blisters, and Robert added that the toes of his left foot also felt cold.

It was with a growing mutual concern that we discussed our dwindling chances of survival. Our ascent of Everest's Kangshung Face had been the best climb of our lives. It had been so enjoyable, so thrilling, so tremendous. And Stephen had summited. As a team, with Paul, by our collective efforts, we had triumphed. Furthermore, we'd become the best of friends. We'd laughed, cried, and shared a great adventure. To be killed now did not seem at all fair.

As the morning waned, the weather turned cloudy, and held off the midday heat as we tried to prepare ourselves to descend. Let's leave by eleven o'clock, we agreed—before our departure time slipped to twelve noon, one, two, and then three o'clock. Try as we might, we could not pack our belongings, or clip on our crampons, or stand up, that most demanding challenge of all. Every exertion had to be willed by a tremendous effort commanded from our oxygen- and energy-deprived brains. As Robert later phrased it, "we possessed the collective energy of a mouse." We talked very little. Had Joe and Mimi and Paul seen us descending? Or had they seen our headlamps last night? If not, then surely they would be looking through the binoculars from Advanced Base for signs of us.

Hours slipped away, fading seamlessly into mere seconds of consciousness. A third attempt at brewing hot water succeeded. Then Stephen discovered a packet of potato flakes, plus some freeze-dried shrimp and clam chowder. He suggested that we eat it, but the mention of food nauseated me. I declined, but he and Robert ate some mashed potato.

As the afternoon ticked away, a single thought kept circling through my mind. "I must get to Advanced Base so Mimi can take care of me." My fingertips looked increasingly ghastly; my frostbite blisters were growing bigger. After first propping myself up on one elbow, I succeeded in sitting up with a great effort. Two hours later, after repeatedly collapsing onto my platform, I had stuffed my sleeping bag. I continued to urge Robert and Stephen to descend. When I left camp at 3:45 P.M., they were still fastening their crampons. It would be dark at six. The fight for our lives was on.

Almost as soon as I departed, the sky congealed into a bleak gray sheet. Snow-laden monsoon clouds thickened around and above me, blending evenly with Everest's undulating snow slopes and ice cliffs. At least the clouds masked the sun's heat, but soon it was snowing again. Visibility diminished to forty feet. But the waist-deep snow was enveloping, somehow comforting.

To sit down for a long rest would be the easiest thing in the world.

Unconscious of any danger, I slid unexpectedly down a thirty-foot-tall ice slab that had been concealed by a two-foot layer of snow. Landing on a powdery bed, I brushed myself off and began angling to my right down a snow ramp leading into a maze of crevasses that we'd threaded through on our ascent. Nervously, I surveyed my surroundings. Near the ramp's base, I knew that I needed to turn sharply left above one of the largest crevasses. The turn was unmarked; we'd been conserving our remaining bamboo marker wands.

My fatigue was growing. Continuing downhill, I tripped over a short icy step and fell forward. My next thought was the unpleasant realization that I was sliding down the mountain head first, on my back. Instinctively, I clutched at my ice ax, jabbed the metal pick into the snow, swung my legs around, pivoted my body uphill, jabbed my boots and crampon points into the snow— and stopped myself—all in several seconds. Trembling with fear and surges of adrenaline, I kicked my crampon points viciously into the hard ice buried beneath the top snow layer, and managed to reestablish myself on the mountain. Then I looked down.

One hundred feet lower, a gaping crevasse leered its icy grin upward, its fathomless blue void wanting to swallow me whole. By the narrowest of margins, I had escaped death again. I looked uphill. Stephen and Robert were descending slowly toward me; I could see their ghostly figures shuffling through the mist and lightly falling snow. Insanity! It would be dark in an hour; what did we think we were doing, descending so late in the day? I realized then that it would be better to return to Camp Two, use our remaining fuel to brew hot water, get some sleep, and descend early the next morning. We had wasted the entire day.

"This is crazy!" I shouted up to Robert. "I just missed falling into a huge crevasse!" Robert soon arrived beside me and promptly slumped in an exhausted heap. A minute later, Stephen joined us. I pointed to the crevasse just below us, recounted my near-death experience all over again for Stephen's benefit, then launched into a high-strung exhortation on the foolishness of continuing our descent. "If we don't climb back up to Camp Two, we'll be sleeping out in a snowdrift!" I knew that I was sounding unduly melodramatic, but I was adamant. To continue descending in such poor visibility, unroped, surrounded by hidden crevasses, risking a forced bivouac in the open, could easily have fatal consequences. In fact, to do so I thought would be suicidal.

Stephen eventually agreed with me, that we had no option but to retrace our steps back up to the Flying Wing; Robert was too tired to care. Accepting

LHOTSE
(27,890 feet)

MOUNT EVEREST
(29,035 feet)

South Summit

Second

Everest's
Southeast Ridge

Camp Three
(26,000 feet)

Everest's
East Face

South Col

Camp Three ▲ (26,000 feet)

Lhotse's
North Face

Camp Two
▲ (25,000 feet)

Camp One
▲ (23,500 feet)

Flying Wing ▲
and
Camp
Two   (24,500 feet)

Trinity Gullies

NEVEREST
BUTTRESS
(USA, UK,
Canada, 1988)

▲ Helmet
Camp   (22,000 feet)

AMERICAN
BUTTRESS   (USA, 1983)

Jaws of Doom

Camp ▲ (22,500 feet)
One

Pinsetter Camp
▲ (20,500 feet)

Big
Al
Gully

Bowling
Alley

Base
of
East
Ridge

▲
Snow Camp
(19,000 feet)

Advanced Base Camp
(17,800 feet)

Advanced Base Camp
(17,500 feet)

Kangshung Glacier

Lhotse and Everest at dawn from the Kangshung Base Camp, with routes marked on Everest's East Face.

our fate, we willed ourselves uphill towards Camp Two. What had taken one hour for us to descend required three killing hours to reverse.

Just below camp, we were stopped by the thirty-foot, sixty-degree ice slab we'd slid over on the way down. With only one ice ax between the three of us, I was wondering how we would negotiate this section. Somewhat comically, Stephen and I balanced up on our front points, climbing side-by-side, while each holding onto the ice ax. Then, while Stephen clung on tightly to my jacket, I swung the ax until the pick lodged. After repeating this procedure several times, we reached easier angled snow.

Robert watched questioningly from below. "Don't forget to leave that ax!"

"Okay, I'll leave it here, partway up," I replied, then climbed down a move and slammed the pick firmly into the ice. The only problem was that the ax was still two full body lengths above him.

"How am I supposed to climb up to it?" he demanded. I wasn't quite sure, but Robert was inventive. He'd figure something out. He would have to!

Stephen and I continued to camp. It was pitch dark by the time all three of us were resettled under the Flying Wing's ice canopy. We collapsed, having eaten virtually nothing in two days. I made a brew of hot water, and we shared several meager grit-filled mouthfuls. We absolutely had to get an early start in the morning. My strength was dwindling and I knew that our chances for escape had almost run out.

* * * * * * * * * * * * * *

The sun rose gold over Tibet. Feeling the sun's warmth penetrate into my sleeping bag, I peeked outside to see towering Makalu resplendent in the dawn light. Inside my sleeping bag, I was deliciously warm. I could have stayed there forever. That was the problem. I struggled to prepare to leave, made two brews of hot water, and invariably knocked over the stove once or twice. Every action was made with a fragile economy of effort and in the slowest possible motion. Stephen and Robert were awake, too, but they had hardly stirred.

I hounded them. "Stephen," I half-joked, "you're not going to be famous unless you get down alive."

We also talked about the mountaineers who'd perished on K2, the world's second highest mountain, two years earlier. Trapped in a storm at 25,900 feet on *The Abruzzi Spur,* they ran out of food and fuel and died in their sleeping bags, or soon thereafter, making a last ditch effort to descend the mountain.

Amongst those killed were two of Britain's best mountaineers, Alan Rouse and Julie Tullis. It was a tragedy we did not want to repeat.

I remembered what an ordeal it had been to stuff my sleeping bag, so I decided to abandon both my sleeping bag and my parka. By carrying an absolute minimum of weight, I hoped to increase my chances for living. But by abandoning my survival gear, I was irrevocably committing myself to descending to Advanced Base Camp in a single day—or I'd be stranded this evening without a sleeping bag or any warm clothing. I dressed in my capilene expedition-weight underwear, my one-piece pile suit, a pile jacket, hat, and wool mittens. In my pack, I carried half a quart of water, my two cameras, and the rolls of film that I had taken at the South Col and above, on summit day.

Again, I left first, departing from the Flying Wing at about 10 A.M. Robert and Stephen said they were coming but, glancing over my shoulder occasionally, I didn't see them for a couple of hours. Our Everest climb had become a battle. We could encourage each other, we could lend moral support, but physically, we could not carry each other back down Chomolungma. Ultimately, the determination to survive was an individual commodity. Robert later told me that when he'd left Camp Two that morning, he did try to get Stephen moving, but Stephen hadn't budged from his sleeping bag. Would he lie there and die? Robert couldn't tell, but finally Stephen did muster himself to stand up and follow us.

I waded through the softly enveloping snow like an automaton. More snow was falling from the heavens. My leadened limbs moved as if by magic, by rote muscle memory, driven by the primal instinct to live. I wasn't going to give in without a fight. My almost seething anger at our shared frostbite and our possibly impending deaths remained, but I sternly reminded myself not to do anything rash. I had to think my way out of this nightmare. I had to create my own destiny if later I wanted to live it. There had to be a way to escape from this crevasse-riddled, snow-walled prison. I realized, too, that my will to live had also spawned a deep hatred for Everest. Chomolungma, mountain of my dreams, how could you kill me? Our brief views of heaven had come at an enormous cost.

Soon I reached the ice step where I'd stumbled and self-arrested the previous afternoon. Sitting down in the soft snow, resting, I decided I'd gone too far right before. I gambled instead on traversing left around a steep snow rib to look for a big crevasse I remembered vividly from our ascent six days ago. But how much the mountain had changed! It was nearly impossible to recognize landmarks because of the tremendous amount of new snow and the smothering clouds. There remained only the slender hope that I could somehow choose a safe path and not be swallowed alive by a lurking crevasse.

But if I did fall into a crevasse, well, what then? I held our only remaining ice ax in my left hand. We no longer had a climbing rope. Even if I fell into a relatively shallow crevasse, I still might not be able to escape. Death would come quickly, I rationalized, and Stephen and Robert would see which trail *not* to take. It was better to make the effort, to reach out for life no matter what the consequences, than to sit down in the snow and passively die.

Using every route-finding skill that I'd learned in twenty years of climbing, I began breaking trail through the crevasses in an increasing blizzard. I excavated a trench to my left through a deep snow bank, climbed down a steep fifteen-foot incline, and saw several crevasses directly in front of me. None of them looked familiar. Cautiously, I waded toward them, holding my ice ax at the ready in case I fell in. A snow bridge spanned the first crevasse; gingerly I trod out onto it and pooled enough energy to jump over the weak-looking midsection. Breathing easier once I reached the far side, I then jumped a second crevasse and plowed straight ahead, thinking now that maybe I knew the correct direction of our route to Camp One. Not altogether positive of the way, though, I moved ahead slowly and cautiously, and prayed that some higher power would guide me.

Then, through the cloud, I caught another glimpse of orange. I'd found the next bamboo wand! *We were on our route!* The marker wand also gave me a tangibly solid connection with my not-so-distant past. I stopped in my tracks. Paul, Mimi, Joe, Pasang, and Kasang; they were all waiting for us below. We were not completely alone. Finding that slender stem of a once-growing plant shook me from my dream world and gave me new incentive to return to earth.

There was still no sign of either Stephen or Robert, but I was convinced that my partners were alive and would soon be coming. Though they'd been far from energetic looking when I left camp, I never once imagined that they were dead or in trouble. We had survived so much already through our collective will and by sticking together that I began to assume that probably we would all live. Death was a possibility, yet it no longer seemed as certain as it had the day before. But we still had over five thousand vertical feet to descend.

I repositioned myself in my mind's eye at where I thought I was along our route, then set off downhill toward the next landmarks, Stephen's Ice Pitch and the next big crevasse. Halfway down the slope, I located another wand, fallen over and half buried by the new snow. "Keep going," I chanted under my breath, my optimism growing. "Keep going, keep going, keep going, keep going."

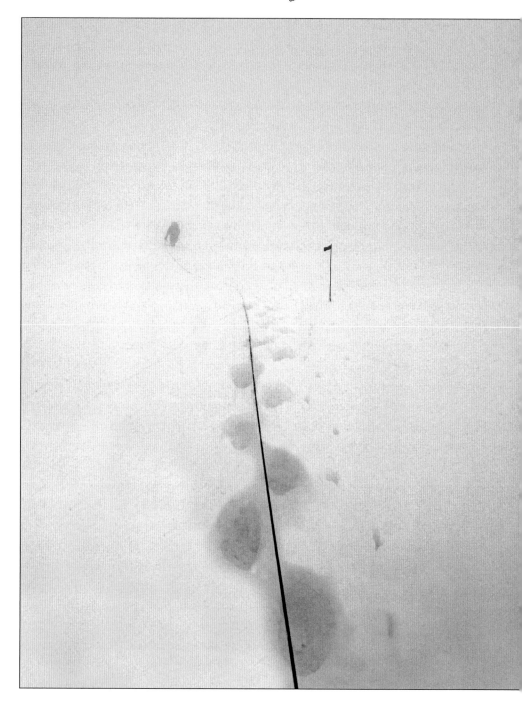

Although this picture was taken on our ascent, eliminate the bamboo marker wand and rope, and it duplicates the conditions we encountered on most of our descent.

I felt as if the clouds surrounding me, thick as ocean fog, could have been sliced like a loaf of bread. Downhill through this misty uncertainty was the only direction that my legs would carry me. As I plunge-stepped down the smooth snow slope, my sixth sense prickled with awareness. An avalanche trap! The gently curving slope was smothered in three feet of new-fallen snow. Had the powder had time to bond with the old layers beneath it? I kicked at the snow with my boots. The adhesion seemed vaguely secure. I continued. What choice did I have? The lambs were being fed to the wolves for breakfast. I vowed with every stumbling forward and downhill step toward safety that if I did live through this climb I would never, ever, do another route that was this dangerous.

What I would have given to be transported virtually anywhere else from the hell of this frozen, frostbitten world! I fantasized warm, white sandy beaches, or sunny Colorado, or the normal everyday things in life—going for a walk, eating dinner with friends. Or events that perhaps too often I'd taken for granted. As soon as I escaped from this hated mountain, I would revel in the mundane.

My strength faltered. My arms began to feel light and buoyant. My legs were lead bars. I breathed from the hollow pit of my empty stomach. My breath gave me back energy to move, but my motions became jerky and slow, one foot placed marginally in front of the other as I pushed through the snow like a human plow, moving closer to salvation and a release from this wretched cage. I couldn't recognize any landmarks, but I knew I must be getting near the steep incline of Stephen's Ice Pitch.

My mind began to falter. Just keep moving, I told myself. Don't dare stop or you'll never start up again. Pace yourself, don't hurry. You don't have the strength to hurry! Don't even bother to think, just let your legs move. Walk. Walk slowly. Breathe. Breathe slowly. Slowly, breathe, slowly.

I heard a shout. Robert was one hundred yards above me.

My companions were alive! In my heart, I'd known all along that they were okay. Once more, I began my halting, awkward movements downhill. The next crevasse was 150 feet lower. It was wide—and unfathomably deep. One slip and I'd disappear without a trace.

Tilted straight into the crevasse, the snow slope I was standing on was church-roof steep. I began to traverse left across it, toward the snow bridge we'd used to cross this impasse on our ascent. The snow was bottomless. Each footstep collapsed into the one below it. I realized that I'd descended too far. I would have to climb back up and make a higher diagonal traverse. I began retracing my steps, and yelled up to Robert to head left earlier than I had.

"Left?" he responded weakly. I nodded, too exhausted to speak. I'd eaten nothing in over two days, and had consumed only a few cups of tea and a bowl of noodle soup in over four days. I thought the climb back up those hundred feet would finish me off. Moving against gravity at that altitude, in our condition, was an incomprehensible trial.

"I'm not feeling very good, you know that?" my brain said.

"Neither am I," answered my body.

"Well, don't let me down now," said my brain.

"What do you mean?" my body replied. *"You always told me you liked a challenge. You're getting one now, aren't you?"*

My eyelids grew heavy; my head began to swim.

"Well, you always said you wanted to experience the ultimate challenge, to feel what life was like on the edge," yelled my body to my brain. *"And guess what, you idiot—I have news for you. THIS IS WHAT YOU WANTED, AND THIS IS WHAT IT'S LIKE! How much longer do you think you can hold on?"*

I managed to take another uphill step. Through the mist and the clouds I saw a second stumbling figure appear. It was Stephen! "So you're alive, too," I thought. Good for you.

We had reached Stephen's Ice Pitch, now buried beneath several feet of powder snow. Angling left, we carefully plowed a trench down the slope. After passing Robert, Stephen and I tiptoed along a ledge underneath a vertical ice wall, across the snow bridge spanning the crevasse, and began the final slog toward the top of our fixed ropes, still a thousand feet below.

Again, I went in front, breaking trail. The snow bridge and ice wall were solid landmarks I remembered from our ascent. We were definitely on route, and I felt a new burst of energy. However, we'd placed far too few wands to mark this section, and I followed my instincts down the short ridges and small snowfields that characterized this portion of the route, relieved that the worst of the avalanche and crevasse danger was at last behind us.

Eyes shifted nervously from side to side, searching for the correct route. Here? There? Maybe that way. Legs faltered, stopped, then started. Energy, what was energy? Air was food. My muscles had degenerated into near uselessness, but with each downhill step I began to gain nourishment from an invisible ally. My oxygen supply was being boosted by the increasing atmospheric pressure.

Move legs, move! You've got to keep moving! I remembered Fritz Wiessner's words, and began to chant them over and over again in a solemn incantation:

"Sometimes you've got to fight it."

"You've just got to fight it." Rest. Breathe.

"Sometimes you've got to fight it."

"You've got to fight it." A few more staggering steps.

"You've got to fight it."

"You've just got to fight it."

My breath became labored. Stay in control! Left foot, right foot, another few steps. Good!

"You've got to fight it."

"Fight it!"

I found another bamboo wand at the start of a snowy prow. I walked to the end of the plank; the ridge was corniced and overhung on both sides. We must have climbed up one side. I returned to the wand. Stephen and I walked to the drop-off for a second look.

"I think we went this way," he said with surprising conviction, and began to descend a steep snow trough. Suddenly there was a loud crack, then a *whoosh,* and Stephen was caught in a small avalanche. Riding atop the wave of falling snow, he flew down a fifty-foot drop and landed in a huge mound of soft snow on the flat terrace below. Springing up out of the drift like a hippo jumping out of a mud hole, Stephen shouted cheerfully: "Yes, that's definitely the right way!"

Shaking my head in disbelief, I returned to the wand. A shorter trough led down to the left. Several steps later, I was also avalanched, and fell twenty feet. I brushed myself off. We continued. Stephen broke trail. We could no longer see Robert, but Stephen assured me he had seen him coming.

Then I noticed Stephen had stopped. I joined him.

"Don't you think we should try over there?" I suggested, motioning to our right down the next snow slope.

"What?" Stephen said, seemingly perplexed.

"Well, it looks better that way to me," I replied.

"Ed! We're at the fixed ropes!" he blurted out, pointing to a short piece of orange eight-millimeter rope emerging from the snow.

My gaze settled fondly on the colored length of rope. I couldn't believe it. We were going to live! I reached over, embraced Stephen in a bear hug and shook him in celebration. All we had to do was rappel three thousand feet to the glacier. Maybe we could still get to Advanced Base Camp tonight. Before starting down the ropes, we glimpsed Robert some distance above us.

"You okay?" I shouted up to him.

"See you at Camp One!" he yelled, adding that he was fine, just slow.

"No—not at Camp One. We're going to Advanced Base no matter what!" I shouted in reply. Robert waved back, and Stephen and I once again began to descend. We dug our harnesses and descenders out from under three feet of new snow (we'd cached them here to save carrying their extra weight any higher), and I strapped on my harness and immediately began racing down the ropes, hurrying from one anchor to the next across the Jumble. I'd been so concerned with staying alive that, until I started rappelling, I hadn't given my stiff, wooden fingers much attention. It took a while to get used to holding the rope, and for the first time I began to realize that my fingers, especially those of my left hand, were very, very cold. I now began to worry. My fingers were not mending as I had hoped. In fact, they felt much worse.

Laboriously, I ripped the fixed ropes out from under their snow mantle. I felt a surge of relief seeing that the Jaws of Doom crevasse had not widened or collapsed. But the seracs had definitely moved downhill, because the ropes spanning the Tyrolean traverse were stretched tighter than ever! I crossed Jaws and continued down to the Webster Wall. There, the rope disappeared into the snow, so I unclipped from my rappel and walked without a belay to the edge of the seventy-five-foot overhanging ice cliff. The pink, eleven-millimeter rope down the Webster Wall was buried deeply, but by stamping out a platform and carefully peering over the edge, I just caught a glimpse of it hanging free.

I dug the rope out of the snow and rappelled to Camp One. It was 5:30 P.M. when Stephen joined me. We had a short discussion about whether we should continue down, or remain here for the night. What little body warmth I still possessed I was rapidly losing through my frostbitten fingers. Since I no longer had a sleeping bag or a parka, I told him that at all costs I must keep moving, to generate heat and to stay warm.

When we'd left Camp One almost nine days before, we'd collapsed our two tents to protect them from damage. They were now buried under several feet of snow. I hardly recognized the campsite. Stephen pointed out a large trough created by an ice fall of recent vintage, directly over where our tents had been pitched. It would have taken us an hour of hard work to excavate them, and since the descent from Camp One to Advanced Base took two hours in good conditions, I lobbied strongly to continue. Reluctantly, Stephen agreed.

I started down the snow slope below camp. The fixed rope here was also completely buried. All of our nine- and eleven-millimeter static fixed ropes were white in color (we'd gotten a good discount on the price) which made them virtually impossible to detect (hence the cheap cost!) against a white snow slope. Now where was that darned rope? Unroped, I gingerly climbed as far down as I dared, and began digging with my ice ax. Below me was a two-thousand-foot drop straight into Big Al. As I continued to chop at the snow, suddenly I heard a pronounced crack—and the slope avalanched just *above* me. Two feet of silky snow cascaded through my legs and into the fearsome abyss. I gripped my ice ax with a burst of adrenaline—and didn't fall.

"Oh, there's the rope," I said matter-of-factly, spotting it at the base of the avalanche fracture. Stephen volunteered to go first, and we rappelled to the bottom of Paul's Ice Pitch, with Stephen digging out each rope length from under the snow. It was a peaceful evening, the bad weather was clearing, and I remember even being nostalgic rappelling past the Greyhound Bus—the first Cauliflower Tower—thinking fondly that I'd never see it so close up again.

Once more, we were about to be caught out in the dark on the mountain. I became increasingly worried, and told myself to stay calm and in control. We'd soon be down. Paul, Mimi, and Joe would take care of us. It was getting dark, no stopping it, and we had no choice but to deal with the situation like we'd dealt with the rest of this hellish descent. Which was as best as we could.

As darkness closed upon Everest, we discovered that neither of our head-lamps worked. Then Stephen fumbled and dropped his spare headlamp bulb.

When Stephen couldn't pull up the next section of fixed rope, I rappelled down and joined him at the bottom of Paul's Ice Pitch. Taking my ice ax with him, Stephen headed down and chopped the rope free, inch by inch, from beneath a two-inch-thick layer of ice that had frozen over it during the previous week. It was painstaking work—and one poorly aimed blow could cut through the rope. I hadn't thought our situation could worsen. It just had. I was shivering so hard my limbs trembled. For the next several hours, all I could hear was Stephen's chopping, then his much anticipated signal of "Right!" or "Off!" which meant that he'd reached the next anchor and it was my turn to descend.

But something wasn't right. I looked down. The toe bail of my right crampon had come unclipped. Held by its ankle strap, the crampon dangled uselessly below my boot. With frostbitten fingers, I couldn't fix it. Rappelling down the ropes at night with no headlamp, frozen fingers, and only one crampon became an endless nightmare. Multiple sections of rope were so well-frozen into the mountain's icy coating that it was impossible to pull up enough slack to clip our figure-of-eight descenders in for a proper rappel. The painful alternative was a wrist rappel. This meant clipping the rope into a short safety sling and a locking carabiner attached to our harness, then wrapping the ice-encrusted rope around our wrists and forearms for friction. Gripping the rope as tightly as I could with my useless fingers, I would begin to slide down the rope. Several times I lost my grip, and proceeded to fall, slide, and bounce down the slope until my safety sling stopped me at the next anchor attaching the rope to the mountain. I prayed that a stupid mistake wouldn't kill me when I was now so close to safety.

Stephen led the entire descent down the buttress. We were more dead than alive when we reached the Kangshung Glacier at about 1 A.M. Using our short length of eleven-millimeter rope stashed at the resting rock, we roped up. The recent warm weather and monsoon clouds hadn't allowed the glacier surface to freeze at night, and the crust was now in about the worst possible condition. Instead of well-frozen snow which would have supported our weight, a thin, breakable snow skin masked over a mush of unstable depth hoar—loosely packed snow resembling large Styrofoam pellets. When the crust broke, as it did about every thirty feet, it was like plunging feet first into a jar of marbles. Extricating oneself was extremely difficult, especially in our weakened state.

We attempted to keep our sense of humor about the situation. This, too, became impossible. Hopefulness and grim determination gave way to anger and sudden outbursts. I slipped back into my old habit, getting pissed off at Venables for moving too quickly, for pulling the rope tight and yanking me off my feet, while Stephen became increasingly angry with me for not moving faster to get back to camp.

About halfway to Advanced Base, Stephen began a ceaseless tirade for a hot cup of tea. *"Paul! Mimi! Joe! TEA!"* he shouted at the top of his lungs about every five minutes. I was craving a hot orange drink and Stephen wanted his bloody cup of tea. That wasn't too much to ask for, was it? We stumbled across the glacier, got lost, finally found our way through the crevasses, and inched progressively closer to camp—to safety, to warmth, to our friends.

"Paul! Mimi! Joe! TEA!"

Suddenly, I fell into another pit of unstable snow. We were roped together about fifty or sixty feet apart to safeguard each other from hidden crevasses. Stephen's patience grew thinner and thinner as I struggled to escape from this new bear trap. But my right leg—and the loose crampon dangling uselessly beneath my boot—remained firmly rooted in the oatmeal-thick concrete.

"Ed, can't you do something?" Stephen protested after watching me struggle in vain for fifteen minutes. I could tell his patience was at an end.

"You look like a bloody floundering bird!" he bellowed.

We were in the middle of a now-starry Everest night, barely alive, and it seemed we were never going to reach camp, even though safety was probably only minutes away. Stephen was angry, my leg was firmly stuck, and all he wanted was a hot cup of tea. I didn't know what to do. I couldn't budge my leg or my boot, and I was completely exhausted. I leaned back against the snow to catch my breath. We were so close to camp, but I couldn't escape from this damn hole! Then I glanced back up toward Stephen—but Stephen had gone.

After untying from his end of the climbing rope without a word, Stephen headed toward camp. I watched his ghost-like figure disappear into the darkness. Moments later, from the crest of the moraine ridge off to my left came a sudden and animated commotion. Other voices rang out, friends' voices, Paul's and Mimi's voices, shouting and exclaiming, and I knew we were safe. I struggled again to free my boot from its slushy prison, but I couldn't. Slumping backwards, I simply waited and looked up at the stars.

Then, momentarily, a wavy beam of light ran along the moraine beside me and a familiar soothing voice shouted out my name. It was Paul Teare. I had never been so happy to hear a friend's voice, a voice which a day or two earlier I was not sure I would ever hear again. I shouted his name back, and Paul bounded across the snow toward me, falling in and leaping back out like a gazelle, springing forward until he reached me and threw his arms around my neck.

"Why didn't you let us know you were alive?" Paul demanded. My attempt to signal from Camp Two with my headlamp had obviously been unsuccessful. Paul asked if I was all right, and I had to admit that . . . well, actually, I wasn't. I told him that my hands were frostbitten, but that my feet, I thought, were alright. In his exuberance over our survival—that we were, amazingly enough, still alive—our frostbite was fairly inconsequential.

"I'm so glad you guys are okay!" he exclaimed. Then Paul asked after Robert, about his condition, and where he was. I replied that Robert was fine, just a bit slower, and that he would be following us down soon.

With Paul shouldering me, I pried my right boot out of the snow and we retraced his tracks back to the moraine where the walking was easier. Minutes later, back in camp, I was greeted with a joyous welcome home hug from Mimi. Joe was in Base Camp, sending word to the Chinese for a helicopter to come look for us, and Paul and Mimi had been so distressed, thinking we had all died, that they could only sleep by taking sleeping pills.

It was 4 A.M. on May 17.

The long hike home: the last few hundred yards to Advanced Base Camp.

I collapsed beside Stephen inside my dome tent, grateful, so very grateful, for sleep and rest and warmth, just to lie down flat and rest and be warm, and to drink a hot drink, even if it was grapefruit juice, to feel it trickle past my parched lips and down my scratchy sandpaper throat before consciousness failed me. I do not really remember what happened during the next two days. I can recall only a string of hazy dreams: Paul putting me on warm, hissing oxygen, the clear plastic mask slipping over my face, while Mimi tenderly soaked Stephen's and my fingers and toes in sterile warm water baths and fed us soup and crackers, and later, Kasang stared blankly at us, not understanding and very worried, and Ang Chu's brother, Sonam, was crouched beside Kasang, and Sonam's body was trembling, he was so frightened and concerned for us, but then Pasang's fatherly face looked down at me, gave me his comforting smile, and his calm hand reached out to gently hold my shoulder and reassure me that everything would be all right, before Robert, after spending the night sitting alone in the mountain snows one last time, finally returned safely to camp with Joe who'd hiked out to help him, and Robert stood in the sunshine outside our tent before he bent over, peered quizzically at Stephen and me lying inside, looking like death—and Robert said to us, grinning that Robert grin: "So, boys, how are we feeling today?"

What I remember most is the sweet delicious sensation of being alive, of lying in my warm sleeping bag on the soft foam pad inside of the yellow tent, and of savoring that simple radiant joy, that great gift, of having survived.

And drinking the hot grapefruit juice drink.

Chapter 14

Rhododendron Blossoms

I went into the woods because I wished to live deliberately, to front only the essential facts of life, and see if I could not learn what it had to teach, and not, when I came to die, discover that I had not lived.

—Henry David Thoreau

*M*imi and Paul selflessly devoted themselves to our care, making round after round of soup and tea to bring us back to life. Our wounded hands and feet were sterilized in warm water iodine baths to help thaw and cleanse our injured tissue. The life-giving oxygen flowing into my lungs and body gave me the slender hope that some of my frostbite might be reversible. Later, inspecting my frozen fingertips with Mimi, I realized to my horror that during Stephen's and my epic nighttime descent of the fixed ropes, while clenching the ice-covered rope in my frozen fingers, I'd ripped open the frostbite blisters on eight of my fingertips. On only two fingers, my right thumb and index finger, were the blisters intact. The remainder were

Left: Rhododendron blossoms in the sacred valley of the Kama Chu, Tibet.

shredded. The first time I saw my fingertips, I stared at the torn skin in incredulous shock, but consoled myself that the underlying tissue was red. I clung to the positive belief that, obviously, my fingers would heal, and my companions encouraged me to maintain my optimism.

Paul's descent from the South Col had gone considerably better than expected. He'd managed to descend the entire face to Advanced Base—nearly eight thousand vertical feet—alone and in a single day! Our tracks in the snow had made the going easier for him, Paul told us, and although exhausted and dehydrated, he felt better as he lost altitude. He had arrived in camp by 6 P.M., much to Joe and Mimi's considerable surprise.

Robert, Stephen, and I were four days overdue returning from the summit. But because we'd previously discussed alternate descent routes with Mimi and Joe—that if trapped by storm at Camp Three on the Col, we might descend via the *South Col Route* into Nepal—that possibility had been weighed by them after we had disappeared. With increasing despair, Paul, Mimi, and Joe had concluded that either we were dead, or we had descended the mountain by another route. Joe rushed to Base Camp to report to Mr. Yang and Mr. Shi in Kharta that three climbers were missing and that a helicopter search was needed.

By mid-May, the expedition had already taken longer than anticipated. Back in New York, Wendy Davis telephoned China, seeking information on our whereabouts. What she learned was the news from Lhasa: that the expedition was overdue because three climbers were missing. "My impression was that three climbers were missing—and presumed dead," she later told me.

Without additional confirmation of our rumored fate, however, Wendy decided to wait before informing others on our support team, or the media, which meant she suffered her dark fears in private. Robert had instructed her to return to Beijing if anyone died, so she went about renewing her Chinese visa, "with tears rolling down my face," she told me. "I was totally consumed by the news. It wasn't until a week later that I learned everyone was alive, and that Stephen had reached the summit."

After our return to Advanced Base Camp, Mimi and Joe began the tiresome chore of packing our gear and tents for the Tibetan villagers from Kharta to carry out. After two days of horizontal recuperation at ABC, I finally crawled from my tent. Robert and Stephen were already up and about. They seemed surprisingly fit, I thought, even though we were all bandaged and patched to varying degrees. Feeling extremely unsteady, I eased my swollen feet into Sorel boots, grabbed a ski pole for support, and began the long hobble to Base Camp.

I had never before grown to hate a climb or a mountain, yet I now definitely hated Everest. Stopping for a rest along the trail, I could not even bring myself to look at the route we had climbed.

Years of practice had taught me how far I could physically push myself on a climb, but on the hike back to Base Camp, when I had real trouble walking, and noticed that my breath came in unpleasant agitated gulps, I realized that our foodless four-day descent from the South Col had pushed me farther than ever before. While Stephen and Robert returned to Base in the speedy (for invalids) time of six and a half hours (the usual journey took two), I crested the final moraine after a nine-hour ordeal. I had been transformed into a feeble old man.

A wet mist blowing up valley softly parted in front of me to reveal the colored tents of our cherished meadow home. After two months of sensory deprivation, there was no more joyous a sight than spiky green grass and tiny clusters of pink and white alpine flowers. Pasang's smile was wide and welcoming; his flock had returned to roost. "This time I very happy," he told me. "Nobody die." We had survived the mountain, but by the slenderest of margins.

The next morning, one by one, Mimi called Stephen and Robert and me into the Base Camp cook tent to bath and sterilize our injuries, and to change our dressings and bandages. When it was my turn, I sat among her medical supplies, staring blankly at my frostbitten fingers while she carefully snipped away the vile coagulated layers of blood and pus-soaked cotton gauze.

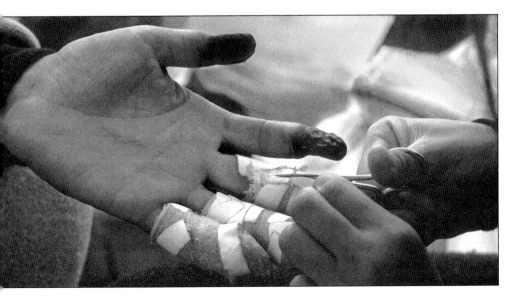

Two days after my frostbite blisters broke, my fingertips had mummified. Joe Blackburn

Until that moment, I had never imagined that I would lose even part of a finger or a toe. But when my eyes saw the black and lifeless, hard, desiccated end joints of eight of my fingertips, I realized with sickening revulsion and overwhelming grief that I was very badly injured. The mountain of my dreams had exacted a horrible price. Everest had killed my fingers and toes.

Images of sunny rock climbing in Eldorado Canyon near my Colorado home suddenly floated in front of my vacant stare, and my brain faltered, switching back and forth between the golden vision of Eldorado and the dead reality of my coal-black, mummified, ruined fingers, especially those of my left hand. Sobs wracked my body until they reached the deepest recesses of my soul; tears flowed uncontrollably down my cheeks.

I am left-handed, I thought. Will I ever be able, again, to hold a pencil or a pen? Write a letter to a friend? Or sign my name? All these thoughts flashed through my mind in those first seconds of disbelief. I was convinced that my life as a climber—a life of adventure and challenge, the life I cherished—was now ruined. I had destroyed the only life that I knew through a preventable, careless mistake—taking off my outer gloves on summit day. I had allowed myself to get frostbitten. Mimi tried to comfort me, but through my moaning and anguished sobs I could no longer hear her soft spoken consolations.

The grim reality of Stephen's left foot—three months after the climb. Stephen Venables

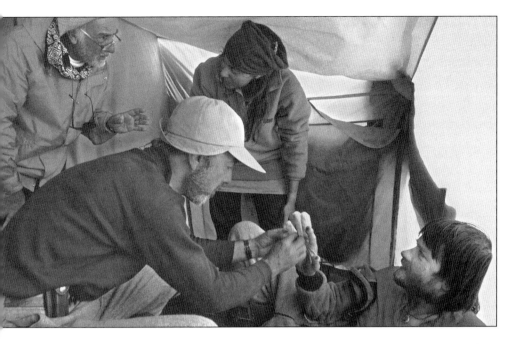

Mimi confers with Dr. Fero Sadeghian and Dr. Nas Eftekhar. Joe Blackburn

That same morning, by fortunate coincidence, a small American trekking group, including two New York surgeons, Dr. Fero Sadeghian and Dr. Nas Eftekhar, wandered into our Base Camp. During the entire expedition, they were the only outsiders we saw. After examining my wounds, the doctors reassured me that my fingers would heal and probably to a greater extent than I now thought possible. They also assured Mimi that her daily treatment regimen of sterile warm water baths, fresh dressings, and preventative antibiotics was the best protocol to follow for treating such serious frostbite injuries.

Stephen and Robert, too, were badly injured. Nearly all of Stephen's left toes had been frostbitten—the dividing line between the dead and healthy tissue was sickeningly evident. His toes were black; his foot was pink. And amazingly, his fingers were entirely unscathed. Robert had frozen the tips of nine of his fingers and part of two or three left toes. When my frostbite blisters had broken open during our nighttime rappelling down the buttress, precious fluid had been lost. Now, in just the past two days, my fingertips and toes had virtually mummified, turning jet black and rock hard. (We each wore different brands of boots, but interestingly—by some physiological fluke—all three of us were frostbitten on our left foot only. Our right feet were fine, just extremely tender.)

The surgeons recommended that Stephen and I be carried on stretchers to Kharta to minimize further trauma. Robert was less injured; he decided to hike.

I had known two mountaineers who died on Everest, Víctor Hugo Trujillo and Roger Marshall. Certainly, before our Kangshung Face climb began, I knew that the goal of climbing Everest—particularly by a new route and without bottled oxygen—might demand the ultimate sacrifice, the loss of my own life. For months in advance, I had tried to mentally prepare myself to face this possibility. During our first days on the *Neverest Buttress* in April, I'd imagined that death or injury, if it did come, would be decidedly swift: from a fall, an avalanche, a collapsed serac, or rockfall. I had accepted the possibility that I or one of my teammates might die. The risks, I had felt, were justified by the opportunity to test ourselves on a new route up the world's highest mountain.

Staring through my tears at my black and dead fingertips, I felt my life pivot. And I wondered, certainly not for the last time, if the risks had been justified. In twenty-one years of climbing, I had never been badly injured as a result of my own actions. Now this. I had always been so careful to protect and promote my body's good health. Obviously, I felt a particularly strong affection for my fingers, hands, and toes, the bodily instruments of my desire. As a rock climber and mountaineer, my life blood flowed through them. Now I had made an all-too-human error, a misjudgment, and I must learn to live with my mistakes. Removing my outer mitts to take the sunrise pictures on May 12 initiated my frostbite, though it was additional events and circumstances—bivouacing without a sleeping bag at 27,000 feet, wading through deep snow without food for three days, holding my metal ice ax in my left hand—that had sealed my fate.

I slowly began to accept the lingering agony of my frostbite and that my life had irrevocably changed, but merging theory and fact was painfully difficult. In a strange way, during these first few days as an invalid, my brain actually began to help make my transition easier: I rapidly forgot what it had been like to have functioning hands. During the next three weeks, I learned that all the fingertips on my left hand, three fingertips on my right hand, and parts of three toes on my left foot, eventually, would all have to be amputated. I also was reminded of Maurice Herzog, the great French mountaineer who in 1950 made the first ascent of Annapurna, the first eight-thousand-meter peak climbed—and lost all of his fingers and toes to frostbite. Yet in the years since, Herzog had led an exemplary life, becoming Minister of Youth and Sports under de Gaulle.

Although I tried not to dwell on my frostbite injuries, it was nearly impossible to ignore my physical and mental pain, and those several days at Base Camp waiting for the porters to come were amongst the most agonizing of my life. What would I do with my life? I found that I could no longer smile, or join in, or laugh. My sociability, my future, my very humanity—each had been irrevocably stripped from my being, stolen and ravaged by one careless impulse.

The evening before we departed Base Camp, we celebrated our success, and I felt temporarily revived. First, we toasted Stephen's accomplishment in reaching the summit, and his becoming the first Briton to do so without using bottled oxygen. Then Stephen proposed a toast to John Hunt, our honorary expedition leader, whose personal recommendation had made Stephen's Everest dream come true. We also toasted our sponsors, Kodak, Rolex Watch USA, Burroughs Wellcome Pharmaceuticals, and American Express, who had believed in our dream. Then there was "our dedicated photographer," Joe, and "our marvelous doctor," Mimi, who'd each supported us so tirelessly. Mimi was also awarded extra praise for so graciously enduring the company of seven generally unwashed men—and for setting the new high-altitude tap dancing world record of 18,500 feet. Whisky and *chang* flowed freely during our toasts to Pasang and Kasang, whose presence had also been invaluable. Lastly we toasted British Everest pioneer George Mallory, whom we recognized for his inspiration.

After dinner, I passed around my copy of *The Mystery of Mallory and Irvine* for my friends to sign. I must admit I was very touched when Stephen wrote, "To Ed, with thanks for getting us alive down the Neverest Buttress."

* * * * * * * * * * * * * *

We departed Base Camp on May 23. The previous day, 130 Tibetan men, women, and children converged on our camp like bees swarming after summer nectar. We gave them extra food and promised them our highly prized, blue plastic barrels if they got us safely to Kharta. A return note from Mr. Yang and Mr. Shi said, not surprisingly, that a helicopter rescue was completely out of the question. Receiving Paul's updated note that the three climbers had been found, but were injured, they promised to send stretchers, but these never came. Luckily, we had several stout wooden poles at camp from which Paul, Joe, and Pasang constructed two sturdy stretchers, weaving climbing rope between them as support netting. Paul took my bolt kit—never used on the mountain— to drill holes in the wood to fasten metal pipe cross-pieces between the poles.

Our two campsites were each cleaned, all rubbish burned and then buried in a deep earthen pit. Although we left the Kama Valley cleaner than it was

The villagers from Kharta carried me away from Everest. Pasang Norbu Sherpa

when we arrived, we sincerely regretted not being able to strip our equipment and ropes from our climb and our camps, as we had always intended to do on our final descent. In the end, we'd had strength enough only to save ourselves.

For a change, the villagers were delightfully eager to shoulder their loads. Stephen and I appraised the two groups of Tibetans, eight men and boys of varying ages, who would carry us. To prevent any one person from tiring, they worked rotating shifts in two teams of four, with one person holding each corner of the stretcher. Dressed for warmth in my spare expedition suit, I lay down, albeit a bit nervously, on the stretcher. Pasang laughed heartily, taking pleasure in anchoring me to it with a loop of climbing rope tied securely around my waist; then we were off.

The ride was rough, a constant up and down jostling similar, I imagined, to the lurching of a camel. I was thankful to be off of my feet, which in recent days had grown increasingly painful. Every ten to fifteen minutes the Tibetans switched positions, one group alternating with their friends who, in turn, carried the communal camp kit, their patched and worn tent, some blankets, pots and eating utensils, a supply of *tsampa,* and a couple of containers of *chang.*

As the Tibetans grew confident of their ability to carry Stephen and me—no mean feat—they ran boisterously downhill whenever a section permitted.

For possessing a photograph of the Dalai Lama, this man could be jailed—or worse.

I'd been frostbitten—that seemingly most preventable of mountaineering injuries—yet it had not, at the time, been avoidable.

Spring had transformed Lhatse, our "pre-Base Camp," into an unrecognizable grass lawn. I straggled in last and immediately lay down next to Stephen, who was curled up in a protective fetal ball on the ground, and already fast asleep.

But today there was no stopping the Tibetans. The home fires were burning. Our carriers jogged eagerly along the trail transporting Stephen and I like charioteering emperors toward the next campsite, at the junction with the Kharta Chu. Pasang and Kasang ran beside us, reporting that Ang Chu had rushed on ahead to his house to pick up his wife's specially prepared *tomba,* a favorite local brew made by pouring boiling water over fermented barley.

Suddenly, my crew careened off route, running down a steep boulder- and bush-strewn hillside in an apparent shortcut to camp—if we didn't crash. Stephen's gang played it sane, following the normal path along the hillside, but there it was, competition right to the very end! Whooping with success and relief, we finally reached the valley floor, passed a goat herder's tent pitched by a burbling stream, and startled a covey of young Tibetan girls chopping wood.

With both of my hands bandaged like cloth clubs, I found it hard to be much help setting up camp. I sat on a boulder watching the porters trail in, while Paul dashed from job to job, erecting my tent so I could lie down, shouting at the porters to leave the loads in a pile, and rummaging through the blue barrels for sleeping bags, foam pads, and ingredients for the evening meal. As the only one of the four of us to survive the climb unscathed, Paul worked tirelessly during our return to Kharta.

The after-dinner drinks at the Kharta Chu camp were a joyful release for everyone, although the celebration proved too demanding for Stephen, who periodically passed out and had to be propped up for his ritual sips of *tomba.* Drunk communally through bamboo straws out of a single bowl, the homemade brew was delicious. Ang Chu's dimples had never been more pronounced. He and Kasang were obviously relieved to be almost home. Our camaraderie was sublimely enjoyable. We had indeed become one family, and this was our last night to enjoy the radiant faces of those who had made our expedition so very memorable. Pasang, Kasang, and Ang Chu soon locked their arms around each other's shoulders in a traditional Tibetan dance, stamping out the heavy beat with their feet. Later, so I heard—a rock 'n' roll disco got into full swing with Mimi and Paul demonstrating new dance steps to their eager pupils—but by then, I'd long since collapsed in my tent.

Victory! Ed, Mimi, Stephen, and Robert at ABC, May 19. Joe Blackburn

Ed sterilizes his fingers in an iodine bath at Base while Mimi helps. Joe Blackburn

Stephen after his bath at Base Camp. Joe Blackburn

Top Left: *Rhododendron blossoms in the Kama Valley.*

Top Right: *Ed leaves Base Camp, carried by the Kharta villagers.*
Pasang Norbu Sherpa

Below: *Paul, Pasang, Kasang, and Ang Chu celebrate.* Stephen Venables

Above: *Reinhold Messner inspects
Ed's frostbitten fingers in Lhasa. "Pshht!!"*
Joe Blackburn

Below: *Jane Pauley prepares to interview Robert Anderson on
The Today Show. Note Anderson's black, mummified fingertips.*
Joe Blackburn

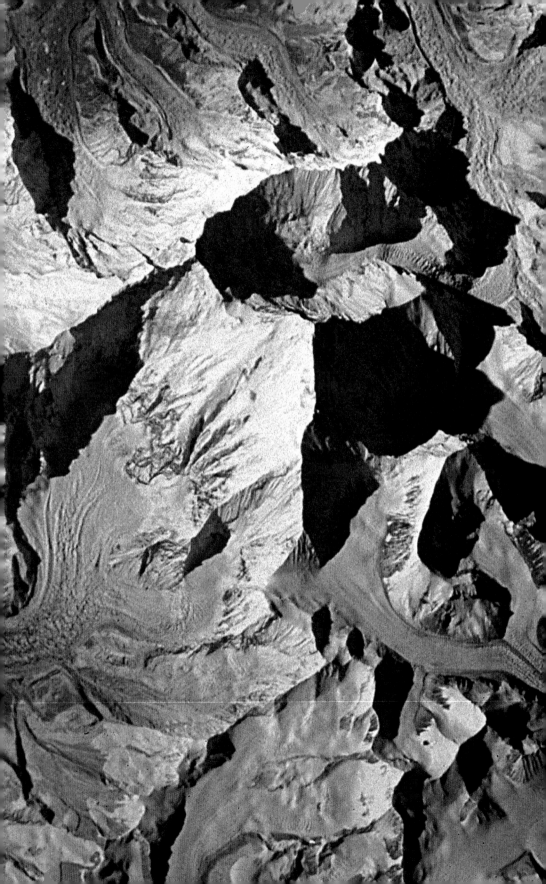

The Mount Everest massif
photographed from the
Space Shuttle in 1996.

Mount Everest at left center;
Rongbuk Glacier on right.

John M. Grunsfeld / NASA

Lenticular clouds cover the summits of Everest, Nuptse, and Lhotse. Glenn Dunmire

Moonrise out of Mount Everest's South Col, captured during a seven-hour time exposure from Gokyo Ri. Ed Webster

The Big View from the summit of Cholatse:
of Everest, Nuptse, Lhotse, and Makalu.   Ed Webster

Moonlight bathes Chomolungma's Kangshung Face, Tibet.

Viewed from Mallory's Meadow Camp at Pethang Ringmo. Dale Vrabec

Our one-year reunion at Joe Blackburn's studio in New York City in 1989.

Left to Right:

Norbu Tenzing Norgay
Mads Anderson
Sandy Wylie
Joe Blackburn
Wendy Davis
Robert Anderson
Roland Puton
Miriam Zieman
Miklos Pinther
Ed Webster
Billy Squier

Sitting:

Paul Teare
Stephen Venables

Ed climbing Valkyrie *(VS or 5.7) on the Roaches in England in March, 1991.*
Julian Freeman-Attwood

Paul never lost his humor or enthusiasm on our hike out. The lake is Shurim Tso.

A young porter carried me piggy-back to Ang Chu's house the following morning. As I sat high on his shoulders, he ran down the hill below camp, then across fields and irrigation ditches to Ang Chu's home where a throng had assembled. I noticed Robert and Pasang in the midst of the crowd. Pasang had rented a horse for Robert to ride! With a jaunty wave of his hand, Robert set off bouncing down the trail on the back of a small but sturdy Tibetan pony.

I was again escorted downvalley on my elevated throne. Ahead, I noticed three western trekkers alongside the trail. Each held a camera armed with a zoom lens, and all three cameras were pointed at me. One of the trio was Joe.

"What's the spectacle?" I yelled.

"You are," Joe said. "I thought I'd bring Galen Rowell to help photograph."

And there was Galen, athletically hopping from rock to rock with two Nikons at the ready. We had never met. I said hello, and Galen told me about his *National Geographic* assignment to photograph local Tibetans chopping down the endangered forested habitat of the lower Kama Valley. After a couple of pleasant miles, Galen ran on ahead to meet his wife Barbara at the roadhead.

The day grew hotter as we traveled alongside the Kharta River. Children spilled out from the villages to greet us, laughing and shouting at the unusual caravan proceeding past their doors, and this funny-dressed man being carried aloft. Carefree and boisterous, my team began singing in full throat. Then, at long last, we rounded a bend and saw two Nissan jeeps parked by the wooden bridge where we'd camped on the first night of our approach, three months earlier.

The Rowells kindly squeezed Stephen and me into their jeep, and we rode the last five miles to the Kharta compound in modern luxury. Robert came galloping in on his steed, and we thanked Galen and Barbara for their help and assistance, before they continued on with their journey to western Tibet.

After an initially cordial welcome by Mr. Yang and Mr. Shi, our reunion rapidly soured into a string of loud shouting matches. We'd sent word to them over a week before to arrange for jeeps to transport us to Lhasa and Kathmandu, but the jeeps hadn't arrived. With our wounds increasingly in danger of infection, it was imperative that we reach medical care as soon as possible.

Then a worse problem arose. Our Liaison Officer, Mr. Yang, hadn't brought enough local Chinese currency (renminbi, or RMB) to pay the local villagers their remaining wages for portering our loads for us. Robert had spent every yuan of his Chinese currency to get us to Base Camp. "How were you intending to pay?" Mr. Yang asked, trying to shift the onus onto us. I gently reminded him that it was the CMA's responsibility to pay for all of our local expenditures, and it wasn't our fault that he didn't bring enough cash along. Foreigners were not even supposed to have "the People's Money." When Mr. Yang tried to hold us accountable for other newly discovered expenses, Robert exploded in anger.

We roomed for three hot days in the dusty Kharta compound. And still no vehicles came. As our food dwindled, we attempted to make the best of a bad situation. My teammates would no longer talk to Yang and Shi, but I felt we had to if we ever wanted to leave Kharta. Hobbling the forty feet to their room, I tried to arbitrate, but when Mr. Yang threatened me with, "Even when the jeeps come, until you pay your bills you will not be allowed to leave Kharta," I too lost my composure. Considering our urgent need of medical care, I found Mr. Yang's statement to reveal an especially callous attitude toward his fellow human beings. When I pointed my bandaged hand at him, and said that we'd contact the American ambassador in Beijing and see that he lost his job, Mr. Yang merely smiled his smug cadre smile, lit a cigarette, and blew a smoke ring into the air. I felt angry and powerless, and unable to respond to his coldheartedness.

During the three days that we spent in Kharta, the pain in my thawed feet became excruciating. I was only able to roll out of bed and stand up with great agony. On the first and second days, I shuffled the eighty feet to the cook room to eat, but by the third day, I couldn't walk. Paul carried me piggyback. I'd hit bottom. At dinner that evening, I felt my resolve suddenly come unglued.

"I can't stand it any more," I sobbed. "I can't walk, I can hardly get out of bed, my hands are bandaged, my foot is bandaged. I can't do anything!"

My teammates consoled and hugged me, and Mimi put me on stronger painkillers to numb the pain in my feet and hands. But I'd begun to doubt that I'd ever get better, or heal. I felt like my life was ruined.

After the others had gone to bed, Pasang drew me aside. We had a heart-to-heart talk about my frostbite. Pasang began by describing his feelings after Roger Marshall fell and was killed on Mount Everest in 1987.

"When you die, your life is finished, gone," Pasang said, using uncharacteristic language for a Buddhist. "Friends remember you, but you can do no more with your life. Life is over," he added with a slow horizontal sweep of his hand.

"Every day now, when you feel bad you must say, 'I no die. I alive!' And you smile! Say: 'I no die, I alive!' " As he looked at me with his caring eyes, I knew that Pasang Norbu Sherpa was a true friend. I would miss him.

"Ed, you come down alive from the mountain, so please, you be happy," Pasang said, breaking into his broad, jovial grin.

"You remember, please. Your life not over."

Chapter 15

Home

In great things it is enough to have tried.

—Erasmus

At last the jeeps arrived. Mr. Yang relented on his ultimatum when we offered to bring the Chinese' favorite Kharta village headman to Lhasa with us, to change our traveler's checks, and pay off our porterage debt. After bidding Kasang and Ang Chu good-bye, we drove to Shekar, and the next morning, we split into two groups. Paul, Stephen, and Pasang traveled overland to Kathmandu, while Robert, Joe, Mimi, and I headed to Lhasa before flying back across China to Beijing. The expedition was over.

At the Lhasa Hotel, we reunited with Pamela Steele, the intrepid Australian we'd encountered months earlier in Zhangmu. Several other mountaineers were also at the hotel: Britain's Chris Bonington, Jess Stock, and Andy Fanshawe, fresh from making the bold first ascent of the West Summit of Menlungtse, one of Tibet's loveliest mountains. And—Reinhold Messner was also in town.

Left: *Heaven on Earth: the sun's first rays illuminate the Khumbu peaks of Nepal.*

When we met him, Messner said mysteriously: "You should not even ask me why I am here." So we didn't. Yet it soon became evident that, coincidentally or not, Messner and Bonington were each seeking something considerably more elusive than the summit of an untrod Himalayan peak.

They were looking, we discovered, for the Abominable Snowman.

"Where have you been climbing?" Reinhold asked Chris, in an understated and yet measured tone of voice, his piercing blue eyes focused and intent.

"Um, on Menlungtse," Chris admitted.

Messner examined every nuance of Bonington's answer. "Ah, yes," Reinhold said. "That is a very good place to see the Yeti." Bonington smiled.

"What do you think the Yeti looks like?" Chris wanted to know.

Reinhold puzzled over this for a minute. "I have a very good idea of how the Yeti appears. He has light gray or brownish fur. He can walk on all fours or upright. He eats fruits and vegetation, but also meat on occasion. And he likes to live in areas with dense trees, but sometimes he goes walking on the glaciers."

"Then you're convinced that they're real?" Chris persisted.

"Yes, of course they are real," Reinhold answered, then paused slightly before exclaiming: *"I have seen one!"*

This, however, was completely top secret Yeti information—and Reinhold abruptly ended the conversation. Sharing such lively discourses, and tales of our respective ascents of the Kangshung Face and Menlungtse, we gathered around tables in the dining room at meals, and spent two evenings in the bar.

Chris Bonington, Mimi Zieman, and Robert Anderson in Lhasa.

Ed shares a laugh with Reinhold Messner.
Joe Blackburn

How I wished Stephen and Paul could have joined us. When, as we were sitting down to have our picture taken, I told Reinhold that people often said that I looked like him, he replied quickly: "Oh, no—first you must lose some more toes and I must lose some fingers."

Earlier, I'd pulled off a bandage to get his opinion of my desiccated black fingertips. Reinhold shook his head. *"Pshht!"* he said, making a swift, scalpel-like slice with the edge of one hand. Then, Reinhold unabashedly showed me the end results of his own frostbite amputations, injuries he had suffered on his very first Himalayan expedition, in 1970, to Nanga Parbat. He had one little toe left on each foot.

"Just be sure to tell your surgeon to smooth and round off the ends of the bones when they amputate them," Reinhold said matter-of-factly, as though having your fingers or toes cut off were an everyday event, or a relatively minor mountaineering hazard, even something to be expected. "If they make a straight cut across the bone," he explained from personal experience, "you'll have a sharp edge there which will push onto the nerves, and your rock climbing will hurt like hell."

Then, musing on our successful ascent of Everest's Kangshung Face, Reinhold added a short postscript. "You were very lucky on your climb," he said, "but then again I have often been lucky, too."

*   *   *   *   *   *   *   *   *   *   *   *   *   *

One week and six plane rides later, I arrived in Boston, Massachusetts, where my father had arranged for my initial medical care. Later, in Denver, Colorado,

I underwent seven separate sur-
geries from July to December of
1988. By the following February,
for the first time in eight months
all of my fingers and toes were, at
long last, healthy and pink. No
more "black bits," as Venables
called them, no more daily bandage changing; no more potential
to be cast as the lead in a B-movie
horror film. My high-altitude photography had cost me dearly.
And the digital losses of my partners? Stephen lost four toes on his
left foot, and Robert, half his big
toe, also on his left foot.

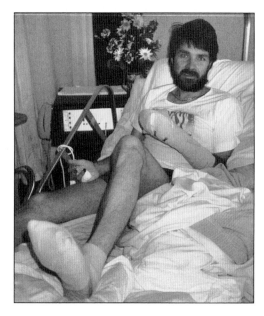

In hospital after the first amputations.

The doctor's appointments
seemed endless. My girlfriend,
Randa Hessel, was a constant support, driving me to appoinments, and helping
me endure the endless trips to the hospital, the seven operations to amputate
my fingertips and toes, the general anesthesia and painkillers (morphine and
Percocets), the "shooting pains" (which zapped like lightning bolts through my
fingers, hands, arms, toes, feet, and legs), the thrice-weekly physical therapy sessions (that lasted one and a half years), the limping and walking on crutches,
and the recurring bouts of lethargy, light-headedness, and systemic weakness
that plagued me during the long dark months of my recovery.

Although the physical damage to my fingers and toes were by far the most
obvious wounds that I suffered on Mount Everest, I also experienced an invisible injury that was far more devastating than the loss of some fingers and toes.
In November, 1988—just when I thought I might be able to resume a relatively
normal life—the bottom of my world fell out.

My new symptoms began just days after my sixth surgery, which was a
general anesthesia. Feeling abnormally weak and fatigued, I began to sleep for
several hours at midday. Then, not knowing exactly what was happening to
me, I began to have panic attacks. The combination of overwhelming tiredness
and irrational fear was absolutely debilitating. I could no longer drive
or go to work, run errands, or visit friends. Randa again rescued me while

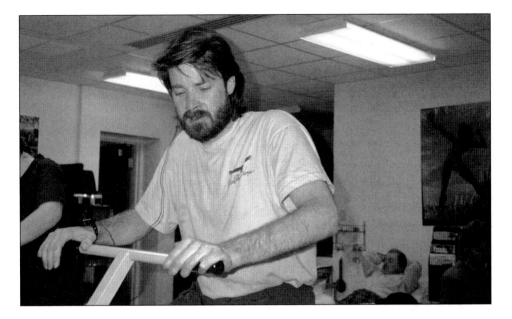

Physical therapy sessions lasted one and a half years.

I sought out new forms of treatment. Acupuncture, biofeedback training, massage therapy, more physical therapy, psychological counseling, I tried them all. At one point, I was going to a dozen doctor and therapy appointments every week.

But, my panic attacks continued. As my neurologist candidly told me, the true experience of a panic attack is unfathomable unless you have personally experienced one. Words barely begin to describe the panic attack sufferer's crippling feelings of dread and anguish. You do not merely feel nervous. You feel an absolute terror that springs from the utter conviction that your death is 100% imminent, that you will die within the next minute or so, and that no one will be able to prevent your death—right there, on the floor of the grocery store or the bank or the movie theater. However, you do not die. You continue to live, but you are utterly convinced that you *still are dying,* or *will soon die.* And the accompanying physiological symptoms of your panic attack—the constricted throat, feelings of suffocation, hyperventilation, light-headedness, dizziness, the racing pulse, and vertigo—can take from thirty minutes to an hour to subside.

During the spring of 1989, I experienced panic attacks on a daily basis. Shopping in the supermarket, I felt bombarded by the noise and bright lights, and often—in the midst of an attack—I had to abandon my cart and groceries to bolt for the doors. In the bank, a waiting line for a teller of more than five people was often too long; and at my initial "try" to go to a movie, after enduring only the first five minutes, I thought I would suffocate before I could run out the exit; and when driving (easily the most panic attack-inducing activity), I rapidly realized that I was a hazard to other motorists. I didn't dare to get behind the wheel of my truck for the next six months.

Had I suffered a brain injury? More tests revealed that I had a "slightly abnormal" EEG, but otherwise my doctors could find no single, identifiable injury. Friends and therapists suggested that I might be suffering from post-traumatic shock syndrome, the illness common to war veterans. However, neither Robert or Stephen ever experienced any similar panic symptoms, and no physician that I spoke to was familiar with any high-altitude mountaineer having suffered panic attacks after serious frostbite and amputations.

With my life turned upside down, I no longer knew who I was—or for that matter, who I once had been. Striving to follow up our Everest climb with what, for me, had become a normal catharsis, I wrote several articles about our new route up the Kangshung Face, even a twelve-page story in *Sports Illustrated*, but what did it really matter? My life as a mountaineer was over.

My neurological and physiological symptoms persisted into my second year of recovery. Then, once my fingers finally had healed, I forced myself to rock climb again. I felt compelled to disprove all of the people who said I would never climb again, and slowly, very slowly, I re-learned how to climb. After two years of training (including one year of practice on an indoor climbing wall), I had regained my sense of balance and roughly half of my previous endurance and strength. The painful sensitivity of my nerve-damaged fingertips also gradually subsided, and my panic attacks—apparently caused by 'oversensitive' neural transmitters—were slowly curbed by anti-depressants.

"Something has clearly happened to your brain," my neurologist told me, "but whether it was the lack of oxygen at high altitude, when you passed out near the summit, or the effects of the general anesthesia, we'll never know."

By 1990, I began to excitedly gauge my recovery by how well I was climbing. After hiking up six of Colorado's 14ers (the state's fourteen-thousand–foot peaks) that summer, the following spring—three years after our ascent of Everest's Kangshung Face—I led a rock climb of 5.11 difficulty. My life as a climber had continued.

Fritz Wiessner, my mountaineering mentor, had been right. Nearly climbing Mount Everest by a new route and without bottled oxygen was by far the best experience of my life—and the worst. The mountains, Fritz once told me in a hushed and heavy voice, can bring you the greatest joys in life, and the worst of sorrows. Certainly, after Lauren Husted's tragic death, and the amputation of my fingertips and toes, I, like many climbers before me, have experienced both of mountaineering's emotional extremes. But no matter how life changing these accidents and injuries have been for me, I have continued to accept the risks and dangers of being in the mountains. As long as I am capable of climbing, how can I not? For my entire life has been directed and led by the optimistic and enthusiastic outlook that my climbing has engendered. Ever since I was young, I have always emphasized the positive in both people and the happenstances of life.

Yet, when I look back upon Lauren's accident and on my storm years on Everest, I must admit that in deeply private ways these two sad and tragic events—her death, and my frostbite—will always shadow and haunt me.

On the slopes of Everest, I stretched my physical and spiritual selves to new heights. And, even after the subsequent pain and uncertainty in my life, the seven operations, panic attacks, and living with the reality that parts of my body are gone forever, I will always revere my three Mount Everest expeditions as amongst the most meaningful and finest of my life's experiences. For during those many long and cold months, my Everest partners and I reaped what the mountains bestow so generously: the bonds of friendship and camaraderie that grow between climbers who share adversity and hardship. On the precipitous flanks of the Kangshung Face, Robert, Paul, Stephen, and I shared life at one of its most elemental thresholds, when all that was left in the world were the infinite possibilities of striving and living and energy and creation, or the stark finality of death. That my teammates and I also had a rare and privileged glimpse of heaven on earth makes me believe that our supreme struggle to climb Everest as a small group of friends was worth the resulting cosmic measure of suffering.

My passion for climbing and the mountains has begun anew. I am back rock climbing again, and for that I am extremely grateful. Life has continued for me in all of its lucky, unexpected, and unbelievable ways. My strength is improving, and I am already looking forward to returning to the most powerful and awe-inspiring mountains on earth, the Himalaya, as soon as I possibly can.

I know, too, that I am lucky to be alive. I will never forget Pasang's wise words to me: "Every day, you must say: 'I no die. I alive.' And smile!"

Nor can I ever forget Lauren Husted's beautifully simple statement that she wrote in her diary several weeks before her death:

"Life surpasses all, and that is why I want to climb."

The Mysteries of Mallory and Tenzing

Noel Odell's diary entry for June 8, 1924.
Courtesy of Peter Odell

*I*n 1990, Paul Teare and Robert Anderson returned to Tibet to attempt the *Super Couloir* on the North Face of Mount Everest. I, in turn, had completed the first draft of this book—and I wanted to track down an unpublished photograph of George Mallory. As Mallory and Guy Bullock were the first Westerners to see Everest's Kangshung Face in 1921, I wanted to honor them. My photographic search led me to contact the family of Mallory's 1924 Everest companion, Noel Odell. On June 8 of that year (see above), Odell was the last person to see Mallory and Andrew Irvine alive as they ascended Everest's Northeast Ridge before disappearing into the mists. In England, Odell's grandson, Peter Odell, graciously loaned me the negatives of the marvelous photographs on these pages—and a copy of his grandfather's 1924 Everest diary.

Left: *George Mallory on a hike near Rongbuk Base Camp in April, 1924.* Noel Odell

The blessing ceremony photograph above—never before published—shows Geoffrey Bruce, Mallory, and Norton at the team's May 15, 1924 *puja* at Rongbuk Monastery. Mallory's gaze is revealingly candid: determined, yet strikingly wistful. On June 3, 1924, Edward Norton reached a record altitude on Everest of 28,126 feet, without oxygen. Five days later, Mallory and Irvine disappeared. In 1990, I sent four of Odell's Rongbuk photos back to Everest with Paul and Robert—which they gave the monks at their own Everest *puja*. Then, one week after Mallory's body was found on May 1, 1999, the so-called "mystery photo" of the 1924 blessing ceremony was "rediscovered," ironically, at Rongbuk.

Blessing photograph, Noel Odell. *1924 Noel Odell portrait,* John Noel, Courtesy Sandra Noel

Andrew Irvine with his 'improved' oxygen gear in Shekar, Tibet. Noel Odell

Rongbuk Monastery's Head Lama was the Dzatrul *Rinpoche* (right), whose name was Ngawang Tenzin Norbu. Born in Kharta, Tibet in 1866, he became the preeminent historical religious leader of the Rongbuk-Tingri-Khumbu regions surrounding Chomolungma. In 1902, he garnered the necessary funds and patronage in Tingri to build Rongbuk Monastery; in 1916, he asked Lama Gulu to found Tengboche, the Sherpa's most revered monastery, in Nepal's Khumbu region. (The Dzatrul *Rinpoche* also personally consecrated Tengboche on its opening in 1919.) Following these successes, he initiated the establishment of other important monasteries in Nepal, at Thame, Takshingdu, and Chiwong.

Locally, the Dzatrul *Rinpoche* was understandably revered. Furthermore, he was believed to resemble the historical Buddha, in his mental clarity and in the quality of his teachings. Children reputedly would point at him and call him *Sangye* (Buddha, in Tibetan), and he became known as *Dzarongpu Sangye*— the Buddha of Rongbuk. Although he viewed British mountaineers as heretics, he presided over the 1922 and 1924 Everest Expedition *puja* ceremonies held at Rongbuk, and on each occasion, he gave his blessing to George Mallory.

But the lama's story does not end there. It was also the Dzatrul *Rinpoche* who gave his blessing—and a new and more fitting name—to a young child from Kharta, the lama's own village. As Tenzing Norgay writes in *Tiger of the Snows*, "When I was born [my name] was not Tenzing. It was Namgyal Wangdi. But one day I was brought to a great lama from Rongbuk, who consulted his holy books, and he said that I was the reincarnation of a very rich man who had recently died in Solu Khumbu [Nepal], and that because of this my name must be changed. The name he suggested was Tenzing Norgay ... and the reason was that, like the lamas from Tsa-Chu, he predicted great things for me. Norgay means "wealthy" or "fortunate." Tenzing means "follower of religion," and it has been *the name of many lamas, and indeed, of this lama himself* [emphasis mine]. Anyhow, "Wealthy-Fortunate-Follower-of-Religion" sounded like a fine all-round name to go through life with, so my parents made the change, and hoped for the best."

When Ngawang Tenzin Norbu died in 1940, the reincarnate lama, or *tulku*, who took his place at Rongbuk was Tulshig *Rinpoche* (yet another Kharta native son) whom the Dzatrul Rinpoche knew and had already recognized as the reincarnation of his own teacher, the former Tulshig *Rinpoche*. After the Chinese invaded Tibet, the current Tulshig *Rinpoche* fled to Nepal. He is now Head lama of Thupten Choeling Monastery in Junbesi. Quite interestingly, the present Tulshig *Rinpoche's* father, in a matter of enduring family pride, was the first cousin brother of none other than Dokmo Kinzom—Tenzing Norgay's mother.

The Dzatrul Rinpoche, Ngawang Tenzin Norbu, Head Lama of Rongbuk. Noel Odell

Tenzing Norgay was born in the Kharta region of Tibet in 1914. Tenzing Norgay family collection

Knowing of these interrelationships, it is possible to look at the early drama enacted on the slopes of Chomolungma and Mount Everest in a new light, an illumination that shows three of the key participants knew or had met one another in a closer, more human, and sympathetic way. I am convinced that these three uniquely gifted men—George Mallory, Ngawang Tenzin Norbu, and Tenzing Norgay—crossed each other's paths in ways we have hitherto not imagined.

I like to imagine that the story, at least of Tenzing Norgay and George Mallory, might have gone something like this.

It was the first week of August, 1921. An energetic seven-year-old with the newly given name of Tenzing Norgay was playing in the vicinity of his home in Moyun village, or perhaps tending his family's yaks amongst the lush meadows of the Gangla—when he saw an oddly dressed, fair-complexioned man, George Mallory, making the first approach by any Westerner toward the base of Mount Everest's great eastern, or Kangshung, face.

On August 2, 1921, Mallory's partner, Guy Bullock, wrote in his diary: "At the Red Monastery [Tharpa Choeling Monastery, Kharta's central monastery, built next to Moyun village, but destroyed during the Cultural Revolution], Gyaljen [their interpreter] and Dupa were behind, and M. [Mallory] went to look for them.... He went back to the last village, and also missed his way, so that although I followed him, I failed to find him. We both overtook the coolies [porters] at the last village, where we had lunch."

This diary entry proves that Bullock and Mallory spent most of a day in the vicinity of Tenzing's village—lost!—and what young boy wouldn't have wanted to see the Western Sahibs from far away who had come to climb their greatest mountain? There can be little doubt Tenzing also heard stories from his parents, and from the thirty-two villagers from Kharta who portered the British climbers' loads of food and gear up the Kama Valley to Chomolungma and Kartse.

Thirty-two years later, this same young boy, Tenzing Norgay, the "Wealthy-Fortunate-Follower-of-Religion"—now a highly experienced mountaineer—became the first, with Edmund Hillary, to stand upon Chomolungma's lofty summit. And during the fifteen exhilarating minutes that the pair stood on Mount Everest's summit, Tenzing Norgay, the man from Kharta, probably cast his gaze down and east into the lands of Tibet, let his eyes wander down the length of the Kangshung Glacier to the sacred valley of the Kama Chu, and joyously smiled when he recognized the yak pastures of his youth at Gangla, and the small side valley holding the lake of the life-giving waters, Tshechu, where (very likely) he was born.

Bibliography

Dunn, Robert   *The Shameless Diary of an Explorer,* The Outing Publishing Company, New York, 1907

Gardner, John   *The Art of Living, and other stories,* Alfred A. Knopf, New York, 1981

Irving, John   *The World According to Garp: A Novel,* E.P. Dutton & Company, Inc., New York, 1978

Lawrence, T.E.   *The Seven Pillars of Wisdom, a Triumph,* Doubleday, Doran & Company, Inc., New York, 1935

Theroux, Paul   *The Old Patagonian Express*: By Train Through the Americas, Houghton Mifflin, Boston, 1979

Winthrop Young, Geoffrey   *Mountain Craft,* Methuen & Co. Ltd., London, 1920

Mountaineering & Mount Everest, History & Reference Books

Boardman, Peter   *The Shining Mountain, Two Men on Changabang's West Wall*
Hodder & Stoughton, London, 1978 / E. P. Dutton & Company, Inc., 1982

Bonington, Chris   *Great Climbs* (US edition: *Heroic Climbs*), *a Celebration of World Mountaineering*
Mitchell Beazley, London / The Mountaineers Books, Seattle, 1994

Bonington, Chris   *The Climbers, A History of Mountaineering,* BBC Books / Hodder & Stoughton, London, 1992

Fanshawe, Andy, and Stephen Venables   *Himalaya Alpine-Style, The Most Challenging Routes on the Highest Peaks*
Hodder & Stoughton, London / The Mountaineers Books, Seattle, 1995

Faux, Ronald   *Everest, Goddess of the Wind,* Chambers, Edinburgh, Scotland, 1978

Franco, Jean, and Lionel Terray   *At Grips With Jannu,* Victor Gollancz Ltd., London, 1967 (the first ascent of Jannu)

Frison-Roche, Andre, and Sylvain Jouty   *A History of Mountain Climbing,* Flammarion, Paris and New York, 1996

Gillman, Peter   *Everest, The Best Writing and Pictures from Seventy Years of Human Endeavour*
Little, Brown and Company, Boston and London, 1993

Kielkowski, Jan   *Mount Everest Massif, monograph, guide, chronicle,* Explo Publishers, Poland, 2000

Lenser, Gerhard   *Pumo Ri,* Orell Füssli Verlag, Zürich, Switzerland, 1963 (first ascent of Pumori)

Mantovani, Roberto   *Everest, The History of the Himalayan Giant*
White Star, Vercelli, Italy / The Mountaineers Books, Seattle, 1997

Mason, Kenneth   *Abode of Snow, A History of Himalayan Exploration and Mountaineering from Earliest Times to the Ascent of Everest,* Rupert Hart-Davis, London, 1956

Murray, W.H.   *The Story of Everest, 1921-1952,* J.M. Dent & Sons, London / E.P. Dutton & Co., Inc., New York, 1953

Neate, Jill   *High Asia, An Illustrated History of the 7,000 Metre Peaks*
Unwin Hyman, Ltd., London / The Mountaineers, Seattle, 1989

O'Connor, Bill   *The Trekking Peaks of Nepal,* The Crowood Press, Wiltshire, England / Cloudcap Press, Seattle, 1989

Ridgeway, Rick   *The Boldest Dream, The story of twelve who climbed Mount Everest*
Harcourt Brace Jovanovich, Inc., New York and London, 1979

Sale, Richard, and John Cleare   *On Top of the World, Climbing the World's 14 Highest Peaks,* HarperCollins, London, 2000

Salkeld, Audrey, and John Boyle   *Climbing Mount Everest, The Bibliography, The literature and history of climbing the world's highest mountain,* Sixways Publishing, Clevedon, Avon, England, 1993

Salkeld, Audrey   *World Mountaineering, the World's Great Mountains by the World's Great Mountaineers*
Mitchell Beazley, London / Bullfinch Press, Boston and New York, 1998

Terray, Lionel   *Conquistadors of the Useless, From the Alps to Annapurna—and Beyond*
Victor Gollancz Ltd., London, 1963 (the first ascents of Annapurna, Chomolönzo, Jannu, and Makalu)

Tichy, Herbert   *Himalaya,* Hale, London / G.P. Putnam's Sons, New York, 1970

Ullman, James Ramsey   *Kingdom of Adventure: Everest, A chronicle of man's assault on the earth's highest mountain, narrated by the participants, & with an accompanying text*
William Sloane Associates, Inc., Publishers, New York, 1947 / Collins, London and Glasgow, 1948

Unsworth, Walt   *Everest, the Mountaineering History,* Bâton Wicks Publications, London / The Mountaineers Books, Seattle; first edition, 1981; second edition, 1989; third edition, 2000

Unsworth, Walt   *Hold the Heights, The Foundations of Mountaineering*
Hodder & Stoughton, London / The Mountaineers Books, Seattle, 1994

Younghusband, Sir Francis   *The Epic of Mount Everest,* Edward Arnold & Co., London, 1926

Bibliography

Mount Everest - Expedition Accounts

Bonington, Chris   *Everest Southwest Face,* Hodder & Stoughton, London, 1973

Bonington, Chris   *The Ultimate Challenge, The Hardest Way up the World's Highest Mountain*
       Stein and Day Publishers, New York, 1973 (US edition of *Everest Southwest Face*)

Bonington, Chris   *Everest The Hard Way,* Hodder & Stoughton, London / Random House, Inc., New York, 1976

Bonington, Chris, and Charles Clarke
       Everest: The Unclimbed Ridge, Hodder & Stoughton, London, 1983 / W. W. Norton, New York, 1984

Boukreev, Anatoli and G. Weston DeWalt
       The Climb, Tragic Ambitions on Everest, St. Martin's Press, New York, 1997

Bruce, Brigadier-General C.G.
       The Assault on Everest, 1922, Edward Arnold & Co., London / Longmans, Green & Co., NY, 1923

Burgess, Al, and Jim Palmer   *Everest Canada, The Ultimate Challenge,* Stoddart, Toronto, 1983

Coburn, Broughton   *Everest, Mountain Without Mercy,* National Geographic Society, Washington D.C., 1997

Dickinson, Matt   *The Death Zone, Climbing Everest Through the Killer Storm,* Hutchinson, London, 1997

Dittert, René, Gabriel Chevalley, and Raymond Lambert
       Forerunners to Everest, The Story of the Two Swiss Expeditions of 1952
       George Allen & Unwin Ltd., London / Harper & Brothers, New York, 1954

Douglas, Ed   *Chomolungma Sings the Blues, Travels Around Everest,* Constable and Company Ltd, London, 1997

Fellowes, Air-Commodore P.F.   *First Over Everest, the Houston-Mount Everest Expedition, 1933*
       John Lane, The Bodley Head Limited, London, 1933 / Robert M. McBride & Co., New York, 1934

Fuchs, Rodrigo Jordan   *Everest, El Desafío de un Sueño, Los Primeros Sudamericanos en la Cumbre*
       (*Everest, The Challenge of a Dream, The first South Americans on the Summit*)
       Published by Rodrigo Jordan Fuchs, Santiago, Chile, 1992

Gammelgaard, Lene   *Climbing High, A Woman's Account of Surviving the Everest Tragedy,* Seal Press, Seattle, 1999

Greig, Andrew   *Kingdoms of Experience, Everest, The Unclimbed Ridge,* Century Hutchinson Ltd., London, 1986

Hillary, Sir Edmund, and George Lowe
       East of Everest, An Account of the New Zealand Alpine Club Himalayan Expedition to the Barun
       Valley in 1954, Hodder & Stoughton, London / E.P. Dutton and Company, Inc., New York, 1956

Hornbein, Thomas F.   *Everest, The West Ridge*
       The Sierra Club, San Francisco, 1965 / George Allen & Unwin, London, 1971

Howard-Bury, Lieutenant-Colonel C.K.
       Mount Everest the Reconnaissance, 1921, Longmans, Green, and Co., London and New York, 1922

Howard-Bury, Charles, and George Leigh Mallory
       Everest Reconnaissance, The First Expedition of 1921, Hodder & Stoughton, London, 1991

Krakauer, Jon   *Into Thin Air, A Personal Account of the Mount Everest Disaster*
       Villard Books, Random House, Inc., New York / Macmillan, London, 1997

Krakauer, Jon   *Into Thin Air, A Personal Account of the Mount Everest Disaster, The Illustrated Edition*
       Villard Books, Random House, Inc., New York, 1998

Kropp, Göran, with David Lagercrantz   *Ultimate High, Everest By Bicycle,* Discovery Books, New York, 1999

McCallum, John D.   *Everest Dairy, based on the diary of Lute Jerstad one of the first five Americans to conquer*
       Mount Everest, Follett Publishing Company, Chicago, 1966

Noel, Captain John   *Through Tibet to Everest,* Edward Arnold & Co., London, 1927

Noel, Captain John   *The Story of Everest,* Little, Brown and Company, Boston, 1927

Norton, Lieutenant-Colonel E.F.
       The Fight For Everest: 1924, Edward Arnold & Co., London / Longmans, Green & Co., NY, 1925

Ruttledge, Hugh   *Everest 1933,* Hodder & Stoughton Limited, London, 1934

Ruttledge, Hugh   *Attack on Everest,* Robert M. McBride & Company, New York, 1935 (US edition of *Everest 1933*)

Ruttledge, Hugh   *Everest, The Unfinished Adventure,* Hodder & Stoughton, London, 1937

Sayre, Woodrow Wilson   *Four Against Everest,* Prentice-Hall, Inc., New Jersey / Arthur Barker Limited, London, 1964

Smythe, Frank S.   *Camp Six, An Account of the 1933 Mount Everest Expedition,* Hodder & Stoughton, London, 1937

Tilman, H.W.   *Everest 1938,* Cambridge University Press, London, 1948

Ullman, James Ramsey, and other members of the expedition
       Americans on Everest, the official account of the ascent led by Norman G. Dyhrenfurth
       J.B. Lippincott Company, Philadelphia and New York, 1964

Bibliography

Mount Everest - Without Bottled Oxygen

Habeler, Peter   *The Lonely Victory, Mt. Everest '78,* Simon & Schuster, New York, 1979
Habeler, Peter   *Everest Impossible Victory,* Arlington Books Ltd., London, 1979 (UK edition of *The Lonely Victory*)
Hall, Lincoln   *White Limbo, The 1st Australian Climb of Mt. Everest,*
                      Weldons Pty Ltd, McMahons Point, Australia / The Mountaineers Books, Seattle, 1985
Messner, Reinhold   *Everest, Expedition to the Ultimate,* Kaye & Ward Ltd., London / Oxford University Press, NY, 1979
Messner, Reinhold   *The Crystal Horizon, Everest—The First Solo Ascent,* The Crowood Press, Wiltshire, England, 1989
Venables, Stephen   *Everest Kangshung Face,* Hodder & Stoughton, London, 1989
Venables, Stephen   *Everest Kangshung Face,* Pan Books Ltd., London, 1991
Venables, Stephen   *Everest: Alone At The Summit,* Odyssey Books, Bath, 1996 (reissue of *Everest Kangshung Face*)
Venables, Stephen   *Everest: Alone At The Summit,* Adrenaline Books, Balliet & Fitzgerald, New York, 2000

George Mallory & Andrew Irvine

Anker, Conrad, and David Roberts   *The Lost Explorer, Finding Mallory on Everest,* Simon & Schuster, New York, 1999
Breashears, David, and Audrey Salkeld   *Last Climb, The Legendary Everest Expeditions of George Mallory*
                      National Geographic Society, Washington D.C., 1999
Carr, Herbert   *The Irvine Diaries, Andrew Irvine and the Enigma of Everest 1924,* Gastons-West Col, Berks, 1979
Gillman, Peter and Leni   *The Wildest Dream, Mallory His Life and Conflicting Passions*
                      Headline Book Publishing, London / The Mountaineers Books, 2000
Green, Dudley   *Mallory of Everest,* Faust Publishing Company Limited, Lancashire, England, 1990
Hemmleb, Jochen, Larry A. Johnson, and Eric R. Simonson, as told to William E. Nothdurft
                      Ghosts of Everest, the Search for Mallory & Irvine, The Mountaineers Books, Seattle, 1999
Holzel, Tom & Audrey Salkeld   *The Mystery of Mallory and Irvine,* Jonathan Cape, London, 1986
Holzel, Tom & Audrey Salkeld   *First on Everest: The Mystery of Mallory and Irvine,* Henry Holt & Co., Inc., NY, 1986
Robertson, David   *George Mallory,* Faber and Faber Limited, London, 1969
Siggins, Lorna   *Everest Calling, Ascent of the Dark Side: The Mallory-Irvine Ridge* Mainstream Publ., Scotland, 1994
Styles, Showell   *Mallory of Everest,* The Macmillan Company, New York, 1967
Summers, Julie   *Fearless on Everest: the Quest for Sandy Irvine,* Weidenfeld & Nicolson, London, 2000

Nepal & Tibet

Aziz, Barbara Nimri   *Tibetan Frontier Families, Reflections of Three Generations from D'ing-ri,* Princeton University
                      Press, Princeton, New Jersey / Vikas Publishing House Pvt Ltd., New Delhi, 1978
Baldizzone, Tiziana and Gianni   *Tibet, On the Paths of the Gentlemen Brigands, retracing the steps of*
                      Alexandra David-Néel, Thames and Hudson, London, 1995
Bell, Sir Charles   *Portrait of the Dalai Lama,* Collins, London, 1946 (life of the Thirteenth Dalai Lama, 1876-1933)
Bell, Sir Charles   *Tibet, Past & Present,* Oxford University Press, London, 1924
Bishop (Bird), Isabella L.   *Among the Tibetans,* The Religious Tract Society, London, 1904
Bonavia, David, and Magnus Bartlett   *Tibet,* Thames & Hudson, Ltd., London, 1981
Clarke, John   *Tibet, Caught in Time,* Garnett Publishing Limited, Reading, England, 1997
Craig, Mary   *Tears of Blood, A Cry for Tibet,* CounterPoint, Washington D.C., 1999
Cronin, Jr., Edward W.   *The Arun, A Natural History of the World's Deepest Valley,* Houghton Mifflin Co., Boston, 1979
Crossette, Barbara   *So Close to Heaven, The Vanishing Buddhist Kingdoms of the Himalayas,* Alfred A. Knopf, NY, 1995
Dalai Lama, Tenzin Gyatso   *Freedom in Exile, the Autobiography of His Holiness the Dalai Lama of Tibet*
                      Hodder & Stoughton, London, 1990
Dalai Lama, His Holiness the Fourteenth, and Galen Rowell
                      My Tibet, A Mountain Light Press Book, University of California Press, Berkeley, California, 1990
Diemberger, Hildegard, Maria Antonia Sironi, and Pasang Wangdu
                      The Story of the White Crystal, based on the manuscript of Ngawang Kalden Gyatsho, a Tibetan
                      Monk who lived in the Eighteenth Century, Ferrari Editrice, Bergamo, Italy, 1995
Downs, Hugh R.   *Rhythms of a Himalayan Village,* Harper & Row, Publishers, San Francisco, 1980

Nepal & Tibet

Fields, Rick, and Brian Cutillo   *The Turquoise Bee, Love Songs of the Sixth Dalai Lama,* HarperSanFrancisco, 1994

Fleming, Peter   *Bayonets to Lhasa, The First Full Account of the British Invasion of Tibet in 1904*
Rupert Hart-Davis, London, 1961

Hagen, Toni   *Nepal,* Kümmerly & Frey Geographical Publishers, Berne / Rand McNally, Chicago & New York, 1961

Harrer, Heinrich   *Lost Lhasa, Heinrich Harrer's Tibet*
Harry N. Abrams, Inc. Publishers, New York and Summit Publications, Hood River, Oregon, 1992

Harrer, Heinrich   *Return to Tibet,* Weidenfeld and Nicolson, London, 1984 / Shocken Books, New York, 1985

Harrer, Heinrich   *Seven Years in Tibet,* Rupert Hart-Davis, London, 1953 / E.P. Dutton and Co., Inc., New York, 1954

Hillary, Sir Edmund   *High Adventure,* Hodder & Stoughton, London / E.P. Dutton & Company, Inc., New York, 1955

Hilton, Isabel   *The Search for the Panchen Lama,* Viking, Penguin Books, London, 1999 / W.W. Norton, NY, 2000

Jerstad, Luther G.   *Mani-Rimdu Sherpa Dance-Drama,* University of Washington Press, Seattle and London, 1969

Knaus, John Kenneth   *Orphans of the Cold War, America and the Tibetan Struggle for Survival,* PublicAffairs, NY, 1999

Landor, A. Henry Savage   *Tibet & Nepal,* A. & C. Black, London, 1905

Matthiessen, Peter, and Thomas Laird   *East of Lo Monthang, In the Land of Mustang,* Shambhala, Boston, 1995

Norbu, Thubten, as told to Heinrich Harrer   *Tibet is My Country,* Rupert Hart-Davis, London, 1960

O'Connor, Bill   *The Trekking Peaks of Nepal,* The Crowood Press, Wiltshire, England / Cloudcap Press, Seattle, 1989

Ortner, Sherry B.   *High Religion, A Cultural and Political History of Sherpa Buddhism*
Princeton University Press, Princeton, New Jersey, 1989

Ortner, Sherry B.   *Life and Death on Mt. Everest, Sherpas and Himalayan Mountaineering*
Princeton University Press, Princeton, New Jersey, 1999

Reynolds, Valrae   *From the Sacred Realm, Treasures of Tibetan Art from the Newark Museum*
Prestel Verlag, London and New York, 1999

Rowell, Galen   *Mountains of the Middle Kingdom, Exploring the High Peaks of China and Tibet*
Sierra Club Books, San Francisco / American Alpine Club, New York, 1983

Salkeld, Audrey   *People in High Places, Approaches to Tibet,* Jonathan Cape, London, 1991

Shakya, Tsering   *The Dragon in the Land of Snows, A History of Modern Tibet Since 1947*
Columbia University Press, New York, 1999

Schaller, George B.   *Tibet's Hidden Wilderness, Wildlife and Nomads of the Chang Tang Reserve*
Harry N. Abrams, Inc., Publishers, New York, 1997

Roerich, George N.   *Trails to Inmost Asia, Five Years of Exploration with the Roerich Central Asian Expedition*
Yale University Press, New Haven, Connecticut, 1931

Schell, Orville   *Virtual Tibet, Searching for Shangri-La from the Himalayas to Hollywood*
Metropolitan Books, Henry Holt and Company, New York, 2000

Tilman, H.W.   *Nepal Himalaya,* Cambridge University Press, London, 1952

Tsering, Diki   *Dalai Lama, My Son, A Mother's Story,* Virgin Publishing Ltd., London, 2000

Waddell, L.A.   *Among the Himalayas,* Archibald Constable & Co., Westminster, 1899

Waddell, L.A.   *Lhasa & Its Mysteries, with a record of the Expedition of 1903-1904,* John Murray, London, 1905

Zangbu, Ngawang Tenzin, the Tengboche *Rinpoche,* and Francis Klatzel   *Stories and Customs of the Sherpas*
Khumbu Cultural Conservation Committee, Kathmandu, Nepal, 1988

Autobiography / Biography

Alvarez, Al   *Feeding the Rat, Profile of a Climber, Mo Anthoine*
Bloomsbury Publishing Ltd. / The Atlantic Monthly Press, New York, 1989

Anderson, J.R.L.   *High Mountains and Cold Seas, A Biography of H.W. Tilman,* Victor Gollancz Ltd., London, 1980

Birtles, Geoff   *Alan Rouse, A Mountaineer's Life,* Unwin Hyman Limited, London, 1987

Boardman, Peter   *Sacred Summits, A Climber's Year,* Hodder & Stoughton, London, 1982

Bonatti, Walter   *On the Heights,* Rupert Hart-Davis, London, 1964

Bonington, Chris   *I Chose to Climb,* Victor Gollancz Ltd., London, 1966

Bonington, Chris   *The Next Horizon, Autobiography II,* Victor Gollancz Ltd., London, 1973

Bonington, Chris   *The Everest Years, A Climber's Life,* Hodder & Stoughton, London, 1986 / Viking Penguin, NY, 1987

Bonington, Chris   *Mountaineer, Thirty Years of Climbing on the World's Great Peaks*
Diadem Books, Hodder & Stoughton, London / Sierra Club Books, San Francisco, 1989

Bonington, Chris   *Boundless Horizons, the Autobiography of Chris Bonington*
Weidenfeld & Nicholson, London / Mountaineers Books, Seattle, 2000

Autobiography / Biography

Breashears, David   *High Exposure, An Enduring Passion for Everest and Unforgiving Places,* Simon & Schuster, 1999
Brown, Joe   *The Hard Years, An Autobiography,* Victor Gollancz, Ltd., London, 1967
Bruce, Brigadier General C.G.   *Himalayan Wanderer,* Alexander Maclehose & Co., London, 1934
Buhl, Hermann   *Nanga Parbat Pilgrimage, A Mountaineer's Autobiography,* Hodder & Stoughton, London, 1956
Buhl, Hermann   *Lonely Challenge, A Mountaineer's Autobiography,* E.P. Dutton & Company, Inc., New York, 1956
Coffey, Maria   *Fragile Edge,* Chatto & Windus Ltd., London, 1989
Curran, Jim   *High Achiever, the Life and Climbs of Chris Bonington,* Constable and Company, London, 1999
Curran, Jim   *Suspended Sentences, from the Life of a Climbing Cameraman,* Hodder & Stoughton, 1991
Diemberger, Kurt   *Summits and Secrets,* George Allen & Unwin Ltd., London, 1971
Diemberger, Kurt   *The Endless Knot, K2, Mountain of Dreams and Destiny,* Grafton / HarperCollins, London, 1991
Faux, Ronald   *High Ambition, A Biography of Reinhold Messner,* Victor Gollancz Ltd., London, 1982
Haston, Dougal   *In High Places,* Cassell & Company Limited, London / Macmillan Publishing Co, Inc., New York, 1972
Hillary, Sir Edmund   *High Adventure,* Hodder & Stoughton, London / E.P. Dutton & Company, Inc., New York, 1955
Hillary, Sir Edmund   *Nothing Venture, Nothing Win,* Hodders, London / Coward, McCann, & Geoghegan, New York, 1975
Hillary, Edmund and Peter   *Two Generations,* Hodder & Stoughton, London, 1984
Hillary, Sir Edmund, and Peter Hillary   *Ascent, Two Lives Explored: Sir Edmund and Peter Hillary,*
   Doubleday & Company, Inc., New York, 1986   (US edition of *Two Generations*)
Hillary, Sir Edmund   *View From the Summit,* Doubleday, London and New York, 1999
Hunt, John   *Life is Meeting,* Hodder & Stoughton, London, 1978
Kukuczka, Jerzy   *My Vertical World, Climbing the 8,000-metre peaks,* Hodder & Stoughton, London, 1992
Leamer, Laurence   *Ascent, the Spiritual and Physical Quest of Willi Unsoeld,* Simon & Schuster, Inc., New York, 1982
Messner, Reinhold   *Hermann Buhl: Climbing Without Compromise,* The Mountaineers Books, Seattle, 2000
Norgay, Tenzing, written in collaboration with James Ramsey Ullman   *Tiger of the Snows, the Autobiography of*
   Tenzing of Everest, G.P. Putnam's Sons, New York, 1955
Norgay, Tenzing, as told to James Ramsey Ullman   *Man of Everest, the Autobiography of Tenzing*
   George G. Harrap & Co. Ltd., London, 1955   (UK edition of *Tiger of the Snows*)
Norgay, Tenzing, as told to Malcolm Barnes   *After Everest,* George Allen & Unwin Ltd., London, 1977
Nunn, Paul   *At the Sharp End,* Unwin Hyman, London, 1988
Scott, Doug   *Himalayan Climber, A Lifetime's Quest to the Great Ranges*
   Diadem Books, Hodder & Stoughton, London / Sierra Club Books, San Francisco, 1992
Shipton, Eric   *That Untravelled World, an Autobiography,* Hodder & Stoughton, London / Scribner's, NY, 1969
Smith, J.R.   *Everest, The Man and the Mountain,* Whittles Publishing, Caithness, Scotland, 1999
Steele, Peter   *Eric Shipton, Everest and Beyond,* Constable and Co., London / The Mountaineers, Seattle, 1998
Stokes, Brummie   *Soldiers and Sherpas, A Taste For Adventure,* Michael Joseph Ltd. / Penguin Group, London, 1988
Terray, Lionel   *Conquistadors of the Useless, From the Alps to Annapurna—and Beyond,* Gollancz, London, 1963
Tullis, Julie   *Clouds From Both Sides,* Grafton Books, London / Sierra Club Books, San Francisco, 1986
Wickwire, Jim, and Dorothy Bullit   *Addicted to Danger, A Memoir about Affirming Life in the Face of Death*
   Pocket Books / Simon & Schuster, Inc., New York, 1998
Whillans, Don, and Alick Ormerod   *Don Whillans, Portrait of a Mountaineer,* William Heinemann Ltd., London, 1971
Whittaker, Jim   *A Life on the Edge, Memoirs of Everest and Beyond,* The Mountaineers Books, Seattle, 1999
Wollaston, A.F.R.   *Letters and Diaries of A.F.R. Wollaston,* selected and edited by Mary Wollaston
   Cambridge University Press, London, 1933

The Eight-Thousand-Meter Peaks of the Himalaya, Books on their First Ascents

MOUNT EVEREST   (29,035 feet) Nepal-Tibet border, Himalaya   (Britain, 1953)

   Evans, Charles   *Eye on Everest: A Sketchbook from the great Everest expedition,* Dennis Dobson Ltd., London, 1955
   Gregory, Alfred   *The Picture of Everest, a book of full-colour reproductions of Photographs of the Everest Scene*
      Hodder & Stoughton, London, 1954
   Gregory, Alfred   *Alfred Gregory's Everest,* Constable and Company Ltd., London, 1993
   Hillary, Sir Edmund   *High Adventure,* Hodder & Stoughton, London / E.P. Dutton & Company, Inc., New York, 1955
   Hunt, John   *Our Everest Adventure,* Brockhampton Press, Leicester, 1954
   Hunt, Sir John   *The Ascent of Everest,* Hodder & Stoughton, London, 1953
   Hunt, Sir John   *The Ascent of Everest,* Hodder & Stoughton, London, 1993, Limited 40th Anniversary Edition

Hunt, Sir John, *The Conquest of Everest,* E.P. Dutton & Company, Inc., New York, 1954

Izzard, Ralph *An Innocent on Everest,* Hodder & Stoughton, London, 1954

Morris, James *Coronation Everest,* Faber and Faber Limited, London / E.P. Dutton & Co., Inc., New York, 1958

Noyce, Wilfrid *South Col, One Man's Adventure on the Ascent of Everest 1953*
     William Heinemann Ltd., London / William Sloane Associates, Inc., Publishers, New York, 1954

K2   (28,251 feet)   Pakistan-China border, Karakoram   (Italy, 1954)

Desio, Professor Ardito *The Ascent of K2,* Elek Books, London, 1955

Desio, Professor Ardito *Victory Over K2, the Second Highest Peak in the World,* McGraw Hill, New York, 1956

Bonatti, Walter *On the Heights,* Rupert Hart-Davis, London, 1964

KANCHENJUNGA   (28,169 feet) Nepal-Sikkim border, Himalaya   (Britain, 1955)

Evans, Charles *Kangchenjunga, The Untrodden Peak,* Hodder & Stoughton, London, 1956

Evans, Charles *Kanchenjunga Climbed,* E.P. Dutton & Company, Inc., New York, 1957
     (US edition of *Kangchenjunga, The Untrodden Peak*)

Brown, Joe   *The Hard Years, An Autobiography,* Victor Gollancz Ltd., London, 1967

LHOTSE   (27,940 feet)   Nepal-Tibet border, Himalaya   (Switzerland, 1956)

Eggler, Albert *The Everest-Lhotse Adventure,* George Allen & Unwin Ltd., London / Harper, New York, 1957

MAKALU   (27,766 feet)   Nepal-Tibet border, Himalaya   (France, 1955)

Franco, Jean   *Makalu, A Team Triumphant, the highest peak yet conquered by an entire team*
     Jonathan Cape, London, 1957

DHAULAGIRI   (26,795 feet)   Nepal, Himalaya   (Switzerland-Austria, 1960)

Eiselin, Max   *The Ascent of Dhaulagiri,* Oxford University Press, London and New York, 1961

Diemberger, Kurt *Summits and Secrets,* George Allen & Unwin Ltd., London, 1971

MANASLU   (26,781 feet)   Nepal, Himalaya   (Japan, 1956)

Japanese Alpine Club *Manaslu, 1954-6*

Maki, Aritsune *The Ascent of Manaslu,* Mainichi Newspaper, Tokyo, 1956

CHO OYU   (26,906 feet)   Nepal-Tibet border, Himalaya   (Switzerland-Nepal, 1954)

Tichy, Herbert *Cho Oyu, By Favour of the Gods,* Methuen & Co Ltd., London, 1957

NANGA PARBAT   (26,657 feet)   Pakistan, Karakoram   (Germany-Austria, 1953)

Buhl, Hermann *Nanga Parbat Pilgrimage, A Mountaineer's Autobiography,* Hodder & Stoughton, London, 1956

Buhl, Hermann *Lonely Challenge, A Mountaineer's Autobiography,* E.P. Dutton & Company, Inc., New York, 1956

Herrligkoffer, Karl M. *Nanga Parbat, Incorporating the Official Report of the Expedition of 1953*
     Elek Books, London, 1954

Herrligkoffer, Karl M. *Nanga Parbat, The Killer Mountain,* Knopf, New York, 1954

ANNAPURNA   (26,545 feet)   Nepal, Himalaya   (France, 1950)

Herzog, Maurice, and Marcel Ichac *Regards Vers Annapurna,* B. Arthaud, Paris and Grenoble, 1951

Herzog, Maurice *Annapurna, Conquest of the First 8,000-metre Peak*
     Jonathan Cape, London, 1952 / E.P. Dutton & Co., Inc., New York, 1953

Bibliography

GASHERBRUM I   (26,470 feet)   Pakistan-China, Karakoram   (America, 1958)

Clinch, Nick   *A Walk in the Sky, Climbing Hidden Peak*
The Mountaineers, Seattle / American Alpine Club, New York, 1982

BROAD PEAK   (26,400 feet)   Pakistan-China, Karakoram   (Austria, 1957)

Diemberger, Kurt *Summits and Secrets,* George Allen & Unwin Ltd., London, 1971
Schmuck, Marcus *Broad Peak, 8047m,* Bergland-Buch, Stuttgart, 1958

SHISHAPANGMA   (26,397 feet)   Tibet, Himalaya   (Tibet-China, 1964)

A Photographic Record of the Mount Shishapangma Expedition, Peking, Science Press, 1966
Scott, Doug, and Alex MacIntyre *The Shishapangma Expedition*
Granada Publishing Limited, London / The Mountaineers Books, Seattle, 1984
(Not the first ascent, but the best account in English.)

GASHERBRUM II   (26,362 feet)   Pakistan-China, Karakoram   (Austria, 1956)

Moravec, Fritz *Weisse berge schwarze menschen. Vom Himalaja Zu Den Riesenkratern Africas*
(*"White Mountain, Black Men, from the Himalaya to the Exploration of Africa"*)
Osterreichischer Bundesverlag, Wien, 1958

Books on the Abominable Snowman or Yeti

Hillary, Sir Edmund, and Desmond Doig
High in the Thin Cold Air, The Story of the Himalayan Expedition led by Sir Edmund Hillary,
Hodder & Stoughton, London / Doubleday & Company, Inc., New York, 1962
Izzard, Ralph   *The Abominable Snowman Adventure,* Hodder & Stoughton, London, 1955
Messner, Reinhold   *My Quest for the Yeti, Confronting the Himalayas' Deepest Mystery,* St. Martin's Press, NY, 2000

The Seven Summits

Anderson, Robert Mads   *7 Summits Solo,* David Bateman, Auckland, New Zealand, 1995
Anderson, Robert Mads   *To Everest Via Antarctica, Climbing Solo on the Highest Peak on each of the World's*
Seven Continents, Penguin Books, New Zealand, 1995
Bass, Dick, and Frank Wells, with Rick Ridgeway   *Seven Summits,* Warner Books, New York / Aurum, London, 1986
Bell, Steve   *Seven Summits, The quest to reach the highest point on every continent,* Mitchell Beazley, London, 2000
Tabin, Geoff   *Blind Corners, Adventures on Seven Continents,* ICS Books, Inc., Indiana, 1993

Books by Sir Edmund Hillary (in order of publication)

Hillary, Sir Edmund   *High Adventure,* Hodder & Stoughton, London / E.P. Dutton & Company, Inc., New York, 1955
Hillary, Sir Edmund, and George Lowe   *East of Everest, An Account of the New Zealand Alpine Club Himalayan*
Expedition to the Barun Valley in 1954, Hodder & Stoughton, London / E.P. Dutton, NY, 1956
Hillary, Sir Edmund   *The Boy's Book of Exploration,* Cassell & Company Ltd., London, 1957
Hillary, Sir Edmund, and Sir Vivian Fuchs
The Crossing of Antarctica, The Commonwealth Trans-Antarctic Expedition, 1955-1958
Cassell & Company Limited, London / Little, Brown & Company, Boston and Toronto, 1958
Hillary, Sir Edmund   *No Latitude for Error,* Hodder & Stoughton, London, *1961*
Hillary, Sir Edmund, and Desmond Doig
High in the Thin Cold Air, The Story of the Himalayan Expedition led by Sir Edmund Hillary
Hodder & Stoughton, London / Doubleday & Company, Inc., New York, 1962

Bibliography

Hillary, Sir Edmund   *Schoolhouse in the Clouds,* Hodder & Stoughton, London / Doubleday & Company, NY, 1964

Hillary, Sir Edmund   *Nothing Venture, Nothing Win,* Hodder & Stoughton, London and Auckland, 1975

Hillary, Sir Edmund   *From the Ocean to the Sky,* The Viking Press, New York, 1979

Hillary, Edmund and Peter   *Two Generations,* Hodder & Stoughton, London, 1984

Hillary, Sir Edmund, and Peter Hillary   *Ascent, Two Lives Explored: Sir Edmund and Peter Hillary,*
     Doubleday & Company, Inc., New York, 1986 (US edition of *Two Generations*)

Hillary, Sir Edmund   *View From the Summit,* Doubleday, London and New York, 1999

Books by Chris Bonington (in order of publication)

Bonington, Chris   *I Chose To Climb,* Victor Gollancz Ltd., London, 1966

Bonington, Chris   *Annapurna South Face,* Cassell & Company, Ltd., London / McGraw-Hill Book Company, NY, 1971

Bonington, Chris   *Everest Southwest Face,* Hodder & Stoughton, London, 1973

Bonington, Chris   *The Ultimate Challenge, The Hardest Way up the World's Highest Mountain*
     Stein and Day Publishers, New York, 1973 (US edition of *Everest Southwest Face*)

Bonington, Chris   *The Next Horizon, Autobiography II,* Victor Gollancz Ltd., London, 1973

Bonington, Chris   *Everest The Hard Way,* Hodder & Stoughton, London / Random House, Inc., New York, 1976

Bonington, Chris   *Quest For Adventure,* Hodder & Stoughton, London, 1981 / Clarkson N. Potter, New York, 1982

Bonington, Chris   *Kongur: China's Elusive Summit,* Hodder & Stoughton, London, 1982

Bonington, Chris, and Charles Clarke   *Everest: The Unclimbed Ridge*
     Hodder & Stoughton, London, 1983 / W.W. Norton & Company, New York, 1984

Bonington, Chris   *The Everest Years, A Climber's Life,* Hodder & Stoughton, London, 1986 / Viking Penguin, NY, 1987

Bonington, Chris   *The Climbers, A History of Mountaineering,* BBC Books / Hodder & Stoughton, London, 1992

Bonington, Chris, and Robin Knox-Johnson   *Sea, Ice, and Rock, Sailing and Climbing above the Arctic Circle*
     Hodder & Stoughton, London, 1992 / Sheridan House, Inc., New York, 1993

Bonington, Chris   *Great Climbs* (US edition: *Heroic Climbs*)*, a Celebration of World Mountaineering*
     Mitchell Beazley, London / The Mountaineers Books, Seattle, 1994

Bonington, Chris, and Charles Clarke   *Tibet's Secret Mountain, The Triumph of Sepu Kangri*
     Weidenfeld & Nicholson, London, 1999

Bonington, Chris   *Boundless Horizons, the Autobiography of Chris Bonington*
     Weidenfeld & Nicholson, London / Mountaineers Books, Seattle, 2000

Books by Reinhold Messner (in order of publication)

Messner, Reinhold   *The Seventh Grade: Most Extreme Climbing*
     Kaye & Ward Ltd., London / Oxford University Press, Inc., New York, 1974

Messner, Reinhold   *The Challenge,* Kaye & Ward Ltd., London / Oxford University Press, New York, 1977

Messner, Reinhold   *The Big Walls: History, Routes, Experiences*
     Kaye & Ward Ltd., London / Oxford University Press, New York, 1978

Messner, Reinhold   *Everest: Expedition to the Ultimate,* Kaye & Ward Ltd., London / Oxford University Press, NY, 1979

Messner, Reinhold   *Solo: Nanga Parbat,* Kaye & Ward Ltd., London / Oxford University Press, Inc., New York, 1980

Messner, Reinhold, and Alessandro Gogna   *K2, Mountain of Mountains*
     Kaye & Ward Ltd., London / Oxford University Press, Inc., New York, 1981

Messner, Reinhold   *All 14 Eight-Thousanders,* The Crowood Press, Wiltshire, England / Cloudcap Press, Seattle, 1988

Messner, Reinhold   *The Crystal Horizon: Everest—The First Solo Ascent,* The Crowood Press, Wiltshire, England, 1989

Messner, Reinhold   *Free Spirit: A Climber's Life,* Hodder & Stoughton, London, 1991

Messner, Reinhold   *Antarctica: Both Heaven and Hell*
     The Crowood Press, Wiltshire, England / The Mountaineers Books, Seattle, 1991

Messner, Reinhold   *To the Top of the World, Alpine Challenges in the Himalaya and Karakoram*
     The Crowood Press, Wiltshire, England / The Mountaineers Books, Seattle, 1992

Messner, Reinhold   *My Quest for the Yeti, Confronting the Himalayas' Deepest Mystery,* St. Martin's Press, NY, 2000

Messner, Reinhold   *Annapurna: 50 Years of Expeditions in the Death Zone,* The Mountaineers Books, Seattle, 2000

Messner, Reinhold   *Hermann Buhl: Climbing Without Compromise,* The Mountaineers Books, Seattle, 2000

Bibliography

Books by Robert Anderson (in order of publication)

Anderson, Robert Mads   *7 Summits Solo,* David Bateman, Auckland, New Zealand, 1995

Anderson, Robert Mads   *To Everest Via Antarctica, Climbing Solo on the Highest Peak on each of the World's Seven Continents,* Penguin Books, New Zealand, 1995

Anderson, Robert Mads   *Antonovs Over the Arctic, Flying to the North Pole in Russian Biplanes* David Bateman, Auckland, New Zealand, 1998

Books by Stephen Venables (in order of publication)

Venables, Stephen   *Painted Mountains, Two Expeditions to Kashmir*
Hodder & Stoughton, London, 1986 / The Mountaineers, Seattle, 1987

Venables, Stephen   *Everest Kangshung Face,* Hodder & Stoughton, London, 1989

Venables, Stephen   *Island at the Edge of the World, A South Georgia Odyssey,* Hodder & Stoughton, London, 1991

Venables, Stephen   *M is for Mountains, Facts and Stories from the Summits of the World*
Pan Macmillan Children's Books, London, 1993

Venables, Stephen, and Andy Fanshawe
Himalaya Alpine-Style, The Most Challenging Routes on the Highest Peaks
Hodder & Stoughton, London / The Mountaineers Books, Seattle, 1995

Venables, Stephen   *Everest: Alone At The Summit,* Odyssey Books, Bath, 1996 (reissue of *Everest Kangshung Face*)

Venables, Stephen   *Everest: Alone At The Summit,* Adrenaline Books, Balliet & Fitzgerald, New York, 2000

Venables, Stephen   *A Slender Thread, Escaping Disaster in the Himalaya,*
Hutchinson, The Random House Group, London, 2000

Books by Ed Webster (in order of publication)

Webster, Ed   *Rock Climbs in the White Mountains of New Hampshire*
Mountain Imagery, Conway, New Hampshire, 1982

Webster, Ed   *Rock Climbs in the White Mountains of New Hampshire Second Edition*
Mountain Imagery, Eldorado Springs, Colorado, 1987

Webster, Ed   *Rock Climbs in the White Mountains of New Hampshire, Third Edition (East Volume)*
Mountain Imagery, Eldorado Springs, Colorado, 1996

Webster, Ed   *Climbing in the Magic Islands*
A Climbing & Hiking Guidebook to The Lofoten Islands of Norway,
Nord Norsk Klatreskole, Henningsvaer, Norway, 1994

Peter Hillary tries on his father's Everest boot.

Index

climbed Pinnacles with Harry Taylor (UK), descended via *North Col Route*, 199

Bridwell, Jim   (James Dennis) July 29, 1944 -
Climbing leader, 20, 33, 38, 59, 66, 68, 70, 73, 81, 84; "advanced group," 32; bivouacs at Camp Four—without a sleeping bag, 85; decision not to mount third summit bid, 87; descends mountain for last time, 88; discusses tactics to climb West Ridge, 43; eloquent speech on sex, fame, and money, 58; load carry to winch base, with resulting argument; 55-57; fixing Lho La headwall, 41, 45, 49; Himalayan experience, first winter ascent of Pumori, 21; illness, descent to Pheriche, 67; leads on West Ridge, 54; nearly killed by rockfall, 41; offbeat locations for birthdays, 53; questions Larson's comments, 72, 76

photographs of, ascends Lho La headwall with Kim Carpenter, smoking cigarette, 60; at ABC with Ang Zangbu, 75; at West Ridge *puja,* 42; with the Hares, 55; *portraits of,* 20, 42

quotations, "All the jet stream has to do is descend a few thousand feet and you're fighting for your life. People can die up there in minutes," 76; "Beginners on Everest," 23; "Climbing Everest is a simple case of mind over matter, mind over hardship, and mind over danger.... I know this will probably be my only chance to summit on Everest. I want to get there, but I also want to come away from this expedition being friends for life," 58; "Give fate too much of a chance," 21; "Go for it, guys! Reckless abandon!" 87; "I think people think we're here on vacation! Our job is to climb the mountain," 49; "Layton, I told you that stove was hot," 70; "Lots of people's summit aspirations are premature," 84; "Mankind is motivated by three primary forces—sex, fame, and money. In all of life's great pursuits, men and women have had to rise above these three primal impulses," 58; "Obviously someone up there likes me," 41; "Remember, it's the tortoise that *always* wins. No hare is going to take first in this race," 68

Bright Star (The Diamond, Longs Peak, Colorado), xiii; first ascent of, 9-13
"Bright Star," (John Keats' sonnet), in full, 7
British high-altitude training methods, 174; *also see* Oxygen, With and Without; *and also* England
Brooks, Choe; British rock climber, 209

Brown, Joe   September 30, 1930 -
legendary British rock climber and mountaineer, 174; first ascent in 1955 of Kanchenjunga, world's third-tallest peak, 175; first ascent in 1956 of the Mustagh Tower, 175; had a brew on, 180; *portrait of,* at ABC below the North Col, 181

photograph of, crossing East Rongbuk Glacier with Anthoine and umbrellas, 182

quotations, "It's always better coming home with a peak in yer pocket," 175;
    "That's the real test on a mountain—whether y'can get down the bugger," 180;
    "What do I need an ice ax for?" 183

Bruce, John Geoffrey   December 4, 1896 - January 31, 1972
nephew of General C.G. Bruce; *portrait of,* 144, 502

Bryant, Leslie Vickery (Dan)   March, 1905 - December, 1957
first New Zealand mountaineer Eric Shipton climbed with; paved way for Edmund Hillary

Buddhism, 24, 25; celebrating with *chang,* 26; *Rinpoches* (reincarnate lamas), 27;
    creating goodness and gaining merit, 28-29; *epigraph,* "If we are facing in the right
    direction, all we have to do is keep on walking," 15

Buhler, Carlos Paltenghe Rockhold (October 17, 1954 -)

Webster's hunch left-hand buttress "would go," 206
photographs of, avalanche roars down Lhotse's North Face with the Kangshung, 207;
    early image of Everest from Sandakphu, Darjeeling, 211; the face in 1921, photographed
    by A.F.R. Wollaston, 200; the face in 1921, photographed by George Mallory, vii
photo-diagrams of, view north across face, with 1983 *American Buttress* marked, 205
Kangshung Glacier, Tibet; a broad, gently inclined, rock-covered river of ice, 300, 303, 472, 504
    photographs of, 303, 306, 320-321, 341, 347, 405, 474-475
Kangshung microclimate, 282, 365, 392
Kangshung Region, Tibet, *map,* 304-305
Kangtega (21,932 feet), Khumbu region, Nepal, 37
    first ascent of peak on June 5, 1963 by Tom Frost, David Dornan (both USA), Michael Gill,
    and Jim Wilson (both NZ); alpine-style first ascent of Northeast Ridge in 1986 by Paul Teare
    (Canada), Jay Smith, Mark Hesse, and Craig Reason (all USA), 207
Karpo La ("White Pass"), Tibet; first crossed by George Mallory and Guy Bullock in 1921, 374
Kartse ("White Peak"; 21,490 feet), Kangshung region, Tibet
    first ascent of peak on August 7, 1921 by George Mallory (UK) and Nyima Sherpa (Nepal);
    hike to, 373-374; views of, 349; *photographs of,* 205, 411
Kasang (Tibet) 1966 - 1988 Everest Kangshung Face Expedition
    Cookboy, age twenty-two Kharta local from Yulog village, 257; carries load to ABC, 359;
    grabs "Charlie," 367; stared blankly at us, 475; Tibetan Paul Revere, 285
    portrait of, serves gourmet meal at Kangshung Base Camp, 367
    quotation, "Goo mournu!" 285, 312, 346
Kata (greeting scarf), 27, 114, 143, 175, 230, 231; *photographs of,* 143
Kathmandu, Nepal; 1985 arrival in, 24-25; 1988 visit, 219-231; illness, 30;
    Monkey Temple, 28-29; mouthwatering cuisine of, 486; pollution and filth, 30; return in
    helicopter, 96-97; want to get back to, 93, 493
Kearney, Kristina 1986 Roger Marshall Everest Solo Expedition
    attends Rongbuk Monastery blessing ceremony, 142-143, 146; circumambulates
    Tashilhünpo Monastery, 120; high altitude record, 139; illness, 136, 146; in Shekar, 122-125;
    leaves for home, 197; member of expedition, 100; not fond of flying, 109; phones Webster
    with news of Roger Marshall's death, 208; Roger Marshall's memorial service, 209;
    stamina of, 107, 128; tours Forbidden City and Great Wall of China, 103, 104; visits Tilman's
    Lake Camp, 165-167; visits British Base Camp, 174; visits Rongbuk Nunnery, 146-147
    photographs of, with Tibetans at Tashilhünpo Monastery, 120
    quotations, "They're party animals, drinking beer and hundred-proof rum, smoking cigars
        and cigarettes! You'd think they might be training for Everest a bit more,"
        174; "Where'd this guy get his license—Sears?" 109
Keats, John; his sonnet, "Bright Star," 7; *epigraph,* "To one who has long been in city pent," 275
Kellas Rock Peak (23,337 feet), Rongbuk region, Tibet
    first ascent of peak in July, 1935 by Eric Shipton, H.W. Tilman, and Edmund Wigram
    (all UK); named for Dr. Alexander M. Kellas, member of 1921 British Mount Everest
    Reconnaissance Expedition, who died on the approach march, 134
Kellas, Dr. Alexander Mitchell   June 21, 1868 - June 4, 1921
        1921 British Mount Everest Reconnaissance Expedition
    noted British early Himalayan explorer and mountaineer, 134
Keller, Helen, *epigraph,* "Life is either a daring adventure, or nothing," 1
Kempson, Edwin   (Edwin Garnett Hone; "G.") June 4, 1902 - May 27, 1987
        1935 British Mount Everest Reconnaissance Expedition
    made first ascent of Kharta Changri on July 29, 1935 with Charles Warren, Rongbuk region,
    Tibet, 134; made first ascent of Khartaphu on July 18, 1935 with Shipton and Warren, Rongbuk
    region, Tibet, 183; John Hunt, Charles Wylie and Michael Ward all learned to climb with "G."
Khamba La pass, Tibet, 119; *photograph of,* 118
Khampa Dzong, Tibet; *photograph of,* 112
Khampas, the warrior class of eastern Tibet; financed by CIA to fight the Chinese in the late
    1950s, 240; *photograph of,* Khampa with bobcat, 239

Perlman, Eric S. (July 30, 1950 -)   1981 American Everest East Face Expedition
    submitted original proposal for the first American Kangshung Face expedition, 203
Permit, *see* Climbing Permit
Pertemba Sherpa
    Sirdar, 1975 British Everest Southwest Face Expedition (summit on September 26)
    Sirdar, 1979 German Everest Expedition
    Sirdar, 1983 American Everest West Ridge Expedition
    Sirdar, 1985 Norwegian Everest Expedition   (summit on April 21)
    Sirdar, 1988 Asian Friendship Everest Expedition
        legendary expedition *Sirdar;* summited on Everest's Southwest Face in 1975 with
        Peter Boardman, 50; reached Everest summit a second time, with Chris Bonington, 77;
        Sirdar of 1988 Asian Friendship Expedition, 237
Pethang Ringmo, George Mallory's fabled Meadow Camp in 1921 in upper Kama Valley, Tibet,
    298; arrival at, 299; on return, 485; *photograph of,* 298
Pethangtse ("Pethang Peak," *or* "Peak of the Icy Plain"; 22,106 feet), Nepal-Tibet border
    first ascent of peak on May 26, 1954 by Norman Hardie, Michael Ball (both UK),
    Brian Wilkinson (NZ), and Urkien Sherpa (Nepal); gleams like obelisk, 366; views of, 410
Petri, the wandering Finn, 55, 57
Pheriche, Nepal; village of, 38; convalescing at, 54, 59, 76; helicoptering past, 95
Photography, 55, 62, 78, 94, 95, 167, 195, 212, 228, 250, 285, 325, 328, 354, 373, 423, 431, 435,
    438, 451, 453, 485
Phuti, Sonam; a Tenzing long lost cousin, 263; "camera-girl," 263; brings Sheik tent, 282
Pilgrims, in Tibet, 114, 117, 120
Pilling, Trevor   1986 British Everest Northeast Ridge Expedition
    solo ascent of Peak 6570, Rongbuk region, Tibet, 173
    photograph by, East Face of Changtse and North Col, 190-191
    quotation, "I was wondering what daft bugger would be wandering about at this time
        of night. I should have known it was you!" 184
Pinnacles, the spiky rock outcrops on Everest's Northeast Ridge, 135
    photograph of, as seen from the East, 199
Pinsetter Camp, *Lowe Buttress,* Everest Kangshung Face, Tibet, 204
Pinther, Miklos   (April 2, 1940 -) 1988 Everest Kangshung Face Expedition
    coming to Everest, most exciting event in life, 270; farewell dinner for support team, 270;
    flies to Beijing at expedition's start, 216; head of Cartography for United Nations, 208;
    pulls out map, 262; wanted to survey Everest with satellite measuring technology, 208
PLA, *see* People's Liberation Army
Pokalde ("the Shoulder"; 18,806 feet), Khumbu region, Nepal
    first ascent of peak on April 15, 1953 by Wilfred Noyce, Tom Bourdillon, Michael Ward
    (all UK), and several Sherpas; a very popular trekking peak, 38
Politz, Andy   (Andrew James)   August 8, 1959 -
        1985 American Everest West Ridge Expedition
        1991 American Everest Expedition   (summit on May 15)
        1999 Mallory & Irvine Research Expedition
            one of team who discovered Mallory's body on May 1, 1999
    21, 62, 76, 81, 84; argument after load carry to winch, 57; "B team" controversy, 33; chops
    steps up icefield, 62; climbing guide on Mount Rainier, 21; climbs to Camp Five, 89; climbs
    with Webster to Camp Two, 64; coughs up blood, 77; discovery of Camp Three, 67;
    enough gas for a few more carries, 80; establishes Camp Three, 67; establishes Camp Four,
    76; illness, 54; intention to work for good of all, 58; Lho La to Camp Three—3,500-feet
    in one day, 80; note from, 38; trades summit slot, 90; wanted to climb Everest without
    bottled oxygen, 66; *photographs of,* climbs to Camp Two, 65; we'd given it our best, 91
    quotation, "I was so happy and it was so cold that tears were running down my cheeks
        and freezing in place," 67; "We've got to get Robert to the top of this
        mountain, that's what we've got to do," 80
Post-traumatic shock syndrome, 497-498

Religion, tenets of Hinduism and Buddhism, 24-29
Renminbi (*also called* RMB *or* "the People's Money"); *see* Chinese currency
Renshaw, Dick   (Richard Michael)   May 28, 1950 -
        1982 British Everest Northeast Ridge Expedition
   noted British mountaineer; attempts first ascent in 1982 of Everest's Northeast Ridge, 135;
   friends with Venables and Webster, 209, 221
Rest step, 84
Reverence for mountains, 37
Rhododendrons, 485; *photograph of,* 476
Ri-Ring (22,822 feet), Rongbuk Valley, Tibet, 154
   first ascent of peak on July 5, 1921 by George Mallory and Guy Bullock, 134
   (The pair initially proposed the name "Mount Kellas" for this peak.)
Rinpoche (a Buddhist reincarnate head lama, or *tulku*); the recognition of a, 27
Rinsing Sherpa   1985 American Everest West Ridge Expedition
   photographs of, on "Potato Chip Traverse," 44; in Camp Two snow cave, 80
River Camp, at junction of Rabkar Valley and Kama Valley, Tibet, 292, 296
RMB (*short for* Renminbi); *see* Chinese currency

"Robert start," (6 or 7 A.M.), 377
Robson, Mount; British Columbia, Canada; *North Face* of, 2, 18
Rock Island; near Kangshung ABC on Kangshung Glacier, Tibet, 306
Rockefeller Center; team holds United Nations flag at, 211
Rocket launchers; used on 1983 American Everest East Face Expedition, 204, 310
Rocky Mountain National Park, Colorado, 8
Rocky Mountain News, in Denver, 20; publishes John Meyer's weekly news dispatches, 68
Rocky Mountains of Colorado, 2, 6, 8
Rolex Watch USA, one of the principal sponsors of 1988 Everest Kangshung Face Expedition,
   209, 211, 217; also sponsored 1953 first ascent of Mount Everest, 209; team makes
   celebratory toast to, 483
Rolling Stones, 232, 268,
Rongbuk Base Camp, Tibet, *see* Base Camps on Mount Everest
Rongbuk Glacier, Tibet, 60; terminal moraine of, 131
Rongbuk Monastery, Tibet, 28, 128; hermitages, 136-137; printing prayer flags, 131; restoration
   begun in 1982, 146; ruins of, 129-130; *photographs of,* destroyed fresco, 130; final
   resting place of monks and nuns, 147; Head lama of, 143; ruins of, 130; Sherpas and
   Tibetans in courtyard in 1924, 130; *stupa* and Chomolungma, 129
Rongbuk Region, Tibet, *map,* 112
Rongphutse ("Rongbuk Peak"; 22,890 feet), Rongbuk region, Tibet; pointed peak due
   north of Changtse; first ascent of peak in July, 1935 by Eric Shipton, H.W. Tilman, and
   Edmund Wigram (all UK)
Roper, Steve (February 13, 1941 -)
   renowned American rock climber and author; suggested title of *Snow in the Kingdom;*
   took portrait of Fritz Wiessner, 214
Roskelley, John   (John Fenton Charles)   December 1, 1948 -
        1981 American Everest East Face Expedition
        1983 American Everest West Ridge Expedition (Tibet)
        1984 American Everest North Face Expedition
        1993 American Everest North Ridge Expedition
   renowned American mountaineer; departs Kangshung Face, 203; declines invitation, 210
"Rotation schedule," Kevin Swigert's plan, 67
Roth, David Lee, rock singer; his album *Skyscraper,* 283
Rouse, Al (Alan Paul)   December 19, 1951 - August 10, 1986
        Leader, 1983 British Everest Winter Expedition
        1986 British K2 Expedition
   noted British mountaineer; summits on K2 in 1986, but perishes on descent, 175, 463-464

Acknowledgments

First, I would like to thank the members of my family, and especially my parents,

Dr. Edward William Webster & Dorothea Wood Webster
for their love and steadfast support

also my parents-in-law,
Philip Nicholas Stamas and Ruth Ingegerd Stamas

—and my brothers and sisters and nephews,
John Webster
Peter Webster
Anne & John Wolfe
Mark Webster
Susan Webster MacPhee
John MacPhee & Jack MacPhee
Micah Webster
Caleb Webster
Nicholas Stamas

When I returned home in June, 1988, my godparents, Judith and Isham McConnell, and their family, Laurie McConnell and Julia McConnell, Hina Hirayama, Charly Steiger, and Mrs. Susan Fisher took care of me while my parents were overseas. I would like to thank them all. Both of my hands and my left foot were bandaged, and as I recalled and relived the events of our Kangshung Face climb, particularly the summit day of May 12 and the difficulties of our descent, my godmother Judith patiently wrote down my diary account of those experiences. Thank you so much, Judy, for being my faithful recorder then, and for taking care of me during those difficult, but happy and memorable, first two weeks home.

Other family members who I would like to give some hugs to are Eleanor Robinson, Barbara Renton, Nigel Renton, Kristin Lewis, Chuck Forsman, Chloe Forsman, Shannon Forsman, Lisa Lewis, Laurie Lewis, Brian Lewis, Linda Henry, Jeninne Milton, Kristen Henry, Anne Stamas, Margaret Bates, Basil Bates, Christopher and Jane Bates, Cathy and Graham Dickerson, Andy and Fiona Bates, Norman Webster, Christine Webster, Harry Johnson, Joyce Johnson, Ed Webster V, & John Webster.

MY THANKS TO THE PHOTOGRAPHERS AND PICTURE SOURCES:

George Mallory
Noel Odell
Captain John Noel
Sir Edmund Hillary
Alfred Gregory
Peter Jackson
Reinhold Messner
Peter Athans
Scott Lankford
Fletcher Wilson
Steve Roper
Jim Detterline
Bill Barker
Ruth De Cew

Trevor Pilling
Robert Anderson
Stephen Venables
Paul Teare
Joe Blackburn
Miriam Zieman
Glenn Dunmire
Dale Vrabec
John M. Grunsfeld
Julian Freeman-Attwood
Das Studio, Darjeeling
Tenzing Norgay family collection
The American Alpine Club Library, Colorado
The Royal Geographical Society, London
The Swiss Foundation for Alpine Research

For his design and layout expertise, and for several year's worth of invaluable creative input into this book, my heartfelt thanks go to designer and digital domain guru, Gordon Banks. No question of mine went unanswered, and the rescues he performed were frequently heroic! Thank you so very, very much, Gordon, for all of your invaluable help.

To the artists whose work is featured in this book, my heartfelt gratitude to Carol Fraser, residing in Switzerland and Rishikesh, India, who painted the enchantingly alive, wondrous frontispiece painting of Chomolungma (whose spirit you captured, Carol); to Japan's Eizo Hirayama, who painted the watercolor of trees and snow at the start of the "Home" chapter; to the Newari painter in Kathmandu who painted the Tibetan Good Luck scroll symbols that start many of the other chapters; and to the unknown Tibetan artist from whose *thanka* I have used other Buddhist icons.

One of my greatest joys has been to be able to include so many of Noel Odell's stunningly beautiful photographs taken on that most famous of the early attempts on Mount Everest: the 1924 British Mount Everest Expedition. I owe a profound and grateful thanks to Peter Odell in England, Noel Odell's grandson, for his friendship over the past decade, and also for his trust in letting me borrow the original 1924 Everest and Tibet negatives to make new prints of them.

Thank you, also, to Sandra Noel, for my use of Captain John Noel's portrait of Noel Odell.

The photographs in this book were scanned and digitally prepared in Photoshop by the staffs of *ImageSystems, Inc.* of Boulder, Colorado (who drum scanned and did match prints for all of the color pictures), and *Photo Craft Laboratories,* also of Boulder, Colorado, who with great care and professionalism printed all of Noel Odell's 1924 silver nitrate Everest negatives. *Photo Craft* also drum scanned all of my 35mm color slides, and converted them into black and white.

At *ImageSystems,* I would like to warmly thank Damon Decker, Jennifer Colton—scanner operators Doug Roma, Mike Deal, and Bryan Starry—Deborah Bain, and Tammy Hamann.

At *Photo Craft Laboratories,* my very sincere thanks go to Roy McCutchen, Ron Brown, Paula David, and Terri Detrano; to Steven Gilmore, who masterfully printed the Noel Odell Everest negatives; to Brad Kaminski, Mike Welch, and Deb Casey in the digital department; and finally, my greatest thanks to Michael Harrison, for his artistry and skill in Photoshop, and for making the vision I had of my black and white images in this book, and their potential, come truly alive.

A special thanks also to James Balog, for sharing your photographic and publishing expertise.

Many people helped shape the manuscript of this book, particularly my diligent and creative editor, Peter Williams, who worked tirelessly, for two years, to help me tell the subtler aspects of my Everest saga, and make this a story that would speak to many people, not just climbers. Various "readers" over the past decade—Steve Roper, Donna DeShazo, Jeff Long, Audrey Salkeld, and Judith Champion, also gave me their "wisdom of the ages" sage advice, and suggestions; more recently, I received valuable feedback from Dr. Hubert Thomason, Laura Thomason, Jason Rider, Glenn Dunmire, Gary Lawless, Beth Leonard, John Owen, Cole Campbell, and Leann Campbell.

For her suggested changes and perceptive additions to my story, her fine ear for words, and for adding just the right amount of linguistic lime pickle, I would like to thank Bhanu Kapil Rider.

And to my proofreader par excellence, Maggie Owen, who endeavoured in the never-give-up tradition of Scott and Shackleton to catch every single typo and misspelling in the entire MS—you have my eternal thanks for the dedication and hard work you have put into my book.

For their help in tracking down, providing, and verifying the various details of and information about the birthplace and childhood of Tenzing Norgay, I would like to graciously thank: the family of Tenzing Norgay—Norbu Tenzing Norgay at the American Himalayan Foundation, and Jamling Tenzing Norgay in Darjeeling, who also kindly allowed me to use two pictures of his father; Kalden Norbu of Tibet Travels & Tours in Kathmandu for his generous and informative email correspondence; also the beloved Tsering Bhuti Dingtsa, for her wisdom and excellent memory; Hildegard Diemberger, for her scholarly and detailed article, *"Gangla Tshechu, Beyul Khenbalung: Pilgrimage to Hidden Valleys, Sacred Mountains, and Springs of Life Water in southern Tibet and eastern Nepal,"* and her radiant book on the cultural and religious history of the Shekar-Kharta region, *The Story of the White Crystal*. Wade Davis and Broughton Coburn, Himalayan visionaries both, I would also like to acknowledge. But my deepest thanks goes to Dale Vrabec, for sharing with me his enthusiasm for the mysterious eastern aspects of Everest and Makalu, and for bringing to my attention the articles, books, and contacts that sent me along the trail of discovery to uncover the story of Tenzing's birthplace. Dale, please accept my gratitude for your help and partnership.

Acknowledgments

The following people also assisted me in researching historical information, obtaining books and photographs, and compiling my Index. Fran Loft, the Librarian at the American Alpine Club Library in Golden, Colorado, helped me with research and loaned me several early Everest photos from the club's picture collection; at the Alpine Club Library in London, Margaret Ecclestone, the AC Librarian, and Sheila Harrison, the Assistant Secretary, kindly researched names and dates of many Everesters, both old and new; and Lindsay Griffin, Mountain Info Editor for High Magazine in England, provided first ascent and peak information for the loftiest Himalayan summits with his usual vigour and uncanny way of knowing precisely which sources to delve into. For assisting with other historical and personal information, I am indebted to Chris Bonington, Joe Brown, Audrey Salkeld, and Peter Gillman (who even paid a visit to the London Family Records Office); Peter E. Odell, Stephen Venables, Ronald Faux, Dick Renshaw, Julian Freeman-Attwood, Caroline Fanshawe, Barney Rosedale, Peter Steele, Rich Marshall, Bruce Hendricks, Karen March, Steve Roper, Jim Bridwell, George Lowe, John Roskelley, Phil Ershler, Jim Wickwire, Peter Athans, David Breashears, Brent Bishop, Greg Glade, Rick Millikan, Eric Simonson, Dr. Geoff Tabin, Lloyd Athearn, Michael Chessler, George Mallory II, Jim Petroske, Bill Petroske, Colin Monteath, and Jan Westby.

At R.R. Donnelley & Sons, my very sincere thanks to Jamie Butcher and Bob Stevens.

My teammates and I would also like to thank some special people we met on our travels:
Tom Dickey & Susan Mitchell
Chester Dreiman & Clare Stocker
Galen Rowell & Barbara Rowell
Chris Bonington, Andy Fanshawe, & Jess Stock
Reinhold Messner
Rodrigo Jordan Fuchs
Rodney Korich & Kim Korich & Arlene Burns
Pamela Steele, The Lhasa Hotel, Lhasa, Tibet
Hari Har Acharya, and Gatha, Atlas Trekking, Ltd., Kathmandu, Nepal
Tsering Dolkar, Himalayan Trekking & Equipment House, Kathmandu, Nepal
Mukund, Mountain Travel, Kathmandu, Nepal
Charlotte Bergstrom & Bill Sindlinger

Additionally, I would like to thank the following doctors, therapists, and institutions:
Nas Eftekhar, M.D., and Fero Sadeghian, M.D.
John F. Burke, M.D., Massachusetts General Hospital, Boston
Robert L. Horner, M.D., and the staff of Hand Surgery Associates, Denver
Kathe F. Morck, Susan Simone, Becky McLean, and Kristine R. Werner, Ph.D. at
The Mapleton Center for Rehabilitation and Boulder Community Hospital, Boulder
George P. Garmany, M.D. at Associated Neurologists, Boulder
and several other Boulder, Colorado therapists, Charles Chace (Acupuncture),
Nancy Johnson (Massage Therapy), Lori Saige (Physical Therapy),
Diana Smadbeck (Biofeedback), and Jack Zellner, D.C. (Chiropractic)
Peter H. Hackett, M.D.
Thomas F. Hornbein, M.D.

and the following Family members, Friends, and Climbing Partners:

Eva & Daniel Baum	Blu	Chris Cline-Cardot
Fred Barth	George Bracksieck	Nick Clinch
Bryan Becker	Carlos Buhler	Alain Comeau
Todd Bibler	Jordan Campbell	Gail Denton
Maureen Troy	Russ Campbell	Gene Ellis
Ellen Blackburn	Carolyn Campbell	Irene Flack
Claire Blackburn	Al Chaffee	Peter Gallagher
Angus Blackburn	Tina Chaffee	Stephan Goldberg, M.D.

Liz Green	Tom Hinds	Louis Reichardt
Rosie Grieves-Cook	Karen Murgolo Hinds	Charley Shimanski
Peter Habeler	Randall Hoffman	Paul Sibley
Andrew Harvard	George Hurley	Allen Steck
Brack Hattler, M.D.	Jean Hurley	David Swanson
Mark Hesse	Kristina Kearney	Janis Tracy
Randa Hessel	George Lowe	Jim Tracy
Paulette Poncar	Steve Matous	Kelly Weir
Bob Poncar	Brent McPhie	Rick Wilcox
Heidi Pfannenstiel	James Morrissey	Kurt Winkler
Roger Pfannenstiel	Gary Neptune	Karin Winkler
Hillary Jacobs	Dan Schelling	Sabina Zieman

EXPEDITION SPONSORS

An expedition to Mount Everest represents the effort, good will, and sponsorship of many people, organizations, companies, and corporations. Everest 1988 was no exception. We would like to take this opportunity to thank the following firms and individuals for generously supporting our endeavor. First, for their Endorsed Support:

The American Alpine Club
The American Geographical Society
The American Mountain Foundation
The Explorers Club
The Mount Everest Foundation
The National Geographic Society
The United Nations

Financial Assistance, Equipment, and Services to Everest 1988 were provided by the three major sponsors of the 1953 British Mount Everest Expedition:

Eastman Kodak — *Kodachrome 25 & 64 color slide film; Ektachrome color slide film, Tmax black & white film, and Kodak paper and chemicals.*

Burroughs Wellcome — *Actifed Plus decongestant, Neosporin, and Cortisporin.*

Rolex Watch USA — *Explorer II & GMT Master II Oyster Perpetual Date Chronometers.*

Everest 1988 also gratefully thanks for their financial backing and generous support:

American Express/Asia — *(Hong Kong office) Travel arrangements in southeast Asia and logistical support in Beijing, China.*
Dow Consumer Products — *Ziplock Brand plastic storage bags.*
Kiehl's, Inc, "Since 1851" — *Skin and hair care, lip balm, sunscreen, and windscreen products.*
Lindblad Travel — *Airline and freight arrangements to China and within Tibet.*
Petroconsultants — *Financial support.*
The Weaver Coat Company — *The Weaver sleeping bag/jacket.*

Additional equipment was graciously donated by the following firms:

Climb High — *Dachstein wool mittens.*
Dolland & Aitchison — *Prescription sunglasses.*
Duggal Color Projects — *Development, slide duplication, and printing of expedition photos.*
Fairydown of New Zealand — *Tents, packs, and clothing.*
Jones Optical Company — *Expedition and travel sunglasses.*
Leki — *Adjustable ski poles.*

Acknowledgments

Metolius Products	*Three cam units.*
Mountain Equipment	*Pants, windsuit, and down clothing.*
Nike	*Trekking boots, socks, t-shirts, and sun hats.*
Seranac	*Gloves.*
Stubai	*Ice axes, ice hammers, ice screws, crampons, rock pitons, lightweight and locking carabiners, figure 8 descenders, wired nuts, and camping tools.*
Ultra Technologies	*Kodak Supralife Alkaline Batteries.*
Wild Country USA & UK	*Friends, Flexible Friends, Alpinist harnesses, and mittens.*

Additional equipment was supplied at cost by:

Berghaus	*Trekking boots.*
Bibler Tents	*Lightweight mountain tents.*
Bolder Designs	*Pile clothing, custom-designed high-altitude down overbibs and down parkas; and Rut's Route expedition sleeping bags.*
Brenco Enterprises	*One Sport Jannu mountaineering boots.*
Cascade Designs	*Therma-Rest inflatable sleeping pads.*
Chouinard Equipment	*Forty-Below lithium headlamps.*
Dana Designs	*Backpacks and duffel bags.*
Denver Drum & Barrel	*16-gallon plastic drums.*
High Adventure Sports	*Aluminum snow pickets.*
Karrimor International	*Backpacks.*
Kenko International	*Asolo AFS 101 mountaineering boots.*
Lowe Alpine Systems	*Rivory-Joanny climbing rope.*
Patagonia	*Pile hats, capilene expedition underwear, liner gloves, and socks.*
Peak 1/ The Coleman Co.	*"The Sheik" Base Camp cooking & dining tent.*
Stevens Press	*Official Expedition color postcards.*
Uniroyal Plastics Company	*Ensolite foam padding.*
Wild Things	*Expedition duffel bags.*

Food & Nutritional supplies were donated by:

Alpine Aire	*Freeze-dried fruit and vegetables, soups, and stews.*
Negroni	*Milano salami and Parma ham.*
Unipro	*Nutritional supplements: Carboplex, Rehydrate, and Sustain.*
Weepak	*Freeze-dried and dried foods.*

Medical supplies were donated by:

Bayer (New Zealand)	Adalat.
Common Brothers, Inc.	Medical supplies.
Johnson & Johnson	First aid supplies.
Roche (New Zealand)	Multivitamins, and Hypnovol sleeping pills.

Travel Arrangements and Administrative help was given by:

Atlas Trekking, Ltd., Thamel, Kathmandu; the Chinese Mountaineering Association, Beijing; CAAC (China Airlines), Beijing; the Lhasa Hotel (Holiday Inns), Lhasa; Lindblad Travel, Inc., Westport, Connecticut; Mercury Travel, New Delhi; Motor Cargo, Denver, Colorado; Mountain Travel, Kathmandu; The Ogilvy Group, New York City; Pan American Airways, New York City; Pro-Service Forwarding, San Francisco; the Shangri-La Hotel, Beijing; the Sheraton Hotel, New York City; Tibet Guest House, Thamel, Kathmandu; and Vasant Continental Hotel, New Delhi.

With many thanks for his invaluable help: William Phillips, The Ogilvy Group, New York City.

Everest 1988 Major Sponsors

American Express, Travel Related Services; Hillary Allman
Burroughs Wellcome Pharmaceuticals; Bryan Carson, Karen Collins, & Tina Hatchard
Dow Consumer Products; Neal Anderson & Rick Depew
Duggal Color Projects; Baldev Duggal, Dinah Davidson, and Judy Tucker
Eastman Kodak Company; Ann Moscicki, Roger Anderson, & Raymond DeMoulin
Kiehl's Pharmacy, "Since 1851"; Aaron Morse and Jami Morse
Lindblad Travel; Lars Eric Lindblad, Jeannie Rodgers, & Carol Bell
Rolex Watch USA; Roland Puton, Tom Annear, & William Sullivan

Equipment Manufacturers for Everest 1988

Steve Byrne *at Wired Bliss*
Todd Bibler, Maggie Owen, Rita Davis, & Nancy Delpero *at Bibler Tents*
the Staff of *the Boulder Mountaineer*
John Connelly *at Brenco Enterprises*
John Cranford *at Kenco International*
Maria Cranor & Peter Metcalf *at Black Diamond Equipment*
David Ellis *at Fairydown, New Zealand*
Karen Frishman & Jane Sievert *at Patagonia*
Kevin Furnary, Paul Chatel, Susan Gore, & Carol Owen *at Mountain Mend / Bolder Designs*
Dana Gleason *at Dana Designs*
Paul Hardin *at The Coleman Company*
Steve Hudson *at Pigeon Mountain Industries / Petzl Equipment*
Jerry Lloyd *at Cascade Designs*
Jeff Lowe, Malcom Daly, & Lynn Rice *at Lowe Alpine Systems*
Fred Meyer *at Omni International Distributors / Stubai Equipment, Austria*
the Staff of *Neptune Mountaineering*
Bob Olsen *at Climb High*
Kate Phillips *at Alpine Sports*
Paul Richards & Paul Williams *at Mountain Equipment*
David Weaver *at Weaver Coat Company*
Rick Wilcox, Bill Kane, & Bill Supple *at Wild Country USA*
Paul Williams *at Bayer, New Zealand*
Mark Vallance & Roger Withers *at Wild Country UK*
John Yates *at High Adventure Sports*

Everest 1988 Additional Sponsors & Suppliers

Denver Drum & Barrel; Steve Kaminsky & Perry Kaminsky
Ogilvy & Mather; Michael Baulk, Vicky Surman, Peter Warren, & Ali-j Wilson
Pan American Airways; Scott Morris
Petroconsultants; Jean-Pierre Javoques
Pro-Service Forwarding; Adrian Pritchard
Ultra Technologies; Judy Kinsky
Uniroyal Plastics Company; Jim Lynch & Mel Terlisner

Food, Beverage, & Nutritional Supplements for Everest 1988

Alfalfa's Market, Boulder
Alpine Aire Foods; Dennis Korn
Celestial Seasonings Tea, Boulder
Unipro; John Williams
Weepak Foods; Ken Fontecilla

Acknowledgments

Science Advisors for Everest 1988

Roger Bilham, *The University of Colorado, Boulder*
William Graves, *The National Geographic Society*
Bradford Washburn, *The Boston Museum of Science*

Media Coverage of Everest 1988

Jim Benemann, *Channel 9 News, Denver*
Annette Carmichael, *BBC Television, England*
H. Adams Carter, *the American Alpine Journal*
Michael Kennedy, Julie Kennedy, Michael Benge, Alison Osius, Penny Ellis,
    Lance Leslie, Mark Thomas, Lynn Thomas, and Jonathan Waterman, *Climbing Magazine*
John Meyer, *the Rocky Mountain News, Denver*
Margaret Sieck, Victoria Boughton, Ramiro Fernandez, & Liz Greco, *Sports Illustrated Magazine*
Harish Kapadia, *The Himalayan Journal, India*
Bernard Newman, Paul Nunn, & Patricia Hughes, *Mountain Magazine, England*
Bruno Cormier & Dominique Vulliamy Lanctot, *Vertical Magazine, France*

Lastly, I'd like to thank the members, friends, and sponsors of my first two Everest expeditions:

The 1985 American Mount Everest West Ridge Expedition

David Saas, *Leader*
Bill Forrest, *Deputy Leader*
Jim Bridwell, *Climbing Leader*
Ang Zangbu Sherpa, *Sirdar*
Udab Prasad Dhungama, *Liaison Officer*
Mads Anderson, *Treasurer*
Dan Larson, *Lawyer*
John Meyer, *Journalist*

Robert Anderson, Peter Athans, Heidi Benson, Kim Carpenter, Randal Grandstaff, Rodney Korich, Scott Lankford, George McLeod, Jim McMillian, Brian O'Malley, Dr. John Pelner, Andy Politz, Greg Sapp, Jay Smith, Kevin Swigert, & Fletcher Wilson.

High Altitude Sherpas: Ang Chering Sherpa, Ang Danu Sherpa, Ang Rinsing Sherpa, Dorje Tsering Sherpa, Lhakpa Dorje Sherpa, Lobsang Sherpa, Mingma Sherpa, Moti Lal Gurung, Passang Gyalchen "PG" Sherpa, Penzo Sherpa, Prithi Bahadur.

Support Sherpas: Ang Tsering Sherpa, *Base Camp head cook;* Chirring, *Base Camp cook boy;* Gyalchen Sherpa, *Camp 1 cook;* Dawa Nuru Sherpa, *Camp 1 cook boy;* Kami Dorje Sherpa, *Camp 1 cook boy;* Ang Tsering Sherpa, *mail runner.*

And: Dick Bass, Chris Bonington, David Breashears, Alison Burghardt & Kurt Burghardt, Ellie Caulkins & the Caulkins Family; the Climbing Nuns (Sue, Mary Ellen, & Jan), John Cruise, Karen Fellerhoff, Patrick Griffin; Eizo, Kazuko, & Hina Hirayama; Alma Husted, Chuck Husted, Chris Husted, and Jenny Husted; Seri Jompanta, Gertrude Koch, Gabrielle Knox, Udom Likhitwonnawut, Eve Nott, Aurapin Pochanapring, Naoe Sakashita, Pertemba Sherpa, and Billy Squier.

My Everest 1985 sponsor, *Eastern Mountain Sports, EMS, The Outdoor Specialists*

And at EMS: Tom Haas, Roy Johnson & Suzanne Johnson, Dick Jones, and Joe Lentini.

1986 Roger Marshall Everest Solo Expedition

Roger Marshall, *Leader*
Ruth De Cew, *Nutrition*
Kristina Kearney, *Support*
Pasang Norbu Sherpa, *Sirdar & Cook*
Li Chen Xiang, *Liaison Officer*
Fu Yide, *First Interpreter*
Ma Qian Li, *Second Interpreter*

And: Mo Anthoine, Bill Barker, Joe Brown, Ronald Faux, Paddy Freaney, Nigel Goldsack, Loel Guinness, Tom Holzel, Dr. Philip Horniblow, Adrian Kearney, Marlene Kearney, and Adrian & Brigette Kearney, Aly Kellas, Paul Moores, Paul Nunn, Trevor Pilling, Dick Pownall, Audrey Salkeld, Brummie Stokes, and Harry Taylor.

1988 International Everest Kangshung Face Expedition

Finally, I could never have had finer companions or climbing partners than I did in 1988 on the East Face on Mount Everest. The experiences, joys, laughs, and tears we shared are some of the most treasured memories of my life—as is my continuing friendship with each of you.

With my greatest affection, to Robert, Paul, Stephen, Joe, Mimi, Pasang, and Kasang—

and also to Norbu, Billy, Miklos, Sandy, Wendy, and Rob.

Ed Webster in 1988 atop the Pang La pass in Tibet, heading toward the Kangshung Face of Mount Everest.

Photograph by Joe Blackburn

ED WEBSTER, born March 21, 1956 in Boston, Massachusetts, is a well known American climber, author, photographer, and lecturer. After graduating from Colorado College in 1978 with a B.A. in Anthropology, he was a contributing editor of *Climbing Magazine* from 1984 to 1994. He has authored two popular guidebooks, which include three editions of *Rock Climbs in the White Mountains of New Hampshire*, and *Climbing In The Magic Islands*, about the Lofoten Islands in Arctic Norway. His articles and photographs have appeared in such diverse publications as *The New York Times Sunday Magazine, Sports Illustrated, Popular Mechanics, Rock and Ice Magazine, Rolling Stone,* and *Climbing Magazine;* and in the books *50 Classic Climbs of North America, Ascent, Heroic Climbs, Himalaya Alpine-Style, Everest, the Best Writing and Pictures,* and *World Mountaineering.* In addition to the three Everest expeditions described in this book, Ed is a veteran of five other Himalayan expeditions—to Bhutan, Nepal, and Pakistan. In 1992, he was the first American mountaineer to climb in Mongolia, where he made the first ascents of several unclimbed peaks.

Ed was awarded the 1988 Seventh Grade Award for "Outstanding Achievements in Mountaineering" from the American Mountain Foundation; the 1990 Literary Award, for excellence in mountaineering writing, from the American Alpine Club; and the 1994 David A. Sowles Award, for saving the life of a fellow climber, also from the American Alpine Club. He lives with his wife, Lisa, in Colorado.